HOUSES OF BOSTON'S BACK BAY

An Architectural History, 1840–1917

An Architectural History · 1840-1917

HOUSES OF BOSTON'S BACK BAY

by Bainbridge Bunting

THE BELKNAP PRESS OF HARVARD UNIVERSITY
PRESS · CAMBRIDGE · MASSACHUSETTS

To Dorie for patience

ACKNOWLEDGMENTS

How does an author begin to express his appreciation for the assistance he has received from so many people in so many ways? Certainly I am humble with gratitude as I recall many instances of
support and encouragement. It was Professor Leonard Opdycke who
suggested the Back Bay as the subject of my dissertation at Harvard
and who has always shown a keen and generous interest in the study.
Without Walter Muir Whitehill's interest and urging, the work would
still be in manuscript form, neatly filed away with thousands of other
dutiful and deserving academic studies.

For every aid and courtesy possible when I was gathering the
material for this work, I am indebted to the administration and staff
of the Boston Athenaeum and particularly to David McKibbin,
Librarian of the Fine Arts Division. In the old days it sometimes
seemed that the staff of the Boston Public Library was not averse to
a few obstacles in the scholar's path, but in recent years no one could
have been more helpful than Sinclair Hitchings and Paul Swanson
of the library's Print Department. Both institutions have been generous in allowing me to reproduce plans, drawings, and old photographs from their collections.

Similarly I wish to thank the directors of the Building and Tax
departments of the City of Boston who gave me, during the winter
of 1941-42, full access to old tax records and building permits which
provided essential information for the documentation contained in
the Appendix.

Sincere gratitude is given to the many persons who allowed me to
see and often to photograph family homes in the Back Bay and to a
number of schools, clubs, and offices which permitted me to inspect
their quarters in edifices which had been built as residences.

To supplement my photographs which were taken more as references on 35 millimeter film, I have been fortunate to solicit the

aid of professional photographers like Bonnie Orr and Henry Sargent. I only wish I had been able to avail myself of their services earlier when more of the old dwellings were in their original state. In selecting illustrations for this work it has sometimes seemed preferable to use one of my old photographs than a recent one of better quality taken after the building had been altered. I am also greatly indebted to Yvan Christ of Paris and Henry-Russell Hitchcock who have allowed me to reproduce old views of Paris from their collections of photographs.

As almost any study which began as a doctoral dissertation, the present work has gone through several transformations. I am grateful to Margaret Paddock, Jacqueline Coker, and Mary Wicker for the perseverance which sustained them through manuscript typing and through endless columns of Appendix. A grant from the faculty research fund at the University of New Mexico defrayed the expense of one typing and of photographic enlargements used as illustrations. The labor of proofreading and criticism performed by Rebecca Salsbury James and Dorothy Feise can only be appreciated by an author who would try to imagine his chagrin had certain slips and downright mistakes not been detected by his proofreaders' careful scrutiny.

CONTENTS

ILLUSTRATIONS

INTRODUCTION 1

The term "Back Bay district" may be used in two ways: geographically it describes an extensive area which was created by filling in the tidal flats of the Back Bay; understood in a sociological sense it refers to the smaller residential district which for a century has been the home of well-to-do Bostonians. As a geographical term, the Back Bay specifies all of the filled land along the Boston side of the Charles River estuary. An extensive section reaching from Charles Dam on the north to Tremont Street on the south, from the western limit of the Common on the east to the new campus of Boston University on the west, it contains some 450 acres (fig. 4). In this larger sense, it is a heterogeneous region including mansions and slums, parks and railroad yards, universities and office skyscrapers.

Sociologically speaking, however, the Back Bay designates a smaller and more homogeneous section. It is Boston's fashionable residential quarter—or so it was until the great depression of 1929 began the gradual conversion of its aristocratic dwellings to more modest uses. Occupying about two hundred acres in the center of the greater filled region, the limits of this smaller area are the river, the Public Garden, Boylston Street, and Fenway Park (fig. 243). In addition, the district prolongs itself for four blocks to the west along Bay State Road and, at its northeast corner, stretches out to include the Brimmer Street neighborhood. It is in the latter sense that we employ the term, implying, thereby, a restricted geographical area and a highly uniform social character.

The Back Bay is interesting to Bostonian and visitor of the present day for a variety of reasons. Some will look at the area as a remarkably complete example of nineteenth century American architecture. Persons interested in this historical and aesthetic aspect of the district are concerned also about its preservation, for there is no example of nineteenth century building and urban planning in America that is comparable to it. Some people with a sociological interest will study the area's changes in property use and occupancy over the last thirty-five years and try to foresee the role the Back Bay is to play in the future development of the metropolitan center. Still others are concerned with the area as a convenient place to live or with property values and tax rates. Whatever one's particular interest in the Back Bay, he soon realizes that it is no ordinary district, and before he proceeds too far with plans or causes he should take a close look at the area's physical characteristics, its history, and its genius. In abbreviated form, therefore, one might attempt to summarize the more important achievements and attributes of the Back Bay district.

With a precision almost unique in American history, the buildings of the Back Bay chart the course of architectural development for more than half a century. Here one can follow, year by year, the changes in architectural style and building technology during the latter half of the nineteenth century. The chart is accurate because it is based on a large number of case studies—almost fifteen hundred—about which fairly complete information is available. The record is the more important when one considers the leading position that Boston occupied as the educational and publication center for architecture in America during the period when the district was being built. The fashions established in the Back Bay were reflected, sooner or later, in other cities of the country.

In themselves the area's buildings are of great architectural value. A close study reveals artistic merits in Victorian architecture to which the last two generations of critics have seemed almost willfully blind. Now, after five decades of neglect, the houses again begin to be appreciated, and if the Back Bay can be spared insensitive remodeling and ruthless demolition for another few years—be spared until the current generation's "blind spot" for Victorian art has been outgrown—it will be appreciated and enjoyed every bit as much as Beacon Hill.

The Back Bay district also constitutes an early and significant chapter in the development of city planning in the United States. With the Public Garden and Commonwealth Avenue, it represents one of the country's first concerted efforts to create a homogeneous urban environment on a grand scale. Later in its history, with the creation of Fenway Park, the district forged the first link of the first metropolitan park system in the nation. Furthermore, the Back Bay demonstrates once again the ability of sound planning to preserve the integrity of a neighborhood. Because of its clearly defined and almost unbreachable boundaries, the Back Bay district has been remarkably resistant to the contamination of slum and nondescript commercial activity. No other nineteenth century urban residential district in the United States has survived with comparable vigor.

A careful study of Back Bay houses also throws interesting light on the sociology of the Boston scene and some of the forces that have tended to shape it. During most of the nineteenth century and despite ample financial resources, Back Bay residences remained modest and conservative because of the old Puritan convictions regarding personal simplicity. Toward the century's end, however, houses tended to increase somewhat in size and splendor as the older tradition weakened and as new families of wealth attempted to make their importance known by means of conspicuous dwellings. A quite different type of sociological force is also illustrated just after the First World War when the automobile began to transport families to the suburbs and when the supply of domestic servants diminished. In a very short time the large town house became out-moded, the Back Bay ceased for the time being to grow, and the large, single-family town houses were converted to other uses.

In a tangible and visible way the Back Bay district also sym-bolizes Boston in its most glorious hour. The area is rich with asso-ciations of people who played important roles in American life and letters and whose works still impinge on our lives today: authors like Oliver Wendell Holmes and William Dean Howells, preachers such as Phillips Brooks, or artists like H. H. Richardson and Wil-liam Morris Hunt. Here lived the great financiers and industrialists who did so much to build America: the Lawrences and Gardners, the Adamses and Ameses, the Forbeses and Thayers. The abode like-wise of legendary Brahmins and ambitious Silas Laphams, the Back Bay has a thousand associations with American thought and action of the later nineteenth century. In brownstone and brick it sym-bolizes its epoch in a way that words and figures alone cannot. The Back Bay is for Victorian Boston what Beacon Hill is for the city's Republican era. And who is to say that the record of accomplish-ment of the later epoch is less impressive or less important than the earlier one? If anything, Boston's cultural leadership in America was stronger in the later period. And the same is true of Boston architecture.

No less interesting than its architectural achievements and historic associations are the present problems and future challenges which face the district. To date the area has demonstrated a remarkable resilience in adapting to types of occupancy other than the one for which most of the buildings were originally designed. With the demise of the large town house, the Back Bay single-family residences were gradually converted into apartments or rooming houses, or divided into offices for professional people. Later came the occupancy by schools and colleges and with them their dormitories. The old residences have proved adaptable and changes have been accomplished without doing violence to the district. Buildings that have proved this adaptable can undoubtedly continue to be useful in the future. The challenge which confronts us now is whether we can forestall the attempt of a few property owners to pull down the present structures and erect new and bigger ones which will destroy the domestic scale and architectural continuity of the district—forestall them long enough for Boston's citizens to awake to the unique architectural importance of the Back Bay district.

A second question concerns the impending commercial development within the area. Although retail shops inside the Back Bay district began to appear along lower Boylston Street in the 1890's, commercial activity has grown gradually and, confined to two streets, not incompatibly with the predominantly residential occupancy. The construction nearby of large life insurance buildings and particularly the recent creation of the Prudential Center have injected new economic forces into the picture. Previously the least desirable and least architecturally interesting area in the Back Bay, upper Boylston Street, now becomes potentially an active and valuable area because of its proximity to the Prudential Center. Already this section has become too valuable for residential purposes, but most recent attempts to provide store and office space by half-hearted modernization have been entirely unsuccessful in terms of urban design.[1] Indeed in much of the recent work there one gets a dismal preview of what may happen elsewhere in the Back Bay if high standards and rigid controls are not enforced. If the shiny resurfaced buildings on upper Boylston or the glass-cubed edifices further down the street are duplicated throughout the neighbor-

hood, what will differentiate the Back Bay from any other congested metropolitan area? What, indeed, will remain to attract people to the district? Clearly present-day problems of the Back Bay
will have to be directed with foresight and firmness if nameless
confusion is to be avoided. But the Back Bay has never been an
average place. One hopes that Boston leaders of the present day
will face the problems of change and growth with the same imagination and largeness of vision, the same dedication to the public
good as the commissioners who laid out the area in the 1850's.

These are the many facets of interest and value of the Back Bay.
The historical limits of the area's growth are easily fixed. The story
begins officially in 1857 when the Commonwealth began to fill in
and citizens to build upon the tidal flats of the bay; it ends at about
the time of the First World War when they ceased to construct
large town houses. During this sixty-year period some fifteen hundred private residences and apartment houses were produced.

The number of houses erected during each year the district was
building is indicated in figure 1. One easily notes the close relationship between house construction and general business conditions.
Thus the panics of 1857, 1873, and 1893 are clearly indicated on
the chart by sharp declines in construction; so also is a minor reces-
sion near the end of the Civil War. Prosperity, on the other hand,
is represented by five waves of building activity: 1853–56, 1859–63,

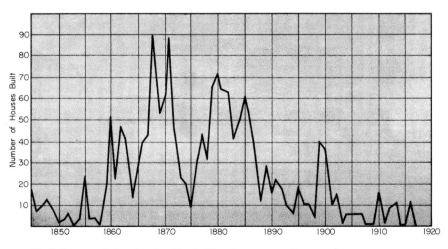

1   Building activity in the Back Bay between 1845 and 1917.

1866–72, 1876–87, and 1899–1902. Especially noteworthy are the housing booms which accompanied the financial spree which followed the Civil War and the solid decade of prosperity from 1876 to 1887.[2]

The concluding date of our study is determined by a new sociological force—rapid transportation. By 1900 the Back Bay residential area had all but ceased to grow. After 1910 only thirty new houses were constructed; after 1917, none at all.[3] Instead of paying high prices for filled land on which to erect a home within walking distance of his office, the potential home builder escaped to the suburbs on the electric trolley or in his automobile. This flight from the city left empty much of the area west of Kenmore Square and adjacent to Fenway Park, and only later was it occupied by nondescript and closely built apartments.

Related to these waves of building activity are changes in architectural fashion. In this study we shall distinguish four principal stylistic eras: a formative and transitional period (1844–1857), a period of disciplined, academic hegemony (1857–1869), an era of almost boisterous individualism (1869–1885), and a final three decades of dignity and impeccable erudition (1885–1917).

Not only the fact that the Back Bay records all these architectural moods but also the orderly way in which she does so is unique. Because the land had to be filled in and because this process was slow and expensive, the supply of new land kept only slightly ahead of the new construction. Filling operations began at the Public Garden and worked toward the west, and a tide of building followed close behind it. Because this front of new construction left very few empty lots in its wake, most of the buildings within each block date from approximately the same time, a circumstance that makes for admirable architectural consistency. As a result of these circumstances a pedestrian starting at the Public Garden and walking westward can review American architectural development of half a century within the confines of a single street. Nowhere else in America is this possible on so impressive a scale.

As the title of the book suggests, this study does not attempt to cover all aspects of the Back Bay development. It is limited to a factual history and description of houses, to an analysis of their architecture, and to a few explanations of their reason for being or their change. Except for brief mention of churches and a few public buildings discussed in connection with the urban plan and growth of the Back Bay, the area's monumental architecture has not been included. Similarly, the gradual spread of commercial activity in the area, which began in one small corner at Boylston and Arlington streets, and the evolution of the district's commercial architecture has been by-passed. Another fascinating possibility that was not pursued is an analysis of the drastic urban changes (such as the Turnpike extension or the Prudential Center) which have come into being in more recent years. To include such topics would clearly have changed the study's whole frame of reference. Although desirable, a complete account of all aspects of the Back Bay—historical and current, urban and architectural, stylistic and economic—would constitute quite another book. For the urgency of the moment, when the fate of the Back Bay as a historical district lies in balance, many interesting aspects of the subject must be put aside.

THE CULTURAL
BACKGROUND
OF THE BACK BAY
DEVELOPMENT

2

Given the stereotyped notion that many Americans have of Boston as a city restrained and refined, sage and immutable, the assertion may seem strange that just over a century ago Boston was a boom town, one of ancient foundation, to be sure, but glowing with optimism and growing in the manner of numerous present-day boom towns from Texas to California. Alive with economic and cultural advance, Boston's population in 1850 was doubling every quarter century. The town, now become a city, was aflame with a new spirit sharply in contrast to the quiet, provincial outlook of the early nineteenth century.

Boston was in such a state of flux that her citizens were almost compelled to think in terms of the future. Nothing indicates the dizzy pace of change better than population figures. In 1800 Boston-town numbered less than 25,000 souls; by 1825 the figure had doubled (58,277); by 1850, quintupled (136,881).[1] The single decade of the forties witnessed a 33 percent increment. This swelling population brought problems. In 1822 the traditional town meeting form of government, having become unwieldy, was abandoned when Boston incorporated as a city. Increasing numbers of Irish immigrants, especially after 1848, resulted in a less homogeneous and cohesive population. And eventually there came the physical problem of where to sleep so many people.

A similar growing out of the small and familiar into the large and untried is evidenced in other phases of Boston life. In volume of trade, in value and diversity of manufacturing, in size and quantity of building, Boston in the years before the Civil War outstripped all of her previous records. Early nineteenth century standards of private wealth and of commercial activity were utterly dwarfed by the scale of mid-century financial operations, while the sea, once Boston's principal source of wealth, became but one among several sources of profit in the city's expanding economy.

At mid-century, however, even the sea trade was still increasing. Under the pressure of growing manufacture and the advent of the railroad, which carried manufactured goods from distant parts of New England to Boston for transshipment, the decade of the 1840's was the most prosperous in Boston's shipping history. It began with the selection of Boston as American terminal for the Cunard Line. In 1849 Boston craft alone carried an estimated 90,000 persons to California. During the fifties, heyday of the clipper ship, which was built in Boston shipyards, Boston shipping soared to a peak with a total carrying capacity of more than half a million tons at a time when an estimated third of the world's commerce was borne by American vessels. The Calcutta trade brought ninety-six shiploads of merchandise to Boston docks in 1857 as against twelve in 1800.[2]

More than any other single factor, however, it was the railroad that changed Boston from a provincial town to a thriving metropolis. In the course of two decades eight railroad lines, built by local interests, were extended from the city in all directions, making suburbs of neighboring towns which for centuries had been independent municipalities, and creating a regional network of railroads with Boston as their center.[3] This new trade area, which extended as far west as the Berkshires, greatly exceeded in size Boston's former trade area, the Merrimac Valley, which had been secured in 1803 by the opening of the Middlesex Canal. For a moment in the early forties, it even seemed that Boston enterprise might extend her domain to the rich Midwest by the building of a direct rail line to the Great Lakes. Indeed, two railroads were pushed through to the Hudson River, and several Boston investors interested themselves in western railroad promotion.

With the growth of rail and sea commerce, Boston manufacturing greatly expanded and diversified. The output in 1800, valued at $6,500,000, had quadrupled by 1840, and it soared another 50 percent to a total of $45,000,000 in 1850.[4] In the early part of the century New England manufacture had been organized on the apprentice system, unaware of the advantages of subdivision of labor and lacking in specialized machinery. Confined to the processing of simple raw materials, it attempted to supply only the most basic needs of the community such as brick, timber, simple metal tools, and beer. Given a first impetus by the Jefferson Embargo of 1807 and later fostered by a high protective tariff, the factory system soon developed; power machinery was introduced, and new methods of financing were devised to secure the necessarily large amounts of capital for large-scale factory building. Boston industry became more diversified, too; from the few basic articles it expanded to include such products requiring highly specialized skills and equipment as shoes, sugar, sewing machines, pianos, and watches. In the 1830's the city also developed the ready-made clothing industry which became the largest undertaking of all. Because New England led the country in textile manufacture, Boston became the dry goods center of the nation; because of her extensive shoe manufacturing, she emerged as the nation's leather market.

Trade so expanded that the old methods of informal meetings among merchants along State Street to effect a sale proved inadequate. Commission houses better prepared to handle the larger and more specialized stocks were founded, and by 1855 the merchants felt it necessary to regularize trading procedure by the establishment of the Commercial Exchange (which later developed into the Chamber of Commerce). Similarly, bankers realized the advantages of a central clearing house in 1857. Thus in commercial and industrial life we witness during the forties and fifties enormous changes in Boston. Men's ambitions soared with the charts of production and records of large profits. Clearly, Boston stood on the threshold of a bright future. The quiet and modest days of the provincial seaport were past.

In the cultural sphere the change was equally significant, even though it cannot be chronicled as conveniently by dollar signs. Although he had long ago ceased to be provincial in literary matters, the cultivated Bostonian at the beginning of the century still saw European culture through British eyes. Sometime before the middle of the century and especially after the inauguration of the Cunard Line made travel much easier, the Yankee student tended to travel more. He now experienced the Continent as well as England. Tom Appleton made the first of his many European journeys in 1833, soon after his graduation from Harvard. Longfellow, a son of Maine, studied abroad in 1826 and 1834 and inspired several Boston students to follow the same course, James Russell Lowell included. That it was more customary for young Bostonians to study in Paris in 1834 than for the youth of either Philadelphia or New York we infer from the letters of the medical student Oliver Wendell Holmes.[5] The post-Harvard travels of Henry Adams or H. H. Richardson and his friends indicate the popularity of a continental *Studentenreise* in the late fifties. Young women traveled, too, for William Morris Hunt married a Boston girl in France in 1855.

Nor was travel confined to the student class. The second generation of the new mercantile families grew to manhood favored with leisure and funds for travel. The type is personified by Bromfield Corey in Howell's novel *The Rise of Silas Lapham*. Some of these men developed a taste for collecting art objects; at least two such collections eventually found their way into public institutions. Colonel T. B. Lawrence's gift of a collection of armor to the Athenaeum in 1871 caught the public interest and resulted in the founding of a public art museum. Thomas Gold Appleton bought engravings in Rome which later he gave to the newly organized Boston Public Library.[6] Heir to an ample fortune derived from textile mills and merchandising, Tom Appleton did not enter business or a profession. He traveled widely and, even before the Civil War, assembled the first large collection of paintings in Boston. Only one generation earlier Boston would have frowned on such unbusinesslike vocations.

Now interest in painting spread with the increase in wealth and cosmopolitan awareness.[7] In the middle of the nineteenth century this interest focused mainly on contemporary French painting and the "old masters," although there was also a substantial patronage of contemporary American landscape and portrait painters. As early as 1826 the Athenaeum held the first of its yearly exhibits; by 1830 there was a commercial gallery, Corinthian Hall; the forties and fifties saw the establishment of three associations of artists, founded, among other things, to organize yearly painting exhibits; in 1847 the new theater, the Boston Museum, was provided with a large permanent collection of old, if somewhat questionable, masters; in

1850 the Athenaeum, settled now in its new home on Beacon Street, devoted its entire third floor to a gallery for sculpture and painting. The fifties brought foreign picture dealers to Boston with stocks of modern French paintings which they sold at substantial prices; by the sixties and seventies several Boston artists traveled abroad to buy for Boston collectors at European sales. This developing interest in art culminated in 1871 in the founding of the long-projected Museum of Fine Arts. Nor were these blessings of art reserved altogether for the upper classes. By 1870 an act of the legislature made art instruction mandatory in all Massachusetts schools in towns with populations of over ten thousand; a normal school was established in Boston in 1873 to train art teachers and supervisors; in 1876 the Museum School was launched as an adjunct of the new art museum.

The forties and fifties also saw a pronounced, almost sudden development of musical interest.[8] Boston had its first season of opera in 1847; an amateur orchestra which performed between 1841 and 1847 was succeeded by a professional organization in 1855 that gave concerts until the Civil War. The Liedertafel Club founded in 1849 was an amateur choral group that took its place beside the Handel and Haydn Society established in 1815. The construction and dedication in November 1852 of the great new Music Hall gave evidence of the substantial nature of Boston's musical interest; to the new hall was added in 1863 the "Great Organ," largest in America to that date. Here was performed in February of 1853 the Ninth Symphony, while another Beethoven concert was organized to commemorate the unveiling of Crawford's statue of the German composer in 1856. What more striking symbol could be found of the city's growing cosmopolitan character? Fittingly enough, Boston also saw the publication of four musical magazines between 1820 and 1839; a professional music school, the Boston Academy, with an orchestra of its own was founded in 1839; and music was introduced in the local public schools before the mid-century.

Three imposing theaters were constructed in these same years: the aforementioned Music Hall in 1852; the Boston Museum (1846), in reality a theater despite its name and its gallery of specious old masters; and the Boston Theatre of 1853, purportedly a copy of Milan's La Scala.

Next a long list of civic improvements and new institutions bear witness to the city's prosperity and optimism and to her new sense of civic dignity. Symbolically enough, the first of a series of civic buildings, the Quincy Market of 1824, was built just two years after Boston was chartered as a city. In turn, there follow the Suffolk County Jail of 1849 and the Deer Island Poor House of 1850, both so important in their time that plans and several columns of description were featured in a contemporary English architectural journal.[9] The Boston Public Library, founded in 1852, was installed in its first home on Boylston Street six years later; a new City Hall was begun in 1861; a Free City Hospital, projected as early as 1852, was finally opened in 1865. Because of its semipublic character, the enlarged Boston Athenaeum of 1847 should also be included here, as should the original Horticulture Hall.

And there were new railroad depots. Each handsomer than its predecessor, passenger and freight depots were erected for all eight railroads serving Boston. The rivalry among the lines came to a climax in the 1872 station for the Boston and Providence line which Boston proudly acclaimed as the handsomest railroad station in all America as well as the one with the world's longest train shed. (Again, one is reminded of similar claims and growing pains in our 1960 boom towns of the Southwest.)

A series of improvements in the field of the public utilities attested likewise to Boston modernity. Between 1853 and 1859 the horsecar replaced the horse-drawn omnibus, and soon seven rail lines crisscrossed Boston and connected it with neighboring towns like Cambridge and Brookline. In 1823 illuminating gas was introduced, only nine years after it appeared in London and four years before New York adopted it; by 1834 gas was already beginning to replace oil lamps for street illumination. An adequate water supply was provided in 1848 when the aqueduct from Cochituate was opened as far as Boston Common amid public rejoicing, and within the year the enormous granite reservoir atop Beacon Hill was in full use. In 1849, following London by only four years, Boston instituted penny postage. To this must be added the construction of three free bridges from Boston to neighboring towns in the 1820's and the successful prosecution of several small filling operations at various places along the waterfront which added to the city's land area.[10]

It is not surprising to find that this economic expansion and civic improvement had a corollary in the field of residential architecture.

The conception and beginning of the Back Bay district symbolizes Boston's wealth and optimism in the late 1850's and the pride and ambition of her civic leaders. In planning Commonwealth Avenue in 1856 as a great boulevard and in constructing in the early sixties blocks of impressive brownstone mansions akin in style to those being built in Paris in the same years, Boston expressed her will to assume a place among the great cities of the world. Here, symbolically, in adopting the new architectural style of Napoleon III's Second Empire, she exchanged her provincial and well-worn garb of the Greek Revival tradition for the more splendid and worldly robes of contemporary Europe.

Eventually, however, this period of turbulent change began to level off. Not suddenly, but unmistakably, the earlier expansive climate yielded to one of complacency and fulfillment. Heretofore progressive Boston now turned her attention to the maintenance of the status quo. No abrupt change of tempo separates the two phases of Boston's life, and it is difficult to say precisely when the change took place, sometime after the Civil War, but certainly by 1890. At first Bostonians were probably unaware of their new outlook—but later they gloried in it.

In the financial world the new attitude expressed itself as a stout conservatism. Rather than the former willingness to risk wealth in an attempt to develop new and larger industry, Boston capitalists now sought safety above all else. If there was no decline in Boston's wealth or population, if, on the contrary, she, with the rest of the country, grew richer and larger as the century progressed, this increase was far less spectacular than it could or should have been. Only by comparing Boston and New York can one understand the magnitude of this change in attitude. In the 1830's and 1840's Boston was a serious contender with New York for the leadership of American finance and commerce. After the Civil War, however, the Massachusetts city, now outdistanced by New York, seemed to rest on her oars. A comparison of the bank clearing records of the two cities illustrates Boston's increasing lag. In 1857, the first year in which Boston had a central clearing house, her total clearings were one-eighth those of New York; by 1880 they had dropped to one-twelfth.[11]

One suspects that this relative decline of Boston's financial operations was partially the result of deliberate choice, that somehow

Boston preferred to retain things as they were rather than to seek ways of enlarging them. An early Boston businessman deplored the fact that his contemporaries were committed to "a policy based on the idea of doing a comparatively small amount of business at a large profit instead of a large amount of business at a small profit." Or was it instead that Bostonians had an instinctive mistrust of bigness? When an early president of the Boston and Maine Railroad was approached with the idea of consolidating four New England railroads in an attempt to push through a line to the Mississippi Valley, he rejected the proposed scheme because it was "too big!"[12] Instead of leading America's expanding economy in the latter half of the nineteenth century, Boston settled comfortably on her existing manufacturing and trade, on her trusteeships and her gilt-edge investments. With few exceptions Boston developed no new large industries in the late nineteenth century; she did not replace her prewar shipping fleet; her dry goods market and the ready-made clothing industry slowly transferred to New York; her extensive western railroad holdings were not used to bolster Boston's waning commercial position. Although Boston financiers had been responsible for building the Burlington, the Union Pacific, the Michigan Central, and the Santa Fe railroads, their descendants in the seventies and eighties were content to sell out at a comfortable profit and invest the proceeds in secure four-percent bonds.

A native son, Frederic J. Stimson, having lived a good part of his life away from the city, was able to view Boston's financial defeat somewhat objectively. In his memoirs, *My United States,* Stimson analyzed why Boston was so outdistanced by New York. He discussed the "spendthrift trusts," that instrument of arch-conservatism peculiar to Massachusetts, which had so stultifying an effect on Boston economy.

Somewhere about 1830, they [the Massachusetts courts] decided that a man could tie his children's inheritance up either by deed or will, so that he could not spend or risk his principal or, indeed, embark in any business. Immense wealth had been accumulated in Boston in the first sixty years of the republic, but instead of trusting their sons and sending them out at their own risks with all their argosies upon life's seas, as they themselves had done, they distrusted their abilities and had them all trusteed. No new enterprise could be undertaken by them for under court decision they had no capital to risk. Perforce they became coupon cutters, not promoters of industry . . . The result of making Boston's youth mere four-percent men was to choke off their own energies and largely to divorce business and the Brahmins.[13]

It was this satisfaction with things as they were that blinded Boston to the essential importance of securing a railroad route to the more agriculturally productive Mississippi Valley. Even when the disastrous effects of this oversight became apparent, Boston was unable to rise above her provincialism in a concerted attempt to rectify the situation by connecting Boston with the rich western lands. In 1859, for example, Massachusetts financiers had a last chance to secure their railroad link with the great midwestern lands when the New York Central system was offered for sale. But because the Boston group was approached on this matter by an "outsider," a "western" man from Springfield, Massachusetts, they were cold to the proposition. Instead the road was bought up by Colonel Vanderbilt for nine million dollars.[14]

Boston ways and Boston attitudes have long been a favorite topic for American writers, both Boston-bred and "western," but perhaps only an outsider could have characterized so clearly Boston's intellectual attitude in this post–Civil War period. Writing in 1906, H. G. Wells devoted a chapter in his book *The Future of America* to the cultural attitudes which he discovered in the United States and especially those which he found in Boston.

In Boston . . . one finds the human mind not base, nor brutal, nor stupid, not ignorant, but mysteriously enchanting and ineffectual, so that having eyes it yet does not see, having powers, it achieves nothing . . . I remember Boston as a quiet effect, as something a little withdrawn, as a place standing aside from the throbbing intercourse of East and West. Boston presents a terrible, terrifying unanimity of aesthetic discrimination. There broods over the real Boston an immense sense of finality. One feels in Boston, as in no other part of the States that the intellectual movement has ceased. Contemporary Boston art is imitative art, its writers are correct and imitative writers, the central figure of its literary world is that charming old lady of eighty-eight, Mrs. Julia Ward Howe. One meets her and Colonel Higginson in the midst of an author's society that is not so much composed of minor stars as a chorus of indistinguishable culture . . . I do not know why the full sensing of what is ripe and good in the past should carry with it this quality of discriminating against the present and the future. But the fact remains that it does so almost oppressively . . . I do not wish to accuse Boston of any willful, deliberate repudiation of the

present, but I think that Boston (the intellectual and spiritual Boston)
commits the scholastic error and tries to remember too much, to treasure
too much, and has refined and studied and collected herself into a state
of hopeless intellectual and aesthetic repletion in consequence. In these
matters there are limits. The finality of Boston is a quantitative consequence. The capacity of Boston, it would seem, was just sufficient but no
more than sufficient, to comprehend the whole achievement of the human
intellect up, let us say, to the year 1875 A.D. Then an equilibrium was
established. At or about that year Boston filled up.[15]

It was this cultivation of the past, this critical attitude toward
the present which enabled her in 1913 to overlook the Armory Show
with genteel equanimity and which drove the Boston-born architect
Louis Sullivan to seek the freer atmosphere of Chicago. Similarly
author William Dean Howells moved to New York in 1889 when he
concluded that Boston was " 'no life' but 'death-in-life.' "[16]

As a corollary to this economic and intellectual development, one
can observe in the field of social relations a congelation of the upper
level of Boston society at about the same time. Cleveland Amory,
chronicler of *Proper Bostonians,* describes Boston's unique system of
"First Families." Among other requirements for this exalted state
he notes two necessary items of lineage: an eighteenth century merchant ancestor, preferably a sea captain, and a nineteenth century capitalist. Though the latter supplied the essential wealth, the
former created the romantic tradition which later Boston generations
were apt to regard with greater admiration. Amory observes that
the family must have been established firmly by at least the 1870's
when, "All of a sudden, as it were, the Golden Gates of Boston's First
Familyland clanged shut and, generally speaking, have remained
shut ever since." He suggests 1879 as the "curfew" date, the death
of John L. Gardner, last of the India merchant-princes. Amory also
describes the extremely conservative character of this elevated level
of society: its dislike for ostentation and hostility to publicity, its
addiction to large family gatherings, and the persistence of such
old-fashioned forms of social intercourse as the sewing circle.[17]

It is more than coincidence that Amory's curfew date of 1879 for
First Family founding, Well's date of 1875 for the symbolic "filling
up" of the Boston mind, and the removal in 1875 of the executive
offices of the Burlington Railroad from Boston to New York fall
within a few years of one another. It is equally important to note

how closely these dates coincide with Boston's budding interest between 1876 and 1890 in the revival of Georgian architecture, a subject that will be discussed in Chapter Seven. The choice of this particular architectural style, however, implies more than "discrimination against the present and future"; it illustrates the effort of the latter-day Bostonian to identify himself with his family-founding, seafaring ancestor. Now in the 1890's, despite ample wealth, Back Bay residents chose to build homes of substantially the same size and architectural style as had their ancestors a hundred years earlier. If one compares these relatively modest town houses with the ostentatious mansions of contemporary New Yorkers, he sees again the fundamentally conservative quality of Boston society and of its mode of living.

Parceled out for the most part in equal twenty-five foot lots and built with substantial dwellings, the Back Bay reflects the fact that it was the home of business and professional men of comfortable wealth. The absence of grandiose mansions, for example, accords with the fact that in 1880 Boston with a population of only 363,000 people had fifty-one banks.[18] These residences also reflect the fact that Bostonians resisted "bigness" in dwellings just as they did in business undertakings, that they preferred to retain the living habits and business practices of their admired forebears.

Although one understands with hindsight the shortcomings of Boston's overly conservative attitude during the late nineteenth century, he must consider other aspects of this self-restraint. The city was indeed more conservative and cultivated than the rest of America at that time—a fact which most Americans of the period admitted, though sometimes grudgingly. Without question life in Boston had less of the willful, noisy, self-assertive vigor that one finds elsewhere in the country. In architectural terms this quality is demonstrated by the houses of the Back Bay. Compared to the energetic but sometimes splendid monstrosities produced by Victorian builders in other parts of America during the last half of the century, the architecture of polite Boston is remarkably discreet. Among the fifteen hundred houses constructed in the Back Bay district, there are not more than half a dozen "shockers."[19]

Henry James, American-born though thoroughly Anglicized, saw the Back Bay in still another way. Of this we read in his chapter on Boston in *The American Scene*:

It is all very rich and prosperous and monotonous, the large lower level [the Back Bay]—but oh, so inexpressibly vacant! Where the "new land" corresponds most to its name, rejoices most visibly and complacently in its newness . . . there the long, straight residential avenues, vistas quite documentary, testify with a perfection all their own to a whole vast side of American life . . . We call such aspects "documentary" because they strike us as speaking volumes for the possible serenity, the common decency, the quiet cohesion of a vast commercial and professional bourgeoisie left to itself. Here was such an order caught in the very fact, the fact of its living maximum. A bourgeoisie without an aristocracy to worry it is, of course, a very different thing from a bourgeoisie struggling in that shade, and nothing could express more than these interminable prospects of security the condition of a community leading its life in the social sun.[20]

Despite Mr. James's recoil from the monotony of this bourgeoisie basking in its own light, the historian will not fail to recognize the existence in the Back Bay of certain socio-economic gradations. Bostonians themselves long since implied these differences when they classed people by the streets on which they lived: the old rich on Beacon Street, the old poor on Marlborough, the new rich on Commonwealth Avenue, and the new poor on Newbury. Within this hierarchy an even loftier rank was conferred on the "water side" of Beacon Street or the "sunny side" of Commonwealth Avenue.

TOPOGRAPHICAL DEVELOPMENT OF BOSTON 1790–1965

3

If by magic or some stroke of science the reader could achieve the mastery of time he now exerts in space, he could push back the years to a given time and then unroll them to observe any aspect of history he wished. A person interested in the topographical development of Boston could benefit especially by this arrangement as he attempts to follow the larger sweep of the development.[1] To obtain such a view, the spectator would also require some vantage point high above the city from which to look down upon the panorama of growth. Today, of course, one would simply anchor his space platform somewhere above the State House dome, but in 1790, when our story begins, the best view of the Boston scene would have been obtained from the great beacon erected on the town's highest hill (fig. 2).

This beacon has symbolic interest about which more should be said. A high Doric column, which crowned the highest summit of Tremont and whose capital stood 210 feet above the harbor, it was erected in 1790 by Charles Bulfinch.[2] Young Bulfinch, just returned from his European travels and embarrassed, perhaps, by the provincial appearance of his native town, replaced at his own expense the dilapidated seventeenth century wooden beacon by this noble shaft. Designed by the man who was destined to become the city's first professional architect, the beacon was the kind of monumental column which might have been found in any up-to-date European

2   Excavating the summit of Beacon Hill in 1811. The State House had
been erected in 1795 on a shelf dug into the south slope, and in 1811
the crest of the hill was cut down to provide gravel for the North Cove
fill. At that time the Doric column erected in 1790 by Charles Bulfinch
to replace the seventeenth century wooden beacon was also demolished.

city of the period. It was also a monument of the type young architects were sometimes asked to design in competitions for the coveted
Prix de Rome between 1790 and 1806.[3] A symbol of Boston's aspirations, this columnar beacon is therefore a fitting observation post
from which to view Boston's progress.

Thus, through a stroke of magic or a flight of whimsy, we find
ourselves back in the year 1790, the year in which, according to the
first nationwide census, Boston had a population of about 18,000
citizens. As we look down upon Boston from our column-top perch,
we are aware of an irregular peninsula that is practically an island
in the center of the Inner Harbor (fig. 3). Almost pear-shaped, with
its tip pointing southwest and its stem an exceedingly narrow isth-
mus connecting the small peninsula with Roxbury Highlands, this
area contains less than one square mile. It is dominated by five
hills, two rather small ones (Fort Hill to the south and Copp's Hill
to the north) and a relatively large one that swells from the center
of the peninsula. Upon closer observation, however, we see that this

largest hill, the one on which our column is built, is really composed of three distinct peaks, thus suggesting its name of Trimountain or Tremont. The town's shoreline is irregular and cut by four deep coves or bays: South Cove to the southwest of Fort Hill; East Cove, or Great Cove, on the northeast which serves as the town's principal harbor; North Cove to the west of Copp's Hill, and the Back Bay. The Back Bay is really the estuary of the Charles River; it cuts behind the peninsula on the southwest and almost isolates it from the mainland. Of the original shoreline of this peninsula, not one foot will remain in 1967, but in 1790 the topography of Boston peninsula was almost as the first Puritans had found it.

On our column-top, let us pause a moment to survey the environs of Boston. The town occupies a relatively small proportion of the peninsula which in turn is isolated by great expanses of water where the Mystic, Charles, and Miller's rivers converge to form the Inner Harbor. This harbor in turn is fringed by a series of small, isolated communities. Across the harbor to the northeast, East Boston is a bleak island, deserted save for cattle and sheep that pasture there; Chelsea is a quiet, riverside hamlet of 472 inhabitants separated from Medford by two deep inlets of the meandering Mystic River; and Charlestown, largest of the mainland towns, is to twentieth century eyes almost unrecognizable without the granite obelisk atop Bunker Hill. To the west we see Cambridge, not yet fused with Charlestown by the acres of sooty railroad yards which will one day obliterate Miller's River. Cambridge is a country village—in all only 148 dwellings scattered on farms or clustered around Harvard College. What will someday become East Cambridge is nothing more than a low hill with a single farm house on it, and Cambridgeport, which in a few years will begin to bristle with activity, is still an uncertain area of salt marshes.[4] Off to the southwest, beyond the two-mile extent of the Back Bay, lie the farms of Brookline, while to the south Roxbury and Dorchester are sleepy villages of 2226 and 1722 population. In a southeasterly direction and separated from Boston by the expanse of the shallow South Bay is an island-like strip of land occupied by a few farms belonging to Roxbury; this area is so unlike its twentieth century configuration that we may have difficulty in identifying it as South Boston. Beyond that to the east are the countless islands of the outer harbor.

Below us Boston's harbor is busy again after long years of war

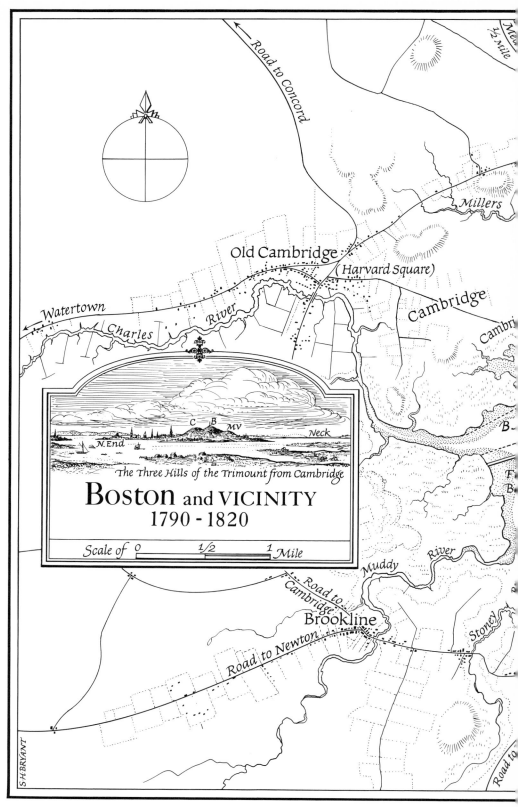

Road to Concord

Millers

Old Cambridge
(Harvard Square)

Cambridge

Cambri

Watertown

Charles   River

B.

F.
B.

The Three Hills of the Trimount from Cambridge

N. End   C B MV   Neck

BOSTON and VICINITY
1790 - 1820

Scale of   0   1/2   1 Mile

Muddy   River

Road to
Cambridge

Brookline

Stoney

Road to Newton

Road to

S.H.BRYANT

3   Map of Boston and vicinity showing the original shoreline and indi-
cating the locations of the Mill Dam and the earliest bridges.

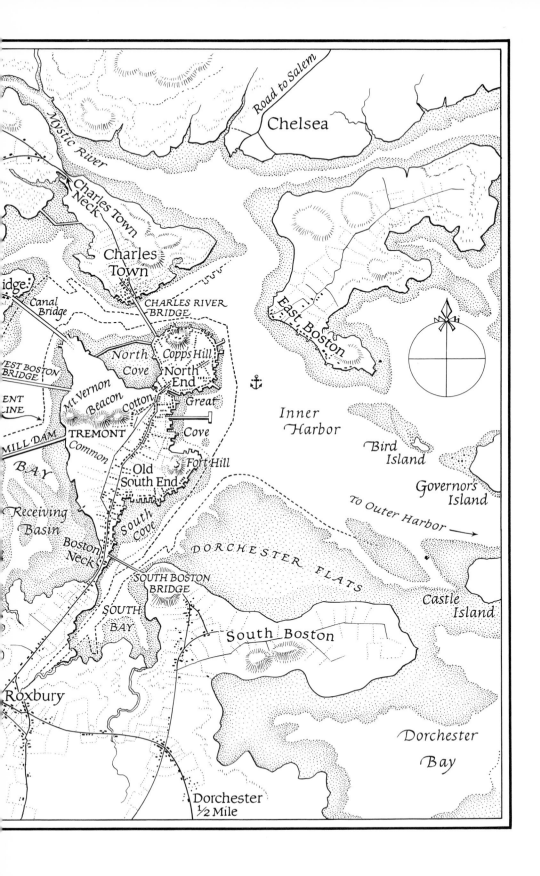

and depression. Save for the Embargo and the short War of 1812, Boston shipping is about to enter on seventy years of unparalleled activity which will carry her ships to all corners of the globe and return great wealth to her merchants. We observe the greatest activity along the waterfront of the Great Cove where there are no less than eighty wharves and quays. The larger ships are moored to Long Wharf which extends almost six hundred yards from the foot of State Street into the harbor. It even projects beyond the remains of the old Barricade, that crescent-shaped breakwater built in the seventeenth century as defense against pirates.[5]

At the head of State Street, commanding a view of Long Wharf, is the Old State House, still the seat of government of the new Commonwealth of Massachusetts; a little to the north is Corn Hill, center of the retail trade. Here we see neat rows of three-story brick houses with shops on the ground floor. The majority of the town's residences, however, are still wooden, often standing contiguous to one another but always with a garden. The North End, dominated by Copp's Hill, is the most populous residential area. Before the Revolution this section was the fashionable quarter, but in recent years a new area known as the South End has arisen in the region between Church Green and the Common. In this latter area the houses appear to be of brick, and they are surrounded by gardens somewhat larger than those of the North End. If we watch the building activity in this neighborhood attentively, we soon discern the graceful spire of Bulfinch's New South Church rising above the housetops, while a group of elegant new houses reminiscent of those currently building in London takes shape along the Tontine Crescent in Franklin Street. Further to the south, as the peninsula narrows down to the Neck, residential building trails off along Washington Street and stops completely at the old earthenwork fortifications erected before the Revolution.[6]

The West End, the neighborhood on the northwest slope of Beacon Hill, stands on the brink of its development. Although long considered a healthful quarter because of the westerly breezes across the Back Bay in summer, and subdivided as early as 1725, it has heretofore attracted few builders. However, Boston's prosperity in the 1790's is attracting numerous artisans from the country round about, and it is they who build the neat but modest houses, a few of which will remain into the twentieth century.[7]

Boston's population, however, is scattered, and unoccupied land still remains to provide living space for a growing population. Most of this free area is just below our columnar perch on Trimountain whose steep slopes have heretofore discouraged house builders. In 1790 the distinctive landmarks known to the twentieth century are lacking. The gold-covered dome of the State House is nowhere to be found; the delicate, ascending spire of the Park Street Church and the somber portico of St. Paul's are as yet unbuilt. Cows graze on Boston Common, the uncertain western limit of which is a salt marsh; and the familiar Public Garden is still a grey mud flat.

But to twentieth century eyes, the most unfamiliar sight of the 1790 scene is the triple summit of Tremont instead of the single rounding crest of the Beacon Hill we know today. The slopes of the three hills are covered with broad pastures and scattered country estates. The most pretentious of these is that of Gardiner Greene, situated on Cotton Hill, easternmost of the three peaks. This mansion, although built before the Revolution, is still one of the finest in Boston.[8] Because of its commanding position, Greene's garden has long been a favorite resort of Boston gentry from which to view the harbor. On the southern slope of Beacon Hill, middle and highest of the Tremont peaks, is John Hancock's house of 1735, while farther down the hill to the west is the more modest seat of John Singleton Copley, the Boston painter now resident in England. Mount Vernon, most westerly of the three summits, contains no buildings. Dr. Joy, the local apothecary, has recently purchased a two-acre pasture between the Hancock and Copley homes and built a modest frame house in order to provide a healthful rural environment for his bouncing family of eleven children. Despite its drowsy, bucolic atmosphere, Beacon Hill is on the verge of great building activity which in less than forty years will obliterate two of the three hilltops described above and change completely the suburban character of the district.

This building boom develops on Beacon Hill in the mid-nineties when interest is focused on the construction of the New State House in 1795. In 1793 the Commonwealth buys the Hancock pasture as the site for this new building and in the following year the Mount Vernon Proprietors begin negotiations for the purchase of the twenty-acre Copley estate.[9] In 1796 this purchase is effected and the Proprietors, having added by other purchases an additional nine acres to their holdings, are ready to launch their new subdivision, the largest real estate operation yet undertaken in Boston.

By the century's end we look down on a scene of great activity and some historic interest. The Proprietors have constructed an inclined wooden track on the western slope of Mount Vernon. Down this plane are drawn carts carrying earth from the excavations on the summit of the hill to fill the shallow tidal flats in the Charles River below. By this ingenious device—some claim for it the title of first railway in America—the crest of Mount Vernon is reduced about sixty feet. Work progresses rapidly and in 1803 Charles Street is laid out and houses rise on the new filled land. Higher up the hill, two of the Proprietors build mansions for themselves—thus setting the fashion for other prosperous Boston gentlemen and establishing a high architectural standard for the neighborhood. The Perkins and the Otis houses stand free on hundred-foot lots and are set well back from the street.[10] By 1826 the Proprietors' entire tract of thirty acres is subdivided and sold except for the northwestern corner which, in this year, is laid out as Louisburg Square and its adjacent building lots. By the mid-forties, practically all of the Mount Vernon subdivision is occupied.

Following Mount Vernon, Beacon Hill is the next peak to be cut down. Actually the demolition begins in 1795 when an ugly hole is gouged in the hill's southern slope in order to secure a shelf on which to erect Bulfinch's State House (fig. 2). Taking their cue from the Commonwealth, various private owners also begin excavations on their property for gravel which is sold to contractors filling in lots along the shoreline. In 1811 the town of Boston sells the plot on which our handsome Doric beacon is situated, and the monument, which only twenty years before was reared as a symbol of Boston's new era, is pulled down. At this juncture we modern Simeons of Stylite shall simply transfer to a space platform, which we anchor above the State House dome, and continue our vigil without interruption.

Before 1820 the site of our erstwhile columnar perch is excavated and the crest of old Beacon Hill reduced by sixty feet.[11] When Cochituate water is piped into Boston just prior to 1850, we can watch the construction of an enormous granite water reservoir on the very site of Bulfinch's column.

The final obliteration of Trimountain comes with the drastic diminution of Cotton Hill. In 1835 the Widow Greene sells her estate, and in less than five months' time more than a hundred thousand cubic yards of gravel are hauled down the hill in ox-drawn carts to fill the old Mill Pond. Fifty feet below the original crest of Cotton Hill, Pemberton Square is laid out, and in October of the same year building lots are auctioned off.[12] Here uniform, bow-front, red brick mansions are immediately erected, thus building over virtually all of the once unoccupied land of the Tremont section.

While our attention has been focused on the area immediately below us, great changes have been taking place in other parts of Boston peninsula (fig. 4). The marketplace about Dock Square is greatly expanded in the twenties. The old covered market area beneath Faneuil Hall, erected in 1763 and enlarged by Bulfinch in 1806, has for years been too small to serve the town which has become a city. In 1823 we can watch the filling of the area near the old City Wharf facing Dock Square and the construction of the gleaming white porticos of Quincy Market. Built as a part of the market but separated from it by wide streets are parallel rows of fine, granite-faced warehouses. Commeasurable also with Boston's new cityship and growing importance is the granite courthouse of 1840 and the rows of granite-front stores built at the foot of State Street.[13] Nor can visitors accuse the new city of provincial ways inasmuch as Tremont House, the most elegant hotel in all North America, has been receiving guests since 1829. Indicative of the luxurious accommodations that the traveler finds here are the banks of water closets situated on each floor in the rear wing of the edifice and a bathing establishment located in the basement. The tempo and magnificence of Boston building increases as the mid-century approaches. Illustrative of this is the new customhouse which Ammi Young builds between 1837 and 1849, a Doric pedimented, granite structure which adjoins the water at the foot of Long Wharf.

Even more symptomatic of changing times is the addition of a series of railroad yards and stations that accumulate on the periphery of the city. In 1834 we observe, from our post of observation, the construction of three long railroad causeways to connect our nearly water-bound city with the mainland. Commencing at the far shores, these gravel-filled and pile-supported roadbeds creep slowly toward the city from three directions: first from the western Roxbury shore across the Back Bay, then from Charlestown on the north, and finally

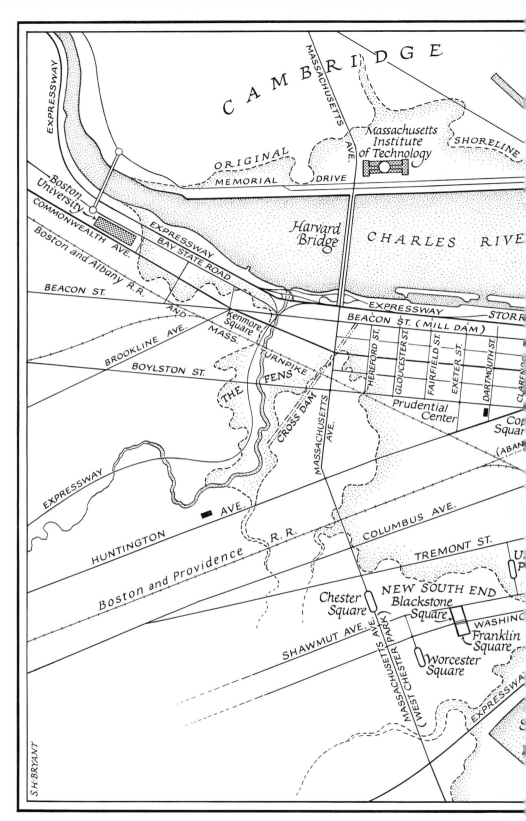

4   Map of the Back Bay district and adjacent areas. This diagram super-
imposes such recent landmarks as modern trafficways and the Prudential Center on nineteenth century streets, railroads, and dams as well as
the original shoreline.

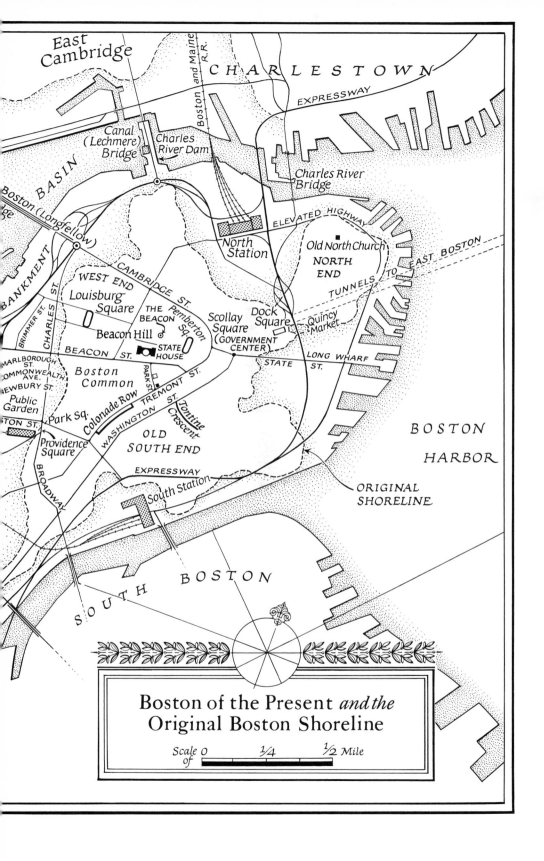

Boston of the Present *and the*
Original Boston Shoreline

Scale of 0   ¼   ½ Mile

from South Boston. By 1850 no less than six of these iron-clad arms reach across the waters. At the city terminals of these railroads, we see the construction of freight houses and passenger stations, at first modest wooden sheds but later expanded into structures of brick and granite, larger even than the warehouses along the waterfront.[14]

Prior to the railroads, even, Boston was linked to the neighboring countryside by a series of bridges.[15] One such bridge, the Charles River Bridge to Charlestown, a 1503-foot-long causeway carried on wooden piles, was already in operation when we took our places upon the Bulfinch Beacon in 1790. Now in quick succession follow the West Boston Bridge to Cambridgeport in 1793, the Canal (or Craigie) Bridge to Lechmere Point in 1809, and the South Boston Bridge in 1805. Soon after Boston is incorporated as a city in 1822 these early toll bridges are followed by four free bridges: the Boston Free Bridge to South Boston in 1828, the Warren Free Bridge to Charlestown in 1828, and two bridges linking newly founded East Boston to Chelsea.

Even more astonishing is the miraculous way in which the actual land area of our small harbor-bound city begins to be expanded in these same years. The shoreline extends on all sides as shrewd Yankee businessmen fill in tidal land for commercial or residential purposes.[16] The gravel for these fills is obtained, as we have seen, from the leveling of the city's five hills. By 1850, 348 acres of land will have been added to the city's original area of 783 acres by means of such fills (fig. 4). The first of these filling operations is carried through between 1804 and the latter part of 1805 by the Front Street Corporation, an association of property owners at the south end of Washington Street who fill a nine-acre area. In 1805 filling activities begin to the north of us in what was the North Cove. Here in 1643 the construction of a mill dam had been licensed by the town in order to provide power for several tidal mills. This original mill dam, which is marked approximately by modern Causeway Street, followed an ancient Indian footpath across the tidal flats. In the course of the nineteenth century, when property has become more valuable for building sites than for milling purposes, the city agrees to the filling of this Cove, and for over thirty years filling operations continue here. At times the work languishes for lack of filling materials. In 1806 the leveling of Copp's Hill in the North End contributes a good deal of gravel fill, but the area is not brought to its final grade until 1835 when enormous quantities of gravel are carted down from Cotton Hill.

Great or East Cove, Boston's old harbor, is gradually built over also. This process, as we have seen, began when the area around the town dock was filled in 1823 to provide space for Quincy Market. It is finally brought to completion in 1874 with gravel obtained from the leveling of Fort Hill, the last of Boston's five hills to disappear.[17] Along the newly made waterfront ever larger wharves are constructed to accommodate the new, iron-hull, steam-driven vessels which after the Civil War replace the clipper ships. Another undertaking is the addition between 1833 and 1839 by the South Cove Associates of fifty-five acres near Atlantic Avenue and Kneeland Street. This fill provides the space required for the new railway yards and stations of the Boston and Albany and the Old Colony lines, and ultimately it will become the site of the modern South Station.

During the second half of the century filling operations become larger and greater areas of land are added to the city. The most spectacular of these takes place in the Back Bay where we shall observe the activity with particular interest.[18] Already in 1814 a great earthen dyke is constructed from the foot of Beacon Street in Boston to Gravelly Point in Brookline. Called the Mill Dam, this dyke impounds the water of the Back Bay and serves as a toll road.

About half way along its length it is intersected by a Cross Dam which divides the enclosed Back Bay into two parts. Between these two reservoirs is maintained a differential in water height which is utilized to power the series of mills situated along the Cross Dam. The construction of this system of granite-faced dykes is slow and expensive. The giant stone blocks and the gravel fill are hauled by barge and horsecart and it is not until 1821 that the project is finally completed. Almost before the water-powered mills are in operation, however, gravel causeways for the steam-powered railroads begin to crisscross the new Mill Pond, and by 1857 the filling of the Lower Basin begins (figs. 5 and 6).

The filling of this great tidal basin is the most drastic single alteration in the history of Boston's changing topography. It adds about 450 acres to the original 783-acre peninsula. Furthermore, this fill fuses Boston to the mainland by increasing the width of the old Neck from a mere 1000 feet to over a mile.[19]

The Back Bay fill seems a fantastically ambitious undertaking. The hills of Boston, heretofore the source of gravel for all fills, have by this time been shaved down and built over, while to bring the gravel by oxcart from the Roxbury highlands would be prohibitively

5   Photograph taken in 1858 from the State House dome looking southwest. A continuation of figure 6, this view shows the Common, the
Public Garden, and rows of houses built along Boylston Street. In the
water-covered Back Bay, the X-shaped forms are the railroad causeways
built in 1834 which impeded the flow of water in the Lower Basin and
diminished the effectiveness of the water power project.

slow and expensive. Indeed, the filling of this region would be quite
impossible without the newly developed railroad. A spur line is laid
from the tracks of the Charles River Railroad along what will later
become Commonwealth Avenue. Over this line, the special gravel
train shuttles between gravel pits in West Needham and the Back
Bay flats (fig. 241).[20] For more than thirty years we see men of Boston
toiling at this project.

As late as 1850 we can still look down on a vast expanse of water
in the Back Bay, though already the city is beginning to encroach
upon the mud flats along the basin's southern edge. An oblong area
running more or less parallel to Washington Street has been filled
and is now being laid out as the "New" South End, a section which

6   Photograph taken in 1858 from the State House dome looking west
along the Mill Dam toward the Brookline shore. Begun in 1814 and
running along modern Beacon Street, the Mill Dam cut off the Back
Bay (left) from the Charles River (right). In the left half of the picture
can be seen a corner of the Common, the Public Garden, Lower Basin,
Cross Dam, Full Basin, and finally the Brookline shore. Along the Cross
Dam, which runs from the Mill Dam to Gravelly Point, are a series
of water mills. The narrow strip of land just west of the Public Garden
but separated from it by a thin body of water is the beginning of the
fill. It widens considerably next to the Mill Dam where construction
on the first houses was begun a year later.

will be built in the early 1850's as a fashionable residential quarter.[21] About the same time a few big houses are constructed along
the north side of the Mill Dam opposite the site of the future Public
Garden.

By the outbreak of the Civil War the Public Garden has been
developed as a green park and the filling of the Back Bay has been
carried as far west as Clarendon Street. A handful of optimistic investors have advanced on the new field and built the first of its brownstone houses. To us these look strange indeed—tall, narrow slices of

7   Commonwealth Avenue and Dartmouth Street. Taken from the tower
of the Brattle Square Church, this photograph shows the Back Bay
in the summer of 1877. The house at the extreme right (number 117
Commonwealth) was finished September 1, 1877; final plans for 303
Dartmouth (the empty corner lot) were not approved until December 21,
1877. Notice that the streets were filled to a higher grade than the lots.
The large building at left is the Hotel Agassiz, erected 1872.

buildings with blank side walls, for the moment often separate from
each other but waiting confidently for their ranks to close. War prosperity spurs building and filling activity in the area, and a tide of
brick and brownstone building sweeps steadily westward across the
old Back Bay, preceded always by a block or two of gravel fill. By
1870 this tidal wave of building reaches Dartmouth Street; by the
late eighties, the Fens (fig. 7). Another decade passes and we see the
last vestiges of the once vast bay disappear as the fill reaches the
banks of Gravelly Point in Brookline.[22]

If the largest, the Back Bay is certainly not the only major land fill in the Boston area after 1850.[23] About that time filling of the South Bay begins and continues intermittently for a century. Here we witness the virtual obliteration of the 200-acre bay by grimy patches of rail yards and factories. Elsewhere the marshy peninsula of South Boston is completely girdled by parcels of newly made land. Along the Cambridge bank of the Charles River, shoreline enlargement absorbs 416 acres more of the Back Bay, almost as much as Boston's fill on the other side of the river. We watch East Boston pushing 370 acres of fill into the Mystic River while in the 1930's the Logan International Airport encroaches on the harbor by several hundred more acres. As we view this extension of the shore line on all sides, we wonder if anything will remain of the once ample harbor and inner tidal basins. In 1841, however, the federal government steps in and establishes a harbor line beyond which future filling operations may not extend.

Even as nineteenth century Boston bulges along her water front, so she advances by land upon her neighbors. By 1912, through the process of annexation, some 24,000 acres of adjacent countryside and neighboring villages are added to the city in an effort to contain its swelling population.[24] Whereas the early city was bottled up on its little peninsula so that a citizen could easily walk to any part of town, things soon begin to change. The construction of bridges and the filling of the Back Bay give direct access to the country in three directions, and the city reaches out long, tentaclelike roadways flanked by newly constructed houses and shops. These long lines of buildings follow the routes of the horsecars and extend far into the country.

In large part the extension of the city beyond the range of a comfortable walk is made possible by the horsecar. First comes the horse-drawn omnibus which crisscrosses the central section of the city with nine routes by 1853. But beginning in that year we observe the laying of iron rails along city streets for the horse-drawn cars, and soon horsecars replace omnibuses. In the 1860's Scollay Square, the terminal for most of these horsecar lines, is a bright and picturesque place. The cars of each line are painted a distinctive color: those for Jamaica Plain are yellow; the West End line, red; the Beacon Street line, robin's egg blue; cars of the Highland Line to Roxbury are decorated with a Scotch plaid. The nine separate lines consolidate in 1877, and by 1889 the first experimental electric car is on the tracks.[25]

On Christmas Eve of 1900 the last horsecar makes a final trip down Marlborough Street to Kenmore Square. Even before this, however, new subway and elevated tracks are under construction. In 1897 America's first subway, under Boylston and Tremont streets, is opened; the noisy elevated train over Washington Street begins operation in 1901.

Such speedy transportation makes it possible for an ever increasing percentage of the total population of Greater Boston to escape from the city to the suburbs. Although the population living within the actual city limits continues to grow at a respectable rate, the growth of the suburbs is much faster, and eventually they house the far larger proportion of Boston's citizens. In 1850, for example, with almost the whole population residing within the city, the population is 136,881; in 1900 the figure has grown to 560,892, one half of Greater Boston's population; by 1950, with the proportion down to 30 percent, the city itself contains 790,863 persons.[26]

Consolidation and crowding within the central city had begun in the 1840's when the last remaining free areas of the peninsula were occupied. From then on the only way to meet the building needs in the heart of the growing city is an ever more intense land use. First to be rebuilt are the residential areas where houses are replaced by commercial buildings; after that small or antiquated blocks of business structures are demolished to make way for larger ones. On Summer Street, for example, the Vassall mansion of 1727 is demolished in 1854 to make way for C. F. Hovey Company's new six-story granite drygoods store, which, in turn, will succumb in 1951 to the gargantuan brick emporium for Jordan Marsh. A similar fate overtakes the neat brick residences of Cornhill and Hanover streets. In the Old South End, Bulfinch's august Tontine Crescent, built in 1789 on Franklin Street, gives way between 1857 and 1859 to a series of five-story granite store buildings. In the 1860's Boston is famous for her business area with its bold, granite facades and high mansard roofs.

Then in November of 1872 the city is devastated by the terrible fire. For two whole days we watch the smoking inferno engulf a sixty-five-acre tract. The very hearts of the retail and wholesale districts are burned out. Though hampered by tight financial conditions, a good many buildings are immediately reconstructed. Among these one may note especially the retail stores along Summer and Hawley streets designed in the currently fashionable, polychromatic Ruskin

Gothic style. These fine stores would do credit to the new Victorian sections of Birmingham or Liverpool. Now also the thirteen-acre tract provided by the removal of Fort Hill between 1868 and 1874 is covered with warehouses of the leather merchants. Teamsters and mechanics are active in the vicinity of Tremont and Broadway jacking up existing buildings in order to raise the grade of the whole area so that it will drain properly now that the Back Bay and the South Bay have been filled in. But most pretentious of all are the structures built for the insurance companies near Post Office Square—tall, granite piles loaded with architectural ornament and capped with ostentatious mansard roofs.[27]

About 1900 a large part of the North End is rebuilt as a tenement district—flats of five and six stories crowded about dark courts and fronting on crooked, narrow streets. By the turn of the century State Street is built over for the third time, now with somber granite office buildings of a dozen stories. In the succeeding years a few new edifices of even greater heights are added in the financial and retail districts. Most spectacular of these is the slender tower of the Customs House and the grim, grey hulk of the Post Office. The era of the skyscraper has arrived, making the narrow, winding streets of Boston seem even more canyonlike than before.

By mid-century we gaze down from our imaginary perch on building activities too numerous to enumerate. If it is impossible for us to follow in sequence the rapid transformation of the city below us, we have, at least, no difficulty in distinguishing recent building projects from those of a century earlier. What an enormous difference in scale there is! Modern construction dwarfs by comparison the most important building of the early and middle nineteenth century. First of the giant undertakings are the two railroad terminals, the North and South stations, built in 1894 and 1899 with their sprawling yards and stations which consolidate the facilities and activities of the eight separate terminals that preceded them.[28] And there is the elephantine Navy Pier in South Boston and the sprawling Navy Yard in Charlestown built on a scale hitherto unknown to Boston Harbor. In every direction our attention is caught by gargantuan power stations and industrial plants, office skyscrapers and warehouses. On both sides of the Charles River university buildings huddle in ever denser groupings and they inaugurate clusters of towers that appear to stretch all the way up to Harvard. High rise building is no longer confined to downtown Boston. In many parts of the metropolis great housing projects can be identified by the way the banks of apartment buildings are set in geometric patterns, while in the direction of the Roxbury and Brookline highlands are hospital complexes set in park-like surroundings.

By 1960 tearing down becomes as prominent an activity as building up. Astonishingly vast areas are leveled as flat as if they had been hit by a bomb: forty-four acres in the West End just behind Massachusetts General Hospital, and another temporary no man's land along Shawmut near what used to be the old Boston Neck. Crews of workmen are busy razing old piers along the waterfront, and swaths of demolition slash through the metropolis as precursors of the never ending extension of expressways, turnpikes, and throughways. Nor can one overlook the great chunks cut out of city blocks in all parts of the city to serve as parking lots. The automobile appears to be the unit of measure now, not the pedestrian.

But as the city grows, the open country recedes. By the 1880's the citizens of Boston begin to realize the value of open areas inside the growing metropolis and of the need to preserve and develop them. For the moment attention centers on the Back Bay area where, in 1893, a promenade one hundred feet wide is added along the south bank of the Charles River. Improvement continues in 1910 when the water level of the river is stabilized by the construction of the Tidal Dam, thus eliminating the ugly mud flats in the basin and suggesting further modifications of the river front with the parklike Storrow Embankment of 1931. But all these improvements are made at the expense of the bay. Between 1800 and 1950 the area of water shrinks to about one third of its original extent. Closed in on both its Boston and Cambridge banks, the original mile-and-a-half-wide bay is compressed to a channel scarcely four tenths of a mile across.

Improvements of a greener sort get underway between 1878 and 1885 when Frederick Law Olmsted is commissioned to develop the famous system of parks extending from the Fens to Franklin Park. In the course of time as the metropolitan area coalesces into a homogeneous network of streets and close-built edifices, these areas of park remain a veritable lifeline of open, green country. And so they remain for many decades until some of them clog up with modern traffic and super highways.

This brings us to the last major topographical change that we

must observe in Boston before we descend from our imaginary vantage point. This has to do with the freeways which have begun to
enmesh metropolitan Boston since the end of the Second World War.
With conventional grade-level streets no longer able to contain the
tidal wave of automobiles that each day sweeps to and from the city,
many miles of superroadways are constructed. The graceful concrete
ribbons of these systems leap rivers and harbor as effortlessly as they
burrow beneath them; they ripple above conventional streets and
float over the very tops of buildings in congested areas; they pile
up in tiers, divide, entwine, dissolve. Girdling the entire downtown
area, this intricate tangle of concrete tentacles reaches out like a
colossal octopus to enfold suburban centers in every direction.

Close by our State House mooring, the skyline has also been
changing. Just beneath us to the northeast of the State House are the
Court House tower and the vast complexities of the new Government Center; on the east, the slender finger of the Customs House,
the grimy cliffed Post Office, and the glossy facades of numerous very
large office buildings constructed in the early sixties. To the southwest stands the brooding hulk of the Hotel Statler, the impudent
little spire of the New England Mutual building, and the aloof silhouette of the Hancock tower. Further away, but stunting all of these
is the phantom height of the new Prudential Center, an apparition
so vast in size that it appears to float above the surrounding district
without being related to it—a brand new microcosm which challenges the sovereignty of megalopolis. As we scan the skyline once
more before descending to the task at hand, we are aware that our
State House dome is no longer the loftiest elevation on the Boston
skyline, the visual hub of this universe. On all sides it is beset by
towering skyscrapers, and even the old dome's golden splendor is
challenged by the gilded roof of a shoe machinery company.

THE TRANSITIONAL PERIOD

1844–1857

4

Prosperity, returning after the austere years which followed the financial panic of 1837, brought with it a great demand for new home sites in Boston. But as increasing numbers of substantial citizens sought suitable homes for themselves and their families, the last free building sites on Boston peninsula were being occupied. The last available areas of Beacon Hill, Pemberton and Louisburg squares, were now developed; and to make matters more critical, commercial interests were beginning to encroach on the residential section in the Old South End. The prices that commerce was prepared to pay for property like the Tontine Crescent on Franklin Street induced householders to give up their old homes and seek residence elsewhere.[1] Boston after two hundred years was outgrowing her small peninsula, and the most likely areas for expansion lay in the shallow tidal flats adjacent to the Neck and along the western fringes of Beacon Hill.

Acting to provide space for its mounting population, the city of Boston authorized filling operations along the Neck in 1850. As a relatively high level was established for the filled area, a healthful, well-drained district was created, and a gridiron plan of streets was laid out with several pleasant parks distributed among them. Building lots sold rapidly; the area was built up with fine brick houses during the fifties; and, for a time, it seemed that this New South End might become the seat of fashion in Boston.

In these same years there was also sporadic filling activity and construction along the eastern fringes of the Back Bay, at the foot of Beacon Hill, and in the Park Square neighborhood. Although the houses constructed here fall within the geographical limits of the Back Bay, they do not constitute an attempt to develop a new residential area. Rather they should be considered as extensions of established peninsula neighborhoods onto adjacent, newly filled lands of the bay. In this sense one might say that Beacon Hill overflowed into the Charles Street neighborhood and onto lower Beacon Street while the Old South End prolonged itself down Boylston Street as far west as what is now Arlington Street.

But these isolated developments were small and hesitant. Few investors would hazard their capital in a neighborhood whose future was so uncertain. It seemed inevitable that these tidal flats would be filled in, but with disputes over ownership no one could be sure to what use the newly made land would be put. In the meantime, the noxious odors of the polluted bay made the district an anything but desirable home site. For a long time even the fate of the Public Garden was unsure as there were repeated attempts on the part of the city to sell this land to industrial interests. But in 1856 a three-way agreement between the Commonwealth of Massachusetts, the city of Boston, and private landowners settled the controversy and fixed property lines. At last it was clear that the Back Bay would develop as a desirable residential neighborhood. Almost before the agreement was reached, private investors began to build houses on adjacent land; in 1857 the Commonwealth commenced the filling of its land, and by 1859 the first houses were under construction on land purchased from the state.[2] From that time on the future of the Back Bay district was assured.

The years 1844 to 1857 form a kind of prelude to the active development of the Back Bay area. There had been little residential building in the area before 1844, but between that date and 1857 some 107 houses were erected. As these houses provide a useful basis of comparison for subsequent Back Bay work, it seems worthwhile to examine them.

Three distinct centers of activity on the filled land may be noted: Boylston Street, extending from Providence Street to the then existing waterline of the bay; Charles and River streets reaching from the Common on the south to Cambridge Street on the north; and finally, lower Beacon Street from Charles Street west along the Mill Dam (fig. 4).

Practically nothing remains today of the houses on Boylston Street, but a record of the sales of lots in this section throws interesting light on the condition of Back Bay property values in the mid-century. In 1843 after some filling had been done, Boylston Street was extended to the waterline, and lots were sold at auction by the city of Boston. The substantial variation in the assessed value of land in this two-block stretch, which today faces the Public Garden, indicates the reluctance with which investors ventured into the region prior to the Tripartite Agreement of 1856. Lots nearest Providence Street and the established Old South End (Bulfinch's Colonnade Row was only a couple of blocks away) were valued for tax purposes in 1844 at $5800, while the same size plots at the far end of the same street bordering the water were worth only $1000.[3] Yet within five years confidence had been established and dwellings of uniformly good quality were constructed upon all these lots. It is interesting also to follow the subsequent increases in property values in this area. By the nineties this land had become too valuable for residential purposes by reason of its proximity to busy Providence Square (now Park Square) and the Boston and Providence Railroad Station; by the turn of the century most of the houses had been replaced by or converted into stores and offices.

In 1967 only the shells of two original houses survive, but a photograph in the files of the Boston Public Library records the street as it was before the gangrenous commercial development set in (fig. 8). Such reminders indicate that originally Boylston Street was lined by a series of red brick dwellings of three or four stories very similar to houses on Louisburg Square. Here one observes floor length, double hung windows; graceful, cast-iron balconies; chaste brick cornices; and moderate pitch roofs with simple dormers. The eighteenth century tradition has been only slightly modified. The interior arrangement followed the usual plan of the Boston town house with formal rooms placed on the lower two floors.[4] To judge from the old photographs, many—perhaps most—of the dwellings had swell-front facades. Called also a bow front or elliptical bay, this feature was a particular Boston one, so much so that Russell Sturgis writing in the 1890's mentions that it was almost unknown in New York.[5]

The second center of activity, Charles Street, early developed as

8   Boylston Street looking east from Arlington Street. The swell-front Greek Revival residences built between 1845 and 1849 had begun to give way to commercial buildings when this picture was taken in 1891. Between 1885 and 1891 five six-story structures similar to those seen in the background had replaced earlier dwellings. Furthermore, additional floors were added to residences to make apartments, and ground stories were remodeled as stores. Street cars are still horse drawn.

the service area for Beacon Hill. As late as 1848 tax records indicate a neighborhood occupied by lodging houses for laborers, livery stables and private coach houses, warehouses and docks, a church for a Negro congregation, a stonecutter's yard, a gas reservoir, and a home for aged women. The Brimmer Street neighborhood was still unimproved mud flats, and both Chestnut and Lime streets ended as cul-de-sacs before reaching the water front. Although the southern end of Charles Street, a section owned by the Mount Vernon Proprietors, was built largely between 1804 and 1844, the street's northern end, between Revere and Cambridge streets, was less systematically developed. Save for scattered wharfs and wooden sheds, most of the territory on the west (the water) side of Charles Street was unfilled or vacant. By the mid-fifties, however, the pressure of population within Boston had created such a demand for building sites that this heretofore run-down neighborhood was reclaimed, and a number of moderately large residences were constructed on the unoccupied land between the Mount Vernon Street church and Cambridge Street. Typical of these were the Oliver Wendell Holmes residence at 23 Charles Street (this would now be 164 if the house were standing), completed in 1859, and that of James Field at number 37 (now 150), which was one of a group of six structures built in 1855 by the speculative builder John Hoppin. The reclamation extended to stable yards and work sheds which, in the course of the sixties, were gradually replaced by rows of uniform brick residences. When the Brimmer Street fill was made after 1863, Chestnut and Lime streets were cut through to Brimmer, which in turn connected with Beacon Street. Thus the area which had been rather a dead end was oriented toward the new Back Bay area, now beginning to blossom. Otis Place and River Place were laid out in the late sixties and in the early seventies were occupied by good residences.[6]

Of the structures erected here between 1845 and 1856 a handful remain, but they bear little relationship to the house type soon to appear in the Back Bay. Typical of the houses built on Chestnut Street are numbers 102, 104, and 106 (formerly 43, 44, and 45), which date from 1855 (fig. 9). The design of this group is conservative. Except for the segmental arches of the facade which take the place of flush stone lintels, little distinguishes it from the houses adjacent to it on the east, numbers 96, 98, and 100 (formerly 40, 41, and 42), built in 1839. There is the same basic plan (three windows wide with a side stair hall), high granite basement, the flat wall surface of pressed Philadelphia brick, the sleek brick cornice of meager projection and the moderately pitched slate roof. Recessed slightly from the street, the 1855 houses today have a pleasant if undistinguished appearance; but their old-fashioned design, together with the stables across the street, clearly reflect the unprogressive character of the Charles Street neighborhood as late as the middle fifties.

9   Facade of 100 and 102 Chestnut Street, 1839 and 1855. Except for the later oriel window, number 100 is a typical Greek Revival town house. Number 102 departs from the Greek Revival vernacular only in the use of brick segmental arches, but its muntin-divided windows, which are original, are old-fashioned.

Of even more conservative design was the group of four houses at 7–12 River Street, built in 1858 by Sam Neal as a rental investment. There is nothing in the design of these structures to differentiate it from the work of twenty years before. The speculative builder, oblivious of the architectural changes taking place in the concurrently building Back Bay section, is content to repeat a familiar tradition that is already passé.

The third center of prewar building upon filled land of the Back Bay is lower Beacon Street. Activity in this section had to wait for the 1827 agreement between the city of Boston and the Boston and

Roxbury Mill Corporation which established boundaries of owner-ship and settled conflicting rights. Immediately thereafter the Mount Vernon Proprietors began to fill their land on the north side of the Mill Dam and by 1828 they had commenced construction of a row of six granite houses (fig. 11). Soon their filling operations extended as far west as Brimmer Street, then called Messenger Street, for tax records of 1844 indicate a house under construction at 84 Beacon Street. Even further to the west and still on the water side of the Mill Dam the Mill Corporation was commencing to fill its prop-erty. By 1850 the line of houses from Charles Street to what is now Embankment Road was practically complete. Although they face what is today the beautiful Public Garden, when they were built these houses fronted dank tidal flats (fig. 10).

10 Beacon Street looking west from River Street. Taken sometime after 1886, the photograph shows a block of six 1828 houses in the foreground and a group of eight four-story houses built in 1849 in the middle-ground.

11 Facade of 72 Beacon Street. A combination of Regency and Greek Revival styles, the white granite blocks of this group of houses begun in 1828 contrast with the brick and brownstone used for other houses in the same block built in the 1840's and 1850's.

Within these four short blocks, we have an instructive illustration of the change that overtakes domestic architecture within the quarter century after 1828. The handsome row of six granite houses at 70–76 Beacon Street erected by the Mount Vernon Proprietors in 1828 are today among the most charming structures in the entire length of Beacon Street (figs. 10, 11).[7] The three-story block is of moderate height since neither basement nor floor heights are excessive, and it is capped with a simple ridged roof of slate interrupted by a single dormer window for each house. The contrast between the rusticated first story and the smooth ashlar surfaces of the upper stories also tends to minimize the apparent height of the houses. This rustication, the segmental arches with their keyed voussoirs, and the recessed panels in which the windows are set is somewhat reminiscent of Regency building in England, but the white granite masonry and some of the detailing indicate that the unknown designer of the block also knew the Greek Revival style which was just taking root

in New England. Several details of the house—the wooden fret moldings, which frame the front door at 73 Beacon and appear to be
original, and the fretlike blocks in the dormer windows are similar
to designs in Asher Benjamin's *Practical House Carpenter* of 1832. The
book did not appear, however, until three years after the house construction.[8] The rather robust wooden frieze with guilloche design
beneath the cornice, which could almost be Italian Renaissance—a
style which would become so popular in Boston twenty years later—
also finds a parallel in Benjamin.

In contrast to these granite houses of 1828 are three dwellings at
the other end of the same block which once stood at 82, 83, and 84
Beacon Street and which were built in 1855, 1850, and 1844 respectively (fig. 12). These structures follow the same three-window, side-

12   Beacon Street looking east from Brimmer Street. This block nicely
     illustrates the development of architectural style from 1828 to 1855.
     The long white block at the right, better seen in figures 10 and 11,
     dates from 1828; reading from the extreme left are 84, 83, and 82
     Beacon Street which date 1844, 1850, and 1855 respectively. Photograph
     taken between 1873 and 1886.

hall plan used in the 1828 group, and they have the same roof slope, but the later designs are slightly taller and the proportions of their windows are somewhat narrower. Most important, however, is the fact that the later architectural details are drawn from Greek Revival and Italianate manners rather than Regency.

A close comparison between 82, 83, and 84 reveals architectural trends at mid-century. Number 84, dated 1844, is a standard Greek Revival town house such as is found in many parts of Boston. (The photograph, unfortunately, shows only two of the house's three front windows.) Built of pressed brick, the surface of the facade is carefully restricted to a single plane. Brownstone window sills and lintels are almost flush and have only a thin molding atop the lintels of the first- and second-story windows to interrupt the continuity of the flat wall surface. Lampblack was mixed with the mortar to obtain a dark color that would minimize the joint and thus emphasize the unity of the facade's plane.[9] The scale of the brick cornice is so light and its projection so meager that it reinforces the sheer, thin elegance of the facade. The only elements that challenge the dominant facade plane are the window shutters and the stone frame of the front door. The entrance is a typical Greek Revival composition whose sturdy pilasters and entablature surround the recessed porch. Worked in brownstone, as opposed to the white granite basement, both the material and the proportions of the entrance contrast too sharply with the rest of the facade, but this solution is so often encountered in Boston that one becomes accustomed to its shortcomings.

Two houses to the east and built in 1855, number 82 Beacon Street demonstrates a marked change in architectural taste if not in basic architectural scheme. The familiar Philadelphia pressed brick has been replaced by brownstone even though the old-style granite basement is still retained. Now, however, all openings are encased by robust moldings and are capped by pediments or a cornice and outside shutters are eliminated. String courses connect window sills; the entrance frame supports two heavy brackets which carry a hood and an oriel window of the second story. The capping member of the facade is a regular cornice and not just a series of thin brick moldings. We observe that the plane of the facade is here subordinate to its overlay of plastic ornamentation and, in addition to its more plastic quality, the 1855 design differs from the earlier one in its greater degree of architectural pretension. The old Greek Revival vernacular is beginning to give way to the more pretentious Renaissance manner that is gaining a foothold in Boston.

Number 83 Beacon Street (1850) is midway between its neighbors in date and style. Windows are not completely encased with framing elements as they are in the later house, but the design of the lintels is more complicated and their projection more robust. The thin brick cornice is substantially the same as before, but the oriel window of the main floor with its bracketed cornice introduces a decidedly plastic note. An example of unsuccessful compromise, the entrance of this house starts as a Greek Revival frame but receives an unrelated, bracket-supported Renaissance cornice. Even the double, bracket-supported dormer window of this house stands midway between the simple design of its earlier neighbor and the more three-dimensional, octagonal organization of the later building.

Attention should finally be called to a splendid group of eight houses that stood at 92–99 Beacon Street. Although only two of the group survive, and these in an altered state, the edifices interest us because of their excellent design and because the contract drawings for them are still preserved. Designed by George M. Dexter and occupied in 1849, the first owners were important shareholders in the Boston and Roxbury Mill Corporation, owner of the land on which the houses stood. The initial contract drawings, dated December 15, 1847, are preserved in volume ten of the Dexter folios at the Boston Athenaeum; they are signed by the various owners, by the builder, C. A. Hall, and by the architect.[10]

This group of four-storied houses once formed one of the finest blocks in the whole Back Bay region. Originally the geometric unity of the group was emphasized by its position as a free-standing block bounded on all four sides by streets. The eight houses, which constituted a total frontage of 240 feet, are grouped by twos with entrances paired. The ground story is of rusticated brownstone, the upper three floors of salmon-colored pressed brick; all windows are framed by heavy stone architraves (figs. 13, 14). The window sills of the upper two floors are supported by stumpy brackets, while the window heads of the second level are treated as pediments and carried on brackets. Projecting considerably beyond the face of the building, the main cornice of stone is carried by brackets of a simple blocklike design. The slate roof has the moderate pitch (a rise of 7 units in 10) characteristic of the early nineteenth century, but the treatment of the

13 Facade of 96 Beacon Street, designed in 1848 by George M. Dexter. One of a row of eight houses built for stockholders in the Boston and Roxbury Mill Corporation, which owned the land on the water side of Beacon Street, this design turns away from the familiar Greek Revival vernacular toward the Italian manner.

dormer windows with the projecting aedicular enframement and low balustrade is somewhat more elaborate. The facade design gains clarity by the variation of floor heights and the presence of the major rooms on the *piano nobile* (the principal floor placed on the second level) is indicated by elongated windows, the pedimented accents of the stone window frames, and a continuous cast iron balcony. Elsewhere windows have a similar width but are framed with a simpler molding. There is a heavy, straightforward quality about all the moldings which suggests that the architect was more accustomed to design for granite than for easily worked brownstone. Nor were larger panes of glass, divided only by a central muntin, available before the late forties. The repetition of fenestration elements, the continuity of unbroken cornice and balcony lines, and ground-floor rustication all give this block of dwellings an unusual dignity and unity.

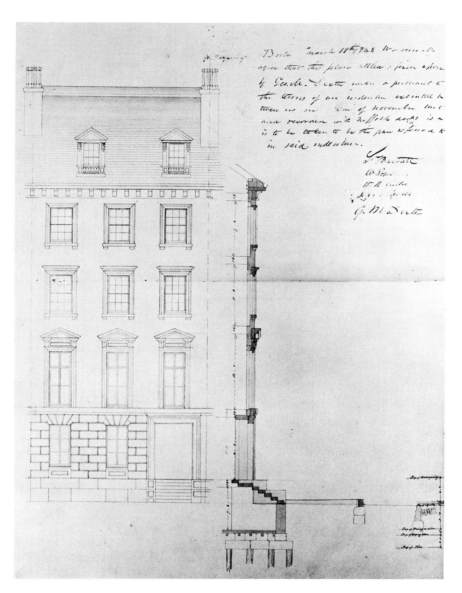

14   Elevation and section from a sheet of the contract drawings for 92–99
Beacon Street. The drawings signed by the architect and five owners
are dated March 18, 1848.

Each house in the block is thirty feet wide and fifty-five feet deep. Such a width allows an ample entrance hall without crowding the adjacent reception room, and the depth of the house is sufficient for a spacious central stair hall in addition to good-sized rooms at the front and back (fig. 15). At the rear is a two-story brick ell. Despite their identical exteriors, these houses vary in actual room arrangement, especially in the placement of the dining room, which might be placed at the front on the first floor or the rear of the second level. Because of drainage problems, the kitchen is not situated in the basement, as becomes usual later, but in the rear of the first floor. The main stair extends only to the second or principal floor, but the service stairs run from basement to attic. Plans of corner houses do not deviate at all from those in the middle of the block.

The Dexter house plans contain quite explicit information about wood framing and masonry construction. Of particular interest is the schedule of wooden piles required to support the foundations of houses in the area (fig. 16). No less than 277 piles were required for each Dexter dwelling. To the precisely inked floor plans, rough pencil markings have been added to show the position of gas outlets for chandeliers and wall lamps in all rooms. Similarly, hot air registers are indicated in the principal rooms on the first two floors but not above that. There is a masonry enclosure in the basement for the furnace, and substantial brick vaults are provided to carry the heavy iron range in the kitchen on the main floor.

The period's fondness for geometric variety in room shapes—an architectural notion that goes back to Adam fashions in England— is nicely illustrated by the circular stair hall in the middle of the house. Here a graceful flight of steps spirals to the parlor floor. In order to accommodate this stair hall the corner of the front chamber has been clipped off, but this is disguised by terminating the room in an elliptical bay. To support the weight of interior transverse walls of the floors above this wide round stair hall, an elaborate wood truss was constructed between the second and third floors (fig. 17). Thus we see what determined effort was required to achieve these varied geometrical shapes.

One final example will serve to summarize the transitional architectural character of this period. A group of four houses at 88–91 Beacon Street was constructed in 1852 by a speculative builder named Fox (fig. 18). The swell fronts, the stolid entrance frames, and the

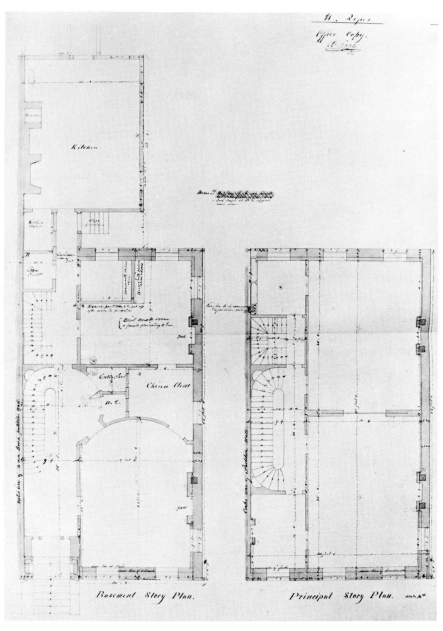

Kitchen

Entrance
China Chest
W.C.

Basement Story Plan.

Principal Story Plan.

15 Plan of the William Ropes house, 92 Beacon Street, showing room
arrangements of the first two floors. The circular stair hall and bow-
shaped wall of the front dining room in the "Basement Story" (really
the first floor since it is seven steps above sidewalk level) are typical
of the Federal style. The kitchen is also placed on the first floor because
real basements were sometimes subject to flooding.

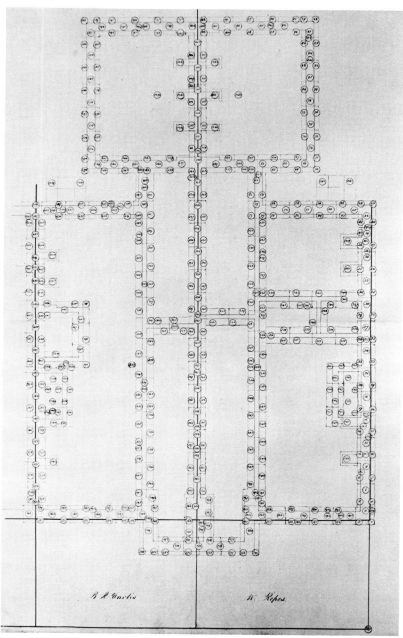

16   Piling schedule for 92 and 93 Beacon Street. Piles under bearing and
masonry walls were alternately double and single and were topped with
a granite capping stone upon which the brick foundation walls were
constructed. Each pile was numbered.

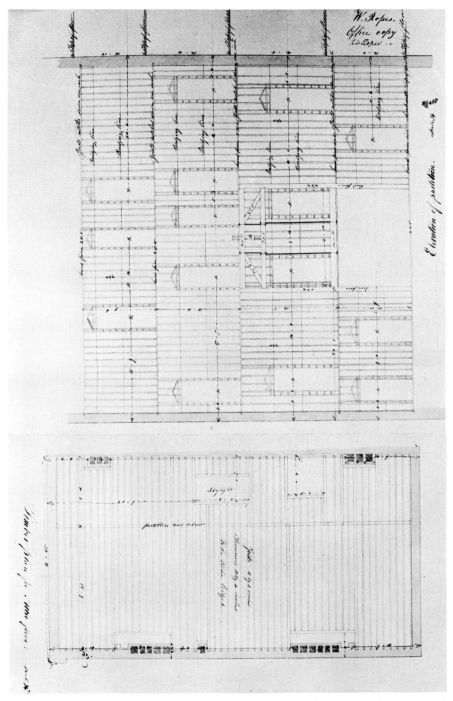

17   Framing of the longitudinal partition of wood between the hall and parlors, 92–99 Beacon Street. The truss in the second story was required to carry the floor above the circular hall on the ground level.

18 Facade of 89 Beacon Street, one in a row of four speculator-built houses constructed by Fox, Standish, and Turner in 1852. The stone brackets of the cornice and the window trim show the growing plasticity of the 1850's. The larger sizes of window glass are also characteristic of the mid-century.

slightly pedimented lintels of the windows demonstrate the tenacity of the old Greek Revival vernacular, but the plastic quality of the ornamentation—projecting window frames of the lower story, pediments and lintels of the second level, a heavy cornice supported on burly stone consoles—look forward to the late fifties. This same plastic quality can be observed in the large, five-sided dormers placed above the elliptical bays. These wider windows with a more complex geometry and the console-supported cornices foreshadow the elaborate dormers of the mansard roofs which appear in the middle sixties. Also indicative of the transitional character of these houses is the selection of the building materials; the granite foundation and lintels, so popular earlier, have been replaced by brownstone, but pressed brick has not yet been superseded by brownstone as the wall material. Although the vigorous, three-dimensional quality of the stone ornamentation presages the sixties, the decided swing to the new French-inspired style of architecture has not yet been made. For this we must wait another five years.

THE PERIOD OF ACADEMIC HEGEMONY 1857–1869

5

The critical decade in the development of the Back Bay district was the 1860's. At this time the distinctive architectural character of the area was established in a manner markedly different from anything that Boston had heretofore known. At this time also the Back Bay asserted its supremacy over the New South End as Boston's fashionable new residential quarter. And the volume of building, in terms of new edifices erected, is unequalled in subsequent Back Bay history.

By 1869 approximately one third of the entire district had been built up. The building boom, which developed in the early years of the Civil War, reached an all-time high for the Back Bay in 1868 when eighty-nine residences were erected. Practically all of Beacon Street below (east of) Dartmouth Street was built in this period; Marlborough Street and Commonwealth Avenue were substantially constructed out to Clarendon Street; Newbury and Boylston streets were lined with houses as far as Berkeley Street, while the Museum of Natural History and the first Massachusetts Institute of Technology building carried the construction still further to the west (fig. 4).

As was pointed out in Chapter Two, Boston in the 1850's was animated by a new spirit which, in all walks of life, distinguished the growing city from the earlier town. A booming population, new commercial importance, and a rapid accumulation of capital gave rise to civic pride which manifested itself in the foundation of new municipal institutions, in the construction of numerous public buildings, and in commercial building on an unprecedented scale. In the field of residential building the Back Bay area is the counterpart of these developments in expressing the new spirit.

From its beginning the district was conceived as an important civic improvement, not merely as another money-making real estate scheme. To understand this one has only to review the widespread discussions of the various proposals for developing the area or to note the repeated demands that the new quarter be handsome and spacious as well as healthful and economically profitable to the Commonwealth. A significant indication of the public ambition for the district is the fact that Massachusetts was willing to devote more than 43 percent of its total land holdings in the Back Bay to streets and parks in order to achieve the desired monumentality.[1] At the same time the state also sought to insure a dignified architectural appearance for the area by incorporating a set of comprehensive building restrictions in the deed that it gave to the individual purchaser. Conceived in the prosperity of the fifties and built largely during the surge of economic activity which came with the Civil War, the Back Bay symbolizes Boston's ambitions in her golden hour.

Both in the plan of the district and in the design of its buildings, the historian finds evidence of a new artistic force at work in Boston. No longer content, as we noted before, with her old position on the periphery of the British world of architectural fashion, Boston, during the late fifties and sixties, seems to have discovered the cosmopolitan art of France. It is significant that this new French manner, so evident in the street layout of the Back Bay as well as in the design of its houses, was also chosen for such important public edifices as the City Hall of 1862 and the Free City Hospital of 1861. In a letter which accompanied his competition drawings for City Hospital, the Boston architect Gridley J. F. Bryant articulated this conscious desire for a cosmopolitan expression when he explained his preference for the new style of architecture: "The particular style chosen is the modern style of Renaissance architecture, a style which, from its own inherent beauties, not less than from its almost universal susceptibility of adoption to structures of a dignified and monumental character, stands confessedly at the head of all the forms of modern secular architecture *in the chief capitals of the world.*"[2]

To understand the decisiveness of this shift from traditional Georgian or long-used Greek Revival to contemporary French ideas, one has only to contrast the Back Bay with earlier examples of residential building in Boston. Especially instructive would be a comparison with the South End, a district similar in terms of date and size and the city's largest residential development undertaken prior to the building of the Back Bay. Constructed largely between 1851 and 1859, this quarter should perhaps be referred to as the "New" South End in order to distinguish it from the older district of the same name built in the neighborhood of Bedford, Sumner, and Franklin streets and fashionable in the years following the Revolution. Occupying filled land for the most part, the New South End lies west of the Neck that once connected Boston peninsula with the mainland. Although there are no definite limits to the district, it is bounded more or less by Massachusetts Avenue, Harrison and Dover streets, and the Boston-Providence railway tracks.

COMPARISON OF THE BACK BAY AND THE NEW SOUTH END

Within the New South End no single axis dominates and three different gridiron patterns of streets connect unpredictably (figs. 244, 245). Save for the railroad, the district has no clear boundaries. Four streets (Tremont, Shawmut, Washington, and Harrison), all major lanes of communication, radiate from the city. With the exception of Tremont these are not wide streets nor are they all straight. In most of the area these traffic arteries are intersected at short intervals by long residential streets lined by trees and parallel rows of houses (fig. 19). Occasionally a block of houses will front on a main artery, but more often the houses face the quieter side streets. Since neither element, the lanes of traffic nor the lines of houses, is strong enough to establish a dominant sense of direction, a feeling of ambiguity pervades.

Nor is there a sense of spatial unity here. The pedestrian's attention is divided between residential streets and busy traffic ways; he discovers no focal points and no dominant and predictable order. Streets have no visual point of beginning or end, and sometimes they shift axis to merge into a new pattern of streets. At several points the region is accented by green parks but these are distributed haphazardly. One

19   Pembroke Street, typical row houses on a cross street in the New South
      End; built about 1870.

stumbles upon them quite by chance. With the exception of Chester
Park (now Massachusetts Avenue), they are aloof and isolated from
the major street system, encircled by houses which screen them from
major currents of traffic and the eyes of less prosperous neighbors.
There is no sense of continuity. To the pedestrian moving through
the area, it unfolds itself by isolated residential blocks. And because
the district is so lacking in continuity, one is hardly aware of variations in the quality of building; mansions cluster about Chester and
Union parks indifferent to factories and wooden tenements only a
block or two distant. There is a cellular quality about this plan.

This type of residential development, lacking a pronounced sense
of direction and characterized by a gridiron plan with an occasional,
isolated park, is certainly English. Originating in Georgian London,
the quiet residential square was imported to Boston in the late eighteenth century and employed here throughout the early nineteenth
century.[3] The first important example in Boston of this pattern was

Bulfinch's Tontine Crescent of 1793 on Franklin Street where a group of sixteen houses was built as a unified composition along one side of a crescent-shaped park. The Mount Vernon Proprietors followed the English model when they laid out Louisburg Square in 1826. It was repeated by the builders of Pemberton Square in 1835. Finally, between 1849 and 1853, in superimposing a series of parklike squares on the pre-existing schedule of streets for the New South End, the city of Boston followed a pattern of residential development which by this time had become traditional.[4]

In sharp contrast to the amorphous quality of the New South End, the Back Bay district is a decided unit. It has definite limits: the Charles River on the north, the Public Garden on the east, the barrier of railroad tracks south of Boylston Street (fig. 243). The western boundary, now Fenway Park, was originally much more clearly defined when the territory beyond the Fens was still open tidal flats. Within these set boundaries a compelling urban unity is established. Five parallel axes are formed by the major streets which are lined with long banks of houses. Interrupted only at long intervals by subsidiary cross streets, these principal streets are also the traffic routes. The coincidence of lanes of traffic, lines of houses, and street directions, each reinforcing the other, creates an overwhelmingly unified urban environment (fig. 20).

In contrast to the cellular aspect of the New South End, a feeling of spacious unity pervades the Back Bay. The green mall down Commonwealth Avenue links the green open areas of the Public Garden and Fenway Park and serves as a channel to bring a sense of open country into the heart of the district. The other parallel streets also act as spacious connecting corridors, an effect that is heightened by the long blocks of houses which face these streets and whose facades function as corridor walls. As the Back Bay was originally built, before the streets were choked with trees and the skyline broken by soaring masses of apartment houses, the pedestrian must have experienced a strong psychological pull which carried his gaze along the street-corridor to the open spaces at each end of the district (figs. 20, 38, 39).

Whereas the inspiration for the streets and parks of the New South End is certainly English, the derivation of the Back Bay plan is unmistakably French. Commonwealth Avenue is a splendid boulevard, wide enough to contain a central mall and planted with four parallel

20   Commonwealth Avenue looking east from Dartmouth Street. Back
Bay streets resemble great outdoor corridors connecting open areas
at each end of the district. More or less uniform house fronts form the
corridor walls, and the sense of direction is impelling. This picture was
taken from the Vendome Hotel in the summer of 1879 or 1880. The
house under construction at number 107, built for J. M. Forbes, was
not begun until May 7, 1879; permission for construction of the dwelling on the empty lot at 119 was granted October 29, 1879, but building operations might not have begun immediately.

rows of trees. Although the American version is more modest than
and in many ways different from contemporary work in France, it
seems clear that these Boston streets were inspired by the famous boulevard system just then being built in Paris for Emperor Louis Napoleon by the Baron Haussmann (figs. 20, 21).

Strikingly different also is the relationship of the individual house
to the total environment in the two Boston districts. Houses of the
New South End were designed with less thought for the street ensemble. The street is lined by a succession of relentlessly independent
house units, each with its separate swell front, its own flight of front
steps, its particular entrance porch (figs. 19, 22). If a block of such

dwellings attains a certain unity, it is because the same unit of design is monotonously repeated. But the separateness of each dwelling is never minimized. About this New South End there is a droning plasticity.

Sections of the Back Bay district built in the 1860's, on the other hand, have a more sophisticated unity. The individual house front counts for relatively little compared to the block in which it is set (figs. 20, 23, 39). The chief responsibility of each facade is to enhance the total street rather than to divert attention to itself. A house front

21   Boulevard Sébastapol, Paris, cut through 1858. View taken about 1865. Typical of the harmonious blocks of buildings which fronted the new boulevards of Paris constructed by Baron Haussmann, such splendid urban improvements inspired the designer and promoters of the Back Bay district.

22 Facade of 458–484 Massachusetts Avenue (formerly West Chester Park).
Erected about 1861, this row combines the old-fashioned bow front
which continued to be used in the South End with the new-fashioned
mansard roof.

is merely one section of the long, continuous wall that defines the
street-corridor. Bow fronts or bay windows, which might destroy the
unity of the continuous corridor wall, are few in number, and houses
are massed in tall, four-story blocks. Even where the designs of facades differ, cornice heights are substantially maintained in adjoining
buildings and the mansard roof is employed uniformly. Rather than
a house front mechanically repeated so and so many times as in the
South End, the Back Bay facade constitutes an integral part of a
larger "streetscape." Whereas the eye sweeps along the relatively flat
facades of the early blocks, taking in an entire Back Bay street at a
glance, in the New South End the eye must proceed by a series of
short jerks, pausing on each projecting swell front.

The style of architecture used in the two districts is likewise quite different. While the South End builder retains numerous characteristics of the earlier Boston tradition, the Back Bay designer looks to the work of the Second Empire for inspiration, and he introduces Boston to such innovations as the mansard roof which quickly becomes the very badge of modernity. For purposes of further comparison, let us describe the facade of a typical New South End house (fig. 24).

The salient architectural characteristics of houses in this area are the bow front facade and the high stoop—the formidable flight of stone steps ascending to the main entrance which is almost a full story above the street. Two or three stories tall above the basement, each house is three windows wide—two contained in the swelling bay

23 Arlington Street looking north from Boylston Street. Although they look like large single dwellings, most of these blocks consist of three or four row houses. The massing, the mansard roofs, and the French Academic style of architecture indicate Boston's attempt to imitate the manner of building then current in Paris. The paved street and electric wires date this photograph in the early nineties.

24   Facade of 450 Massachusetts Avenue (formerly West Chester Park), built about 1861. The non-Academic stone trim of windows and doors and the swell-front facade so characteristic of Boston building of the middle fifties illustrate the conservative quality of the New South End.

and one over the entrance. To this simple scheme is added a quantity of brownstone decoration—undulating lintels, door frames with hoods supported by ponderous brackets, and a heavily rusticated basement. Although ornate, the decoration belongs to no historic style, and it has a heavy plastic quality that dominates the brick wall surface. With the decoration so much brownstone "icing," the finest house is the one with the most elaborate overlay of ornamentation. The main cornice, which contains both modillions and dentils, projects so far beyond the face of the front wall that this capping member, in the interests of equilibrium, must be constructed of wood rather than of masonry. After 1858 the South End adds the mansard roof to this typical scheme.

The precise architectural style of such a design is hard to define. Certainly the basic *parti* (architectural concept) is similar to houses built about Louisburg Square soon after 1828 (fig. 25). The bow front, though common in Boston since the 1830's, came from Regency building in England.[5] The Greek Revival details of Beacon Hill, however, are here replaced by a heavier and more plastic decoration which has some kinship to the bracketed Italianate manner of Sir Charles Barry. But the would-be Renaissance cornices and architrave moldings are designed freely and more emphasis is placed on decorative profusion than on archaeological accuracy. From the detailing, which is often heavy-handed, and from the unimaginative way in which the same house design is mechanically repeated on consecutive lots, one might assume that many of the blocks were designed by speculative builders rather than architects. Surprisingly enough, however, surviving fragments of evidence do not bear out this assumption, because several projects for entire blocks of houses by recognized architects are known.[6] Yet the contrast between this work and that being done at almost the same time in the Back Bay is sharp.

The Back Bay building from the outset is animated by a more discriminating and theoretical spirit. Rather than a repetition of the old Greek Revival body overlaid with varying degrees of decorative elaboration, there emerges a more self-conscious and disciplined architecture. Placing more stringent demands on the designer than did the old vernacular, the new manner is based on abstract principles of composition; ornamentation is architectonic rather than merely profuse; and decorative detail is more accurate archaeologically. Based on theory rather than on intuition, the system of design is one that

25   Facade of 8–10 Louisburg Square, 1842. The bow front, unframed
windows, and shear masonry surface of these large town houses show
how the Greek Revival manner grows out of and yet fuses with the
earlier Federal idiom. The heavy door frame and moderately small
glass panes of the house on the right are most characteristic of the
period.

must be learned. As the ultimate origin of the new movement was
the Ecole des Beaux Arts, we may call it the French Academic manner.

The change from the old vernacular to the new Academic manner
occurred quite sharply in Boston between 1855 and 1859 when the
new style was taken up by the handful of architects who were just

then beginning to emerge as a professional group. At first the whole energy of the group was absorbed in learning and then practicing the French formulas until they could be manipulated competently. By 1860 progressive Boston architects had mastered the style and were at ease with the discipline. The present-day critic may discover a certain pedantry in their architectural exercises, and the buildings do have sometimes the feeling of paper architecture, but, with it all, a dignity and decorum is attained here which produced remarkably handsome streets and neighborhoods when taken as a whole.

FRENCH ARTISTIC CURRENTS IN BOSTON

Before proceeding with an analysis of the new French Academic architecture in the Back Bay during the 1860's, some consideration must be given to the question of French artistic currents in Boston, the extent of their influence, and how they got there. Although none of the evidence examined manages to explain the exact nature of the relation between Boston and Paris, yet the quantity and widespread presence of French artistic concepts in the city suggest that the influence did exist and was important.

A number of factors account for the great artistic prestige that Paris enjoyed during the nineteenth century. Too well known to require more than mention is the position that Paris long held as the artistic capital of the western world. Her pre-eminence in architecture at mid-century was reinforced by the achievements of Baron Haussmann in cutting through Paris a system of great boulevards and in creating a series of magnificent public areas. Less spectacular but strong enough to attract young architectural students from all parts was the fact that France offered almost the only systematic training in architecture to be had.[7] Whereas aspiring young architects in England and America depended on the apprentice system of architectural training, which was followed by all alike no matter to what point they had progressed in the formal school system, the French followed a specialized curriculum that had been in force since the early nineteenth century. After lower school the French student had one year in a government drawing school plus a year or more in a private atelier where he prepared for the entrance examinations of the Ecole des Beaux Arts. Following admission the diploma usually required five years. (Germany also had a system to train architects, but because this program was interspersed with field work as a government inspector, it was difficult for foreigners to follow through to a diploma.) When the many foreign students returned home from Paris, they naturally took current French tastes and practices with them.

The best known of Boston's students to go to Paris was Henry H. Richardson. Though not Bostonian by birth, he was educated at Harvard and eventually opened his office in Brookline. In 1860, immediately after graduation, he departed for Europe and entered the Atelier Jules-Louis André of the Ecole des Beaux Arts.[8] Because of the Civil War, Richardson stayed on in Paris and obtained work with the French architect Théodore Labrouste where he was responsible for the initial studies and possibly the final design of the Hospice des Incurables at Ivry (fig. 31). Richardson is mentioned here not because the Academic French style is imprinted on his work (for he showed great independence in his later work), but because he was the first student from Boston to go to Paris and because he illustrates the manner in which American students worked into the French educational system.

Three other young men who later became important Boston architects studied in Paris in the late sixties. Robert Peabody entered the Atelier Daumet in 1866 after graduation from Harvard and did not return to the United States until 1870. J. P. Putnam worked at the Beaux Arts in 1869 before going on to the Royal Academy in Berlin; Francis Chandler studied in Paris between 1867 and 1869.[9] Unfortunately for tracing the spread of French influences to the Back Bay, we do not know what specific work these men did in the area before 1873 when, quite naturally, the effects of the French training would have been easiest to detect.

William G. Preston, a less definite architectural personality than Richardson, may illustrate the way a more average talent reacted to the French environment. The son of Jonathan Preston, a successful builder-designer in Boston, William Preston went to Paris following his studies at Harvard, but there is no record that he entered an atelier. Indeed he cannot have stayed abroad too long as he is annually listed in the *Boston Directory* after 1861. The sketch for the first Massachusetts Institute of Technology building, which he signed as having been drawn in Paris in 1863, indicates how completely he abdicated to his new environment (fig. 26).[10] Basically the design is

26   The design for the first building of Massachusetts Institute of Technology is reminiscent of the familiar pavilion composition used on the east facade of the Louvre or for the buildings facing the Place de la Concorde in Paris. The rendering, dated "Paris, France, 1863," is signed by the architect, William G. Preston.

nothing more than a reworking of the familiar Bourbon pavilion motif used a dozen times by architects of the ancien régime from the Louvre to the Place de la Concorde and since echoed times without number. Yet such a design demonstrates the virtue of the academic system: if it excludes originality, it insures a certain level of competence and precludes drastic mistakes. Preston's other early works also show strong Gallic influences: the delightful old Museum of Natural History of 1862 on Berkeley Street (still happily preserved as Bonwit Teller) and the A. F. Conant house at 17 Arlington Street (1864). Preston's flirtation with French architectural styles was brief but instructive for it demonstrates the competence in manipulating the Academic formulas that could be gained without prolonged study abroad and also the ease with which the fashion could be discarded when youthful, vivid memories of France had faded. As we trace Preston's career in the forty-eight volumes of his work preserved in the Boston Public Library, we see how soon he exchanged the predictable regularities of the French Academic manner for the vagaries of the Queen Anne style.

If Boston's architectural students were enthusiastic about the opportunities of study in France, her practicing architects were equally aware of its advantages. When, in 1865, William Ware was selected to establish the first school of architecture in the United States at Massachusetts Institute of Technology, he departed for a year's trip to study European systems of architectural education. That he was most impressed by French architectural instruction is evident from the fact that he brought back with him M. Létang to teach architectural design in the new Department of Architecture which opened in 1867.[11] Mention might also be made here that Ware's partner, Henry Van Brunt, made a translation between 1863 and 1872 of the *Discourses* by Viollet-le-Duc, the great French architectural educator.

Finally, there is Arthur Gilman. According to the account of Gilman's life in the *Dictionary of American Biography,* he studied and traveled abroad before 1859 when he married and settled in Boston. The *Boston Directory,* however, lists Gilman as a practicing architect every year from 1843, the first year of its publication, to 1867, the year he moved to New York. The *Directory* also specifies the place where he boarded each year except 1858. One infers, therefore, that this was the year of Gilman's travels despite the fact that he maintained his Boston office. This is of paramount importance because it is Arthur Gilman who is credited with the layout of the Back Bay street system.[12] He also designed the Boston City Hall in 1862 while associated with Gridley Bryant. It is a great pity that Gilman did not record his travel impressions and his later thoughts on architecture. Not only would they have settled many questions regarding Boston's indebtedness to France, but they would have made lively reading.

This traffic of architects was not all one way. At least three architects with French names were in Boston in the early 1850's. An article in the *Boston Daily Courier* for November 8, 1854, noting the opening of the Boston Theatre stated that "in the spring of 1853 a $500 prize was awarded to a Mr. André Noury, architect, for a plan for the new structure."[13] It went on to say that as the plan did not fit the site, it was altered by Jonathan Preston. The *Boston Directory* lists both Noury and a Mr. Launay as architects in 1853; in 1854 only Mr. Noury is listed. Neither is listed before 1852 nor after 1854. Even though the technical accuracy of these gentlemen did not commend them to Yankee builders, they could have served as a channel through which French architectural ideas, books, or drawings reached the shores of Boston.

A third Frenchman, Charles Lemoulnier of Paris, is credited by C. A. Cummings with the design of the old Deacon mansion which was occupied in 1848 (fig. 28).[14] Lemoulnier is listed as an architect in the *Directory* between 1847 and 1850; he appears also as a resident of Boston in 1851 but not as an architect. After that he, too, drops out of sight.

So much for the documentary evidence relating Boston architectural practice to that of France in the fifties and sixties; there remains, however, a sizable amount of internal evidence. The first apartment house built in the United States (except perhaps for New Orleans) was erected in Boston in 1857. Decidedly Continental in its appearance as well as its method of organization, the Hotel Pelham stood at the corner of Boylston and Tremont streets, a site now occupied by the Little Building. Designed by an unknown architect for a Dr. Dix, the hotel again made history when it was raised on jacks and shifted several yards to the northwest in order to permit the widening of Tremont Street. Photographs of the old hotel show a ground story occupied by shops containing a mezzanine and an entrance vestibule which was a full story high (fig. 27). The principal cornice occurred at the level of the fifth floor leaving one story to be treated as an attic and yet another full story in the mansard. Except for the four rather strange balconies that clung precariously to the facade, this building might have been built in a provincial city of France. The significance of the building to our story, aside from its early use of the mansard roof and its exotic appearance, is the early date at which Boston got its first apartment building—prior to New York and only five years after London.[15] The introduction of this type of living quarters illustrates an important change from traditional Anglo-Saxon concepts.

An equally remarkable and somewhat earlier example of French influence in Boston was the Deacon mansion finished in 1848 on Washington Street between Concord and Worcester streets.[16] Of sym-

27   Hotel Pelham, built 1857. Formerly standing at the west corner of Tremont and Boylston streets just outside the Back Bay area, it was the first apartment house in eastern United States.

metrical design with projecting end pavilions, the edifice was capped with a well-designed mansard roof (fig. 28). It was surrounded by a spacious walled garden, and a porter's lodge preceded the entrance of the house on Concord Street. The interior of this mansion was fabulous for Boston of that day. Whole rooms were brought from France to be reinstalled there and furniture and fabrics were imported "by the boatloads." Sections of paneling from the Deacon house are still preserved in the Athenaeum and the Boston Museum of Fine Arts. These pieces are said to have come originally from a Hôtel de Montmorency in Paris—there were several of this name. Here obviously, because of the early date, the design, and the furnishings of this house, one has another important link with France.

Although not directly pertaining to architecture, it is instructive to see how closely other aspects of French art were followed in Boston. French painting had its advocates, the foremost of whom was certainly William Morris Hunt.[17] Although he did not establish permanent residence in Boston until 1862, he was a frequent visitor here after 1856 when he and his wife, who belonged to Boston's prominent Perkins family, returned to America from France. Hunt, more than any other American, popularized French painting in this country, and his art classes became a kind of way station on the road to Parisian ateliers. He was also instrumental in forming several of Boston's first picture collections and in introducing his collector friends to the Barbizon painters.

28   Facade of the Deacon mansion, built 1848, demolished. Designed by an architect from France named Charles Lemoulnier, it was the first building in Boston to have a mansard roof and to show an interest in French architectural fashion.

Thomas Gold Appleton, a friend of Hunt's and an early traveler to the Continent, formed the first collection of paintings in Boston, the only one prior to the Civil War. Among his thirty or more pictures were many French canvases. Appleton traveled constantly in Europe and when, in 1864, he built his own home at 10 Commonwealth Avenue, it was in the current French Academic manner (fig. 51).

Finally it should be noted that in the late fifties French and Flemish picture dealers began to discover the potentialities of the Boston market. In 1857 the Flemish art dealer Gambert brought a group of French pictures to sell to prosperous Bostonians. In this venture he apparently had such success that he returned in 1860 for a second showing at the Athenaeum, on which occasion many Americans were given their first viewing of Rosa Bonheur's work. In 1865 the French dealer Cadart was in Boston with a collection of paintings by Corot. During the war the Wigglesworth and Hitchcock collections were commenced and numerous Boston gentlemen followed suit after 1865. By 1880 more than half of the pictures in Boston collections were French.

The Academic French Style in the Back Bay

Although the material just surveyed does not explain the chain of circumstances through which Boston became the disciple of French architecture, it at least indicates that by the early 1860's the city was well aware of French artistic tastes. Similarly, as we turn to a study of specific Back Bay buildings, we discover a general receptiveness to French ideas if few identifiable influences. In only one instance does it seem that we can point to a clear French prototype, and there we cannot document the relationship.

The block of five residences at 22–30 Marlborough Street was begun in 1863 for the Thorndike estate. The architect of the group is unknown but the basic *parti* resembles the administration building of the Hospice des Incurables at Ivry, just outside of Paris (figs. 29, 30, 31). As Henry-Russell Hitchcock pointed out, this hospital, designed in 1862–64 by Théodore Labrouste, was in no way exceptional in its day; it repeated the same general scheme that Percier and Fontaine had duplicated by the block along the Rue de Rivoli and one

29   Facade of 22–30 Marlborough Street, 1863. This group of houses illustrates the Back Bay preference for tall, narrow massing and correctly
detailed Academic trim. Only twenty feet wide and built on speculation
for the Thorndike estate, the block as a whole is monumental. The
tax value of each house in 1865 was $25,000.

30   Facade of 28–30 Marlborough Street. The design emphasizes the top and bottom limits of the building by means of the heavy cornice and the stone rustication of the lower levels. The three intermediate stories constructed of brick are relatively simple. This straightforward solution recalls such contemporary work in France as Labrouste's hospital at Ivry.

31   Hospice des Incurables, Ivry, Seine, 1862–65, by Théodore Labrouste.
Administration and ward buildings.

that echoed countless other times up and down the new streets of
Paris. The Marlborough Street houses are important to us because
they demonstrate that a Boston architect could reproduce a contemporary French form with understanding and clarity.[18]

In the Ivry hospital the ground floor arcade of cut stone contrasts
with brick walls of the upper stories; the separate blocks of buildings
are related by a constant cornice height and uniform fenestration;
the simple mansard roof is punctuated by unobtrusive dormers. In
Boston this scheme has been modified skillfully to meet the requirements of a series of five single dwellings vertically disposed. Ingenious
double hung windows alternate with recessed entrance vestibules in
an attempt to maintain the uninterrupted succession of arches on the
ground story. The traditional *piano nobile* is recalled by the slightly
elongated proportions of the windows of the second story and their
elaborate window frames. Even the color scheme is reminiscent of
French prototypes: the cream-colored Nova Scotia stone basement and
trim, the salmon brick of the upper stories, and the blue slate of the
prominent roof.

No other Back Bay houses can be related so directly to French prototypes, however. A case in point is the group of three houses that Richard Morris Hunt designed in 1859, within four years of his return from Paris.[19] Erected at 13, 14, and 15 Arlington Street, the site now occupied by the Ritz Hotel, this group is conceived as a free-standing block consisting of a central element three windows wide flanked by projecting pavilions of two bays' width (fig. 32). Four stories tall, it was constructed of brownstone and topped by the customary mansard roof. Despite the unity of the composition, it would never be taken for a Parisian residence. Its vertical organization as a series of row houses rather than as flats and its isolation as a detached building mark it as more Anglo-Saxon that Gallic. Yet the designer was surely conversant with current Parisian architectural styles and practices, for he had recently received a diploma from the Ecole des Beaux Arts and had worked in Parisian architectural offices. The dif-

32   Facade of 13, 14, and 15 Arlington Street, 1859, by Richard M. Hunt. This group of houses, which stood on the site of the Ritz Hotel, was designed within four years of the architect's return from Paris.

ference between French prototype and Back Bay product demonstrates the extent to which an architect was limited by the requirements of the American town house and perhaps also by the force of habit of the building trades of the period. Nevertheless a comparison between the Arlington Street block and earlier Boston town house designs show that the designer had been able to carry over a good bit of French feeling in the grouping of windows and the use of projecting pavilions. The Hunt houses, which are no more French-influenced than a number of other Back Bay mansions of this time, should dissuade the critic from dismissing the hypothesis of direct Gallic influence in Boston merely on the grounds that its residences have substantial differences of appearance and feeling from construction in France at the time.

The most obvious French architectural element observed in the Back Bay is the mansard roof. This particular feature seems to have made its appearance in Boston about 1857.[20] In that year it was used on the Hotel Pelham and, in a somewhat modified form, in the Back Bay at 122 Beacon Street. Adjacent houses at 104–116 Beacon Street, built only one year earlier, had used the traditional moderately pitched ridge roof (figs. 27, 33, 53). The mansard continued in use through the 1870's, but by 1880 it was passé and mostly employed by speculative builders.

In addition to the mansard roof, that symbol of modernity for the late fifties and early sixties, the French Academic fashion requires a facade symmetrically organized and correctly detailed. Appropriate architectural decoration is distributed around door and window openings, on the main cornice, on levels of the various floors, and on the basement (fig. 34). Although not articulated for actual structural reasons, Academic theory dictates accents at these points to emphasize the fact that they are areas of critical architectural importance. Abjuring the merely frivolous or opulent but recalling, instead, a structural form, such ornamentation is termed architectonic.

Quite properly the focal point of the facade is the entrance. Approached by a low flight of steps, the main entrance of the Back Bay house is usually protected by a shallow porch, a projecting hood, or a recessed vestibule. Restrained in design, these elements are composed of correctly detailed Classical forms: flanking pilasters with a lintel treated as an entablature or a porch supported by free-standing columns. At its simplest, the entrance is merely framed by an archi-

33   Facade of 104–116 Beacon Street, 1856. Originally of similar design,
      this row of house fronts combined progressive French Academic details
      worked in brownstone with an old-fashioned ridge roof. The broadly
      projecting cornice is constructed of wood and is reminiscent of the
      Italianate manner. The three copper-clad oriel windows on the second
      floor were added in 1883 and 1885.

trave molding, and sometimes it is not an isolated element of the
facade composition, as at 22–30 Marlborough Street, but is treated
like an element of fenestration (fig. 30).

The window treatment of the Back Bay house offers the designer
another opportunity to demonstrate his command of the Academic
formula, and it differs noticeably from earlier usages (figs. 12, 25, 35).
In the forties the window opening had been unaccented; it caused as
little interruption in the flat plane of the facade as possible; no frame
surrounded the window, and its lintel was set flush with the facade.

34   Facade of 133 Beacon Street, 1863. A typical French Academic design
      which accents openings, cornice, and basement with sober, architectonic
      ornamentation.

35 Window at 8 Commonwealth Avenue, 1864, showing the restrained and correct detailing of French Academic architects in Boston of the Civil War era.

Twenty years later, however, the opening becomes a distinct architectural unit set off from the plane of the facade by a stone frame. Important windows of the lower stories are further accented by a keystone or capped by a pediment or cornice. One should note that the florid lintel, so prominent in the New South End during the fifties (figs. 22, 36), is renounced in favor of more correct Renaissance forms. Outside shutters, common in Boston since the middle of the eighteenth century, are almost entirely abandoned now because they conflict with the architectonic enframements.

Another common though not inevitable feature of the 1860 Back Bay house is its more or less complete entablature whose cornice is supported by modillions or a dentil course (figs. 34, 37). The projection of the cornice is considerably greater than for the thin brick courses that capped the facade of the Greek Revival town house but about the same as the cornice used in the New South End during the fifties. It differs from the latter, in that it usually has a frieze and a suggestion of an architrave, whereas the South End designs ordinarily include the cornice only.

One other architectural feature should be mentioned: the brown-stone balustrade which in the sixties contended for popularity with cast iron fences or railings. Composed of turned stone balusters or plates with a pierced design, these balustrades bordered the sidewalks and front steps of houses, and they were sometimes used on balconies or to cap the entrance porch (fig. 35). Because of their exposed positions, many of these stone appendages have literally melted away from the action of rain and frost, but enough survive to indicate how effective this feature could be. With the exception of 58–60 Commonwealth Avenue, the balustrade is never used as a parapet above the main cornice because its situation there would screen from view the fashionable mansard roof.

36   Window at 44 Union Park, about 1855, illustrating the more florid architectural ornament preferred in the New South End.

37 The facade at 188 Beacon Street, 1864, utilizes numerous string courses
between the floors. It is capped by a more or less complete entablature
instead of the single heavy cornice which prevailed in the New South
End.

It is unnecessary to continue a catalogue of all the architectural
features used by Back Bay's aspiring academicians. Suffice the observation that quoins are used but twice in this entire period, panels
of bas-relief twice, pilasters of colossal order only once as a major

element of facade design; and there is one specimen of pilasterlike panels. The designer seems to have found his facade composition too crowded with necessary window openings to encumber it with additional architectural elements. Also it is possible that the pilaster was considered somewhat old-fashioned by architects of the sixties because it had been used so extensively two generations earlier by Bulfinch and his followers. Horizontal moldings and string courses, on the other hand, abound. Since these members do not occur in the crowded zone of window openings, they could be employed liberally without congesting the design (fig. 37). Indeed, this repetition of horizontal elements helps to reduce the inherent verticality of the town house composition and thereby reinforces the Classical preference for horizontality and repose.

More pertinent to the monumentality of the new French-inspired style than this correct use of Academic details is the manner in which individual town houses are massed in tall blocks of unified design (figs. 23, 32, 38). The aesthetic value of these high, wall-like facades in defining the space of the corridorlike streets has already been noted. We must now explain how such compositions happened to come into being and analyze how they are organized. Most house fronts of early Back Bay dwellings are four stories high to the main cornice.[21] In part this height represents an aesthetic preference (such tall buildings more convincingly resembled contemporary French blocks), and in part it resulted from the fact that the widths of the first Back Bay lots to be built on were considerably narrower than they later became. When a lot is narrow, the house has to go higher in order to provide the requisite number of rooms. Similarly, when the frontage is a mere eighteen or twenty feet, it is difficult to include appendages like bay windows or projecting porches without crowding the facade. Thus both the height and flatness of the early house fronts were in good part due to the narrow width of the building lots.

One nineteenth century historian of Boston architecture ascribes the predominance of this narrow house in the sixties to the great rise in the price of land. As logical as this statement may at first appear, it is only partially correct. That the value of Back Bay real estate rose at a phenomenal rate in the years that preceded the Civil War is certainly the case, but it is also true that the land values rose even more rapidly after the war and continued to increase throughout the century.[22] If the high cost of land had been the determining factor in

38　　Newbury Street, looking west from the Public Garden. Photograph between 1881 and 1889. Occupying the present site of the Ritz Hotel, the house at the extreme right was designed by Richard M. Hunt in 1859.

house sizes, then the narrow lot would have persisted and become even more popular. In actual fact, the opposite is true; a narrow house is rarely found in the 1870's and it all but ceases to be built in the eighties and nineties. Instead of land values, it is more a question of the method by which the filled land of the Back Bay was sold.

Since the Massachusetts legislature was unwilling to advance state funds to defray the costs of filling the Back Bay tidal flats, it arranged to exchange land for fill. Thus, as we shall see in more detail in Chapter Eight, an area of approximately four city blocks was deeded to the contractors Goss and Munson in lieu of a cash payment for filling the area. In addition to this, two large plots were granted to the city of Boston as an indemnity; and several large plots were sold to investors at private sales prior to 1860 before the district had become securely established as a fashionable neighborhood and therefore able to command high prices. Later these lands were sold to individual builders in lots of varying widths, many of them very narrow. As these plots were situated at the northeast corner of the Back Bay, the portion nearest Beacon Hill, they were therefore the first section to be filled in and built upon. By 1869 this property was entirely covered with houses.

By 1860, however, public confidence in the region had been established and the Commonwealth instituted a series of public auctions as a means of selling the remainder of its holdings. For the sake of convenience, the blocks of unsold land were divided into lots of equal size. The width of the lots facing Commonwealth Avenue was standardized at twenty-six feet; those on Beacon, Marlborough, Newbury, and Boylston streets, at twenty-five. At these auctions each lot was disposed of separately, and once these properties had passed into different hands it was difficult to redivide them on a basis other than the standard lot size.[23] The main exception to this concerns corner properties on Marlborough, Newbury, and sometimes Beacon streets. Here a speculative builder might buy the corner plus one or two adjacent lots and erect a group of three, four, or five small houses facing the cross rather than the main street. By and large, the blocks divided into standard lots lie to the middle and western portions of the district, and they were not, therefore, filled in and built up until after 1870.

If the Academic architect preferred the tall, narrow, flat-faced house, he was also aware of the importance of maintaining consecutive cornice and roof heights. This he attempted to do even when forced to construct his blocks of houses one or two units at a time. Take, for example, the north side of Beacon Street between Clarendon and Dartmouth streets, where the block consists of twenty-seven houses built over a period of seven years. In that entire block the cornice line changes but four times, in three of which cases the difference in levels is so slight as to be scarcely noticeable (fig. 39). Twelve consecutive houses in the block, numbers 198 to 220, fall into five separate design groups which were built independently, yet not once in that interval does the level of the cornice or the height of the mansard change. To enumerate all such instances of conscientious respect for existing levels would be to catalogue the building done in this period.

39 Beacon Street looking east from Dartmouth Street. In this block of twenty-seven house units built between 1862 and 1869, the cornice height changes but four times. Photograph about 1885.

Still another means of achieving the desired monumentality is to combine several houses into a single design. By merging relatively small dwellings to form a larger composition, a more impressive architectural effect is obtained. Only by this sort of grouping could the Yankee designer hope to capture something of the unity and dignity of the Parisian boulevard.[24] An analysis indicates that four fifths of the Back Bay houses built between 1857 and 1869 are grouped in some manner.

There are many ways to group houses. In size, a group may vary from two houses to an entire block, from a cluster of edifices set off as a complete free-standing group, to several contiguous houses which constitute a portion of a long block. The short, free-standing block, several examples of which still remain on Arlington Street, is particularly handsome because of its clear geometry (figs. 23, 32, 40). By reason of its spatial isolation, in which all four facades and mansard roof can be seen, the architect has an opportunity to design a three-dimensional building, not just a two-dimensional facade. Such free-standing groups can be treated as either a simple rectangular block with a uniformly flat facade and continuous cornice or as an articulated mass consisting of central block and side pavilions. Numbers 1, 2, and 3 Arlington Street form a dignified composition in which the changes in the plane of the facade are reflected in the mansard roof (fig. 40). Perhaps this group has a slightly cramped feeling with end pavilions too bulky for the central section. Prior to its mutilation, the proportions of its neighbor, 4–7 Arlington, were somewhat better. Consisting of four houses, the single-house end pavilions were not too bulky for the two-house central mass, and they were differentiated from it by grouped windows and corner pilaster panels.

40   Group of houses at 1, 2, and 3 Arlington Street, 1861. A composition of projecting end pavilions about a central block is a typical French Academic solution.

However satisfactory this use of the pavilion as a matter of theoretical design, it must be admitted that it is sometimes ineffectual when seen from the street. The actual three-dimensional projection is so slight that one is hardly aware of the pavilion's existence. At 149–159 Beacon Street, for example, the end pavilions protrude only the width of one brick. Here the architect thought only of his design as it appeared on the drafting board; he had not learned to visualize it as a three-dimensional building. A similar type of free-standing block, though it does not usually employ projecting pavilions, also occurs in the Back Bay for groups of small houses facing the cross streets. Here a simple massing is desirable because the composition is already congested by the close fenestration.

Effective grouping, however, is not confined to free-standing blocks. Within the long banks of edifices which parallel the main streets, several adjacent house fronts may be related with good effect. Either the same unit of facade may be merely repeated any number of times (fig. 59), or several units may be integrated in a single design (fig. 41). If the latter scheme is followed, the composition will surely utilize the pavilion as an axial feature or for balancing end forms. Although this scheme may sometimes be criticized as paper architecture, such groupings of houses impart the sense of unity and coherence to the streetscape which was lacking in the droning monotony of the New South End and which is to be lamentably absent in the heedless competition for variety and individuality in the 1870's.

One of the most accomplished of these integrated designs was built by Snell and Gregerson in 1867 at 401–409 Beacon Street (figs. 42, 43). Of brick with stone trim, the three-story design originally consisted of five units, but the corner house has been replaced by a modern apartment building. Here end pavilions are more than usually effective because both design and a marked projection set them off from the main mass of the building. This effective opposition between central and end forms is reinforced by a number of details. The pavilion has a vertical composition, and the levels of its windows as well as the design of their frames differ slightly from those of the main block. The mansard roof of the pavilion is distinguished from that of the main block by reason of the more complicated dormer windows and the somewhat greater height to which the roof is carried. The center block is dominated by a horizontal feeling due to the rusticated basement, the continuous iron balconies repeated on two

41   Facade of 211–219 Beacon Street, 1866. A unified design that balances
a pair of houses with octagonal bays on either side of a central element
with a flat facade.

levels, and a strong entablature. This horizontality plus the even
reiteration of fenestral elements conveys a feeling of repose and unity
which is checked by the more vertical proportions of the pavilions.

On this main theme of horizontal center and vertical end forms
counter movements are imposed in order to weave the compositional
fabric together. The strong horizontality of the main block is checked

42   Facade of 401–407 Beacon Street, 1867, by Snell and Gregerson. A
      composition of five houses with pavilions that project and are capped
      by a higher roof. The original pavilion at the left was replaced by an
      apartment building in 1925.

by a series of recessed pilasterlike panels in the brick masonry which
rise from the level of the first-story window heads to divide the main
block into bays. Likewise the verticality of the pavilion is moderated
by the subtly accented brick string courses at the second-floor level.
The middle bay of the whole composition is marked by several minor
accents: a dentil course instead of the paired brackets in the entablature, a slight elaboration of window frames at the third story, and a
stone band at the second level which acts as a tie. The middle pilasterlike panel is also eliminated.

There is a fine sense of order in this design, no single element is
thought of as an end in itself but always in relation to the whole composition. The characteristic Snell and Gregerson keystone is reserved
for the central entryways of the first floor, but the main entrance of
the house in the right pavilion is restricted in decoration to maintain

43   Facade of 403–407 Beacon Street. The three houses of the central block are bound together as a single element. Nova Scotia stone and the pronounced keystones over the entry are trademarks of the Snell and Gregerson office.

the harmony of that unit's fenestration. Also the pavilion's stone window frames, in contrast to those of the main body, become simpler the higher one goes.

A more extensive application of the pavilion scheme for group design is found at 110–130 Marlborough Street (1868) where eleven houses are designed as a unit (figs. 44, 45, 46). Both central and end

44   110–130 Marlborough Street, 1868. Erected by a speculative builder, this block contains eleven units—two houses at each end of the group with bay windows which carry into the mansard roof, two pairs of intermediate houses with oriel windows, and a central pavilion of three units. The two houses on the right end are not shown. Although each unit is relatively small (from sixteen to nineteen feet wide), the group as a whole attains a certain largeness and impressiveness.

45 Facade of 118–122 Marlborough Street. Three middle houses of the eleven-unit group shown in fig. 44. These three houses constitute a pavilion accented by a mansard roof, but it is scarcely noticeable since its facade projects but four inches in front of the units adjacent to it. The central axis is marked by a projecting, double dormer window, a rounded pediment on the oriel window, and a central entrance flanked by symmetrical windows. The apparent change in masonry is only a matter of repointed mortar joints of the house on the right.

46   Facade of 128–130 Marlborough Street, detail of fig. 44. Paired houses
      with bay windows form the end pavilions of the larger composition.

pavilions are employed. With a marked verticality, somewhat in the
manner of book ends, the end pavilions enclose the middle portions
of the composition. The verticality of these end members comes not
from the timid break forward of the facade, for the projection is so
slight as to be masked by a drain pipe, but from the strong forms of
the two sets of bay windows which break through both cornice and

mansard. The seven middle houses of the group have a quieter, more horizontal disposition. The second story oriel windows do not destroy the integrity of the facade plane and there is an orderly sequence of windows. The central element of three houses is distinguishable because its mansard is carried a little higher than the rest of the block and its three oriel windows are capped by slight pediments. The composition's center axis is barely marked by a double dormer window in the attic, a segmental pediment for the oriel, and an entrance flanked by small, symmetrically placed windows.

Successful ensembles can also be obtained by merely repeating the same unit of design. Outstanding examples of this arrangement are 24–30 Marlborough Street, 104–116 Beacon Street, and 20–36 Commonwealth Avenue (figs. 29, 33, 47). The last group forms one of the most imposing compositions in the whole district, although the nine individual units in themselves have an insignificant frontage of nineteen feet. The success of this block depends on an unbroken expanse of facade some 175 feet long. The heavy bracketed cornice, the strongly marked stone frieze at the second-floor level, and the even rhythm of the fenestration create such a strong continuity that minor variations can be made in the house widths or in the disposition of doors and windows of the first story without impairing the overall unity. A comparison of these houses, designed in 1860 by Gridley Bryant, with a group built in 1869 at 377–395 Beacon Street (fig. 48) will show how much more effective is the flat facade group than one which employs the bay window. In both cases the individual dwelling has the same frontage. But the Beacon Street row is so fragmented by projecting bays and porches that the individual designs fail to reinforce each other and to create an impressive unit of design.

Before leaving this discussion of the group house, we must note that a large number of the houses were built in pairs. Indeed this solution seems to be a favorite one: it accounts for 24 percent of all houses erected between 1857 and 1869. Of this number, two thirds are paired about a center line so as to form a symmetrical composition (fig. 51). Such an organization of facades is superior to one that merely repeats the design because the bay windows act as framing elements for the continuous flat wall surfaces around the entrances, which become the main plane of reference for the composition. Thus the group reads with somewhat more geometric unity than a block

47 Facade of 20–36 Commonwealth Avenue, 1860, by Gridley J. F. Bryant. Although each house is but nineteen feet wide, the group as a whole forms one of the most impressive blocks in the Back Bay.

fragmented by repeated bay windows. That the architect of the 1860's clearly preferred the balanced formula is indicated by the fact that there are fifty-eight examples of symmetrical grouping as against eight where the unit of design was merely repeated without regard for symmetry.[25]

A small but interesting group of structures is that in which facades of different widths are fused in a unified composition. A good example of this is 38–40 Commonwealth Avenue, built originally as two houses which are now combined to form one section of the College Club (fig. 49). Fifty-feet wide, number 38 was organized in two parts, an octagonal bay and the flat middle section, while number 40 with a width of twenty feet contained but a single octagonal bay. By means of the uninterrupted entrance porch and front steps, the unidentified architect of these houses achieved an impressive and well-integrated composition.

It should be emphasized that duplication of design motifs was not necessarily the result of economy. Two instances can be cited where paired facades appear to have been the result of a deliberate aesthetic choice on the part of the owners. The houses at 135–137 Beacon Street were built in 1860 by related families, the Russells and the Gibsons (fig. 50). The interiors of the two houses vary considerably for the main staircase of number 135 carries to the top of the house while in 137 it only goes to the second floor. There is a difference also in the arrangement of the bedrooms on the fourth floors as evidenced by their

48   Two units of the nine-unit block at 383–395 Beacon Street, 1869. Only three stories high and interrupted by bay windows, this block lacks the unity and urbanity of 20–36 Commonwealth Avenue (fig. 47).

49   Facade of 38–40 Commonwealth Avenue, 1862. Built as two houses
       and not united until 1919. The porch opening on the right originally
       served as the entrance to number 40, which was the smaller dwelling.

fenestration, and the wood trim in the parlors and libraries are not
identical. It is obvious that the architect, E. C. Cabot, prepared separate plans for these two houses and that 135 was considerably more
expensive to build. Yet the facades of the houses are almost identical,
the only difference being the three-window arrangement on the top
floor at 137 as opposed to the two-window scheme of 135. It would
seem, then, that these houses were not built as duplicates in order to
trim expenses, as would be the case today. Instead they are two sepa-

rate dwellings designed to fulfill different living requirements but for which the owners deliberately chose identical facades.

Another such case is 8–10 Commonwealth Avenue (1864, demolished 1963) erected by two friends, Erastus Bigelow and Thomas Appleton (figs. 35, 51). Appleton, heir to one of New England's great fortunes, was a man of taste, widely traveled, and the first Bostonian to form a private picture collection. His biographer states that he spent much

50   Facade of 135–137 Beacon Street, 1860, by Edward C. Cabot. Built for the related S. H. Russell and Charles Gibson families. The Gibson house is today preserved as a museum.

51 Facade of 8–10 Commonwealth Avenue, 1864, demolished 1963. This
    is another example of a facade design duplicated in the interests of
    harmony and unity. Despite the apparent similarity of the two fa-
    cades, number 8 was two feet wider than the other, but number 10
    had a library which extended through the combined widths of both
    houses on the second floor.

time and derived great pleasure from designing and building his new
town house.[26] The interiors of these two houses had many differences,
the most important being the large Appleton library which extended
completely across the rear (south elevation) of the combined houses
on the second floor. Their paired facades, however, followed precisely
the same scheme.

Faced with a solitary design, the Back Bay architect was no less
desirous of obtaining a balanced composition. If the house was sufficiently wide to allow the principal rooms to flank the center hall, a

symmetrical facade presented no problem, as at 5 Commonwealth (fig. 52). It was when the building lot was too narrow to admit such duplication of parts that the designer's ingenuity was taxed to produce a balanced facade. The easiest method of achieving symmetry under such circumstances was to omit the bay window, pair the windows of the upper floors about a center line and balance the entrance against a window on the first floor (figs. 29, 32). If some form of projecting window were desired, an oriel could be used on the upper floors leaving the ground floor free for an axial entrance or an entrance paired with a pendant window (figs. 37, 53). The most elaborate example of this solution, 117 Beacon Street, utilizes an oriel window and balcony

52   Facade of 15 Commonwealth Avenue, 1861. When the lot was wide enough to permit the center hall plan, a symmetrical facade presented no problems. Originally, the windows were not subdivided by muntins.

53   Facade of 122 Beacon Street, 1857. This illustrates the ingenuity expended in achieving the symmetrical composition demanded by the French Academic formula. This house had the first mansard roof in the Back Bay district.

supported by an intricately contrived trumpet-shaped bracket which in turn is carried on a central column (fig. 66). Here the axial composition is still further emphasized by the mansard roof treated as a separate unit and by the dormer window which projects in front of the facade and breaks through the cornice.

When the bay window was incorporated in a narrow house, it interposed a considerable obstacle to the symmetrically arranged facade. The usual solution in such cases was a frank compromise; the bay was placed on center, but one diagonal face of the bay on the ground floor was clipped off and this space thrown into the entrance porch. If the design were paired, the awkward interpenetration of porch and bay could be partially concealed and the mutilated symmetry somewhat restored (figs. 48, 54).

The most successful of all the symmetrical solutions to the single, narrow facade containing a bay window frankly places the entrance on the projecting face of the bay. At 154 Beacon Street the entrance is on the bow front of the house (fig. 55). Here a broad flight of stairs leads to the gracefully cantilevered entrance balcony. There is a dignity in the triple arcade of the first story, and the off-center entrance is hardly noticeable because of the cadence of the three arched openings at this level. Nor is the transition objectionable from the three openings of the lower floor to the handsomely framed paired windows of the upper floors. Finally at 17 Marlborough Street the architect not only places the entrance squarely in front of the octagonal bay, he emphasizes it by adding an arched portico supported by free-standing columns (fig. 56). This is one of the most ingenious and original facades of the entire period.[27]

Variations of the French Academic Style

It was 1860 before local architects had mastered the French-inspired discipline, and for a while they practiced it with considerable artistic success and with evident satisfaction to themselves. But as with any rigid academic system, they soon began to tire of repetition. Once they understood the formula, they became bored paraphrasing it, and by 1868 there were signs of experimentation. Slight at first, these variations are important to note because they illustrate both the

54 Facade of 212 Beacon Street, 1863. The porch masks the off-center position of the entrance and thus maintains the symmetry of the facade composition. Such a projection, which extends the full width of the lot, would have violated property restrictions imposed by the Commonwealth.

beginning of the restlessness which will become so strong in later Queen Anne work and the influence that new building techniques begin to exert upon architectural design after the Civil War.

Confining our remarks to the 1860's, we can note five tendencies which modify the Academic French formula in one way or another. By far the largest group shows a preference for simplification. At first glance, facades of this category do not seem to differ from those of regular Academic design: they employ brownstone, retain the same general proportions, and evince no decided preference for

55   Facade of 154 Beacon Street, 1861. One of the most ingeniously symmetrical and handsome Academic facades in the district. As a curved mansard roof would have been difficult to construct, the attic was recessed behind the parapet.

56 Facade of 17 Marlborough Street, 1863. The porch projecting in front of the bay would seem to violate Commonwealth property restrictions; this may be the reason why this solution was not used elsewhere.

either the flat or the bay window type of house front. Yet on these facades the usual range of architectural decoration is reduced to a few string courses or to thin architraves of stone that enframe windows and main entrance. At 186 Beacon Street, for example, only repeated string courses and a hint of the orders on the entrance porch recall the usual Academic paraphernalia (fig. 57). The facade depends entirely on the proportions of its windows and on an effective contrast of plain wall surfaces with the crisp contours of the string courses.

When the facade is constructed of brick, Academic decoration is restricted to simple brownstone moldings which frame window openings, as at 4 Marlborough Street (fig. 58).

A less numerous group tends toward overdecoration rather than simplicity. Although forms employed are of Classical derivation, they become overladen, and the decoration tends to develop an existence of its own which is independent of the architecture it embellishes.

57   Facade of 186 Beacon Street, 1869. One variation of the French Academic tradition tended to simplicity and omitted intricate moldings about windows and doors. Here the only stone decoration consists of simple string courses.

58 Windows of 4 Marlborough Street, 1864. A simplified Academic design in brick encases openings with plain brownstone architraves and omits the usual component of Classical details.

At 31–47 Commonwealth Avenue, for example, the cartouches over the window heads appear to be almost independent of the stone lintels; they even look as if they were detachable, pieces cut separately and then bolted into place (figs. 59, 60). Such stone ornamentation, incidentally, has much in common with decoration cut in wood. A comparison of the above-mentioned window detail with bookcases in the library of 135 Beacon Street reveals a similar fully modeled, curvilinear, but put-together quality (fig. 61). Facades thus crowded with elements of decoration to the point of restlessness are few in number (ten ex-

59   The facade of 39 Commonwealth Avenue illustrates the tendency to
complicate the Academic formula with additions of carved ornamentation and frequent breaks in the plane of the facade. Built in 1872,
it repeats a design that was followed in nine adjacent houses between
1864 and 1873.

60   Entrance of 39 Commonwealth Avenue. The abundance of intricate
stone carving seen here was achieved at slight cost with mechanized
stone working equipment. The stone cartouches over the window and
door resemble shapes employed in contemporary woodwork.

amples among the 304 houses considered). This figure underlines the
restrained quality which characterized most work done in the Back
Bay prior to 1869, and which continued even into the florid 1870's.

The third of our five tendencies redesigns the details of the Classical
orders while retaining their general proportions and functions. A visual
comparison of two entrance porches illustrates this point (figs. 62, 63).
The earlier example, a porch at 13–15 Marlborough Street (1864),
follows the Academic-Classical formula so quietly that one accepts it
as a matter of course; the later entrance (1869) at 37–39 Marlborough
Street preserves the traditional division and proportions of column,

capital, and entablature, but it demands our attention because of the unusual detailing of the capitals. Here, presumably, is another of those many attempts to design "the American order," that will-o'-the-wisp which was to inspire so many architectural excrescences in the 1870's. Another example at 304 Berkeley Street (1869) illustrates the point in slightly different terms (fig. 64). The critic accustomed to the cohesiveness of Classical forms is here jarred by the heavy, inarticulate brownstone shapes which frame the windows and door. Over the openings are stubborn projecting blocks that look at first like redundant lintels. The window heads are chamfered but this surface is illogically interrupted by square projections which suggest keystones. Closer observation, however, reveals that these ungainly forms are essentially cornices supported by consoles and the chamfered posts are nothing more than architraves which customarily surround window or door openings. To confuse matters further, the frames are spotted with clumsy bosses that suggest pegs of nonexistent wood joinery. This kind

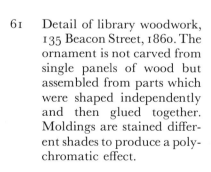

61   Detail of library woodwork, 135 Beacon Street, 1860. The ornament is not carved from single panels of wood but assembled from parts which were shaped independently and then glued together. Moldings are stained different shades to produce a polychromatic effect.

62   Entrance of 13–15 Marlborough Street, 1864. The entrance porch illustrates the preference for correctly detailed Classical orders by architects of the early sixties.

of pointless experimentation, which fumbles with surface detail as it
searches for originality, will plunge the American designer into great
confusion a few years later.

Changes in building technology account for the last two groups that
develop out of the French Academic manner. A new method for orna-
menting stone that appears in the 1860's can undoubtedly be explained
as an attempt to find a less costly way of facing and decorating than
the traditional hand methods. As it proved faster and simpler to smooth

and trim the stone with a mechanical planer and then countersink a design, the traditional technique of carved low relief disappears from ordinary usage. Complex patterns employing an incised line could be cut into the flat stone face with very little effort.

63   Entrance of 37–39 Marlborough Street, 1869. This porch shows the tendency to experiment with the orders which gained popularity in the 1870's.

64   Facade of 304 Berkeley Street, 1869. This design illustrates the tendency
to redesign Classical forms. The stone trim, despite its eccentric detail,
encases openings and accents the cornice and foundation lines in the
conventional Academic manner. The corner oriel window is constructed
of wood.

This type of decoration made its first appearance in a Back Bay
facade in 1861, but the technique attained its greatest currency in the
late sixties and seventies in houses built by speculative builders (fig. 65).

One of the most elaborate examples of the incised line decoration is found at 117 Beacon Street (figs. 66, 67). Here the technique is used to ornament a great variety of architectural forms though not all of the surfaces to be embellished are flat. Nor is all the stone ornamentation of this facade obtained by the incised technique alone; the brackets which support the second story balcony are covered with delicate carved relief. A shield in the dormer window bears the date 1864.

At 16 Marlborough Street (1864) one finds the incised line technique used for both the stone brackets which support the second story

65   Entrance of 327 Beacon Street, 1871; house designed by Fred Pope. As stonecutters' wages increased, technology provided shortcuts to decoration in the form of incised lines. More economical than the traditional carved relief was a design grouted out of a stone surface that had already been mechanically planed.

66   Facade of 117 Beacon Street, 1864. An unusually elaborate example of a symmetrical facade composition in which the axis is carried into the pavilionlike mansard roof.

oriel window and the wooden bottom rail of the oriel itself. The character of the decoration in both materials is so similar as to suggest a common origin of the technique, probably in contemporary woodworking. Certainly this manner of working wood was to be mercilessly exploited by American furniture makers during the seventies and early eighties.

The last variation on the standard Academic French theme that one discerns in the 1860's is a tendency to destroy the importance of the wall surface by breaking it up into a series of panels which project from or sink behind the plane of the wall. The Academic architect at first had used the wall surface as the stable, controlling plane from which to project his architectonic elements of decoration (fig. 34). Somewhat later, however, as the two pairs of houses at 21–27 Marlborough Street (1866) indicate, he occasionally employs the wall surface as a dynamic element in the design (fig. 68). Instead of a stable plane of reference, the wall surface here disintegrates into a series of overlapping panels. In the octagonal bay window, for example, the surfaces of the diagonal walls appear, in comparison to the front wall

67   Entrance of 117 Beacon Street. Stone decoration here is achieved by both incised line (Ionic volutes) and traditional carved relief methods (the brackets which support the balcony).

68   Bays of 21–23 Marlborough Street, 1866. Another variation of the
      French Academic formula is achieved by manipulating the surface of
      the facade with projecting moldings and recessed panels. The impor-
      tance of the plane of the facade is thus minimized.

of the bay, to occupy relatively different levels on various stories. Window moldings sometimes appear to be superimposed directly on the
wall (second story window above entrance), while at other times they
protrude directly from the recesses in the wall (central windows of the
bay). Despite such arbitrary handling of wall planes, the symmetrical
grouping of the two pairs of houses plus the choice of simple Classical
porch details keeps the design within the limits of the Academic tra-

dition. Such manipulation of planes by the unknown architect contains the roots of what we shall identify in the 1870's as the "Panel Brick" style.

PLAN OF THE BACK BAY HOUSE

It is evident that these Victorian houses were built for a way of life very different from that of the present day. For one thing, there was an abundance of inexpensive domestic help since incoming streams of New England farm girls or waves of Irish immigrants kept Boston well supplied. In addition the house was the center of a self-contained family life and families were generally large. It should be remembered also that the house was occupied only during the winter or at most during the school year, and the regime followed there was more formal than that of the summer residence.

The family spent a far greater proportion of its time at home than is the custom today. Here it was that its members sought most of their amusements, entertained their friends, pursued their studies and often kept their account books. The house had to be large and provide rooms for many activities. Entertaining, for example, was almost necessarily done at home. Not until 1872 did the Somerset Club open a dining room for ladies, and even then Boston society was reluctant to abandon the home as the scene of its parties. When dancing parties were staged at home, the parlors were thrown together by opening the large connecting doors, and canvas covering was tacked over the wall-to-wall carpeting. Only in relatively recent years, with the passing of the large town house and the increasing difficulty of securing servants, has entertaining at the club become usual. The debutante party did not move out of the home until the second decade of the present century though social commentators have often noted that by New York standards, Boston parties were traditionally simple.[28]

A person investigating the houses of the sixties is soon aware of an almost standard plan. Practically every dwelling, in addition to sleeping and service quarters, has four main rooms for daytime activity: parlor, library, reception room, and dining room. Because of the variety of family activities, it was necessary to have both a parlor and a library; the former served as a place for entertaining and as a music room, the latter was important not only because the prominent Bostonian was expected to be well read but because the man of the family needed a study. As the Boston merchant's afternoons were traditionally spent at home (the exchange closed at two P.M. and he was home for dinner at three), it was necessary to provide a quiet retreat where he might spend his afternoon in study or with his accounts. A reception room, always adjacent to the main entrance, was required in those days of rigid social decorum as a place to receive persons on less intimate terms with the family.[29] The dining room was as large and formal as the meals served in it, and no informal eating rooms were provided. Very few home builders chose to go beyond these more or less standard requirements. New England conservatism and a dislike of ostentation constrained even the wealthiest citizens to follow the basic plan. Not until the 1890's were very large town houses built or old houses doubled in size by combining them with adjacent structures.

Since the town house was used only during the winter, no special accommodations were needed for the hot months. There were no porches or balconies for outdoor living on the lower levels, no loggias at the top of the house to take advantage of summer breezes across the Back Bay. Neither was any effort made to utilize the back yard as a garden or open living quarter. Instead, this rear area was paved with bricks, and it functioned only as the service yard through which tradesmen entered the kitchen from the back alley; seldom was this area planted with even a tree.

Thus it was that a house with rather standard accommodations was required, and the only variation in the arrangement of the necessary rooms stems from the width of the lot on which the house was built. If the lot was narrow, the house had to be distributed on a greater number of levels; if wide, the requisite rooms could be fitted into fewer stories. But always it is the same basic form, the row house —a long, narrow structure several stories high, squeezed between party walls, and open for windows at its narrow front and rear ends.

Depending upon the lot width, three basic plans for the row house can be distinguished: Type I for the narrow house, Type II for a lot of medium width, and Type III for a wide lot (fig. 69). The narrow plan of necessity is employed for houses less than twenty feet wide, and often it is found in those as wide as twenty-three feet. It allows for two rooms on each floor, one front and one back, and it is usually arranged on six levels. A rear ell is never included, as that would

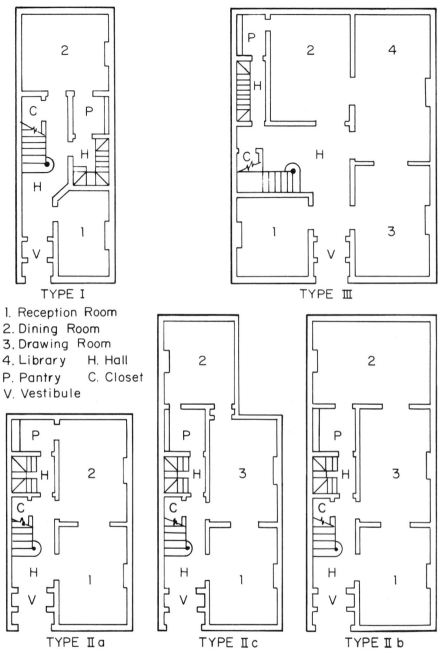

TYPE I

1. Reception Room
2. Dining Room
3. Drawing Room
4. Library   H. Hall
P. Pantry   C. Closet
V. Vestibule

TYPE III

TYPE II a

TYPE II c

TYPE II b

69   Typical plans of Back Bay houses of the 1860's. Type I is for lots less
      than twenty-three feet wide; Type II for lots twenty-three to thirty feet
      in width; Type III for lots more than thirty-five feet wide.

eliminate outside light from the back rooms. This plan for a narrow lot is most frequently found in areas constructed before 1869.

Type II, the plan for lots of twenty-three- to thirty-feet frontage, is wide enough to permit one room plus a side hall. This category can be subdivided into three groups. Type IIa is two rooms deep; Type IIb, a class encountered less frequently in Boston than in New York, is three rooms deep; Type IIc is two rooms in depth but has a rear ell similar to houses of Beacon Hill and to the Dexter houses described in Chapter Four. The second classification, IIb, has the great disadvantage of a middle room without outside windows. In New York this middle room was sometimes illuminated by a large light well fitted with an elaborate system of mirrors for reflecting the light down to the center parlor, but in Boston as far as one can tell, no such system was used.[30]

Today it is difficult to determine the exact popularity of the rear ell plan (IIc) because of the large number of rear additions made to the houses in more recent times. An ell is never added to houses three rooms deep. Type II houses are usually three stories in height plus basement and attic, and it accounts for about one-third of the Back Bay houses of this period. The best examples of this medium-width house are found on Commonwealth Avenue below Clarendon Street.

Type III, the wide house on lots of more than thirty-five feet, permits greater variation in plan. In the sixties the wide plan most commonly encountered has a center hall with rooms placed in the four corners. Because a greater number of rooms are located on each floor, there is no need for a rear ell or for the house to consist of more than three stories plus basement and attic. A good example of a wide house is 15 Commonwealth Avenue (fig. 52).

Although the plans just described are for houses situated in the middle of the block, a corner house usually follows the same scheme. Despite the fact that a long side of such a structure is now free for windows, little advantage is taken of the possibility, and the chimney stacks continue to be built into the long outside wall (figs. 32, 40). Houses which today have the entrance on the wide side rather than the usual narrow end wall, especially when situated at ground level, result from a remodeling. An entrance placed in the long side of the house did not occur before 1869 and then only in small houses; this solution did not become popular until the early 1870's (fig. 70).[31]

Finally, a few atypical plans should be noted. Although built in

the middle of the block, the residences at 5, 36, and 38 Commonwealth Avenue have side yards on one side of the building which permit windows to open on three sides of the house. These edifices, which
in effect become corner houses, continue an earlier practice found
occasionally on Beacon Hill. This variation is not repeated in the
Back Bay after 1868. Mention should be made also of 25 and 27 Commonwealth Avenue. The latter, a Type III house, consists of four
principal rooms on the main floor grouped asymmetrically about a
center hall. Its counterpart, number 25, was built originally in an ell
shape with the open corner to the street and three rooms on the main
floor, but in 1888 the open corner yard was filled in with a room and
basement entrance hall. In the entire district there are but two examples of free-standing single houses, and these date from a later
period.[32]

The peculiar drainage condition which prevailed in the Back Bay
affected the arrangement of rooms. Both sanitary and storm sewers
originally drained into the Charles River. Under ordinary circumstances these sewers drained the houses adequately, as the lowest basement level allowed by law was Grade 12, that is, 12 feet above mean
low tide. Grade 12 is five feet below the level of the Mill Dam (and
street level) and three feet above the average level of high tide (fig. 183).
Sometimes, however, during periods of exceptionally high tides and
strong east winds, the waters of Boston Harbor piled up to levels
considerably above that. There are records of tides as high as fifteen
feet above low tide.[33] When such conditions prevailed, the sewers
backed up into the basements of houses. It was therefore impossible
to place the dining room or any other main room in the basement.
Kitchens, however, were generally situated there although they, too
were occasionally removed to the safer height of the first floor. This
problem also explains why the main entrance in the early days was
never situated in the basement, although modern alteration has frequently relocated it there. The unsatisfactory and unsanitary drainage
condition continued until 1884 when Boston completed its present
divergency sewer system which drains the lowest Back Bay basement
at all times and which pumps the sewage into the outer harbor at
Deer Island.[34]

Because of these factors, the Back Bay architect was prevented from
using the so-called "English basement" which was popular in both
New York and Boston's New South End (fig. 24). This arrangement

70   Facade of 271–279 Clarendon Street, 1869. Five small houses 17 feet wide were grouped together in one block facing a side street. The corner house was organized symmetrically about its entrance, which faced Marlborough Street. In 1890 that entrance was transformed into a bay window when the house was joined with one next door at number 273 and a new entrance made.

placed both dining room and kitchen in the basement, which is only a few steps below the street level, and sometimes employed a subbasement for the furnace. Because of the high ceiling demanded in a formal apartment like the dining room, the level of the main parlor floor was fairly high above the street, and hence the main entrance on that level was reached by a long flight of front steps—the high stoop of the English basement house. In contrast to this, the front steps of Back Bay houses were low, often not more than six risers (fig. 30). This was possible because the basement level could be as much as five feet below the street and because there were no major basement rooms which demanded excessively high ceilings. This difference in the level of the first floor and the absence of the formidable high stoop is one of the most marked differences in the houses of the two areas.

In the large majority of Back Bay houses of this period the kitchen is placed in the rear of the basement where it opens onto the back yard, a step or two lower than the kitchen floor. The service entrance is invariably on the alley, not on the front of the house as in New York where there are no alleys. Often a long narrow wooden shed runs along one side of the back yard serving as a storeroom and woodshed. The middle portion of the basement is devoted to stairs, pantries, storage closets, a water closet for servants, and a furnace room. At the front of the house is a laundry with appended drying room and a large coal bin. Often this bin extends out under the front steps and occasionally a small outside door under the front steps opens into the coal bin (fig. 65). But this is not a tradesman's entrance and it was used only for coal deliveries. Old photographs sometimes show coal wagons backed perpendicularly against the curb (fig. 20). From here the coal was

71   Entrances of 275 and 277 Clarendon Street, detail of fig. 70. Because the lots are shallow, no front yard is allowed, and the facade rises directly from the sidewalk. The entrance steps are therefore recessed within the open entrance vestibule.

carried into the house in baskets. The windows of these front basement rooms are always small and they are often covered by some kind of metal grill.

The disposition of the rooms on the first floor varies with the width of the house. Type I, which is standard for narrow lots, accounts for 61 percent of the houses built in this period. There is but one variation of this plan; if the house is too narrow to admit both reception room and entrance hall, the former is omitted and the entry opens directly into a spacious reception hall.

The main stair is always placed fairly far back in the house. This allows for a room of generous depth on the second floor at the front of the house, and it provides also for a deep entrance hall on the first floor containing two sets of double doors connected by a vestibule as well as an outside porch. Occasionally the outside staircase approaching the porch is recessed, especially in the small dwellings facing the cross streets where the house is placed next to the sidewalk (fig. 71).

The disposition of the second floor is determined by the number of main rooms that could be placed on the first floor. In Type III, where all principal rooms are on the first level, the second floor is given entirely to bedrooms, although an additional upstairs sitting room will usually be provided. In Types IIb and IIc the library is placed on the second floor; in Types IIa and I that level contains both library and parlor.[35] In Types I and IIa the two large rooms, connected by the stair hall, open up to form a particularly fine apartment for entertaining (fig. 72). The main staircase frequently does not carry above the second level and hardly ever above the third. Only the service stairs run through from basement to attic. The ceiling heights for the two main floors vary between twelve and fourteen feet.

Ordinarily Back Bay residences contain two large and two or three small family bedchambers. Again the arrangement of these rooms depends on the width of the house and whether any second-floor area is available for bedrooms. Type I always has two bedroom floors; the lower contains two large bedchambers, one front and one back, while the upper level may or may not be subdivided to form two small chambers across the front or back. In Type II secondary bed or dressing rooms (the so-called "hall room" which was situated above the entrance hall) are included front and back in addition to the large bedchambers. In both Types I and II the middle of the house is given over to stairs, closets, toilets, and a light well. This latter feature is used to illuminate the main stair hall or the middle parlor in the "New York house." Bathrooms and dressing rooms open onto this shaft for ventilation and light. The light wells and the service stairs are illuminated by means of a skylight. In the attic a ladder and bulkhead communicate with the roof.

In residences of the late fifties and sixties the bath and water closet are usually placed in separate rooms; the bathroom communicates through dressing rooms with both main bedchambers but the water closet opens directly on the stair hall. The bath is repeated on both bedroom floors, though often a single water closet serves the two floors. Frequently wash basins with running water are placed in each bedroom or their adjoining dressing rooms. These generalizations are made on the basis of surviving house plans for Back Bay residences, since no house inspected in 1948 retained its original toilet fixtures or arrangement.[36]

The attic is divided into small servants' chambers of which there are never less than three. Sometimes one attic room is fitted as a sewing room with wardrobes and shelves. In a few very large houses (Type III), a billiard room is included in the attic. No plumbing was originally provided on this floor—not even a wash basin.

After such a resumé of the accommodations of the Back Bay dwelling, the modern reader may wonder how such houses could ever have been considered satisfactory. Arranged on five or six levels, they obviously could not be maintained without a large staff of servants. Two servants was the absolute minimum: a cook and a parlor maid who also waited table. Usually there was a third girl to care for the upper floors and to serve as personal maid. A butler might be employed instead of the parlor maid; his duties would include shopping for groceries and running other errands.[37] In addition, there was a laundress and a sewing woman who worked part time, and if the family had a carriage, a coachman was needed.

Even with an adequate staff of servants, there were enormous numbers of steps to negotiate each day with third-floor bedroom, fifth-floor sewing room, first-floor dining room. And what conscientious New England housewife would miss a kitchen inspection at least once a day? Originally there were no elevators in these houses, although the service area or light wells in the middle of the house have frequently been transformed into elevator shafts by later remodelings. It is, of course, this twofold problem of steps and servants which in

72

Stair hall of the *piano nobile* at 22 Commonwealth Avenue, 1861. Two sets of double doors connect the parlor, library, and stair hall to create a splendid apartment for entertaining.

the last forty years has spelled the demise of the large town house.

These houses were seemingly designed with no thought whatsoever of conserving work or steps. Indeed it seemed to matter little whether the smooth operation of a city house took one or a half dozen servants, a fact that is not surprising when one considers the $3.03 average weekly wage of a domestic servant as late as 1875.[38] Perhaps this paltry hire put the housemaid beneath consideration for it is certain that only the barest accommodations were provided for her. Despite the numbers of servants and the twelve to fourteen hours daily which they spent on duty, usually no social room was set aside for them other than the kitchen. Since their sleeping quarters on the top floor were without a water closet or running water, it was necessary for them to go all the way to the basement for these facilities. Attic rooms were also without fireplaces or central heating, though flue outlets indicate that individual stoves could be used.

The kitchen–common room, however, may not have been without its interest for the maids, as it was there that they found their principal contact with the outside world. Here each morning a long procession of tradesmen brought their wares for inspection and purchase: butcher, baker, grocer, dairyman, to say nothing of the succession of delivery boys. The service areas of these houses in the nineteenth century must have presented a much more animated scene than do the desolate alleys and dingy back yards of the same houses today.

INTERIOR DESIGN

In planning the individual room, great emphasis is placed upon symmetry. Doors, windows, and mantelpieces are carefully arranged axially and when a wall falls on axis, it is hung with a long pier mirror. The actual shape of the room, however, is apt to be complicated and irregular; one side will be interrupted by the chimney breast since party walls are not thick enough to encase flues (fig. 102). Another wall will probably be interrupted by the complex surfaces of the polygonal bay window. These frequent breaks in wall plane are accentuated by the way the heavy plaster cornice is carried around all obstructions. Gone is the quiet elegance of rooms of clean-cut geometric shape—ellipses, circles, rectangles—so popular in the 1830's and 1840's. However, the earlier practice of connecting principal rooms by large double doors is continued wherever possible, and the vistas thus obtained between rooms are emphasized by the aforementioned elongated mirrors.

One of the chief beauties of the houses of this period is the interior woodwork. Although fully paneled walls are no longer fashionable by the 1860's, the wooden dado is usual in stair halls and libraries. In other main rooms double doors are especially fine with their large, simple panels that emphasize the satiny textures of the ash and walnut woods of which they were constructed. Openings are encased by wooden moldings that have a generous, full-bosomed quality. The woodwork of the mantels, bookcases, and mirror frames is accentuated with cartouches, scrolls, and brackets which have a vigorous, curved

73

Fireplace at 135 Beacon Street, 1860. Typically elaborate cabinet work of Civil War era. The ornate effect is further emphasized by the use of different colored woods or stains.

design and which contrast effectively with the plain surfaces of the panels. Sometimes, however, this decoration has a "glued on" look: it does not seem to be an integral part of the wooden paneling, an appearance which is heightened by the polychromatic effect derived from the use of contrasting woods or from staining (figs. 61, 73).

Even this manipulation and fussy concern with details cannot destroy the effect of beautiful woods lavishly used. A quality that future generations will surely admire about Victorian architecture will be its bountiful use of fine woods; doors and trim in even the service areas are made of perfectly clear pine of a quality that is virtually unobtainable today. Of excellent craftsmanship also are the inside shutters that fold into window reveals. Exterior shutters, one recalls, were hung only when the house was closed in the summer or for other long periods (fig. 39). When not in use, they were taken off and stored in the basement or back yard shed.

The main staircases also merit comment. The long flights of eighteen to twenty-four steps often bend gracefully at top and bottom so that on upper floors the first and last risers are parallel to the runners. Turns are accomplished gradually and the handrail has an easy flow as it runs through the main floors of the house without interruption (figs. 72, 74, 75). The stairs of the first floor usually terminate in a cascading effect, the three of four bottom steps swelling successively in size and degree of curvature (figs. 76, 77). In the early sixties, when stairs were still finished by hand, such complex curves and surfaces of intricate geometric shape were within the price range of even the speculative builder; but after the Civil War, presumably under the impact of higher wages and machine tools, these subtleties were abandoned for straight flights of steps with straight handrails and runners that extend between newel posts at each landing (figs. 78, 79).

However handsome the interiors of these houses of the 1860's, one gains the impression that as far as the interior design is concerned, the architect functioned as little more than an artistic coordinator who brought together a variety of stock mantels, plaster ornaments, and millwork. An examination of the few surviving sets of working drawings for Back Bay houses of the period reveals an astonishing paucity of interior details or even of rough suggestions for the interior finish. Whereas the schedule for cut stone work of the facade was usually prepared in great detail, one finds, for example, in Bryant's contract plans for 22 Commonwealth Avenue, not a single detail for the woodwork, not a profile of a plaster molding, not a cupboard elevation, nor even a draftsman's note on the plans to indicate the nature of the wood trim.[39] Indeed, from the specifications that accompany these plans, one infers that once a specific sum had been set aside for carpentry work, a certain standard of workmanship and quality of material were implicit. It would seem that the owner was expected to select specific details within an established repertoire which the contractor was prepared to execute for a given price. This impression is strengthened by knowledge that all the plaster cornices were prefabricated and sold at so much a running foot and that they as well as plaster ceiling medallions were glued in place.

74 Main stair on the *piano nobile* at 72 Marlborough Street, 1866, by Charles Kirby. The gracefully curving handrail runs without interruption from the first to the fourth floors.

75 Main stair at 1 Arlington Street, 1861. This doorway leads from the second-floor drawing room to the stair hall.

The Dexter plans of 1847 for 92–99 Beacon Street are scarcely more illuminating on the question of millwork. There one finds one or two schedules for simple dressing-room shelves. And on the reverse side of one sheet containing a floor plan there is a very hasty pencil sketch

76   First floor newel post, 1 Arlington Street. The expense of the carved newel and the gracefully fluid lines of the three bottom stairs and the wainscot was not much greater than ordinary stairs when all staircases had to be fashioned by hand.

77   Main stair of 137 Beacon Street, 1860. The plan of this stair with the five bottom stairs broadening out in a flowing curve is not unlike staircases of the old Greek Revival manner which used scroll newels, but the dark woodwork and details of the eight-sided column and the segmental arches bespeak the Civil War era.

78 Main stair at 10 Commonwealth Avenue, 1864. Straight runs of stairs and handrails extending between newels on each floor became usual after the Civil War.

for a fireplace wall in a library. Unfortunately the house for which this fireplace was presumably intended was completely remodeled in 1902; so it is impossible to check the pertinence of the sketch.

The contracts for carpentry and masonry were let separately, a practice which continued throughout the history of the district. In the case of the Motley house at 22 Commonwealth Avenue, the carpentry was contracted by James Fitch, the masonry by Standish and Woodbury. Incidentally, both contractors occupied houses in this same group: Fitch lived at number 30 and Standish at number 32.

The original floors of early Back Bay houses were of softwood as the fashion of the day dictated wall to wall carpeting. Softwood was also used in the uncarpeted attic. Stairs were carpeted but constructed of hardwood. The cost of carpeting was a substantial item; a new house that sold for $27,000 in 1869 required $862.82 for carpeting.[40]

It is impossible to specify the exact date at which hardwood floors became popular as in many cases a parquet or hardwood floor was later installed when the original carpeting wore out. A reporter at the Paris Exposition of 1867 mentions precut parquet panels as if they were something new, and it is certain that parquet carpets, as they were called, were in extensive use by the time of the 1876 Philadelphia Bicentennial.[41] The first parquet floor (1871) that I have identified in the Back Bay is at 165 Marlborough Street. Here in the main hall a parquetry surrounds a panel of carpet. The remainder of the house, however, is completely carpeted (fig. 101).

Another handsome feature of the Back Bay mansion is the fireplace which is found in all principal rooms and in most bedrooms. These mantelpieces are made both of white marble and of wood. For im-

79   Main stair at 226 Beacon Street, 1864. A halfway landing and the screen of columns are features which Snell and Gregerson will employ consistently for their stair compositions in the 1870's.

portant rooms, the characteristic mantel is one with a heavy lintel which carries the mantel shelf and which is supported by carved consoles (figs. 80, 81). This lintel is decorated by either a series of inset panels or carved bosses in high relief. The consoles are heavy sculptural forms which spring from recessed panels of the vertical jambs. Smaller mantelpieces in the bedrooms usually consist of a projecting marble shelf, one inch thick, and a simple facing whose arched opening is accented by a keystone (fig. 82). From house to house one notices marked similarities in mantel design throughout the decade although the later tendency is toward more decoration.

The construction of the marble mantelpieces is fairly uniform. With the exception of a solid lintel that spans the opening and supports the mantel shelf, these mantels are built up with a series of slabs about one inch thick which, when fitted together, present a very robust and sculptural appearance. It is interesting to note the strong likeness be-

80   White marble mantel in the drawing room at 22 Commonwealth Avenue, 1861. In the sixties mantels for important rooms usually have a heavy projecting shelf supported by consoles.

81

Wood mantel in the library at 22 Commonwealth Avenue. Wood and marble mantels follow the same basic design, but the carved decoration on wooden examples is somewhat more elaborate. When this picture was taken the andirons and objects on the mantel shelf had been wrapped preliminary to closing the house for the summer.

tween the carving of these marble compositions and the brownstone decoration on certain Back Bay facades. The reeded consoles of fireplaces at 22 Commonwealth, for example, are very like the stone brackets used as keystones on the exterior of 122 Beacon Street (figs. 80, 83), while the leaf decoration in the lozenge-shaped panels of the marble mantel of 22 Commonwealth closely resembles that in the triangular spandrels of the stone entry in the same row of houses (figs. 80, 84). Mantelpieces of wood have a basic similarity of form to those of marble except that the wood carving and moldings are understandably somewhat more elaborate (fig. 81).

82 Bedroom fireplace at 407 Beacon Street, 1867. Built up with one-inch marble slabs, such simple, round-headed, stock fireplaces do not vary appreciably from one house to another.

The similarities of these marble mantels to contemporary stone ornamentation and to the wooden mantels as well lead one to the conclusion that they were produced locally. Because of generic similarities, it would seem that they were the work of one or two marble yards rather than the design of different architects. From a supply of ready-made mantels, the owner could select pieces for his house just as he chose gas fixtures or wall paper. The Motley building contract specifies differing cash allowances for mantels in the various rooms.

Unlike most other Back Bay mantels is a group of particularly elaborate white marble compositions which graced the home of William Weld at 1 Arlington Street (1861). These specimens, with their florid leaf and scroll forms, their carved heads and robust cable moldings, are somewhat unusual (figs. 85, 86, 87). Their construction is also different. Instead of the thin slabs finished with mechanical marble planes, the Weld mantels are built of thicker blocks whose moldings and relief decoration are cut by hand. It seems likely that these mantels, and probably another in the parlor at 135 Beacon Street, were imported from Italy. British architectural periodicals of the time contain advertisements of Carrara marble dealers like Gian-Carlo Fabricotti who produced fine marble mantels in quantity at his Carrara marble quarries, transported them to England in his own ships, and sold them in retail or wholesale lots at his London warehouse. Probably a limited selection of imported mantels was also available in Boston. The testimony of such contemporary sculptors as Hiram Powers indicates the technical superiority as well as the economy of Italian over American marble cutters.[42]

The ubiquitous plaster cornice provides us with another example

83   Brownstone decoration of facade of 122 Beacon Street, 1857. The
      console-shaped keystone is similar to the brackets of the marble man-
      tel at 22 Commonwealth Avenue (fig. 80).

84   Main entrance at 24 Commonwealth Avenue, 1861. The character of the stone carving of this door frame is similar to that observed on marble mantels.

85   Mantel of the front drawing room on the *piano nobile* at 1 Arlington Street, 1861. Placed against a chimney breast which is located on the center axis of the room, the mantel is topped by a carved, gilt-framed mirror.

86 Mantel of first floor reception room at 1 Arlington Street. A cast iron coal grate of American manufacture fills the opening.

87 Mantel of the rear drawing room, *piano nobile*, at 1 Arlington Street. The florid design and the more plastic quality of the carving suggest an Italian rather than a Boston origin for this mantel.

88 The drawing room ceiling at 1 Arlington Street is elaborately decorated with a variety of plaster moldings.

of a stock element used to decorate the Civil War house. Placed eleven or twelve feet above the floor, it was necessary that these cornices have a bold design in order to be seen against the big-patterned wall papers (figs. 85, 88). Intricate cornices of plaster were cast in molds and glued to the ceilings. Only the simplest moldings were formed in place by troweling the wet plaster with a template. The Motley contract allows $1.50 per linear foot for cornices of the parlor and library, $1.12 for the dining room, and $.70 for the bedrooms; the working drawings for the house, as mentioned before, contain no cornice details. Other house plans of the period are equally silent on the details of the cornices. Among the plans for a dozen different houses on Beacon Street prepared by William Dexter, there are details of only three plaster cornices.

Another ornament that should be mentioned is the precast plaster rosette affixed in the center of the ceiling about the outlet for the gas chandelier (fig. 89). The floral forms of these units are more than pure ornamentation since they screen a ventilator which connects with the chimney flue and which was placed there to carry off gas fumes from the chandelier.

The gas fixtures were regarded as part of the furnishings of the house, not a part of its standard equipment. In 1869 the fixtures for a typical thirteen-room house cost $346.76. That it was customary for families to take the gas fittings with them when they left a house is attested by the collection of gas wall brackets and chandeliers at the Gibson House Museum, 137 Beacon Street, which derive from three different houses which the owners or their close relatives had occupied.[43]

89   Detail of fig. 88. The chandelier rosette and garland as well as the other ceiling moldings are of precast plaster glued in place. Perforations in the rosette disguise a vent which carried off fumes of the gas chandelier.

Early Architects Working in the Back Bay

Very little is known of the architects who designed the first buildings in the Back Bay. Records of early architectural firms for the most
part have been destroyed, and the Boston Building Department did
not begin to keep complete records of new construction until after
the great fire of 1872. Fragments of information have been gathered,
however, on this tantalizingly incomplete subject.

Office drawings of three early architectural firms have been preserved which document a few Back Bay buildings and which give
important information on matters of construction, mechanical equipment, and architectural procedure. Eldest of the three architects whose
drawings have been preserved is George M. Dexter. His activity falls
prior to the large-scale development of the district as he gave up practice in 1852 and he designed only two groups of early Back Bay houses:
67–69 and 92–99 Beacon Street (figs. 13–17). The former was demolished long ago; the latter, built in 1849, was discussed at length in
Chapter Four. Just reaching the active part of his career in the early
sixties was Nathaniel J. Bradlee who maintained an architectural
office from 1853 to his death in 1888. His many commissions seem to
stem from his business acumen and friendships rather than his ability
as a designer. By 1873 he had already designed twelve residences in
the district. Youngest of the three architects is William G. Preston. In
addition to the initial sketches for the first Massachusetts Institute of
Technology building and the old Museum of Natural History, Preston
designed thirteen Back Bay houses and the first section of the Hotel
Vendome.

The documentation of activity in the Back Bay area of other Boston
architectural offices is, unfortunately, a hit and miss matter. From
surviving working drawings and the building contract dated 1860
once preserved by Warren Motley for the family home at 22 Commonwealth Avenue, Gridley J. F. Bryant is known as the architect of
the block of nine houses numbered 20 to 36 (fig. 47). Although this is
our only proof of Bryant's activity in the district, it is safe to assume
that his office, the largest in Boston, did much work there. Bryant's
associate at the time, Arthur Gilman, is credited with the layout of
the district and the design of the Arlington Street Church.

The only early Back Bay house of H. H. Richardson, mentioned by Henry-Russell Hitchcock on the basis of drawings preserved in Richardson's office, is 164 Marlborough Street (fig. 126). Although of related design, the authorship of two contiguous houses at 312–314 Dartmouth Street is questioned by Hitchcock. They were built a year later (1871) than 164 Marlborough.[44]

Personal recollections of early owners assist us to attribute two other early house groups. The late C. H. Gibson recalled that the residence of his family at 137 Beacon Street (today the Gibson House Museum) was designed by E. C. Cabot in 1859 and built the following year (fig. 50). The late Mrs. W. C. Endicott, Jr., remembered that the firm of Snell and Gregerson designed her house at 165 Marlborough Street (figs. 97–103). The design of the three-house group of which the Endicott residence is one unit corresponds in style with documented work of the firm after 1873.[44a]

Elsewhere, passing references give clues to the authorship of a few more pre-1873 edifices: the Hotel Hamilton (now demolished) at the northwest corner of Commonwealth Avenue and Clarendon Street, built in 1869 by Ware and Van Brunt (fig. 90); the Hotel Agassiz (1872) at Commonwealth and Exeter Street, by Weston and Rand; Richard M. Hunt's three dwellings (1859) at 13, 14, and 15 Arlington Street (fig. 32); and four small houses by an obscure designer named A. C. Martin.[45]

Thus of approximately 730 residential structures built in the Back Bay between 1855 and 1873, it is possible to ascribe with certainty only 52 to known architects, an unsatisfactory state of affairs which is aggravated by C. A. Cummings' statement that these houses "were widely different from any heretofore built and very generally under the charge of professional architects."[46]

One is tempted to make attributions on stylistic grounds, but several factors are dissuading. The similarity in the detailing of stonework on some facades may derive from the fact that the stone was cut in the same yards. The interiors offer little assistance on the problem of attribution because the architect did relatively little original work here. As we have seen, plaster ornaments and marble mantels were derived from open stock, and the millwork was probably determined by what the carpenter was prepared to do for a certain fee rather than by what the architect chose to design. Indeed, so little concerned with interior design was the Boston builder that there are

90   Hotel Hamilton, 260 Clarendon Street, 1869, by Ware and Van Brunt
(now demolished). The first apartment house in the new Back Bay
district, this design combined an Academic pavilion composition with
an inventive use of brick detailing. The octagonal bay at the left of
the picture was added in 1887 by Van Brunt and Howe.

instances in which the architect's services were required only for the design of the facade.[47]

A more serious drawback to this work of attribution is our inability to establish the stylistic character of the different architects and architectural firms at work in the Back Bay in the 1860's. Boston had forty-nine architects in 1857, seventy-two in 1869. Of this large number, we can identify the work of only twelve different individuals or firms. Although it is improbable that all or even most of Boston's architects were commissioned to design residences in the district, such prominent contemporaries as Luther Briggs or Hammatt Billings must surely be represented there.

Despite these drawbacks, one can make some good guesses as to who designed some of the Back Bay's buildings beyond the fifty-two structures just mentioned. Several houses predating 1873 are ascribed to Charles K. Kirby on the following grounds: Kirby, who designed the first Boston Public Library, is listed as an architect in the *Boston Directory* between the years 1852 and 1882. At one time or another tax records between 1860 and 1872 show him as the owner of eighteen different houses under construction; after that date city building permits frequently designate him as architect, builder, and owner. We have, therefore, made the assumption that he designed all the houses with which he is connected. It might further be stated that Kirby took no interest in the affairs of the Boston Society of Architects, which considered it unethical for an architect to act both as contractor and architect for a building.

For similar reasons a number of houses are ascribed to Fred B. Pope before and after 1873. Although he is listed as an architect in the *Boston Directory* between 1871 and 1893, he is mentioned neither in the history of the Boston Society of Architects nor in any account of early Boston building. The group of designs ascribed to him seems to be little more than an echo of current architectural fashions (fig. 65).

One is tempted to try to form a group of attributions about the firm of Ware and Van Brunt. These partners were among the most influential of the younger architects who came into prominence after the Civil War, and they were continually in the forefront in the search for new forms. Their firm was the first in Boston to provide aspiring draftsmen with some systematic architectural training beyond the routine duties of the apprentice. In the late 1860's a series of buildings was built in what we shall call in Chapter Six the Panel Brick style. The principal characteristics of this group are a preference for pressed brick laid with thin joints, intricate brick cornices, and a fondness for small-scale panels of brick decoration worked into the masonry surface. These decorative panels both recede and project from the wall surface; often they take the shape of crosses. Several early examples of the style were designed by Ware and Van Brunt: the old Hotel Hamilton of 1869, one of the first examples of the style in Boston (fig. 90); Weld Hall, Harvard, of 1872, which employs intricate brick work; and probably the house for Charles E. Ware (1869) at 44 Brimmer Street (fig. 91). The Panel Brick style was too diffused to be the work of one office only, and Ware and Van Brunt are by no means restricted to this manner since in these very same years they were seriously involved with Ruskin Gothic concepts at Memorial Hall, Harvard University (1867). Nevertheless one is tempted to associate them with the emergence of the Panel Brick style for residential architecture.

The work of Snell and Gregerson, on the other hand, possesses a stylistic consistency too strong to pass unnoticed.[48] Houses designed by their firm in the mid-seventies (and therefore documented by city records) bear too many similarities to certain houses dating from the sixties to leave any doubt of their authorship. While many of their contemporaries merely manipulated Classical forms, Snell and Gregerson, more perhaps than any other contemporary Boston firm, demonstrated a sympathy and understanding of orderly, Academic design. Although disciplined, their designs are not the rigid mechanical exercises which less gifted academicians so often produced in the name of Classicism. Usually they demonstrate a good deal of freedom and originality in handling Classical detail but these decorative variations never obscure the architectonic clarity of the composition. In their hands the French Academic formula is both dignified and adaptable, and it merits comment (figs. 42, 97).

Specifically their houses can be identified by the following stylistic characteristics: One, an invariable preference for brick walls with a trim of cream-colored (Nova Scotia) sandstone used to accent such architectural features as entablatures, string courses, rusticated basements, and framing members; second, window openings framed with an architrave of considerable projection, the sills usually supported by small corbels; third, window and door openings capped by flat arches, sometimes spanning the whole width of the opening, but more frequently accenting only the three center voussoirs as a kind of large

91   Number 41 Brimmer Street, 1869, probably by Ware and Van Brunt.
An early example of the Panel Brick style so popular in the 1870's.

keystone; fourth, use of an unusual console-supported entablature
where the console is not treated as a modillion with leaf design and
a horizontal axis but reeded and with a vertical axis; fifth, use of an
oriel instead of a bay window to permit a more symmetrical composition and to maintain the integrity of the flat, limiting plane of the
facade; sixth, the first floor kept unusually low (only six or seven steps
above the street) and the kitchen placed on the first floor and dining
room on the second; seventh, facades of adjoining houses are related.
In eight out of ten cases the main cornice level of a Snell and Greger-

son house is made to align with that of an adjoining house which preceded it in date of construction. In all, twenty-nine Back Bay residences are ascribed to this firm: fourteen of them documented in the records of the Building Department, fifteen by attribution.[49]

THE STATE OF THE ARCHITECTURAL PROFESSION

The years immediately following the Civil War were difficult ones for the architectural profession. Not only was the practitioner faced with a rapidly changing world, he was forced to redefine the job which he had always done. Caught between the speculative builder on the one hand and the increasingly complex field of engineering on the other, the value of the architect was sometimes questioned, and the architect had to justify his services in the eyes of the public. He had in addition to reorganize his office proceedings and devise a more efficient system of architectural education, and to make matters more difficult, he was faced with alarming competition within the ranks of those who called themselves architects.

Between 1830 and 1867, while Boston's population quadrupled from about 61,000 to 250,000, the number of those who styled themselves "architects" increased ninefold, from eight to seventy-two.[50] With a ratio of one architect to approximately every 3400 citizens, competition in 1867 was cutthroat. There were no recognized standards of professional conduct, no qualifying examinations to determine the practitioner's proficiency. And most vexing of all to the architects of the period, there was no agreement on fees or professional responsibility.

During the three quarters of a century between Bulfinch's first work and the Civil War the architect had been primarily a purveyor of taste. His principal service, in the field of residential architecture, had been to advise his clients on matters of style and to prepare for them elevation drawings utilizing architectural ornamentation based upon one of the several approved styles. In city houses there was little variation in room arrangement, problems of construction were still so simple that builders' rule of thumb methods were quite adequate to solve them, and questions about mechanical equipment were practically nonexistent. Thus it was that a reasonably accurate knowledge of historical styles and current British developments and an ability to incorporate these details in designs of some coherence were the things that distinguished the architect from the housewright. As a result, the architect's education was one long search for erudition. Despite this, however, the endless succession of hopelessly unauthentic though naïvely charming Italian villas, Swiss chalets, Tudor cottages, and Greek temple-houses indicates how rare indeed was an accurate knowledge of the historic styles. As very few early nineteenth century American designers had firsthand experience with European buildings, they were dependent upon the engravings which illustrated the architectural books of the period. But these pictures sometimes led them astray. Even those who had once traveled in Europe found it difficult to achieve European results in America where craftsmen were slow to give up the long-used Georgian-Greek Revival vernacular. Too often a given style of architecture was little more than a set of structurally irrelevant details applied to an ordinary frame or masonry structure.

If in the first half of the nineteenth century America had not always been able to differentiate between naïve inventiveness and archaeological erudition, in the late fifties and early sixties it began to make the distinction with some assurance. This was undoubtedly more true in Boston than in most other parts of the country, because of the city's traditional orientation toward Europe. Here a European study trip soon became a part of the architect's professional preparation, and helped to set him apart from the design-mongering speculative builder.

The profession also had to face competition with the rapidly advancing field of engineering. In the early years of the nineteenth century the structural problems involved in erecting most wood or masonry buildings were such that any man of practical experience could solve. After 1850, however, society began to demand larger and more complex buildings and the growing use of ferrous materials posed problems for the trained engineer. If the architect viewed with secret alarm this growing importance of engineering, he often tried to minimize it by segregating the lofty realm of art from the merely utilitarian world of engineering. But all the same he probably sensed that sooner or later he would have to come to terms with the technical advances in the field of engineering. Ruskin might protest that true architecture was above utilitarian considerations, that only the traditional building materials were worthy for monumental building, but the esteemed Edward M. Barry, professor at the Royal Academy, advised his young pupils that the architect's duties were twofold. He must at once be an artist in his design and a man of science in its execution; his architecture "externally may indulge in grace of form . . . but internally she must accept the obligation to combine convenience and fitness with beauty."[51]

An important indication of change on the Boston architectural scene was an attempt to provide adequate training for young men who wished to become architects. Up to this time American architects had been trained under the old apprentice system. The few who had attended college received no practical preparation for the profession, and following graduation they still had to acquire technical information while serving as apprentice draftsmen. In 1863, however, W. R. Ware and his partner Henry Van Brunt organized informal classes in their office. Here regular apprentice duties were supplemented by lectures on design and architectural history as well as instruction in free-hand drawing. They modeled their instruction on that given in Richard Morris Hunt's New York studio, where both Ware and Van Brunt had studied. Hunt's program in turn, was copied from the course of instruction in the French ateliers where he had studied. Although the success of the experiment was immediate, it was apparent that only a full course of study would meet the architect's increasing need for specialized training. As a result, Ware was asked in 1865 to form the first school of architecture in the United States at the Massachusetts Institute of Technology. A four-year course was outlined with emphasis on architectural design, free-hand drawing, construction, and architectural history. Instruction began in September 1867. Similar schools appeared in rapid succession at Cornell (1871), Illinois (1873), Syracuse (1873), Michigan (1876), Columbia (1881), Pennsylvania (1890), and Harvard, (1894).[52]

Another visible sign of the change is the development of the large specialized office. The best example of this in Boston is the office of Gridley J. F. Bryant. In his years of activity Bryant developed a practice that was regional in scope and turned out an incredible quantity of work. He is credited with the building or remodeling of nineteen state capitols and city halls; thirty-six court houses; fifty-nine hospitals, schools, or other public buildings; sixteen railroad stations; sixteen custom or post offices; and eight churches. This takes no account of his private commissions! When, for example, the great fire of 1872 devastated Boston's central commercial district, it destroyed 152 structures designed by Bryant; of that number he was engaged to rebuild 111. Clearly such a volume of work could not be handled by one man. Bryant, an active, energetic administrator, was constantly on the move inspecting jobs in distant cities, meeting with building committees, and arranging new commissions for the firm. He was the prototype of the modern "contact" man, so often the most widely known and best remunerated member of the present-day architectural firm. In practice for himself at the age of twenty-one (1837), Bryant was associated between 1860 and 1867 with Arthur Gilman, but one infers from the *Boston Directory* that he did not enter into a direct partnership until 1868 when he combined forces with L. P. Rogers. The best work of the Bryant office was done in association with Gilman. With an income sometimes amounting to $20,000 annually, Bryant lived well and entertained liberally but died in poverty in 1899.[53]

An example of the efficiency with which his office was run is seen in the aforementioned printed specification form for the Motley house at 22 Commonwealth Avenue (see note 39). Already in 1860 Bryant was using this time-saving standardized form which the association of Boston architects was still discussing eight years later.

Finally, the founding in 1867 of the Boston Society of Architects indicates that the profession was attaining a certain maturity.[54] Although trailing by some ten years its New York counterpart, this organization had pioneer work to do. The purpose of the founders seems to have been twofold. On the one hand, they hoped to establish the standing of architecture as a learned profession; on the other hand, they sought a kind of polite trade union which could present a united front against clients who tried to exploit the heretofore disunited body of architects.

The "highbrow" element within the society thought of the organization as an instrument for discussion and debate which would perform a function somewhat similar to that of the Royal Institute of British Architects. They hoped thereby not only to improve their own minds but to assure their position among the older, established, learned professions. The more pragmatic members sought merely to cope with such practical matters as standardization of fees, rules by which architectural competitions should be conducted, an agreement among the members regarding advertising and underbidding one another, and the proper relationship of architect to client and contractor.

Despite some evidences of tension between the two groups, they managed to work together. The minutes of the society's early meetings reveal programs of balanced interest. During the first year of its existence, for example, the topics under consideration at the biweekly meetings included: architectural fees, publicity measures, inventions useful to architecture, the usefulness of printed form specifications, the employment of women, Sir Charles Barry's work, and the influence of monastic orders on Romanesque architecture. The Boston Society of Architects did not immediately achieve its ends. By 1871, however, in union with the American Institute of Architects, they reached agreement on a standard fee for architects. And by 1895 the national American Institute of Architects, its Boston chapter included, was able to agree on the first professional code of ethics which decreed that no architect might solicit commissions, advertise, or enter competitions without compensation; nor might he enter a partnership with a contractor or manufacturer in building an edifice of his design.

The society took a great interest in the newly founded department of architecture at Massachusetts Institute of Technology and some of its members were eventually to teach there. When the Rotch Traveling Fellowship, the first architectural scholarship in America, was established in 1883, the society was asked to make the awards for the first four years.[55]

Thus it was that the profession accommodated itself to the changing conditions of the American architectural scene. In retrospect practice in the 1860's sometimes may seem to stand near to the rule-of-thumb practice and the superficial style-conscious point of view of the early nineteenth century, but it is important to realize how substantial were the changes that took place in this decade. For the first time the American architectural profession felt the full impact of the cosmopolitan building of Europe and was moved by the changing complexion of American building. It found itself somewhat like an awkward youth just come of age with a position to establish among mature competitors. Its members, some of them men without college background or European study, were faced with the problem of lifting themselves by their own artistic bootstraps. But with the characteristic vigor and self-confidence of the period, they set about to do all that had to be done: gain a working knowledge of the historic styles of architecture; master current European fashions and adapt these to the American scene; reconcile architecture with engineering progress or at least define the province of each; provide the young men of the profession with an adequate technical training; organize their professional ranks; and establish the profession's standing and importance. It might be added that the vigor and resourcefulness with which these problems were tackled is reflected in the architectural designs of the following decade.

THE DECADES
OF INDIVIDUALISM

1869–1885

In terms of architectural style the 1870's represent the most individualistic and the most complex period in Back Bay history. Architectural fashion changes with the season, and at any single moment several
different movements compete for public favor. Bored with Academic
competence, architects after the Civil War seemed to consider the
idioms Boston had used before confining. Yet instead of developing a
radically new architecture based on function, the profession turned
to an ever wider eclecticism. During the seventies designers generally
subordinated historical precedent to fancy or to the requirements of
the machines with which they worked. In this process they sought to
improve, that is, to elaborate upon older models; novelty and decorative abundance were the desired objectives. Somewhere after 1880,
however, they commenced to turn toward a somewhat more faithful
reproduction of some historical style. This period, therefore, is a curious
mixture of personal invention and historical selection. As witness to
the active search for a satisfactory architectural vocabulary, whether
inventive or archaeological, we find at least nine distinct stylistic tendencies flourishing in the Back Bay between 1869 and 1885.[1]

Before losing ourselves in this welter of stylistic innovation, however, let us think for a moment of the geometric relationship of the
single house to the larger block in which it is placed. As we saw earlier,
a block of houses in the 1840's was composed of a series of adjacent
units of similar size and shape. The block presented a homogeneous
appearance because of the basic similarity of the several units of which
it was composed. Its form was simply and clearly defined by a few

large planes: sloping roofs, contiguous facades, and end walls. The uniform banks of houses gave definition to the calm open space of the street between them. Two decades later the individual house was still an integral part of the larger block though the geometric appearance of that unit had altered. Loftier than before, because of an additional story and a high mansard roof, these massive blocks of dwellings loomed above the street and constricted its space; the only outlet seemed to be at the ends of the street. To the pedestrian the contiguous house fronts appeared as great walls lining the street corridor. And although projecting elements such as porches or bay windows sometimes occurred, they were distinctly subordinate to the continuous corridor walls (figs. 38, 39).

In the seventies, however, the compelling geometric unit of the block begins to dissolve as the individual house disengages itself from the larger unit. One factor which contributes to this process of dissolution is the variety of roof forms that appear. Flat, gable, hip, or mansard roofs replace the uniform moderately pitched roofs of the forties or the ubiquitous mansards of the sixties. As a result the rectangular mass of the block is no longer covered with a more or less uniform lid as in earlier generations. The variations in roof design create frequent changes in cornice height and give a serrated silhouette to the streetscape, an effect which is all the more exaggerated when seen foreshortened from the street. Nor is it only the roofline which is interrupted. The plane of the facade is broken with increasing frequency by the bay window, a feature which had become almost standard by the 1870's. Often the bay window is carried above the cornice and capped by a roof of its own which is visually distinct from the roof of the house behind it (figs. 115, 116). In this way the bay develops a geometric independence of the rest of the block. As the pedestrian looks along a typical Back Bay street of this decade, he sees not a single large geometric unit as before but an array of independent though contiguous forms (fig. 92).

At the same time that these basic changes in geometric composition were taking place, one can observe the gradual growth of a more plastic architectural decoration. In the forties, except for the gentle bowing of some house fronts, the principal plane of the facade was scarcely interrupted by decorative features: Lintels were set flush and sills minimized; the brick cornice protruded hardly at all beyond the face of the facade; there were few bay windows and no projecting

92   Beacon Street, numbers 336–354, constructed between 1876 and 1886.
This row of houses illustrates the way in which the former compelling
harmony of the streetscape dissolves as individual houses strive for
individual notice.

entrance porches, only recessed entrance alcoves (figs. 10, 12, 25). In
the fifties the ornamentation took on a more plastic quality: lintels
and sills were pushed out in front of the brick facade and enlivened
by knobby corbels; the recessed entrance porch developed a projecting
hood supported by heavy brackets; and the main cornice, carried on
brackets rather than by thin courses of corbeled brick, became much
heavier (figs. 13, 18). By the late fifties and early sixties the limiting
plane of the facade, though still easy to distinguish, had been subordinated to an accretion of architectural forms: window frames, string
courses, and cornices. Architraves were carried around almost all windows and robust pediments were employed over the more important
openings of the main stories; the octagonal bay window had begun

to appear and projecting entrance porches supported by free-standing columns were common (figs. 34, 59). The cornice now projected so far in front of the wall that, for the sake of equilibrium, it often was constructed of wood rather than of heavier masonry. In the mansard roof, dormer window compositions became steadily more ornate and three dimensional. Finally in the seventies and eighties this growing sense of plastic form tended to disengage individual houses from the simple geometric limits of the block (fig. 92).

The proportions of the facade also changed considerably. In the 1840's the house had a relatively broad appearance. Its height from street level to cornice was approximately one and three-quarters times its width. Windows had about this same proportion although there was some variation between floors. In the sixties the typical town house increased in height to form a ratio of about two and one-half to one. During the seventies it is no longer possible to specify a characteristic proportion for the facade because of the many variations caused by the different roof styles employed. Generally, however, the height of the house is relatively less than a decade earlier.

In a similar way windows differ markedly from one decade to the next. As late as 1840 window design was still controlled by the size of available glass. Panes differed but slightly, from eight to ten inches wide and as much as sixteen inches long, and they were generally set 6/6 (six lights in each of the two sashes of a double hung window). The division of the sash by thin muntins insured a consistency of scale even though the window lengths might vary between floors (figs. 9, 25). About 1850 it became possible to manufacture glass in larger sheets and the 2/2 window design made its appearance (fig. 18). Here each sash was divided by a single vertical muntin into two glass panels about 15 inches wide and as much as 3 feet long. In the early seventies the size of available plate glass increased to the point that a single sheet could fill each sash.

Choice of building materials also changed decidedly during these decades. A pressed brick of terra-cotta color had been the uniform building material of the forties and fifties.[2] During the late fifties and sixties brownstone generally replaced brick as the principal building material. Although pressed brick was still employed in this period, it was subordinated to the more fashionable brownstone trim that was used for basements as well as window and door frames. Other architectural elements constructed of wood, such as dormer windows or the main cornice, were painted to resemble brownstone and sometimes sanded (sand dusted on the wet paint to create a rough sandpaper-like surface that resembled dressed stone). Thus the overall effect of a block erected in the sixties was one of brownstone construction. It might be noted in passing that a putty-colored Nova Scotia sandstone was also used a good deal in this period, but the lighter shade of this stone was so quickly obscured by city grime that its color variation did not destroy the homogeneous appearance of early Back Bay streets. In their use of materials builders of the seventies differed widely from earlier practices. In additition to the ubiquitous brown and cream-colored sandstones which continued to be used by more conservative builders, there now appeared a considerable variety of building materials and textures: several kinds of brick and stone, glazed polychromatic tile, terra cotta, slate in several colors, pressed copper and iron, and wrought iron.

Indeed, one detects quite a new attitude on the part of the architect of the seventies in this regard. In the earlier decades building materials had little influence on design; they were merely the matter out of which the design was to be wrought. In the 1840's it would appear that the designer had used brick walls and granite basement almost as a matter of habit. When brownstone replaced pressed brick in the sixties, the change was motivated by fashion and economy. As the delicate Academic details could not accurately be reproduced in brick nor duplicated with any degree of economy in granite, the designer turned to the more tractable medium of brownstone. In contrast, many designers of the seventies and early eighties began to display a sensitivity to the texture and color of the materials with which they worked, and at times they even went so far as to eliminate the customary carved decoration in order that the texture used could be clearly appreciated. This respect for the unique properties of a material reached a high level about 1885.

Finally in the matter of group design, one can also trace a steady evolution between 1845 and 1890. In the forties there seems to have been relatively little attempt to group a series of houses into a single design. Such unity as did prevail resulted from a repetition of the same basic unit (fig. 8). In the sixties an impressive ensemble was sought deliberately by combining several houses into a single unified group (figs. 41, 47). After about 1870, however, the idea of group impressiveness was superseded by individual distinction as each house attempted to capture the spectator's attention with lively and original display (fig. 92). Finally, in the early nineties, when architects had rediscovered the value of architectural decorum, they sought to endow each house with sober monumentality although little attempt was made at grouping.

Underlying these developments, the historian can detect a gradual but fundamental change in point of view; he senses an evolution that begins with the unconscious architectural vernacular of the forties, that changes to the self-conscious idiom of the sixties, and finally develops into the self-assertive expression of the seventies and eighties. In the forties the similarity of size and massing of structures, the use of traditional building materials, and the absence of distinctive architectural features bear witness to the builder's unconscious allegiance to the old Greek Revival vernacular. The pretension of the sixties, the substitution of up-to-date brownstone for provincial brick, the tendency to overlay the facade with a panoply of correctly detailed Renaissance forms, the grouping of houses into tall, balanced groups—these are the evidences of a self-conscious cultivation of the sophisticated Academic French style. Finally, the self-assertiveness of the seventies and eighties is attested by the architect's experimentation with building materials, his unwillingness to be satisfied with established proportions or with quiet, geometrical compositions, his attempt to dissociate each house from the block and make it stand out as an independent unit. His restlessness is also apparent in the way he discards the Academic manner in favor of no less than nine distinct architectural manners which flourish more or less concurrently.

In spite of these changes, it is essential to remember that the town house retains certain fundamental and little-changing qualities. It is a single-family dwelling arranged on four to six levels; it has a long, narrow plan confined between party walls and open for windows (usually three per floor) at the narrow ends only; it is constructed of masonry, and is set back a uniform distance from the street line. During the half century that this study covers, one finds relatively little variation in the size or the internal arrangement of the Back Bay dwelling because it was built to meet the requirements of a class whose way of life did not alter.

The graph in figure 93 provides a visual picture of the chronological relationship of the various architectural styles which flourished in the Back Bay district over the years. One will note the supremacy

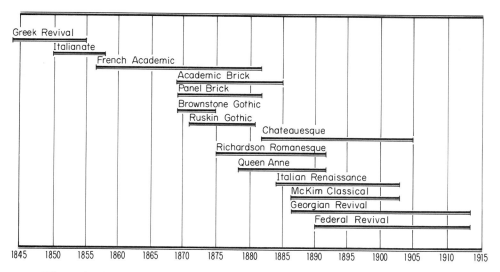

Greek Revival
Italianate
French Academic
Academic Brick
Panel Brick
Brownstone Gothic
Ruskin Gothic
Chateauesque
Richardson Romanesque
Queen Anne
Italian Renaissance
McKim Classical
Georgian Revival
Federal Revival

1845 1850 1855 1860 1865 1870 1875 1880 1885 1890 1895 1900 1905 1910 1915

93   The principal architectural styles in the Back Bay and the years in which they flourished.

of the old Greek Revival vernacular in the forties and the relatively sharp transition in the late fifties from that style to the Academic manner which entirely dominated building of the 1860's. At the very end of the sixties there is a swift upsurge of new architectural styles, and during the seventies, eighties, and early nineties still other idioms make their appearances. Even though the Georgian Revival establishes itself as the district's dominant architectural idiom by 1900, it never attains the relative strength of the old Academic manner in the sixties.

Speaking in percentages, six major architectural movements competed for prominence between 1869 and 1885.[3] In this period Academic Brownstone accounts for 21 percent of the houses in the Back Bay; Academic Brick, 26 percent; Panel Brick, 19 percent; Gothic styles, 19 percent; Queen Anne styles, 8 percent; and Richardson Romanesque, 4 percent. Three percent of the houses do not fall into these categories.

It is instructive to compare this wide dispersion with the homogeneity of the previous decade when 89 percent of the 304 known Back Bay designs fell within the French Academic tradition. Yet it is important to realize that the old Academic manner was not suddenly abandoned. Two variants, which we shall call the Academic Brownstone and the Academic Brick styles, taken together constitute 47 percent of the period's total construction (268 out of 570 houses available for classification).

THE ACADEMIC BROWNSTONE STYLE

The old Academic style built in brownstone continued to be reproduced in diminishing numbers down to 1882. However, its use for 120 houses after 1869 must not obscure the fact that historically and aesthetically this group is relatively unimportant. Late examples add to the old tradition nothing which had not already been achieved in the sixties. Two houses of adequate Academic design were built as late as 1876, but with one exception late brownstone examples of Academic design are built as repeating single designs.[4] Not conspicuously bad, the performance is merely routine, and the designs lack the distinction and the incisive detailing of Academic buildings erected fifteen or twenty years earlier. Architects and clients who would have had the knowledge and money to reproduce correctly the old French Academic idiom now chose to work, instead, in a more up-to-date manner. Almost wholly this late work is the routine performance of speculative builders, and its principal historical interest lies in the manner in which it demonstrates the way an old and tried tradition is transmitted to the level of everyday building, to the vernacular.

Number 321 Marlborough Street (1874) illustrates late and somewhat degraded Academic usage (fig. 94). The general organization of the facade with a recessed entrance and a bay window which carries into the roof is typical of the early seventies, while the mansard roof, the use of brownstone, and the general emphasis placed on the windows and door frames or along the cornice relates the design to the Academic tradition. A quantity of ornamentation exists, but it lacks consistency. In some areas surface ornamentation is achieved by the incised line technique (window lintels, the "capitals," and the chainlike figure of the upper string course); in other areas a countersunk and paneled decoration appears (lower string course and the panels below the first-story windows); a conventional architrave molding is used only for the depressed, almost flat arch of the entrance. These three techniques are unrelated in scale and character and they illus-

94   Entrance of 321 Marlborough Street, 1877. One of a group of three houses built by a speculative builder at the same time but each of a slightly different design. It illustrates the garbled way in which the old French Academic manner was handled in the 1870's.

trate the designer's undiscriminating efforts to achieve large amounts of decoration with minimal labor costs. Although such a house has no great merit as an individual design, it possesses the moderate virtue of much vernacular architecture of fitting unobtrusively into its environment and of providing the background out of which more important buildings may emerge.

What happened to the Academic Brownstone manner in the 1870's illustrates the eventual fate of all architectural idioms. Falling into disfavor among better architects, it was left to third-rate practitioners who discredited it. The style makes its final Back Bay appearance in 1882 at 264–266 Commonwealth Avenue. For a more creative use of the Academic tradition, we shall have to turn to the Academic Brick style.

THE ACADEMIC BRICK STYLE

The spirit of the old Academic tradition is much better preserved in the 1870's by architects who built in brick rather than in brownstone. Although not using the same strict Classical vocabulary as before, this group continues the logical, architectonic quality which motivated the best work of the sixties. Walls are plain brick relieved by moderate quantities of ornamentation placed at critical points and usually cut from a light-colored stone. Probably this combination of materials was preferred because the contrast emphasized the importance of the architectonic forms. Now, however, instead of the rigorously correct Classical elements which had been utilized earlier, the detailing is developed with a certain inventiveness and simplification which indicate that the designer was no longer timidly preoccupied with Academic perfection.

The Academic Brick designer also continued the creditable practice of relating adjacent house designs in order to enhance the harmonious appearance of the street. Although the projecting gutter blocks and fire walls which were required by Boston's new building laws made it difficult to fuse separate dwellings into a single block as in earlier practice, there are notable attempts of Academic-minded designers to achieve group unity. Five contiguous houses, for example, were erected between 57 and 65 Commonwealth Avenue in three separate building operations between 1874 and 1879 by two architectural firms.[5] It is interesting to note how the facade of number 61, the last of the group to be constructed, was accommodated to the adjacent facades in order to unify the group (fig. 95). By judicious repetition of the basement, first floor, and window heights of the houses on the left and by continuing the lines of the cornice and mansard of the houses on the right, the middle design succeeds in tying the five dwellings together. At the same time, one will observe that the

95　Facade of 59, 61, and 63 Commonwealth Avenue. Three in a sequence of five houses constructed between 1874 and 1879 in three separate building programs by two architectural firms. They illustrate the way in which the harmony of the old Academic tradition is generally retained by architects working in the Academic Brick manner.

designers did not restrict themselves to a slavish copy of Renaissance ornament. In all cases details of the orders have been considerably modified though their main Classic proportions and their architectonic function have been retained.

These same two firms worked harmoniously with Shaw and Shaw to create a group of five houses at 131, 133, 135, 151 Commonwealth Avenue and 303 Dartmouth Street. Four more residences at

96   So similar are the facades of the two houses built at 261–263 Commonwealth Avenue (at right) that it is hard to believe that they were designed by different architects in 1880. Although one story lower, numbers 265 and 267 attempt to prolong the levels of string courses and cornice height where possible.

261–267 Commonwealth Avenue, built as late as 1880, found the firm of Peabody and Stearns cooperating in a similar manner with Snell and Gregerson as well as Shaw and Shaw (fig. 96). It is hard to believe that numbers 261 and 263 were designed by different firms, so similar are they in spirit and detail. Nor was the Academic Brick style lacking examples of houses organized into a single, well-knit architectural unit, as 252–260 Beacon Street proves.[6] This group dates from 1870, just a few years before building laws required the use of the divisive fire wall.

The most successful Academic Brick design (and perhaps the hand-

somest house in the whole Back Bay) was built in 1871 at 165 Marlborough Street. Designed by Snell and Gregerson for T. F. Cushing
but acquired soon after its construction by William C. Endicott, this
house was occupied until 1958 by Mrs. William Endicott, Jr. Because
it so well exemplifies the values of the Academic Brick style and because of its architectural merit, both on the interior and exterior, the
design will be considered in some detail.

Standing on the northwest corner of Marlborough and Dartmouth
streets, the house is part of a group of three closely related structures.
Although each house is a complete entity, the three units of design
fit together to create an impressive whole. Seen from Dartmouth
Street (figs. 97, 98), the two end houses form pavilions which rise
half a story higher than the center section, a relationship which is
effected by a clever manipulation of floor levels. The end pavilions
are marked by bay windows that are carried through the cornice, and

97   Three houses grouped to form an impressive unit: 165 Marlborough
      Street and 326–328 Dartmouth Street, 1871, by Snell and Gregerson.
      The dormer window at extreme right is not original.

98   Facade of 326 Dartmouth Street, detail of fig. 97. Changes in floor levels and in detailing of the stone trim differentiate this central unit from the end houses but do not impair the unity of the larger composition.

they are accented by a double dormer window plus a slight forward projection in the mansard roof. The pavilions serve to emphasize the self-contained quality of the composition. The entrance of number 328 has been inserted in the right octagonal bay in order to maintain a just balance with its pendant on the other corner. The independence of the central body of the design (the middle house) is indicated by its lower height (two stories instead of three), the higher level of the main floor, the somewhat wider proportions of its windows, the use of round-headed windows in the dormer (that at number 328 is obviously a remodeling), and its heavier bracket-supported cornice. Within the larger compositon, this central section is a self-sufficient element, provided with its own center axis (the rusticated, light-colored stone entrance porch with a bay window above it) and balancing wings (the rectangular bay windows which, breaking forward from the facade, are carried into the mansard). The proportions throughout the whole group are so excellent and the relationships of its various parts so skillful that one receives the impression of a building much larger than it actually is.

The Marlborough Street facade (fig. 99) is no less skillfully integrated. Here again octagonal bays create framing elements for the flat, central area which contains the entrance. That the principal rooms are ranged on the second level explains the diminished height of the ground story and the lofty proportions of second-story windows. The central panel of this facade is adroitly composed. Beginning with the heavy-shadowed portico, the eye moves up to the ornate but less plastic composition of the second-story window frame and from there to the rather flat, simple architraves which enframe the third-story windows. There is an obvious pyramidal composition of which the segmental pediment of the second-story window is the apex. The window openings are also ranged in numerical sequence from bottom to top: five units of the first floor (three bays of the portico plus adjacent floor-length windows, all capped by the same entablature), a four-unit window of the second floor, three separate openings on the third floor, and two simple dormers in the mansard. This composition is nicely contained by the delicate verticals of the pilaster-like brick planes and by the more vigorous verticals of the bay windows.

The Endicott house well illustrates the change that took place in the early seventies as Boston architects, impatient of a slavish copy of rules that had been mastered, sought individual expression by means of imaginative and ingenious modifications of the old Academic formula. Here the frieze of the entrance portico has "triglyphs" which have been changed into bracket forms, the cornice is enlivened with superimposed rosettes, the Tuscanlike capitals are provided with a curious egg and dart cushion in place of the usual echinus, and the four faces of the abacus are relieved with rosettes similar to those of the cornice (fig. 99). The treatment of the second-story four-part window is highly original. A symmetrical placement of the windows

99   Facade of 165 Marlborough Street, detail of fig. 97. A carefully integrated sequence of five units of design on the ground floor reduces to
four on the second, three on the third, and two in the mansard.

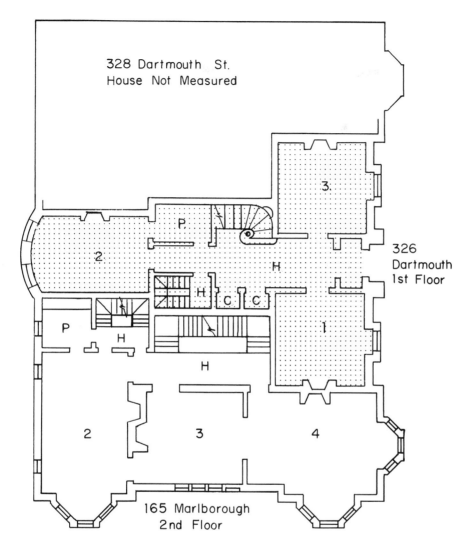

328 Dartmouth St.
House Not Measured

3.

326
Dartmouth
1st Floor

P.

2

H

P

H

H   C   C

H

1

H

2   3   4

165 Marlborough
2nd Floor

1. Reception Room   V. Vestibule
2. Dining Room   C. Closet
3. Drawing Room   H. Hall
4. Library   P. Pantry

100   Plan of principal floor, 165 Marlborough Street and 326–328 Dart-
       mouth Street.

101 Entrance hall at 165 Marlborough Street. The landing and the screen of columns in front of the stair is a Snell and Gregerson characteristic; the banister is cast iron.

on the exterior would have required an asymmetrical interior arrangement; to avoid this discrepancy the designer made the right section of his window solid, disguising this fact by a shutter. The segmental pediment, which covers only the two center openings, is quite unconventional; yet the architraves which surround the end windows are fused to the pedimented middle frames with ease.

The interior arrangement of these three houses is unusual. For one thing, the kitchens of the two end houses are placed on the first floor, not in the basement as was customary and as was done in the middle house, where the first-floor level is considerably higher than its two neighbors.[7] In 165 Marlborough Street and its pendant, 328 Dartmouth Street, the importance of the first story is minimized as the main rooms are lifted to the second level. In the former the ground floor contains kitchen, pantry, reception room, a large entrance hall, and a small conservatory; the second story contains a large corner library, an intermediate drawing room, a dining room, and a pantry; the third floor is devoted to three principal bedchambers with appended dressing rooms; the fourth, to minor chambers and servants' rooms. The plans of these three houses key together in a most ingenious fashion (fig. 100). The middle house is formed in a T-shape, with the wide bar toward the street and the stem at the rear where the house narrows down to a single room fifteen feet wide.

The interior of the Endicott house is handled with the dignity characteristic of Snell and Gregerson. In the entrance hall the pilaster treatment of three walls is repeated along the fourth side of the room as free-standing columns which support the second floor (fig. 101).[8] The main stair, recessed behind these columns, rises to the second level in four easy stages. Below, the ceiling is low, about eight feet, but on the second floor it is fourteen feet. On the upper level the library is a particularly spacious room, completely carpeted, hung with red velvet drapes and red damask wall covering (fig. 102).

102   Library on the *piano nobile* at 165 Marlborough Street. Typical of the sixties and seventies, the active spatial organization of this room, which has many changes in plane to accommodate the chimney breast and bay windows, is further accentuated by breaks in the elaborate plaster cornice.

It contains a heavy wooden mantelpiece built of richly contrasting woods. Decorative details of the plaster cornice and ceiling are accented in gold. Here strict symmetry has been maintained even at the cost of introducing a large double door toward the stair hall, only half of which actually opens since the hall does not continue far enough along the library wall to permit a full double opening.

Until the sale of the house in 1958, the dining room retained the decoration and furnishings provided by the first owner (fig. 103). The ebony furniture, mantelpiece, wainscoting, and cornice are said to have been imported from the Orient as were the yellow porcelain plaques set above the fireplace and over the mirrored chimney-breast, and the yellow-green wallpaper.[9] The chandelier, which could be adjusted for height, was originally a whale-oil lamp. It is a pity that a room such as this one could not have been preserved as a record of American taste in the last half of the nineteenth century. Indeed this entire residence and its furnishings merited preservation as a museum house.

If the work of Snell and Gregerson illustrates the Academic Brick group at its best, the style also occurs in numerous less refined examples. A more pedestrian design by Peabody and Stearns was repeated numerous times in the Back Bay between 1876 and 1880. It was used for six houses at 271–281 Beacon Street in 1876 and 1877,

103   Dining room at 165 Marlborough Street. The ebony woodwork and furniture and the tile insets were executed in the Orient for the dwelling's first owner, T. F. Cushing.

104   Facade of 275–277 Beacon Street. Two of a row of six houses designed in 1876–77 for the builder G. W. Freeland by Peabody and
Stearns. With minor modifications, this Academic Brick design was
used for eighteen Back Bay dwellings.

for seven houses at 121–133 Marlborough Street between 1877 and
1880, and, in a slightly smaller variation, for five houses at 128–136
Newbury Street in 1877 (fig. 104).

The Academic Brick manner continued to flourish as late as 1885.[10]
After that, it shaded off into the Georgian Revival and various phases
of the Classical Revival. The style is important because it provided

the medium of expression for the more conservative branch of the architectural profession in the 1870's and 1880's. Even though these architects sought to retain the orderliness and sobriety of the old Academic tradition, they could not escape entirely the exuberance and self-confidence which animated all architectural activity in the seventies and which manifested itself in the greater freedom of detailing.

THE PANEL BRICK STYLE

The third architectural style to flourish in the Back Bay area during the 1870's can be called the Panel Brick style. As the more conservative Academic manner from which it derives, Panel Brick ornamentation is centered at points of critical architectural interest although no attempt is made to reproduce Classical forms. Cornices, pilasters, window and door enframements, and similar elements are used, but despite the quasi-structural placement of these forms, one feels that they are employed as lively elements of surface decoration rather than for architectonic emphasis. As often as not, what might at first appear a logical, structural form is violated by the capricious interruption of some nonstructural projecting or indented panel. Nor is ornamental emphasis restricted to critical areas, for the regular wall surface is often divided into panels of ornament that vie for attention with the window or door frames.

As the name indicates, this style utilizes brick masonry in which a variety of decorative patterns have been worked by means of projecting or receding brick panels. Trademarks of the Panel Brick manner are stepped corbel tables, string courses with nimble, geometric indentations, and a variety of cross-shaped panels which animate the facade with a play of crisp, staccato patterns. Designers also are fond of "surprise" elements such as a corbeled chimney stack (fig. 105). But being formed of common brick, this decoration is an integral part of the masonry fabric of the building, and its scale and character stem from the material itself. Examples of this style are 2 and 63 Marlborough Street, designed in 1871 and 1875 (the latter by J. P. Putnam) and the related houses at 397 Beacon and 1 Gloucester Street, designed in 1870 by W. G. Preston (figs. 106, 107).

105   Facade of 101 Marlborough Street, 1872. This chimney is characteristic of the tendency of the Panel Brick style to create intricate
patterns and original shapes by the way in which the bricks are
laid.

106   Facade of 63 Marlborough Street, 1875, by J. P. Putnam. The vibrant, decorative quality of this brick masonry is characteristic of the Panel Brick style. The basement entry was added in 1917.

When one attempts to specify exactly when Panel Brick decoration makes its appearance in the Back Bay, he realizes that in part at least it is an outgrowth of two earlier building traditions in Boston. Already in the late sixties we noted among certain Academic architects working in brownstone a tendency to handle Classical forms freely and to subdivide the wall area arbitrarily into receding and projecting planes. In the Panel Brick style these tendencies are exaggerated but one should not find it difficult to recognize their origin. It can also be argued that the Panel Brick manner grows out of crisp and delicate Greek Revival brick work in which masons had learned to suggest a dentil course or even the whole entablature within the restricted module of a common brick.

The Panel Brick idiom's first Back Bay appearance in developed form was in 1869 when six new edifices, of which 41 Brimmer Street is typical, made use of the characteristic brick technique (fig. 91). Intimations of the technique can be found, however, as early as 1864 at 16 Marlborough Street. Here in the capitals of the pilaster strips the usual classical forms are replaced by a simple pattern of brick set edgewise to the facade (fig. 112). By 1867 at 104 Marlborough

107   Facade of 397 Beacon Street, 1870, by W. G. Preston. The manipulation of the plane of the facade by means of projecting and recessed panels is typical of Panel Brick design. The bay window was added in 1889.

Street a developed Panel Brick cornice had already appeared. The style is most popular between 1869 and 1879. After that it would appear that the novelty of intricate brickwork diminished and that the energies of designers and masons were channeled into experiments in the Romanesque and Queen Anne styles. It is difficult to put a terminal date on the fashion because it shades off almost im-

108   Facade of 7, 9, 11 Hereford Street and 435 Beacon Street, 1879, by R. S. Bither. Building permits for these houses indicate that they were planned as two stories with a mansard roof. Fourth stories were added for purchasers to two of the houses by the speculative builder before the row was finished.

109   Entrance of 9 Hereford Street, detail of fig. 108. This house illustrates
that the Panel Brick style retains a good deal of vitality even in the
hands of a speculator builder.

perceptibly into these new stylistic experiments. The idiom had vitality, however, for even in the hands of speculative builders, in the
early eighties, the sprightliness of its brick ornamentation is not entirely obscured (figs. 108, 109).

Historically the Panel Brick style occupies a crucial position in the evolution of Back Bay architecture. Its appearance in 1869 marks the first clear-cut departure from the old Academic discipline; it shows Boston architects throwing aside restraining Classical canons in a deliberate play for individual freedom. Secondly, the clearly experimental manner in which brick designs were substituted for Classical details is a prelude to the individualistic "Free Classical" forms of the Queen Anne style. Finally the Panel Brick style may be regarded as an early attempt to design a building which deliberately reflects the specific nature of building materials of which it is constructed, an attitude which looks forward directly to the work of Richardson in the 1880's. Thus the style reaches back to the Greek Revival of the 1840's at the same time that it looks forward to the Queen Anne and Richardson Romanesque experiments of the 1880's.

If a desire to explore the nature and possibilities of brick as a building material was father to the Panel Brick style, then economy was its mother. It is evident from the discussions of the Boston Society of Architects that designers at this time were beset by a sharp increment in labor costs. The minutes of the society for May 7, 1869, record that Mr. Preston "read a paper on artificial stone, predicting its use in place of customary freestone which was becoming more expensive because of quarry combinations in price and the exorbitant labor rates of the stonecutter's union." Mr. Preston's complaint about high labor rates is confirmed by the record, but the sharp rise in wages was not confined to the stonecutter's trade alone. The average weekly wage paid during these years to all employees in Massachusetts is as follows.[11]

1860	$ 9.87
1872	15.64
1878	12.63
1880	10.54
1881	13.29
1883	14.99

It will be noted that the big increase takes place before 1872, during the very years in which the Panel Brick style was formulated. The contention that this sharp rise in wages after the Civil War encouraged the Panel Brick style is based on the reasonable assumption that brick masonry, even when laid in complicated patterns, is less expensive than carved stone. Although not directly proving this point, John

Sturgis' apology for the use of terra cotta for the old Museum of Fine Arts will shed some light on the costliness of stone construction in the early seventies. At the June 1876 meeting of the Boston Society of Architects, Mr. Sturgis countered criticism of the museum building by stating that it cost $41,000 less to construct it of richly decorated terra cotta than of undecorated stone.[12]

It is also true that masons' wages in America were far above those in Europe. While the average mason in America between 1860 and 1880 received $2.79 per day, the American commissioners to the Paris Exposition of 1867 could report that expert marble workers' daily hire in Paris was but $1.00 to $1.50. The commissioners to Vienna in 1873 reported that stone masons in that city were currently paid but $1.25 a day for eleven hours of work. In 1883 the average stone mason's weekly wage in Massachusetts was $14.39, or 41 percent higher than the $10.16 paid his British counterpart.[13]

THE GOTHIC STYLES

An account of nineteenth century Gothic Revival architecture in the Back Bay or elsewhere can become very complicated. In any decade of the century one can find "Gothic" buildings of some sort, although the particular brand of revivalism produced at different times is apt to vary greatly. Looking to England for illustration, one can distinguish at least five varieties of the mode. In the early 1800's there was "Gothick," primarily a literary affair, which regarded the Medieval style simply as another assortment of exotic decorative forms. With the building of the Houses of Parliament, in the thirties, there developed "Pugin Gothic" which approached the architecture of the Middle Ages in a more systematic, archaeological way. Toward the middle of the century "High Victorian Gothic" flourished under the primacy of Gilbert Scott; built frequently of brownstone, it had a moderate acquaintance with English architecture of the thirteenth century. During the sixties and seventies there flourished the polychromatic "Ruskin Gothic" influenced in large part by Medieval construction in northern Italy. Finally, at the century's end and extending into the present century, the use of the Medieval style became very diversified. Appearing in as many variations as there were different prototypes in the Middle Ages, these Late Gothic Revival buildings while respectful of archaeological accuracy were strongly conditioned by practical requirements.

So great are the differences between these revivals that they certainly cannot be lumped together as a single movement, yet, a rigid separation and discussion of each phase can become so splintered that our overall view is lost. Add to this difficulty the facts that chronologically these styles overlap and that builders of the period, being eclectic, often combined various phases of Gothic within a single structure. For present purposes it is enough merely to be aware of these different currents of the Gothic Revival as points of reference.

In the Back Bay one will recognize architectural references to the last three of the Gothic Revivals which flourished in England. As in the case of the various styles which flourished in Britain, these classes have little in common beyond the use of the pointed arch. They are: The Brownstone Gothic, Ruskin Gothic, and Late Gothic. The first corresponds roughly to the High Victorian Gothic of Scott; the second echoes the movement of the same name in England; the third parallels the diversified revivals at the century's end. We shall consider the first two of these classes immediately; the last will be deferred for discussion in Chapter Seven.

THE BROWNSTONE GOTHIC

Brownstone Gothic can be dealt with quickly. There are only three examples of it in the district: 165 Beacon Street, built in 1869; 76–80 Commonwealth Avenue, 1872; and 117 Marlborough Street, 1873 (figs. 110, 111). These performances strike a naïve if charming note so ungainly is their medievalism: panels of stiff tracery, squat pointed arches, columns with clumsy, foliate capitals, and fanciful wooden dormers in a mansard roof, the whole exercise looking more like colored cardboard cutouts than Medieval construction. Nor should we overlook the fact that decorative effects which were supposed to be Gothic were produced by means of the money-saving incised line technique.

Because its interior was drastically remodeled about 1905, one cannot say whether Gothic inspiration at 165 Beacon Street, the best of the specimens, continued behind the brownstone veneer. The interior

110 Facade of 165 Beacon Street, 1869. The first indication in the Back Bay of the Gothic style, it is a timid reflection in brownstone of High Victorian Gothic architecture in England.

111 Facade of 76 Commonwealth Avenue, 1872. One of a group of three narrow dwellings whose Gothic quality is confined to the brownstone facade. The apartment house at the left replaces the center unit of the original group.

of 76 Commonwealth Avenue, however, was equipped with mantels, staircase, and woodwork similar to any residence of Academic design.

Mention should also be made of several earlier houses whose exteriors might possibly be construed to be "Medieval." One cannot quite decide whether the deeply recessed, segmental-arched entrance ways of 135–137 Beacon Street were intended by E. C. Cabot to be Medieval (fig. 50), and the same uncertainty surrounds 18–20 Marlborough Street. But there is little doubt about the wooden oriel and wooden dormer at 14 Marlborough Street (1863) which evidences a touch of Ruskin influence as well (fig. 112).

Outside of these meager examples, the Middle Ages are poorly represented during the 1860's in the Back Bay domestic architecture. This is rather surprising when one considers how creditably Ware and Van Brunt handled the style in the 1867 design for First Parish Church. Possibly it was not so much a lack of interest in Medieval architecture which restrained the Back Bay architect as the practical difficulty of adapting rambling, picturesque Medieval forms to a cramped city facade.

The Ruskin Gothic Style

In the seventies the rising tide of individualism was not slow to discover the Ruskin Gothic style as a vehicle of expression, and the architect eagerly seized upon polychromy, profuse decoration, and picturesqueness as a means of enlivening his house, demonstrating his impeccable taste, and advertising the fact that he was strictly up to date. According to the new gospel of Ruskin, our Back Bay architect sought to kindle the Lamp of Sacrifice with conspicuous ornamentation even though economic circumstances forced him to replace hand carving by machine decoration; he paid lip service to the Lamp of Truth, though long usage had accustomed him to accept the eight-inch veneer of stone or four-inch layer of face brick that overlaid a structural core of common brick; he dreamed of picturesquely irregular roof lines only to modify his ideal silhouette to provide adequate head room in the attic; he designed facades gaudy with polychromy only to have city smoke dull them; he projected romantic bowers from his facades only to have municipal fire laws say that he must

112   Facade of 14 and 16 Marlborough Street, 1863 and 1864. The wooden
oriel window, the dormer window, and the stone voussoirs of the
segmental arches on the left building somewhat recall John Ruskin's
version of Gothic forms. The pilaster capitals of the right house are
an early indication of Panel Brick work.

113   Facade of 109 Newbury Street, 1871. Designed by the prominent architect Charles A. Cummings as his own residence, this design seeks to compress too many "Medieval" forms into a dwelling on a modest 25-foot corner lot.

cover his half timber work with tin. But his enthusiasm for Ruskin did not diminish.

The first Back Bay dwelling to carry the Medieval guise beyond an occasional pointed window is the 1871 home of the architect C. A. Cummings. Much spoiled by commercial alterations, the house at the corner of Newbury and Clarendon streets still proclaims its romantic antecedents (fig. 113). The basic shape of the house is a rectangular box capped by a truncated pyramidal lid, but our architect would trick us into believing that it was two massive cylindrical donjons with conical roofs. In attempting to preserve the effect of these towers and yet to provide practical head room in the attic, the design loses its way in a welter of interpenetrating gables, mansards, cone-shaped towers, chimney stacks, spires, and dormers—a geometer's nightmare.

Enough is left of Cummings' house to demonstrate his penchant for contrasting materials: salmon-colored pressed brick, cream-colored Nova Scotia sandstone, black (tar-impregnated) brick, and slate in three colors. Ingenious brick masonry also adds a note of fancy to the design; the brick cornice suggests diminutive machicolations while other courses of brick are set in a basket-work pattern. In segmental window heads, voussoir lengths are irregular and of contrasting materials. In its day this house must have made its mark for in the next year Cummings was chosen to design New Old South Church, the first unit of which (the parsonage) was built in 1872. A somewhat more convincing medievalism, it might be noted, was achieved by another architect, J. Pickering Putnam, in a house designed for himself a few years later (1878) on the far corner of the same block, at 277 Dartmouth Street (fig. 114).

Also typical of Ruskin Gothic designs in the seventies are 121 and 165 Commonwealth Avenue. The first was designed in 1872 by Cummings and Sears; the second, in 1879 by an unnamed architect[14] (figs.

114   Facade of 277 Dartmouth Street, 1878. Designed by J. P. Putnam, another prominent architect, as his home, this example is somewhat less restless than fig. 113.

115　Facade of 121 Commonwealth Avenue, 1872, by Cummings and Sears. Perhaps the most characteristic Ruskin Gothic facade in the Back Bay, this design employs a variety of building materials: two shades of brick, cream-colored stone, wood, polychromatic tile, slate of two colors, and wrought iron.

116　Facade of 165 Commonwealth Avenue, 1879, probably by Cummings and Sears. The bay window with its independent roof tends to disengage itself from the block.

115, 116). As the designs of these two houses are so similar, particularly the entrance treatment and the dormers over the bay windows, one is inclined to attribute the second house to Cummings' office. The panels of colored tile and the courses of masonry in contrasting colors show that Cummings, in addition to knowing Ruskin's approval of poly-chromatic effects, agreed with H. H. Holly that if the facade of a city structure, by reason of the economic necessity which forced the utilization of every inch of ground area for building, could not achieve an interplay of geometric forms which cast deep shadows, at least that facade could be enlivened with color.[15] Number 165 enhances its facade with a profusion of stone carving which simulates various textures and Gothic patterns. Both houses also achieve a striking and irregular silhouette by carrying the bay window through the cornice into the attic and giving the whole projection a roof that is independent of the mansard behind it. When seen from the street level, these towerlike bays pull away from the roof of the house with startling relief. Engaging for their vertical thrust, compositions such as these stand out with a bold impudence which does much to destroy the geometric unity of the entire block. But this independence is nothing when compared to the puny exhibitionism of the "modernistic" entrance which a misguided remodeling has in the early 1960's imposed upon number 121.

The best Ruskin-inspired house in the district—best perhaps because less preoccupied with superficial Ruskin detail and more concerned with craftsmanship and an effective use of materials—is 191 Marlborough Street, built in 1881 for Edmund Dwight (figs. 117, 118). A thirty-two foot lot gave the architect, Carl Fehmer, an opportunity to design a facade which is less cramped and vertical than most of its contemporaries. Only three stories high in front (though the rear portion goes higher), the convincing thing about this facade is its existence as a three-dimensional composition. It is not just a paper design which fails to take plausible form in three dimensions as is the case in the early Gothic edifices of this district. In this house the spectator observes the forward thrust of gable and bay window countered by the inward pull of the deep and spacious entrance porch. The reduction in the number of fenestration units in the left bay as they go higher and recede into the plane of the facade is also designed with sensitivity.

This facade design is nicely integrated. The vertical shapes of bay windows and the gable are balanced by the rather squarish proportions

117 Facade of 191 Marlborough Street, 1881, by Carl Fehmer. Somewhat wider (32 feet) than usual, this design is less cramped and hence has a more convincing massing and proportion than the average Medieval style house in the Back Bay.

118 Entrance of 191 Marlborough Street, detail of fig. 117. The quality of stone carving and the ironwork make this one of the handsomest dwellings in the area.

of the entrance recess, the triple window above it, and the hipped dormer. Yet the two sides of the composition are related by a series of horizontal string courses and by the three vertical subdivisions of the second-story windows to the right which pick up the vertical accent of the left half of the composition. Especially fine is the carving of the Nova Scotia stone about the portal and along the balustrade of the entrance steps. A handsome wrought iron grille fills the upper part of the generous arch of the entrance porch and ironwork appears again on the roof of the bay window. The interior of this dwelling was completely remodeled in the 1920's.

In contrast to the Fehmer house is a series of Gothic houses built by the contractor Asa Caton at 226, 319, 321, and 323 Commonwealth Avenue (fig. 119). It is not clear from the city records whether Caton also designed these houses, but if he did, he was responsible for the ugliest buildings in the Back Bay. At number 226 six different shapes and sizes of arches vie for attention on a facade already tortured with string courses, relieving arches, and panels of sculptured relief. Strangest of all are the overhanging corners atop the towered bay window and the hood above the entrance which somehow give the effect of a design craning forward. Almost the only "horrors" in the entire district, these houses are among the few edifices which satisfy the last generation's morbid expectations of outlandish Victorian architecture. Still these houses are important to Back Bay history because they show us by comparison the restraint and dignity of the vast majority of Boston residences in this period. For all our modern condescension toward the Victorians, these structures contain a moral which some present-day designers have not yet learned: Don't try to crowd too many architectural features into too little space!

It might also be noted that a number of contemporary Back Bay houses utilize Ruskin polychromatic effects even though they are not cast in specifically Medieval forms. Chief among these are several edifices designed by W. Whitney Lewis. English by birth, Lewis was in Boston by 1871 and in practice for himself in 1875. Typical of his numerous houses in this period are 20 Fairfield Street, 1875, and 226 Marlborough Street, 1881 (fig. 120). The Ruskin Gothic manner was popular until the late seventies; the last reference to that style in the Back Bay is to be found in a group of speculator-built houses at 254–278 Newbury Street, erected in 1882.

Before leaving this phase of Gothic, attention should be called to

119   Facade of 226 Commonwealth Avenue, 1881. Built by a speculator named Asa Caton, this house is one of the few outlandish "Victorian" designs in the entire Back Bay.

the interiors at 86 Marlborough Street designed in 1872 by Sturgis and Brigham. Here the stair hall creates a rather striking first impression with its oak paneling and strapwork balustrades, but closer inspection reveals the detailing to be crude (figs. 121, 122). The strapwork is not carved; it is simply sawed out of inch-and-a-half planking

120   Facade of 20 Fairfield Street, 1875, by W. Whitney Lewis. The contrasting bands of black brick, salmon-colored brick, and light-colored
sandstone are characteristic of the Ruskin Gothic style. The top
story was added in 1887.

121   Stair hall at 86 Marlborough Street, 1872. The strapwork is cut out
       of two-inch oak planks with a jig saw.

with the original faces left plain. The dining room has interesting
decorations which reflect contemporary British fashion (figs. 123, 124).
Here the overmantel is filled with painted tiles which illustrate gas-

122   Detail of fig. 121.

tronomical nursery rhymes: "Sing a Song of Sixpence," "Little Miss Muffet," and so forth. The tile borders of the overmantel are filled with rinceaux entwining about birds, beasts, and heraldic devices; a Medieval knight and lady painted on canvas are set in the niches of the mantel shelf. The cove above the sideboard is decorated with panels of flowering fruit boughs. On the ceiling the coffers are filled with a four-color, stenciled pattern while the cove contains alternating canvas panels representing the chase and a fruit tree pattern. Obviously related to contemporary English work, this decoration was executed, so the *American Architect and Building News* informs us, by J. Moyr Smith of London.[16] British influence is also evident in the facade of this edifice which one would classify stylistically as Ruskin Gothic (fig. 125).

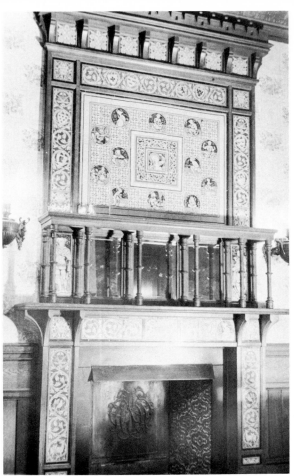

123 Dining room mantel at 86 Marlborough Street. The mantel is set with tiles illustrating gastronomic nursery rhymes. The dining room was decorated by Moyr Smith from London.

124 Painted cove and stencil design on ceiling of the dining room at 86 Marlborough Street.

125

Facade of 86 Marlborough Street, 1872, by Sturgis and Brigham. Although the exterior is unimpressive, the interiors were much publicized when they were done (see figs. 121–124).

THE ROMANESQUE STYLE

Another style to flourish in the Back Bay in this period is the Richardson Romanesque. Characterized by a mood that is best described as gloomy robustness, this style evinced a marked preference for the round arch, expansive wall surfaces of rough-textured masonry, areas of contrasting polychromy, and accents of fine-scaled, Byzantine-like sculptured decoration.

The Richardson Romanesque is sparsely represented in the Back Bay during this period. In all, less than one seventh of the structures constructed between 1869 and 1900 were designed in this manner.

That is, out of 952 houses which are still standing or destroyed houses of which a photographic record has been found, only 124 are recognizably Romanesque. More surprising than this, of these 124 designs only 23 (less than $2\frac{1}{2}$ percent of the total construction) are reasonably "pure" Romanesque stylistically speaking. The other 101 designs, largely the work of speculative builders, are architectural hybrids in which the Romanesque strain, though predominant, is diluted with other styles.

This indifference on the part of Back Bay residents to Romanesque as a style for their homes seems strange when one considers the widespread favor that the style enjoyed in the same years for churches and public buildings. Four of the district's twelve churches, for example, and two of its four schools are Romanesque. It is even more curious that Richardson himself was commissioned to do so little residential work in the district. For despite the national prestige he had gained as the result of his Trinity Church design and his personal friendship with many of Boston's leading citizens, some of whom were building town houses at this very time, Richardson was employed to design only three Back Bay houses: the rectory for Trinity Church, the H. L. Higginson house at 274 Beacon Street (built in 1881; now demolished), and the B. W. Crowninshield residence at 164 Marlborough Street. Moreover, the Crowninshield house was designed in 1870, before Richardson had developed his characteristic manner, and its deft brickwork is closer to the contemporary Panel Brick style than to the master's mature work (fig. 126). One wonders, for example, why Carl Fehmer replaced Richardson as architect for the Oliver Ames town house in 1882 or why the Frederick Ames family in the same year entrusted the remodeling of their house at 306 Dartmouth Street to John Sturgis yet retained Richardson for two store buildings, one of which was commissioned the same year as the house.[17]

The paucity of Richardson houses in the district cannot be ascribed to a disapproval of the Romanesque style nor to the fact that his houses were too expensive, since many Commonwealth Avenue dwellings must have cost quite as much as the Higginson house. One possible explanation may be that between 1879 and 1886, the years when the Back Bay's greatest mansions were being built, Richardson was occupied with such large commissions as the Allegheny County Buildings, the Albany City Hall, stations for the Boston and Albany Railroad, and various libraries. Perhaps his Boston friends realized

126   Entrance of 164 Marlborough Street, 1870, by H. H. Richardson. Designed before Richardson had developed his characteristic Romanesque manner, this house evidences an interest in intricate brickwork similar to the Panel Brick style.

127   Trinity rectory, 233 Clarendon Street, 1879, by H. H. Richardson,
       original state. It represents an imaginative handling of a house on
       a restricted city lot.

that under the pressure of this work, Richardson would be forced to
relegate his residential commissions to assistants, a practice, Hitchcock
indicates, that was all too common in the office.[18]

A simpler explanation, however, is that Bostonians judged that a
massive Romanesque style was ill-suited to the requirements of the
narrow multiwindowed city house. Nevertheless one regrets that Richardson had no occasion to turn his hand to the problem of the typical
twenty-five-foot-wide, four-story, row house—his Back Bay Commissions were for large houses or for corner locations. To judge from his
drawings for the Henry Adams house in Washington, however, his
solution to this problem would have been creditable.[19]

The Trinity rectory is certainly the best of Richardson's Back Bay
dwellings (figs. 127, 128). It was built as a two-story house in 1879;
a full third story was added in 1893 and the roof reconstructed according to its original design when a rector with a family succeeded
bachelor Phillips Brooks. As originally designed the deeply recessed
entrance porch spanned by the broad Syrian arch dominated the
facade more effectively than it does today. Despite asymmetry, the

numerous shapes of windows, and the variety of brick decoration, the facades of this house are beautifully organized.

The coherence of the Clarendon street elevation results from the complex equilibrium which the architect maintains between a sequence of interrelated though diverse elements. The crux of the design is the placement of the seven second-story windows. Identical in shape but spaced at slightly varying intervals, these windows are separated by three panels of cut brick decoration. At each end of the house, two windows enframing a brick decorative panel form a unit of design which aligns with the banks of the windows in the first story and with simple gables on the third level. As the brick panel between the right pair of windows is wider than that on the left, there is space for four mullioned first-floor windows on the right side but only three on the left. The larger right-hand gable further reflects this irregular spacing of second-story openings. Two second-floor windows, also separated by a decorative panel, are set symmetrically over the wide arch of the

128   Trinity rectory, present state. The third story was added in 1893 and the roof reconstructed according to the original design.

entrance porch. The seventh window of the series establishes the position of the single transomed window of the first story and the smaller dormer in the roof. Thus the unsymmetrical but orderly spacing of these seven second-story windows is echoed in all parts of the facade.

The balance one senses in this composition results from a living equilibrium of parts rather than a static symmetry. Although the opposing gabled units use identical elements, that on the right is considerably larger than the left, with a wider bank of mullioned windows, larger panel of brick decoration, and bigger gable with round-arched window. This greater size and the way that the right section is isolated from the rest of the facade by the downspout give it a weight that its counterpart on the left does not have. Counterbalancing this emphasis on the right section, however, is the deep-shadowed arch of the entrance porch and the larger dormer window above it which are located left of center. This equalization of weights is facilitated by a repetition of identical window shapes in both halves of the composition, a repetition which allows the eye to move freely across the facade in a horizontal direction. Furthermore, the varied window shapes on all floors are unified by the use of window panes of almost equal size. The composition is also held together by four bands of smooth stone which carry across the facade, three related to the first-story windows and one at the height of the main cornice.

The quality of the brick masonry in this house is especially fine. Window openings of the second floor are deftly framed by an edge roll molding of brick while relieving arches are indicated in the masonry over the lower banks of windows. The expanses of masonry are sometimes modified by setting the brick in patterns or by the introduction of panels of crisply cut brick decoration, but these variations in texture do not detract from the massive quality of the masonry nor its uniform color. As in the case of Sever Hall at Harvard, both face and decorative cut brick for this house were produced in the brick yard of M. W. Sands in North Cambridge.[20]

The restrained elegance with which Richardson designed the rectory can best be appreciated by comparing it with 21 Fairfield Street, a house built a year later and obviously patterned after it. Not only did W. Whitney Lewis, the later architect, copy the rectory scheme of recessed entrance way and gabled end wings, he openly cribbed the chimney-stack design with its appended quarter-round windows (fig. 129). Beginning with the basic Trinity *parti* he went on to outdo

129 Facade of 21 Fairfield Street, 1880, by W. Whitney Lewis. The basic organization of its design is the same as Richardson's Trinity rectory except that additional decorative elements have been added and the design is sadly lacking in unity.

Richardson in size, in quantities of applied decoration, in varieties of textures, and in the addition of numerous little architectural "features." The result is a welter of competing forms—complete artistic indigestion. This is a typical instance of the way Richardson's contemporaries misunderstood and misused his style of architecture.[21]

The rectory's interior details are worthy of note. The architectural foci of the library and drawing rooms are recessed fireplaces or

130   Library in Trinity rectory. The inglenook is a characteristic Queen Anne feature, but the sensitive use of materials is Richardson's. The terra-cotta lunette is not part of the original scheme and the warmth of the natural surfaces has been somewhat dulled by later coats of paint.

131   Detail of fig. 130. Carved wood ornament. The sunburst in the soffit of the arch is another Queen Anne motif.

inglenooks. The most elaborate of these is situated in the first-floor library (figs. 130, 131). Here the wooden posts and lintel which separate the alcove from the rest of the room are carved with a beautiful hexagonal diaper pattern while the reveal of the opening contains a panel carved with a typical Queen Anne sunburst motif. The mantel is vigorously designed with rough-hewn stone consoles, and a smooth stone shelf thrusts boldly forward above the pressed brick jambs of the fireplace opening. The original Lincrusta Walton embossed wallpaper, though painted over, is still on the walls and adds yet another texture to contrast with the surfaces of rough stone, smooth brick, and crisply carved wood. On the floor above, the drawing room fireplace is lighter in scale since it is carved in wood. Here the casing which surrounds the marble facing of the hearth is cut with a delicate reed pattern which toward the floor flattens into the plane of the upright members (fig. 132).

Other interior details are treated with characteristic Richardson finesse. The lintel over the opening to the shallow fireplace alcove of the dining room is rather similar to that used in the library though it lacks the carved diaper design (fig. 133). Adjacent to the front

132   Second floor drawing room, Trinity rectory. Originally the woodwork was not painted.

133

Dining room fireplace, Trinity rectory.

134

Entrance hall, Trinity rectory. The scroll newel and the curving plan of the lower stairs return to a solution which had long been popular in Boston. The free design of the spiral post in the alcove illustrates the Queen Anne style's love of inventive details.

135

Second floor bedroom, Trinity rectory.

door and opening into the stair hall is an intriguing little alcove which serves as a diminutive reception room. Raised one step above the level of the hall and separated from it by a parapet and an oddly turned column, the alcove is paneled above the built-in bench and lighted by an outside window (fig. 134). The main stair terminates in an unassuming scroll newel. On the second floor the principal bedroom has a simple but decidedly graceful Queen Anne fireplace with posts which flare out like brackets to support the mantel shelf (fig. 135).

The Henry Lee Higginson house at 274 Beacon Street, designed in 1881, demolished in 1929, was one of Richardson's less successful compositions. The circular tower is not well integrated with the plastic mass of the structure; the sprightly, steep-sloped dormer window is quite out of keeping with the mansion's stolid mood; and the stubby stone blocks used to frame the entrance are much too small and inconsequential for their rugged, quarry-faced finish. But whatever the shortcomings of this house, it appears relatively successful

136   Numbers 270 and 274 Beacon Street, 1881. The H. L. Higginson house on the left was Richardson's only large Back Bay residence but not one of his most successful works. The more accomplished house on the right for C. A. Whittier was by McKim, Mead and White. Both houses were demolished in 1929.

when compared with 234 Commonwealth Avenue which is a clumsy reworking of the Higginson scheme (figs. 136, 137). Built eight years after Richardson's, this structure was designed by the same W. Whitney Lewis who earlier parodied Trinity rectory. About the facade of the Commonwealth Avenue house there is an ungainly, pot-bellied feeling caused by an unfortunate disparity in scale between the big undivided sash of the second story and the diminutive recessed openings of the tower. This facade gives the impression that somehow it is bending over backwards.

The interior of the Lewis house, especially the stair hall and second-floor library, presents an interesting fusion of Richardson, Eastlake, and Shaw. Separating the two parts of the second-floor library is a triple arcade filled with Eastlake tracery of turned wood which is carried on twisted wooden columns with Byzantine capitals (fig. 138). An exotic note, too, is the window with three arches filled with stained glass and a wooden grille which opens from the rear wall of the library into the stairwell (fig. 139). The trim in the upper and lower halls has a somewhat Byzantine character and, as in the library, the oaken woodwork is stained a dark color.

The firm of Allen and Kenway was the most consistent exponent of the Romanesque tradition in the Back Bay, and they had a dis-

137

Facade of 234 Commonwealth Avenue, 1889, by W. Whitney Lewis. A smaller and less successful version of the Higginson house, its fenestration lacks a consistent scale.

138 Second-floor library at 234 Commonwealth Avenue. Detail of the triple arch that divides the library. The arch marks the position of the lateral bearing wall of wood which was required by building regulations in houses having a width of twenty-five feet or more.

139 Second-floor library at 234 Commonwealth Avenue. Above the built-in divan the grilled and stained glass window opens into the stairwell.

tinctive way of handling it. In five of the ten Romanesque houses they designed in the district between 1881 and 1888 they substituted balustrades or heavy horizontal cornices for the usual gabled roofs and thereby sacrificed the picturesque massing which is one artistic merit of a good Romanesque design (fig. 140). And perhaps because they thought the broad Syrian arch was unsuited to the pinched, vertical quality of the usual city facade or because its heavy spandrels reduced available window areas, they also omitted this conspicuous Richardson element. Instead they capped their entrances with tight, stilted arches surrounded by heavy archivolts carved with an acanthus leaf pattern. The firm was also fond of Auvergnat marquetry (colored stone set in geometric patterns) and areas of intricate Byzantine-like decoration carved in brownstone.

140   Facade of 282 Commonwealth Avenue, 1884, by Allen and Kenway. A run-of-mill work in the Richardson Romanesque manner.

141   Facade of 222 Newbury Street, 1884, by S. D. Kelley. Kelley was an architect who turned out designs for several Boston speculative builders. In this facade he combines Richardson Romanesque and Queen Anne features.

142   Facade of 43 Bay State Road, 1889, by S. D. Kelley. One of a row of four houses, this design combines Richardson-like rough-textured stone with Georgian-inspired doorways.

The majority of Romanesque houses produced in the late eighties and early nineties have little to recommend them. The most elaborate if not the most successful Romanesque house which remains in the district today is 347 Beacon Street, an edifice designed in 1884 by J. H. Besarick. Here one is oppressed by the gross profusion of carved brownstone decoration while the facade's "unsymmetrical symmetry" produces distinctly unpleasant tensions. More typical of this late work are the six row houses designed in 1891 for 461–471 Commonwealth Avenue by S. D. Kelley. These structures bear witness to the degradation which overtook Richardson's personal idiom in most parts of America and even, on occasion, in Boston when speculative builders exploited the style. Although they echo the master's fondness for mixing heavy Romanesque elements with light forms of late Gothic origin, these houses lack unity as a group or as single units and their individual elements compete for the spectator's interest. Number 308 Commonwealth Avenue is a Romanesque version of an apartment building which becomes progressively less Romanesque the higher the eye goes. Indeed in all of these last-mentioned buildings, it is only the use of rough-faced brownstone and an occasional use of the round arch that labels them Romanesque—superficial guides for classification which need not detain us.

As Richardson's aesthetic principles were vulgarized and his personal style reduced to a series of artistic clichés, the dividing line between it and several other styles tends to disappear. When a decorative detail was chosen only for its richness or inventiveness, it mattered little from which archaeological style it was derived. As an example of this running-together of styles, one can instance 222 Newbury Street, 1884 (fig. 141), or the group at 13–24 Bay State Road, 1889. These structures, picked at random, illustrate the fusion of the Queen Anne and Romanesque manners. S. D. Kelley, the architect for both, was even able on occasion to fuse Georgian details on forms that suggest the Romanesque (fig. 142).

The day of the Romanesque was fairly brief. In domestic architecture the style makes its Back Bay debut in 1879 at Trinity rectory, and by 1892 it had run its course. After 1892 but three houses were erected in that manner; the last structure to incorporate Romanesque features appeared in 1895 at 137 Bay State Road.

The Queen Anne Style

Before discussing examples of Queen Anne architecture in the Back Bay district the term must be explained, because few architectural terms have been so loosely used. Employed in a purely historical sense, the term denotes the reign of Queen Anne, 1702–1714. In more recent architectural usage, however, Queen Anne's name has been usurped by a group of nineteenth century British architectural styles which have almost no connection with that lady and frequently little relation to each other. Thus the term is sometimes used to denote a manner which is chiefly Medieval in inspiration, at other times to refer to buildings which appear almost Georgian. Popularly and often with little discrimination, it is used for any architectural eccentricity produced in the last quarter of the nineteenth century. Obviously our use of the word must be restricted if hopeless confusion is to be avoided.

The appellation as well as the architectural style known as Queen Anne originated just a century ago with a group of British architects. These young men, the most prominent of whom were R. Norman Shaw, W. Eden Nesfield, and Philip Webb, faced with the disintegration of craftsmanship in the building trades before the onslaught of the machine, sought to revive the old tradition of good craftsmanship which they felt had existed in England as late as the reign of Queen Anne.[22] Their idea was to transport British architecture back to this happier era of sound craftsmanship and then allow it to develop freely and functionally from there. As their architectural training, for the most part, had been in the offices of such champions of the Gothic style as Pugin and Street, these young innovators at first quite naturally utilized Medieval forms as a medium of expression. Once embarked on this course, each man evolved a personal style which changed with the passing years. Of the three, Norman Shaw's career was the most spectacular, and his name is most closely associated with the Queen Anne style.

At least four distinct manners can be distinguished in Shaw's work. In the late 1860's his designs are Medieval in character, emphasizing such qualities as a rambling, informal plan and a utilization of half-timbered construction. This stage is admirably represented by country houses like "Leys Wood," Sussex (1868), and "Pierrepont,"

Surrey (1876). In the seventies Shaw developed a more urbanized style. Utilizing brick and evincing a preference for large double-hung windows, this second phase exploited the hybrid architectural forms of the early eighteenth century produced by the fusion of the traditional Medieval vernacular of England and the corrupted Renaissance manner of the Netherlands. Examples of this phase of Shaw's work are: "The New Zealand Chambers," Leadhall Street, London, 1872; the architect's own house on Ellerdale Road, Hampstead, 1872; and the Bedford Park subdivision of 1876–78, a well-designed, medium-priced suburb and the forerunner of the modern garden city. By 1891, when he designed "Chesters" in Northumberland, Shaw had exchanged his early picturesque idiosyncrasies for a disciplined style not unlike eighteenth century Georgian work. His last building, the Piccadilly Hotel of 1905, and his unused designs for the Regent Street Quadrant show yet a fourth way of working and approximate the modern Academic Baroque manner to which official British architects and city planners remained addicted through the 1930's.

Shaw's theories and example inspired similar experiments among his contemporaries and soon many different personal experiments, which drew inspiration from various phases of eighteenth century architecture, were flowering in England. These British developments were not long in being transported to America. By the mid-seventies Shaw's first or Medieval style was reflected in several informal, half-timbered country houses from the H. H. Richardson office, typical of which are the Watts Sherman house in Newport, 1874, and the projected Cheney house of 1875. These designs exploited half-timbered work well before the appearance in 1878 of Shaw's *Sketches for Cottages and Other Buildings*.[23] Because of the restrictions on the exterior use of combustible building materials as well as the style's demand for a picturesque massing, this Medieval work was not readily adaptable to city dwellings. Somewhat later and in suburban settings, this fashion, reinforced by the late nineteenth century passion for architectural authenticity, developed into Tudor Revival or "English Style" residences of the late nineteenth century.[24]

Shaw's second manner was especially popular on this side of the Atlantic and was enthusiastically hailed as the "Free Classic." But the uses to which Shaw's ideas were put in urban and suburban architecture in America were very different. In the cities the Free

Classic recommended itself by reason of its flexible proportions, its large window areas, its informal if copious decoration, and the fact that it is almost entirely constructed of brick. The suburban architect, on the other hand, exploited the rambling, informal plan and seized upon the style's picturesque vagaries which he developed in wood construction rather than the masonry used by Shaw. Whereas city building, at least in the Back Bay, followed the parent style rather closely, suburban design used the English work only as a point of departure and went on to develop something that was distinctly American.

The impact of Shaw's third or Georgian manner is less apparent in America than its predecessors because, being more archaeological, it is not easily distinguished as a specific influence. After 1890 one finds it very difficult to differentiate Shaw's British Georgian manner from the revival of the Yankee's own American Georgian. This does not mean that Shaw had ceased to interest the American designer. Indeed it can be argued that the revived interest in Colonial architecture in America was partly Shaw's doing, for by his successful adaptation of British seventeenth and eighteenth century precedent, Shaw encouraged Americans to draw on their own Georgian heritage.[25] One might think of Norman Shaw as the godfather of the Georgian Revival in America. Finally, be it observed, Shaw's last phase had relatively little influence in America, and since it chronologically follows the active period of building in the Back Bay, one finds no evidence of it here.

Primarily then, it is Shaw's second manner that directly influenced Back Bay design. Looking one moment again at this parent work, one observes that it features good craftsmanship and an atmosphere of informal comfort. The plan of the Queen Anne house is informal and unsymmetrical; coziness is prized, and rooms are replete with alcoves, inglenooks, and bay windows. The house grows from the inside out; the exterior expresses the informal plan and delights in asymmetry, in a variety of steep-gabled wings which protrude from the building, in large windows, and in numerous tall chimney stacks that bespeak hospitality and comfort within. Double hung windows are used because they are thought to be more convenient than casements. The element of good craftsmanship is stressed on the interior by elaborate plaster work, by paneled wainscots and overmantels, and in an abundance of turned woodwork. The exterior boasts a craftsmanlike combination of many different materials. Brick masonry especially is handled with skill and ingenuity; the warm red brick is often molded in unusual architectural shapes or decorative patterns are carved in the brick wall. The Queen Anne architect enlivens his facades with Renaissance details, but Classical regularity and symmetry are not allowed to overrule irregularities of massing or fenestration demanded by the interior. It is not the Classical prototype that is important but the quality of the work that the craftsman produces when he is inspired by it.

The new Queen Anne movement was attentively received by Boston designers. The programs of the Boston Society of Architects for February and March of 1877 were devoted to a spirited discussion of the new British development, and long articles in the Boston-published *American Architect and Building News* for April 28 and October 6, 1877, appraised the style's merits and limitations. If Shaw can be said to have given full expression to the new style first in 1872 (the New Zealand Chambers), the historian will see how promptly the new movement was echoed in the Back Bay where a fully developed Queen Anne residence was under construction in 1878.[26] It would seem that Boston designers had availed themselves of the enforced leisure of the depression years to study Shaw's work and that they were thoroughly acquainted with and ready to use the new style without preliminary experiments when construction picked up in the late seventies. As a consequence, there is no transition period; the style appears in the Back Bay in full blossom.

In adapting Shaw's second manner to their needs, different Back Bay designers used the new style in various ways. Some architects, accepting the Queen Anne as a bundle of new architectural tricks, succeeded in duplicating Shaw's decorative features; others discovered in it an excuse for all kinds of artistic license; still a third group, comprehending the basic problems with which Shaw was grappling, concentrated on the comfort and good craftsmanship of the structures which they were designing.

Typical of the group which successfully copied British decorative forms is 135 Marlborough Street, built in 1880 (fig. 143). The most interesting thing about the house is its ornamental use of brick. Pilaster and cornice forms are made of molded brick while the frieze under the main cornice is filled with floral patterns of cut brick. A characteristic Queen Anne decorative detail, also wrought of cut

143 Facade of 135 Marlborough Street, 1880, by Cabot and Chandler. An effective use of both pressed brick and cut brick ornament which had been popularized by Queen Anne architects in England. Fourth story added in 1935.

144 Facade of 178 Marlborough Street, 1879, by Cabot and Chandler, who were the Back Bay's most competent designers in the Queen Anne tradition. The picturesque dormer window is a characteristic feature.

brick, is the sunburst relief over the second story window. (The relief decoration was carved in the bricks before they were fired; after they were taken from the kiln the bricks were laid in regular courses in mortar according to a pattern which would produce the design planned.) Before the structure was remodeled with the addition of a full story, brick dormers undoubtedly added an animated element to the composition. Number 178 Marlborough Street (1879), which delights in a similar use of brick ornamentation, retains its elaborate dormer (fig. 144).

Cabot and Chandler, architects for these two dwellings, were also the authors in 1879 of the charming little house at 12 Fairfield Street for Georgiana Lowell (figs. 145, 146). Here the entire decora-

145   Facade of 12 Fairfield Street, 1879, by Cabot and Chandler. Despite its richness the brick ornamentation remains subordinate to the broad areas of brick masonry and to the simple mass of the dwelling.

146 Detail of fig. 145. Ornamentation consists of no less than twenty different patterns of brick. Molded brick can be seen in the cornice, string courses, the jambs of the lower window, and the beaded voussoirs of the upper arch. Cut brick were used for the square flower relief and for several sections of the console that supports the oriel window.

tion is achieved in brick, a satisfactory state of affairs as it allows large quantities of ornamentation yet subordinates it to the simple mass of the house. Because ornamentation and plain wall surfaces are formed of the same warm red brick, the decoration is absorbed into the structure's broad areas of masonry. Although the eye enjoys such detail, it is not distracted by it. One is able at a glance to grasp the essential form of the edifice as a whole—a cubic block capped with a moderate hipped roof which clusters around a single chimney stack. The main cornice is drawn at the level of the third-story window sills while the juncture of the roof and walls receives minimum architectural accent. This solution emphasizes the compact, blocklike mass of the structure. Contrasting with this solidity is the delicate, flickering counterpoint of brick ornamentation. Particularly fascinating are the string courses of brick molded in blunt pyramidal forms or as half cylinders. About the window openings a lively pattern of rectangular bricks alternates with those shaped with an edge-roll molding. The base of the oriel window, shown in figure 146, gives an idea of the variety of decorative elements that can be wrought in brick. No less than twenty different shapes of molded brick are used on this facade.

Boston architectural firms produced some exceptionally good work in the Queen Anne vein. For vigor of design and caliber of craftsmanship, a number of Back Bay residences are comparable to contemporary British work; it is only in size that they are inferior. Cabot and Chandler followed by Peabody and Stearns produced the most Shaw-like dwellings in the district though the most exuberant Queen Anne design is W. R. Emerson's Boston Art Club of 1881 on the corner of Newbury and Dartmouth streets (fig. 147).

When a new architectural style appears upon the stage of history, it is the superficial details that first gain popular attention and are copied; the fundamental concepts involved are understood more slowly and by fewer architects. The spread of the Queen Anne style to America well illustrates this process. Even some Back Bay practitioners who used the idiom saw in it little more than a novel system of ornamentation that could be served up in the name of modernity; these men were little more than style peddlers. In their work each architectural element is apt to be separate and unrelated; each opening has a different size and proportion, and often these forms are in active competition. One is sometimes reminded more of doll's house architecture than of serious urban design.[27]

Flagrant examples of this architectural attitude are found in two houses designed by Allen and Kenway in 1882. At 346 Beacon Street the same unit of fenestration is scarcely repeated (fig. 148). The contrasts between round and square-topped windows, narrow and wide openings, is utterly confusing as is the absence of vertical alignment. Single elements such as the dormer and entrance porch detach themselves from the rest of the design because of their exaggerated picturesqueness. This last point is also illustrated by the two-story oriel window at 386 Marlborough Street.[28]

The less perspicacious designer could also seek variety by mixing the architectural styles at his disposal. It is quite unnecessary to dwell upon the stylistic crossbreeding of Queen Anne with various architectural consorts, for there seems no end to the shapes and colors of

147   Entrance of 270 Dartmouth Street, the Boston Art Club, 1881, by
W. R. Emerson. This entrance, with cut brick ornamentation, is the
handsomest Queen Anne detail in the Back Bay.

her progeny. All that we shall do here is point out the three principal
hybrid forms which spring from the parent stock.

Number 119 Commonwealth Avenue, designed in 1879 by Bradlee
and Winslow, illustrate a fusion of the Queen Anne and Academic
traditions (fig. 149). Reminiscent of the latter are the smooth-sur-
faced brownstone facade, the mansard roof, the rather correct architraves about the windows, and the main entablature. Explicable

148   Facade of 346 Beacon Street, 1882, by Allen and Kenway. Characteristic of Queen Anne search for the picturesque, the fenestration of this facade is merely chaotic.

149   Facade of 119 Commonwealth Avenue, 1879, by Bradlee and Winslow. This facade combines Academic features (window enframements and use of brownstone) with Queen Anne elements (hooded entrance and dormer windows). The dormers are made of pressed metal painted to resemble brownstone.

only in terms of the Queen Anne are the curious sweeping consoles which support the balcony over the entry and the steep pediment of the attic dormer (which, surprisingly enough, is made of pressed metal painted to look like stone). The freer fancy of the Queen Anne manner can be detected also in the playful console of the third-story window sill.

At other times the Queen Anne style merges with the oncoming Georgian Revival, a combination also found in the work of Norman Shaw at a certain point in his career. The handsome town house at 211 Commonwealth Avenue designed for W. P. Mason by Rotch and Tilden is illustrative of this stylistic confluence (figs. 150, 151). Free of Queen Anne's usual decorative excesses, this composition with its bowed bay window is almost regular enough to suggest early nineteenth century precedents. An affinity for the picturesque, however, which was born of Queen Anne, induces the designer to reor-

150   Facade of 211 Commonwealth Avenue, 1883, by Rotch and Tilden. This design illustrates the Queen Anne architect's tendency both to handle the Georgian style with freedom and to try to improve upon it by adding decoration.

151

Detail of fig. 150. This entrance composition purportedly reworks an idea found in two recessed Boston doorways dating from the early nineteenth century.

ganize the usual Renaissance door frame in a capricious way, sink the whole composition in an elliptical recess, and introduce diminutive broken pediments over each jamb of the door. Great ingenuity is evidenced in the way the various freely interpreted Classical forms are related to the warped surfaces of the niche.

According to a note by the architect Ogden Codman preserved in a miscellaneous file in the Boston Athenaeum, the Mason entrance recalled a doorway used by Asher Benjamin in two earlier Boston houses: one for Judge Jackson at Bedford and Otis streets, another for Otis Everett's dwelling on the corner of Washington and Oak streets. Mr. Codman's note has historical interest since it underlines the connection between the Queen Anne and Georgian traditions, and his further comment that it was a "very bad copy" illustrates the condescension of the later purist (speaking about 1915) toward the picturesque whimsies of Queen Anne designers.

And finally, as we have already seen, Queen Anne and Richardson Romanesque can merge as at 222 Newbury Street (fig. 141). It is hardly worth lingering over family traits here, but one can see at a glance that Queen Anne is responsible for the characteristic stepped gable and the playful uses of material, with Richardson the progenitor of the round arch, the quarry-faced brownstone surfaces, the stubby columns, and the drip molding whose ends transform into Byzantine-like leaf forms.

In contrast to these variations of the Queen Anne style which rely on a superficial manipulation of decorative features, there is the third group of structures which concentrate upon a sensitive use of building materials. Instead of being something that is applied, such quality as this group possesses derives from the materials of which the edifice is built. The architect here was aware of the texture as well as the color of his material and it is apparent that he found beauty in a juxtaposition of materials, that he sought to adapt such decoration as he employed to his material, and that he prized good craftsmanship.

This new attitude is in direct opposition to the one which prevailed in the sixties where the material merely furnished the stuff, the almost inconsequential matter, out of which preconceived architectural forms were created. It is also very different from the contemporary attitude demonstrated by 119 Commonwealth Avenue (fig. 149) where the material (dormer windows of pressed metal painted and sprinkled with sand to resemble brownstone) was deliberately falsified for the sake of economy and fire protection.

A few architects in the 1880's sought liberation from meaningless archaeological formulas. Sloughing off such architectonic ornamentation as window frames, pilasters, and pediments which suggest a structural use but are not structurally requisite, and relieved of the need to follow the theoretical order of some historical style, the designer focused his attention on the actual proportions of the facade and the materials with which he was working. As they had a structural purpose, window and door lintels were retained; frequently they were accentuated by a contrast of materials or by the method in which the material was laid in place.

Some of the most successful of these houses are built entirely of brick and evince an unusually sensitive attitude on the part of the architect toward his material. At 357–359 Beacon Street (1885, Carl

Fehmer) flat arches and jambs of all openings, string courses, quoins, and cornice are constructed of buff-colored brick which contrasts mildly with a darker and warmer brown hue used elsewhere (fig. 152). This light brick trim protrudes so slightly from the main plane of the facade—less than half an inch—that it is all but indistinguishable except when observed in the raking light of the late afternoon sun. The brick cornice also has barely enough projection to differentiate it from the rest of the facade.

Number 505 Beacon Street (1888), also by Fehmer, has an equally chaste interplay of geometric shapes and textures—this time smooth brownstone and brick (fig. 153). Number 195 Marlborough Street (1883) is handled the same way though quarry-faced stone is employed in the basement. The facade at 248 Marlborough Street uses brick ornamentation in as lively and imaginative a way as was ever devised by the Panel Brick style, but richer textural contrasts are here achieved (fig. 154). The big blocks of rough brownstone, which form the continuous band above the first-floor openings, appear strong and impressive against the plain brick surfaces of the lower stories. Simple expanses of brick are also an effective foil for the green-patinaed pressed copper surfaces which cover the bay window and for the staccato designs worked into the fourth-floor windows and cornice. The arched windows with their archivolts suggest Richardson Romanesque, but clearly the architect was more interested in the scale and play of light and shade than in the historical precedents of his design.

Three houses built at 251–255 Marlborough Street between 1883 and 1886 by two firms give additional proof of the excellence of this class of Queen Anne houses.[29] Photographs, unfortunately, do not do justice to the sensitive yet clear way in which the stone and brick surfaces have been used. In these examples flush brownstone lintels have been substituted for flat arches of brick, but because of the similar colors of brick and stone and the fact that the stone members rigorously preserve the plane est 'blished by the brick, contrast of textures is achieved without destroying the continuity of the masonry.

As refreshing as this simple brick style is, one should not fail to realize that it is related to earlier traditions of Back Bay building. In eliminating extraneous ornamentation from the facade so that the simple sheet of brick could be appreciated for its own value, the

152   Facade of 357–359 Beacon Street, 1885, by Carl Fehmer. Architectural accents on this facade, used at such critical points as openings, corners, and cornice, are confined to a slight projection and a change in the color of the brick.

153   Facade of 505 Beacon Street, 1888, by Carl Fehmer. Such decoration as this excellent facade possesses comes entirely from the contrasts in texture and color of the building materials employed.

154   Facade of 248 Marlborough Street, 1885, by Hartwell and Richardson. The ornamental relief of the facade comes naturally out of the materials employed. Leaded windows of the second floor were added in 1919.

designer of the eighties revived the brick work of the 1840's and early fifties. At the same time the crisp, small-scale brick decoration with which the facade is accented refers back to the Panel Brick style of the early seventies.

While speaking of this distinctive use of brick in the eighties, mention should be made of the variety of new brick shapes and colors which came into use. The salmon-colored Philadelphia pressed brick which had served the builder since about 1830 was in the late seventies and eighties supplemented by bricks of brown, yellow, buff, and cherry-red hues. Brick sizes also varied; in 1875 the Boston Society of Architects sent a circular to brickmakers in the neighborhood of Boston calling attention to the serious lack of uniformity of brick sizes.[30]

Still other houses built during the 1880's in the Back Bay utilize strong, rough textures of quarry-faced stone with good effect. This innovation, of course, is not without local precedent. Ever since the opening of the Middlesex Canal in 1803 had placed the granite quarries of Chelmsford within economic reach, unfinished granite had been popular with Boston builders. It had been used, for example, in several blocks of warehouses in the vicinity of the old Long Wharf and in the late forties for the impressive water reservoir atop Beacon Hill. In 1882 when the reservoir was demolished, the granite blocks were reused for the bridges designed by Richardson over the Back Bay Fens.[31] Rough stone masonry had also been popular for churches, outstanding among which were Ware and Van Brunt's First Church of 1867 and Richardson's Brattle Square and Trinity churches of 1871 and 1875. Given this precedent it is not surprising to find quarry-faced stone used also for domestic architecture.

Rough-surfaced brownstone makes its first appearance in Back Bay residential building in 1876 when it is employed at 303 Dartmouth Street for a rusticated basement. In 1880 the same material is featured on the entire first story at 251 Commonwealth Avenue (fig. 155); the first house faced completely with rough brownstone is 318 Beacon Street, 1881. The material last appears as a major element of design in 1892.[32] After that, rough brownstone is replaced by smooth, light-colored limestone, a material more compatible with the tastes of the Classic Revival.

Although sometimes employed for an entire facade, rough brownstone is more effective when contrasted with areas of smooth brick.

155   Entrance of 251 Commonwealth Avenue, 1880, by
Shaw and Shaw. The
quarry-faced brownstone
of the lower story is the
first large-scale use of
rough masonry for a Back
Bay house.

Impressive simplicity is achieved, for example, at 283 and 285 Beacon
Street and at 257 Marlborough Street, houses built in 1885 and 1883
by Cabot and Chandler. At 283–285 Beacon not only do the rough
stone lintels contrast with the expanses of plain brick masonry but
the size of the lintels over basement and second story openings is
monumental (fig. 156). In this Spartan composition all carving is
avoided, and the only variety comes from two copper gutters and the
wrought-iron balustrade which caps the circular bay. At 257 Marlborough the rustication of the lower stories modulates to smooth
stone lintels in the upper two floors (fig. 157). Also the finely cut capitals of the loggialike openings on the top floor enhance by contrast
the strong rustication in the lower part of the house.

    De-emphasis of architectural trim had beneficial effects. It made

156   Facade of 283–285 Beacon Street, 1885, by Cabot and Chandler. The only decorative relief in these two houses derives from the contrasting textures and colors of the stone lintels and brick masonry.

for a more congruous urban scene by minimizing the uniqueness and separateness of the individual house, and it focused attention on a meaningful use of building materials. This latter point is verified by comparing a row of houses at 336–354 Beacon Street with dwellings of similar size at 245–275 Marlborough Street (figs. 158, 159). Both groups use the same materials, brownstone and pressed brick, but in the Beacon Street group the importance of building material as an aesthetic asset is subordinated to a panoply of superimposed architectural features.

These same blocks also demonstrate how the streetscape achieves greater harmony when less emphasis is placed upon architectural style, especially when more than one style is used. The Marlborough Street row was built between 1880 and 1887 by six different architects. Although each retains individual characteristics as to height, proportion, and design, the several houses do not compete with one another. Uninhibited by archaeological considerations, their designers were free to consider the basic problem of a multiwindow facade on a wall-bearing structure. The similarity of the problem and the straightforward solutions result in an admirable consistency within the row of houses. In contrast to this but built in almost the same years, 1876–1886, the ten dwellings on Beacon Street employ five different archae-

157

Facade of 257 Marlborough Street, 1883, by Cabot and Chandler. The quarry-faced stone of the lower story contrasts effectively with the flush stone lintels and smooth brick masonry of the upper floors. The loggialike top story is also skillfully designed.

158   Numbers 336–354 Beacon Street, 1876–1886. Ten dwellings built
within a decade, each of a distinct style of architecture, create a
restless streetscape.

ological systems which necessitated frequent variations of cornice
heights and bay window design. Such constant change imparts little
unity or repose to the street.

Undoubtedly the Back Bay's most original work was done in connection with a simple use of materials, and, in a sense, this movement symbolizes Boston's artistic maturity. Here her architects produced something of their own. After twenty years of schooling in the
Academic style followed by a restless adolescent search for self-
expression and a subsequent discovery of the values of craftsmanship
through contact with the Ruskinians and the Queen Anne men, Boston designers stood on the threshold of an indigenous architecture,
even as Chicagoans of the same decade were pioneering in the field

of architectural engineering. Along with Richardson, who would seem to be a fellow seeker rather than teacher of this group, they developed a vital understanding of the nature of the materials with which they worked, and they were ofttimes freer than he from an inhibiting allegiance to a pre-established system of archaeology.

Whether or not this artistic frame of reference could have provided the foundation from which to build a modern architectural expression or produce an idiom congenial to an industrial society is a matter of question. Although it showed a healthy independence of archaeological precedent and a sensitive feeling for material, this style had little connection with the machine age. It made no attempt to utilize the new materials or systems of construction produced by industrial society. Instead, it cherished the craftsman's attitude toward architecture and

159   Numbers 245–275 Marlborough Street. Erected between 1880 and 1886, these ten dwellings rely upon a sensitive use of material instead of applied ornamentation. This creates a somewhat more harmonious streetscape than when each house is in a different architectural style, but the ubiquitous bay window and the absence of a uniform cornice height deprive the block of the unity it would have had in the early sixties.

was most successful when applied to masonry structures that were wall-bearing. In any case, this progressive and indigenous style was soon cut short by a new wave of Classical revivalism which appeared on the Boston architectural scene at the end of the 1880's.

FIRE LAWS AND PROPERTY RESTRICTIONS

Another factor, one quite beyond the realm of artistic taste and fashion, had considerable influence on the appearance of the Back Bay house during this period. This was the corpus of building laws which the city of Boston drew up in the early 1870's for all structures built or remodeled in the central part of the city. These building requirements departed in many respects from earlier usage and they affected directly the exterior appearance of new construction.

It is interesting to note that the enormous body of building and hygienic controls exerted today by the modern city grew originally out of attempts to control fire hazards. All aspects of building regulation and enforcement in New York City were under the supervision of the Fire Department until 1862.[33] Only then did the city establish a Building Department and charge it with the inspection and certification of new construction. Boston followed suit in July 1871, when an act of the legislature authorized a department for the survey and inspection of buildings. The same act established minimum building standards and safety precautions, and it charged the new department with their enforcement. These regulations were strengthened in 1872 and, after the disastrous Boston Fire in November of that year, both building regulations and their enforcement were tightened by the acts of 1873. Few additional changes were made until 1892.

These laws of 1871, 1872, and 1873 regulated every phase of building from the driving of the pile foundations to the construction of heating ducts and roofs. Sufficient for present mention are those requirements which specifically affected the appearance of the Back Bay residence. According to the new regulations, party walls had to be carried some distance above the level of the roof; a gutter stone or masonry corbel had to separate the cornices of adjacent houses; an ordinary mansard roof could not exceed one story in height; exterior trim, such as cornices more than forty-five feet above the ground had to be made of or covered with noncombustible material; above the second story bay windows could not be constructed of wood. For buildings wider than thirty feet, a maximum span of twenty-five feet for wood joists was established, and intermediate bearing partitions were required.[34]

The most striking artistic effect of these new laws was to make it illegal to build the blocks of closely integrated houses which had been the happy achievement of the 1860's—blocks of houses fused into a single imposing unit by a continuous roof surface and unbroken cornice. Instead of harmonious coexistence, a restless striving now emerges caused by the constant interruption of the roof by party fire walls, and the incessant checking of the cornice by bulky gutter stones or brick corbels. Even where the same facade is repeated or where adjoining designers attempt to preserve a sense of continuity and unity, the individual house fronts are set off from one another by these mandatory fire barriers. A brief comparison of the houses at 22–30 Marlborough Street (1861) and a group built two decades later (1880) on the same street (numbers 381–391) illustrates how much the fire measures cost in terms of architectural unity (figs. 29, 160).

In addition to the laws set down by the Building Department, there were certain property restrictions which the Commonwealth imposed on the filled land when it transferred title to private ownership. It is interesting to see how these regulations affected the specific architectural character of the facade. Most pertinent is the regulation creating a mandatory setback of twenty (or twenty-two) feet from the sidewalk.[35] Although the main facade of the house could not project in front of this line, the owner was permitted to construct such appendages as steps, porches, balconies, or bay windows in the area. As this gave the builder who constructed a bay window a bonus of from thirty to forty square feet of floor area, the effect of the provision was to encourage the multiplication of plastic appendages on the facade. The bay window was popular for other reasons also: it formed a pleasant sun trap during the winter months in which the house was occupied, and it provided a better view of the long streets than could be obtained from regular windows. These practical considerations reinforced the already strong individualistic tendencies which impelled designers in the 1870's to emphasize the plastic entity of the house design.[36]

160 Facade of 385–389 Marlborough Street, 1880, by O. F. Smith. When compared with similar sized houses of 1863, fig. 29, these facades illustrate how bay windows and other appendages destroy the continuity of later rows of houses. The gutter stones and fire walls were required by fire laws.

  The provision in the deed specified that no projection could extend more than five feet beyond the building line nor exceed seventenths the width of the lot (with a maximum total length of 18 feet); the corner of the projection could not form more than a 45-degree angle with the front corner of the building (fig. 161). The restrictions were spelled out in somewhat more detail in deeds given after 1863 and amplified and interpreted from time to time in the annual reports of the Commissioners on Public Lands (after 1879 called the Harbor and Land Commission). In the 1883 report the commission opined that projections into the reserved area preceding the facade could not overlap, that if a porch or door step were attached to a projecting bay window, the combined projections could not exceed the prescribed five feet. Under such an interpretation 17 Marlborough Street (1865) would appear to have been an infraction of the law, but as title for the land on which this house was built had been given in 1862, before the tighter restrictions of 1863 were imposed, its owner could not be prosecuted (fig. 56). The strengthening of the restrictions, however, may explain why this very satisfactory design was not repeated.

In addition to its other duties, the commission was charged with the enforcement of the deed restrictions. Although these limitations existed from the outset, the matter of enforcing them did not come up before 1879 and no legal action was taken under them until 1883. Probably the most important test of the Commonwealth's power to enforce the restrictions was posed by the Algonquin Club. As designed in 1887 by McKim, Mead, and White the basement story of the club was treated as a projecting bay which extended the entire eighty-two foot length of the facade (fig. 191). In 1889 the Massachusetts courts decreed that this projection was in violation of the property restrictions, and they required the club to alter the facade to its present state. The commission also decided, and the courts sustained, that bay windows or other forms could not project over alleyways. As a result, the owner of the Hotel Kensington at 687 Boylston Street (corner of

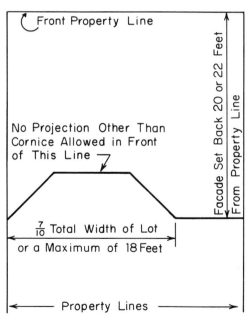

161   A summary of setback requirements for Back Bay structures.

162   Facade of 176–178 Commonwealth Avenue, 1883, by Charles Atwood.
The continuous line of bay windows and entrance porches would
seem to violate property restrictions that limit projections beyond the
building line to seven tenths of the lot width, but Massachusetts
courts deemed these examples conforming.

Exeter) was required to remove the bay windows above the alley at
the back of that structure.[37]

Although the Harbor and Land Commission in 1883 had stated
that "if front porches are enclosed or attached to the house next or to
the bay window . . . they are subject to the same restrictions as first
class [that is, regular bay window] projections," the Massachusetts
courts in 1894 decided that the combination of bay windows and open
porches at 176 and 178 Commonwealth Avenue did not violate the

regulations (fig. 162).[38] A somewhat similar but earlier (1865) solution has already been seen at 212 Beacon Street (fig. 54). As this house was built on the north (water) side of Beacon Street on land purchased from the Boston and Roxbury Mill Corporation, which had not imposed as strict building regulations on its land as had the Commonwealth, its design was not circumscribed in the same way. Despite the court ruling in the 1894 case, a reasonable fear that such a design might not be lawful may have discouraged other architects building on property derived from Massachusetts from using this very satisfactory solution. Another house design frequently utilized in the late sixties on Beacon Street (239–251, 377–395, or 419–431) would appear to violate the regulation since the bay window is fused to the entrance porch and together they exceed seven-tenths the width of the facade (fig. 48). No proceedings, however, are recorded against any of these householders.

PLAN AND INTERIOR ARRANGEMENT

When one looks behind the facade of the Boston town house of the 1870's and 1880's, he finds few important changes in plan or parts. To be sure, there is a multiplication of such mechanical features as bathrooms and heating units and, in the late eighties, the gradual substitution of electric for gas illumination. There is even the availability of the hydraulic elevator which was used in a few dwellings. But despite these innovations, the Back Bay house did not change drastically in its organization.

There is a tendency after 1880 to make a few houses larger and more ostentatious than heretofore, but the 25- or 26-foot-wide house continues to account for the great majority of the edifices built. Such variations in lot sizes as did exist can be explained by two factors: desire for greater display and differences in land ownership. Dissimilar methods of land division were used by the private companies and the Commonwealth who held initial title to the Back Bay. With a few early exceptions the area between the Public Garden and a line midpoint between Exeter and Fairfield streets was divided into standard lots and sold by the Commonwealth at public auctions. Situated nearer Boston this area was filled and built over first. Further to the west or north of Beacon Street and owned by two private corporations, the remaining area was sold privately rather than at auctions, and it was possible for the individual house builder to buy whatever size lot he desired. Although the 25-foot lot persists from force of habit and convenience and accounts for the majority of parcels in the area, there is more variation in lot sizes here than in Commonwealth land.

Most of the large houses were located on the north "sunny" side of Commonwealth Avenue or the water side of Beacon Street—areas in the Back Bay which were regarded as particularly desirable. Generally these larger lots vary from 35 to 40 feet in width and seldom reach 50 feet, the size of a double lot to which the large house of an earlier decade would have had to extend. There was also some division into very narrow lots, but this trend comes later and is most evident in less fashionable blocks or on the periphery of the district. One sees it, for example, in speculator-built rows like 110–128 Bay State Road, constructed between 1910 and 1913, or in the more interesting groups of small town houses facing Charles River Square (1910) or West Hill Place (1916).

The tendency of a few householders to build somewhat larger dwellings can also be seen in the way several wealthy men acquired the house next door and opened it into their own residence. When 1 Commonwealth Avenue was combined with the corner house at 12 Arlington Street in 1893 by Montgomery Sears, its entrance and staircase were removed and its entire second story was remodeled into a huge music room. Likewise Mrs. Jack Gardner, whose father, David Steward, had built a conservative twenty-two-foot residence for her in 1861 at 152 Beacon Street, in 1880 bought the adjoining dwelling at 150 and combined it with her old house. There she lived until her Fenway palace was finished in 1902. And Dr. Holmes acquired the adjacent house at 294 Beacon Street as a library extension to the old family residence (number 296, now demolished). In still later times wealthy owners, desiring an impressive dwelling in an old and established Back Bay street, would sometimes purchase two narrow brownstones dating from the sixties and replace them with a single new one. E. S. Draper in 1904 demolished Mrs. Gardner's double house at 150–152 Beacon Street, built in the early sixties, to make way for the white stone mansion which occupies the site today. Similarly the Bayard Thayer and H. P. King houses at 84 and 118 Beacon Street, dating 1911 and 1907 respectively, replace smaller and earlier structures. A. C. Burrage demolished a house in 1899 which was only eighteen years old in order to obtain sufficient room for his chateau at the corner of Commonwealth Avenue and Hereford Street.

Proper Boston, however, never quite took to these showpieces. Judge Grant, in his delightful novel of 1909 entitled *The Chippendales,* gives the flavor of Boston's resistance to such combined houses or to overly large new ones. And when one compares Boston dwellings with those of New York, the conservative nature of Back Bay tastes is unmistakable. One type of house enlargement which apparently did not offend Boston propriety was the addition of a rear ell. After the introduction of the electric light in the late eighties, preservation of daylight in back rooms of town houses was no longer so important and large ells that covered a fair proportion of the back yard were sometimes constructed. Between 1873 and 1908 five such ells were added to older houses on the north side of Beacon Street between River and Dartmouth streets.

One modification that occurred during the late 1870's in the standard house plan concerned the arrangement of the main stairway which was pushed into the middle third of the house (fig. 163). In order to fit the staircase into this new space, the old straight flight of the sixties, whose axis ran parallel to the party wall, was changed to a series of short flights arranged in a U-plan, as at 74 Commonwealth Avenue (fig. 164). As it now contained no stairway, the width of the entrance hall could be reduced, thereby leaving greater width for the front room. This solution resulted in less waste space on the upper floors as well.

Although partly a matter of planning efficiency, this modification also stemmed from the designer's desire to create a more varied and dramatic stair composition than had been achieved before. Better illustrations of this new outlook are found, of course, in the more elaborate residences of the period. An interesting example is 151 Commonwealth Avenue, the house that architect Robert Gould Shaw built for himself in 1876 (fig. 165). Although nothing could have been simpler in this particular situation than a straight flight of steps parallel to the party wall, the architect-owner, seeking a suitably dramatic composition, broke the main ascent into four separate flights and boldly pushed the bottom section into the middle of the lower hall. This intricate massing wasted space and cost money, but it made the climb to the second floor an aesthetic adventure.

1. Drawing Room
2. Dining Room
P. Pantry
H. Hall
V. Vestibule

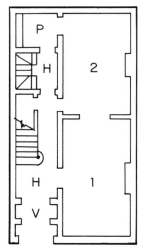

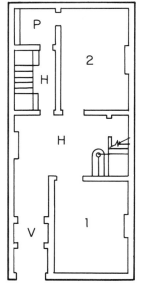

House of 1860's with side hall and straight flight of stairs

House of 1870's with stairs in middle hall and divided into three runs

163   Placement of the staircase in residences of the 1860's and the 1870's.

Another fine stair in terms of its geometric form and spatial composition was designed in 1891 by Hartwell and Richardson for the large Proctor residence at 273 Commonwealth Avenue (fig. 166). Here the visitor is led from the central hall up three stairs and through three well-proportioned arches into a splendid paneled stair cage. Four distinct ascents, two spacious landings, four changes of direction, and an abundance of light from outside windows makes the ascent to the second floor leisurely and effortless.

From the exterior 231 Commonwealth Avenue does not appear to be an unusual residence, but it has one of the most beautiful stairways in Boston (figs. 167, 168, 169). Situated in the usual middle section of the building, this handsome stairway rises to the top of the house in a splendid spiral. Within the impressive volume of the stair

164

Main stair at 74 Commonwealth Avenue, 1870. Rather than one long flight running parallel to the party wall (see figure 78), the typical stair composition of the seventies and eighties breaks into several runs with changes in direction.

165   Main stair at 151 Commonwealth Avenue, 1876, by Shaw and Shaw. This complicated composition utilizing three landings and four changes in direction illustrates the growing taste for dramatic stairways.

166   Main stair at 273 Commonwealth Avenue, 1891, by Hartwell and Richardson. Beyond the entrance hall the stairwell occupies an area some twenty by thirty feet and rises through two stories. The oak paneling and intricate massing recall Queen Anne compositions, but the arches and Ionic capitals herald approaching Classicism.

hall one is almost drawn to the upper levels by the sensuous curl of the spiraling handrail and the flood of light from the ample skylight above. An arcade runs around the stair well at the fourth level; through this arcade one can distinguish a minor stairway which continues to the uppermost floor. The architects, Rotch and Tilden, were also imaginative in the detailing of the dark mahogany newel posts and the graceful continuous banister.

The house at 306 Dartmouth Street was enlarged by the Frederick L. Ames family soon after they bought it in 1882. The result of this alteration, done by John Sturgis, was the creation of the most palatial room in the Back Bay (figs. 170, 171). The ample proportions of the great living hall, eighteen by sixty-three feet with an eighteen-foot ceiling, are augmented by a grand staircase which rises through three

167

Main stair of the J. C. Rodgers house, 231 Commonwealth Avenue, 1885, by Rotch and Tilden. The cylindrical stair cage is approached between carved mahogany newel posts and a rise of two steps.

168   Main stair at 231 Commonwealth Avenue. Second floor banister.

169   Main stair at 231 Commonwealth Avenue. The skylight provides a
flood of light and repeats the shape of the spiraling staircase.

stories. The cloister-domed ceiling of the stair well is covered with
murals on canvas by the French artist Benjamin Constant;[39] the stained
glass windows were executed by John La Farge (fig. 172). The stair
landing, as large as an ordinary room, has a monumental Jacobean
mantel cut of the same warm oak with which the rest of the hall is
paneled. This hall and the remainder of the new wing were specifically designed for large-scale entertaining. It was so planned that
guests arriving by carriage could enter the house by a side door from
the porte-cochere, take an elevator to the second floor where wraps
could be deposited, and then make a formal entrance descending the
grand staircase into the reception hall.

As we have seen, by relocating the stairway in the center of the
house it was possible to widen to eighteen feet the front room of the
typical twenty-five-foot house of the late seventies. As this was spacious enough to serve an important function, the area usually became

the drawing room, previously accommodated on the second floor. The old reception room adjacent to the entrance was then omitted. The back portion of the first floor remained the dining room as before. The second floor contained the library and one main bedroom; the upper floors as usual were devoted to minor bedchambers and servants' quarters.

In the larger houses of these years a noticeable characteristic, and one which is quite in keeping with the period's desire for invention and variety, is a tendency to contrast the various formal rooms by

170   Reception hall at 306 Dartmouth Street by John Sturgis. This monumental stair and reception hall constitute the most palatial space in a Back Bay residence. It was added in 1882 when the house was remodeled for Frederick L. Ames.

171 Reception hall at 306 Dartmouth Street. The hall was designed so that guests could ascend from the porte-cochère to the second floor by elevator, leave their wraps, and then make an entry down the grand staircase.

utilizing different styles of decoration and different woods. No better example of this could be found than the old William Powell Mason residence at 211 Commonwealth Avenue designed in 1883 by Rotch and Tilden. The interiors of this residence were maintained in their original condition by Miss Fannie Mason, who lived in the house until her death in 1950.

The library, constructed of quartered oak, has a paneled wainscot and a heavy wooden cove which almost produces the effect of a vault (fig. 173). A carved oak cornice carries around the room below the cove and the walls are covered with Morris-like tapestry. Quite different is the drawing room with delicate white woodwork, light-colored furniture, and intricate plaster ornamentation on both ceiling and frieze (fig. 174). This plaster bas-relief has a minute, delicate scale, and its designs are basically classical though they are embellished with a lighthearted fancy that distinguishes them from the serious archaeological copy work that will flourish in the nineties.

For the oval-shaped dining room of this extraordinary house, Arthur Rotch designed both woodwork, with its deep niches and mantel, and furniture (figs. 175–178). Of modified Duncan Phyfe design, the funiture is constructed of the same dark mahogany as the paneling. Both furniture and paneling, according to Miss Mason, were manufactured by the Boston cabinetmakers Davenport and Company, a firm later absorbed into Irving and Casson of Cambridge. One finds

172   Skylight in the stairwell at 306 Dartmouth Street. The stained glass was designed by John La Farge; the murals were painted by Benjamin Constant.

173   Library at 211 Commonwealth Avenue, 1883, by Rotch and Tilden.
The room has a cove ceiling and is finished in quartered oak.

statements to the effect that Boston interior trim and staircases sometimes were manufactured in England. Although it may occasionally
have been economical to employ British workmen, the Mason dining
room proves that Boston cabinetmakers in this period were not inferior to foreign shops.

Like the dining room, the stair hall of this house is paneled in dark
mahogany (fig. 179). The very ornate newel post and balustrade panels
and the highly original designs of the stairs, with closed stringers and
exposed boxing, well illustrate the inventiveness of the designer. It
also demonstrates the high level of craftsmanship which existed in the
1880's. This hall, illuminated by an arched, recessed window at the
level of the landing, is carried only to the second floor; above that,
a smaller, steeper staircase ascends to the third level. Even this minor

174

The drawing room at 211 Commonwealth Avenue is finished in ivory-colored woodwork and has delicate frieze and ceiling decoration of plaster.

175

Dining room at 211 Commonwealth Avenue. The rose and cream-colored marble mantel contrasts with the dark mahogany overmantel and wainscot.

176 Dining room niche at 211 Commonwealth Avenue. Furniture as well as woodwork were designed by Arthur Rotch and illustrate his freely inventive use of Georgian forms.

177 Dining room chair for 211 Commonwealth Avenue, designed by Arthur Rotch.

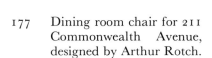

178   Detail of fig. 175. Plaster ceiling
of the oval dining room and the
silver chandelier originally made
for candles and a whale oil lamp.
The holes in the plaster ceiling
medallion carried off fumes
from the lamp.

179   Main stair hall at 211
Commonwealth Avenue.
The dark mahogany finish
and the detailing resemble
the stair of the Rodgers
house (fig. 168), which
was designed by the same
architect two years later
(1885).

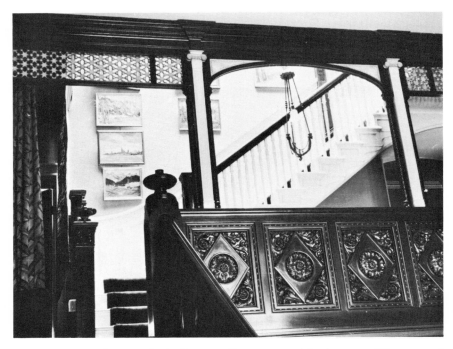

180   Second floor stair hall, 211 Commonwealth Avenue. The carved panels in the foreground are a continuation of the balustrade of the main stair; in the background is the stair to the third floor.

stairway is elaborately ornamented with delicate balustrades and an Eastlake screen of turned wooden spindles which separates it from the larger hall (fig. 180). The principal bedrooms and dressing rooms have a delightful series of Queen Anne mantels with an assortment of hoods, shelves, recesses, and cabinets (figs. 181, 182).

In terms of overall development, the changes that take place in the plan and interior design of houses of the 1870's and early eighties are of the same sort that occurred on the facade. While working with essentially the same basic elements that had been used one and two decades earlier, there is now an attempt to use these forms in a more personal and varied manner. A greater variety of woods and other kinds of building materials are employed and within a single house an attempt is made to contrast the materials and design of one room with another. Even in more modest undertakings where interior wood work and furniture were not made to order for the house, individual

181 Bedroom mantel at 211 Commonwealth Avenue. The architect, Arthur Rotch, enjoyed whimsical detail, and gave each of the house's dozen mantels a quite different character.

182 Dressing room mantel at 211 Commonwealth Avenue. The odd shelves and the charming but nonfunctional hood over the mantel are characteristic of Queen Anne work.

impressiveness was attempted by the use of ornate mantels, doors, and trim. Despite their elaboration, these parts were moderately priced because they were made in quantity with the aid of machinery.

CONSTRUCTION OF THE BACK BAY HOUSE

With the exception of a very few fireproof dwellings constructed in the late nineteenth or early twentieth centuries, the typical Back Bay house, in the terminology of the Boston Building Department, is a Class II structure. That is, its exterior walls are masonry, but its interior partitions and floor supports are of wood. In such a dwelling construction is quite simple: the longitudinal party walls of brick support the transverse floor joists; the front and back facades are free of floor loads except for the negligible weight of the floor in a bay window. Although the weight of simple ridge roofs and the steep lower slopes of the mansard are partly carried by the front and back facades, almost the entire roof load, including flat roofs and the upper slopes of the mansard, are supported on the party walls in the same fashion as floors.

With the loads of each separate floor thus transferred to the solid party walls, a great freedom is allowed in the disposition of interior partitions. As transverse partitions (those parallel to the facade) are carried independently on each floor by doubled joists, there is no necessity for a vertical alignment of these partitions on the various floors. This flexibility in the location of interior walls is especially noticeable in the placement of partitions between the stair hall and bedrooms on the upper floors (fig. 183).

When, however, brick party walls are more than twenty-three or so feet apart, an intermediate bearing wall of wood is customarily employed.[40] Running parallel to party walls, this intermediate wall is constructed of two-by-six uprights (studs). It is placed between the entrance vestibule and the adjacent parlor in the front section of the house, and between the dining room and pantry in the rear (fig. 184). Story by story, this intermediate timber wall was erected as a separate supporting member. In the basement, however, the bearing wall was customarily built of brick. Although the second-floor drawing room is sometimes extended the full 25-foot length of the house, the longi-

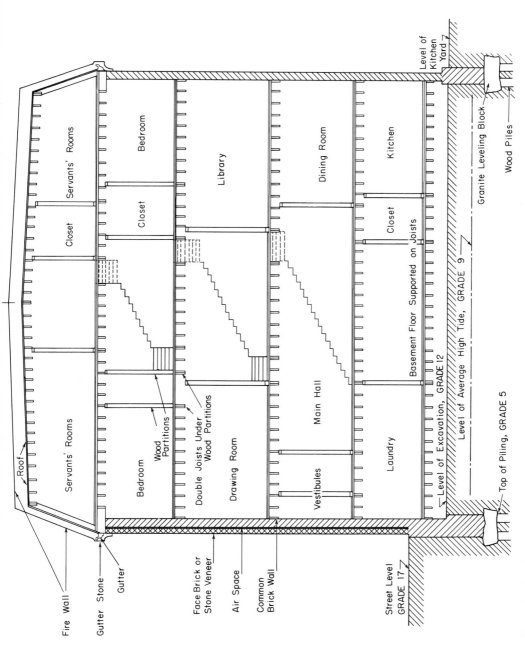

183   Longitudinal section of a typical Back Bay house of about 1865 showing transverse partitions and important grades.

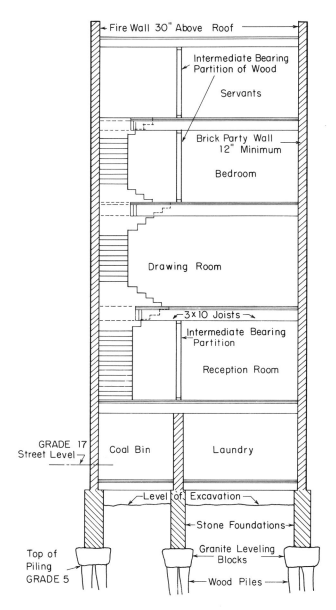

184　Transverse section of a typical Back Bay house showing lateral partitions.

tudinal bearing partition often interrupts second-floor libraries, dividing them into a main section and an alcove which are connected by some kind of arched opening or doorway (fig. 138).

In selecting the sizes of his floor timbers, the designer chose the side of safety. For example, on a twenty-foot span he would use three-by-twelve joists, twelve inches on center; a modern builder would probably reduce joist sizes to two-by-twelve and place them on fifteen-inch centers.[41] Such oversized timbers, their good quality and proper seasoning, are responsible for the excellent state of preservation of ceilings with ornamental plaster work in Back Bay houses.

It is difficult to say exactly when iron beams were added to the repertoire of the house builder, as few house plans survive to give information on the subject. Neither the Dexter nor the Bradlee drawings indicate iron beams for headers, trimmers, or for partition supports in residences. City building permits indicate that as early as 1877 I-beams were used under partitions at 65 Commonwealth Avenue, and by the middle eighties this practice had become common. Working drawings for the Loring house at 2 Gloucester Street, built in 1893, carefully prescribe twelve-inch metal beams under all interior partitions. But despite these changes, throughout the period building practices remained substantially the same as they had been in the early nineteenth century, and one can safely say that no structural advances were pioneered here. As far as one can tell from an examination of building permits, the first fireproof house was 420 Beacon Street, built in 1892 for Emily Sears after Peabody and Stearn's designs.[42]

The peculiar subsoil conditions in the Back Bay required special attention in the preparation of house foundations. Because the land on which most Back Bay houses were built had been filled, it was necessary to set the foundation walls on wooden piles which had been driven down to hard gravel. From the building permits, one learns that piles of thirty-five feet were required in the neighborhood of Dartmouth Street and at the eastern end of Bay State Road; near Gloucester Street they were less than twenty feet long; but at Kenmore Square no piles at all were needed. First by common practice and then by law, the tops of the wooden piling were cut off at Grade 5, that is, five feet above mean low tide or some twelve feet below the surface of Beacon Street (fig. 183). The piles were spaced from eighteen inches to three feet on centers and they were arranged in double rows (fig. 16). They were capped by granite leveling blocks which had to be at least four feet underground. On these leveling blocks the actual foundation walls were begun.[43] As basements were allowed no lower than Grade 12, the basement floor was at least seven feet above the top of the wooden piles. In usual practice, however, only the furnace room with its brick floor was placed at Grade 12. The kitchen, laundry, and other rooms were situated a few feet above, thus leaving a shallow air space under the basement floor of wood which was supported by joists just as any of the dwelling's upper floors.

In the course of Back Bay history some change occurs in the thickness of masonry bearing walls. Houses built in the sixties, prior to the enactment of the city building laws, often used party walls no more than eight inches thick. Even if structurally sufficient, this wall was an inadequate fire barrier, since the holes left for floor joists frequently pierced the entire eight-inch wall and thus could permit the passage of fire from one house to the next. This practice was sanctioned in the law of 1871 but it was remedied in 1892 when a twelve-inch thickness was specified for walls carried above thirty-three feet. Recesses for flues or pipe chases could be reserved in the wider wall, but its effective thickness could never be less than eight inches. New York's requirements were more stringent in this matter: a twelve-inch wall was required by 1862 and in 1871 this was increased to a sixteen-inch wall.[44]

Exterior walls, even those which did not carry floor loads, had to have a thickness equal to the party-bearing walls. Facades were often veneered with stone or face brick; the veneer was separated from the common brick core by a two- or three-inch air space. Kilham states that in the middle third of the century the brick veneers were often poorly bonded to the core, sometimes going as much as seventeen courses (about four feet) without a tie.[45] After 1872, however, the facing was required by law to bond with the core every two feet. The air space between the core and veneer provided some insulation as well as a barrier to moisture which so easily penetrates the porous sandstone veneer.

Mechanical Equipment of Buildings

One can discuss the early sanitary facilities in Back Bay dwellings only in terms of working drawings because the original fixtures and bathroom arrangements have been subject to repeated modernization. The Dexter plans for 92–99 Beacon Street, as mentioned in Chapter Four, sometimes indicate a bath for each bedroom floor, at other times but one facility for the two major bedroom floors; no running water was provided in the attic. The tub, wash basin, and water closet which now constitute an ordinary bathroom unit were separated in the forties. Wash basins were placed in individual bed or dressing rooms, the bath was located in a walk-through closet which communicated with both front and back bedrooms, while the stool was placed in a small closet (hence the name, water closet) which opened off of the main stair hall. Substantially the same arrangement was repeated in Bryant's 1860 plans for 22 Commonwealth Avenue, and it is not until the seventies that we have clear evidence of all three conveniences located in a single room, as Whitney Lewis' plans of 1875 for 504 Boylston Street show.[46] Even in large houses plumbing installations were meager. The three main bedrooms on the second floor of the palatial Mason residence at 211 Commonwealth Avenue, built in 1883, were served by a single large bathroom. It must have been in the 1890's before separate baths for individual bedrooms were generally installed in even the most luxurious houses. All major bedrooms at 303 Commonwealth Avenue, 1895, were provided with private baths. By the eighties, at long last, the servants' quarters were also equipped with an upstairs bath.

In the course of three quarters of a century substantial advances were made in the methods of heating houses. The traditional wood-burning fireplace was replaced in the early nineteenth century by coal grates when first canals and then railroads connected the seaboard cities with the coal-producing hinterland, thus bringing coal to the consumer at reasonable prices. In Boston an early furnace was in operation at the Massachusetts Medical College by 1816, but two elegant town houses built at 77–79 Mount Vernon Street in 1834 were not equipped with furnaces. By 1859 the *Boston Directory* listed eleven persons or firms as furnace builders. Furnaces in the Back Bay in the 1860's were placed in a vault about 6 by 9 feet and enclosed by brick walls, which presumably were for fire protection. From all indications these early furnaces were far from efficient, for as late as the early eighties two furnaces were required to heat a typical Back Bay house. In the forties and fifties only principal rooms on the first two floors were heated by the furnace. Hot air was introduced there by means of large floor registers set in a circular soapstone frame. In summer these registers were covered with carpeting. Upstairs rooms depended on old-fashioned coal grates for warmth.[47] As late as 1848 the Dexter plans for 90–99 Beacon Street indicate floor registers on only the first two floors. (The finished drawings make no reference to heat ducts or registers, but rough pencil additions show both heating fixtures and illuminating gas outlets.) None of these early furnaces, of course, remains in operation. From the large number of new furnace installations for which city building permits were issued during the eighties in houses which had been built in the sixties, one infers that either substantial improvements were made in furnace design in that decade or a surprising number of old furnaces wore out at just the same time. By the middle seventies circulating hot water systems were in use and it was possible to heat even the attic rooms by this means.

An important piece of equipment in all large homes of the period was the kitchen range which heated water for the household as well as cooked its food. Typical of these is the range at 72 Marlborough Street, a house built in 1868. Recessed in a brick alcove and set on a brick hearth supported on a brick vault, the heavy cast iron stove was heated with coal (fig. 185). The fire box of the range was fitted with water pipes for heating water, and the warmed water was led off in copper pipes to an adjacent copper storage tank from whence it was piped to the baths and wash basins of the upper floors. The range was selected as the source for hot water because it was kept burning day and night as long as the family was in residence. The furnace, on the other hand, would not be operated in mild weather.

Mention should also be made of the typical laundry. Its equipment consisted of a triple-compartment soapstone sink, a special built-in copper tub for heating water, a small coal stove for heating flatirons, and a special drying room off the laundry. This closetlike drying room was fitted with an ingenious revolving wooden drying crane of which very few remain (fig. 186).

185

Typical kitchen range set into a brick recess. The coal range also heated water for the household and stored it in a copper tank barely distinguishable to the right behind the stove pipe. This range was patented in 1870 by Carpenter's of Boston, as the cast inscription above the warming oven indicates. As the house in which it was photographed was built in 1866, the range must have been added at a later date.

186 Drying room adjacent to basement laundry at 226 Beacon Street, 1864. Equipped with a rotating wooden clothes crane, the drying room was warmed by means of a special coal stove which also served to heat flatirons.

Gas for illumination was introduced into Boston in 1823, three years after Paris, four years before New York, and fourteen years before it was made available in Philadelphia. This, of course, remained the standard method of lighting the Back Bay house until the nineties. In October 1879 Thomas Edison demonstrated the incandescent lamp for the first time; in 1882 the first commercial installation of electric lights in Boston was made in the Hotel Vendome.[48] Here a private eight-horsepower generator provided the current for fifty lights in the dining room and ten bulbs in the offices. By 1883 the Pennock Electric Company could offer private plants of five-hundred-light capacity for three thousand dollars, the yearly maintenance of which would amount to three dollars per bulb. A public supply of electric current was available in the Back Bay in the autumn of 1886. Another use of electricity was for the buzzer which replaced the old system of call bells centered in the kitchen (fig. 187).

With the introduction of the electric light, of course, the need for interior light wells diminished, and as more stringent fire laws also discouraged these wells, they ceased to be built. Skylights were sometimes retained, however, in the main stair halls. Here the ceiling aperture was filled with ornamental tracery and stained glass, the whole composition being retained more for purposes of decoration than illumination.

187   Call bells at 72 Marlborough Street, 1866. Situated in the basement kitchen, each bell had a slightly different tone and was connected with a pull in another room of the house by means of a taut wire. Such complicated mechanical systems became obsolete with the introduction of electric buzzers.

Relieved of the necessity of providing the maximum amount of outside light for the principal rooms, the architect was also apt to add rear ells to his house. This feature can be seen in some of the larger dwellings at the western end of Commonwealth Avenue and in the remodeling, after 1900, of numerous older houses nearer the Public Garden. W. P. Mason's music room seems to be the first Back Bay interior specifically designed to take advantage of electric illumination (fig. 235).

In the period under consideration, the hydraulic elevator also made its appearance. This feature was first employed in a private Back Bay house in 1876 though it had been installed in the area five years earlier in two apartment buildings. As late as 1890 the elevator was still an exceptional feature, there being in all the district only forty-four installations.[49] Thought of at first as no substitute for stairs but as a utilitarian trunk and furniture hoist, this feature was situated in the service hall. When later the elevator became an accepted method of vertical transportation for people, it was promoted to the front hall and the elevator shaft enclosed. Fortunately for later owners desirous of installing an elevator, the light wells and banks of interior closets so common in the earlier houses often provided accessible elevator shafts.

Beginning in the late 1880's changes caused by the use of an elevator affected a modification in the exterior appearance of a few large Back Bay residences. Of rare occurrence and late date is the reservation of the top story of the house for a major room such as a studio or ballroom. The only residence that seems to have been designed in this way was Ogden Codman's mansion of 1911 for Bayard Thayer at 83 Beacon Street. Several houses, such as 76 Beacon, built in 1847 and remodeled in 1906, installed an elevator and enlarged the top story with a studio.[50]

A second modification has to do with lowering the main entrance to about street grade while placing the principal rooms on the two levels above it. Although this results in a facade that looks quite different, the room arrangement does not vary radically from previous usage (fig. 229). Except for placing the entrance hall on the same level as the kitchen and service areas, the floors are left much as before. The first floor is occupied by a front library or family living room and a rear dining room; the second floor—still the *piano nobile* with the highest ceilings in the house—contains such formal cham-

188   Facade of 147 Beacon Street, corner of Berkeley Street, 1861. Originally the main entrance was on the first floor and fronted Beacon Street; the present grade-level entrance on Berkeley Street was substituted about 1900.

bers as drawing, music, or ball rooms. The placement of these formal rooms two full flights above the entrance, however, would have been impractical without an elevator. Within such houses a formal stair often runs only to the second principal floor where it is retained more for ceremonial purposes than for communication since most traffic between floors was carried by the elevator.

Contrary to what one might assume, there is no sure correlation between the height of a house and the use of an elevator. None of the six-level houses of the 1860's seems to have had elevators originally. In the eighties, when houses tended to shrink to four or five levels, the presence of an elevator is not necessarily indicated by a taller house. Of ten consecutive five-level houses built between 1881 and 1885 on the "sunny" side of Commonwealth Avenue between Exeter and Fairfield streets, seven have elevators, three do not. A safer generalization is that any costly house built after 1895 has an elevator regardless of its height.

The placement of the main entrance at street level requires some explanation. We saw in Chapter Five that in the Back Bay house of the 1860's the front door was placed about five feet above street grade, and approached by a flight of outside steps (figs. 44, 47). This flight was not as long as those of South End entrances which often had a dozen steps or more.

During the late 1880's, however, entrances begin to appear at grade level, an arrangement made possible by the construction of a new sewer system in 1884 which protected the basement against flooding in times of high tide. Street-level entrances are of three kinds. One solution places the entrance hall slightly below grade in the basement. It is particularly evident in remodeled houses where the old laundry room or coal bin was converted into an entrance vestibule, the old exterior steps removed, and a new interior staircase constructed to the basement entrance (fig. 106). The former vestibule on the main floor would be incorporated into the drawing room and sometimes an elevator installed.

A second solution, ordinarily found in corner locations, places the entrance on the long side of the house. Level with the street, the entrance foyer is a low-ceilinged room situated several steps above the other basement rooms. From it one ascends six or eight steps to the main floor where the principal stairs begin. This solution is found in both new houses, for example, 49 Bay State Road, 1893, and in remodeled ones, such as 147 Beacon Street, 1861, modified about 1900 (figs. 188, 222).

A third solution places the main entrance hall and a minor reception room only two or three steps above grade, and begins the principal stairs at this level also. Although this makes an imposing entrance, it reduces the basement area below to an almost unusable space with barely six feet of headroom. When this system is employed the kitchen is placed on the ground floor, not in the basement, and the dining room is on the *piano nobile.* As a result, this solution is restricted to large residences. Introduced to the Back Bay in 1884 by McKim, Mead, and White at 32 Hereford Street, the arrangement was used in all their later houses in the district (figs. 189, 190).

The convenience of baths, artificial illumination, elevators, and better heating was obviously not achieved without financial cost to the householder. Some indication of the expense of these mechanical improvements will be seen by comparing two residences built in 1834 and 1869. In his thorough book on Beacon Hill property, Allen Chamberlain records that a fine house at 77 or 79 Mount Vernon Street in 1834 cost $7500, excepting the price of the land.[51] Thirty-five years later we find that a considerably smaller house at 128 Marlborough Street, now only nineteen feet wide as against the twenty-seven-foot width of the Beacon Hill example, sold for $27,000. Allowing $6000 for the Back Bay lot and 25 percent for the builder's profit, this house must have cost somewhere in the neighborhood of $16,500 to build.[52] Of course, building materials and labor costs had risen in the interim. A carpenter's average daily wage rose from $1.40 in the 1830's to $2.40 in the late sixties; mason's pay, from $1.37 to $2.69. Although brick prices actually decreased from $10.00 per thousand in 1809 to $7.41 in 1874, lumber, which is a larger item of construction, increased from $16.00 per thousand feet in 1823 to $26.00 in 1874.[53] If, then, the cost of labor increased roughly 87 percent and materials perhaps seventy, one can estimate that actual building costs rose between 70 and 80 percent from 1834 to 1869. Thus it would have cost about $13,500 to reproduce the Beacon Hill house in 1869. Theoretically, at least, a house two-thirds that large (the size of the Marlborough Street structure) could have been built for $9000. Actually, however, it cost about $16,500. Much of the difference must be attributed to the added mechanical equipment. The Beacon Hill house had been provided with no means of heating except coal-burning grates; had no plumbing beyond a pump and well in the back yard, and presumably had only an outside privy since no other sanitary facilities are mentioned; neither was there provision for illumination.[54] The Marlborough

Street house, on the other hand, was provided with a hot-air furnace; baths and water closets on both third and fourth floors, water closets on the first floor and in the basement; a laundry and kitchen equipped with tubs, sinks, and running water; a separate system of hot water which circulated through the house; and illuminating gas piped to all rooms, halls, and large closets. It would seem, then, that these utilities cost only slightly less than the structure itself. Sixty years later Lewis Mumford, in discussing the development of modern architecture of his time, will observe that, "every new mechanical utility, however indispensable, has increased the cost of the modern dwelling, by diverting to machinery energy and money that used to go into the bare shell."[55] The tendency which began a century ago continues today to increase in almost geometric proportions.

THE AUTHENTIC REVIVALS AND TRIUMPH OF THE GEORGIAN STYLE
1885–1917

7

The Back Bay district, as we have already noted, offers a unique opportunity in which to examine the many styles of architecture that flourished and competed for favor in nineteenth century America. The matter of style emerges as the most interesting and variable aspect of Back Bay architecture since other factors, which ordinarily influence architectural development so strongly, remain constant. Because building budgets, the objectives of the builders, and the uses to which the structures were to be put vary so little, the changes that took place in architectural style emerge all the more clearly. When to this we add the facts that the buildings are both documented and well preserved, we realize the importance of the Back Bay to the history of American architecture.

In quick succession we have observed the modified Greek Revival vernacular of the 1840's and a growing preoccupation with French forms in the late fifties and sixties. The hegemony of the French Academic manner was followed by a variety of individualistic experiments and personal styles during the seventies. The middle eighties saw the beginning of a greater awareness of historical prototypes though designers still delighted in the picturesque. In the present chapter we shall observe the swift dispersal of the picturesque and personal idioms before the "Authentic Revivals," a variety of styles

of greater archaeological accuracy than any of the fashions which
hitherto had flourished in the Back Bay.

The moderate-sized houses of the 1840's, though largely eighteenth
century in composition, had been decorated with discreet accents of
Greek Revival ornamentation. Little attempt was made by the individual house to vie with its neighbor in architectural display; ornamentation was restricted to the plain brick cornice and a sturdy door
with fan and side lights set under the flush lintel of the main entrance. Since each house was conceived as an independent unit of
design, it would appear that the group attained such unity and
congruity as it had by reason of a strong and persistent tradition, not
because its designer had consciously sought that end.

In the 1850's the simple Greek Revival forms were gradually
replaced by robust but freely interpreted Renaissance details as the
sheer brick facade burgeoned with applied brownstone details: architraves, window pediments, bracket-supported hoods, stout cornices,
and an occasional oriel window. Gradually these details assumed
more importance than the flat plane of the facade to which they had
been grafted.

After 1857 Back Bay architects entered on a decade and a half of
French discipleship which used the mansard roof almost exclusively
and required that the brownstone details be used with Academic
rectitude. Thinking wistfully of the great banks of structures which
lined the new boulevards of Paris, the Back Bay designer sought
order and impressiveness but realized that he could never emulate
these if he designed the house fronts that bordered his streets in
twenty-five-foot slices. But as the social and economic structure of
Boston required no monumental palaces and but few apartment
blocks, our architect learned to organize his dwellings in groups, to
fuse narrow, separate, row houses into larger unified blocks. From
the point of urban design, the district's handsomest residential streets
were erected under this inspiration.

In the seventies the unifying force of the Academic formula dis-
solved before an individualism which expressed itself in ingenious
but sometimes undisciplined versions of Richardson Romanesque,
Ruskin Gothic, and Queen Anne styles as well as in exaggerated
variations on the old Academic theme. By reason of eccentric architectural design, variety and contrast of building materials, and an

insistent plasticity, the house in this period began to dissociate itself from its neighbors. Asserting its uniqueness and its importance, each structure bristled with distinctive, sometimes bizarre, ornamentation, and its many separate decorative features competed for the spectator's attention.

Then, just before 1890, aggressive individualism gives way to erudition and a return to quieter forms. Although the individual house strives for autonomous impressiveness, it does so by means of an accomplished use of historic architectural forms which are skillfully adjusted to the requirements of the town house. Competition among houses is less overt; one feels that the designer seeks the spectator's intelligent approval rather than his startled attention. The preponderance of taste once again calls for the Classical manner or some Renaissance variation of the Classical, and, as the century draws to an end, Boston shows a growing preference for her old Federal style.

In this sequence of architectural fashions, one can follow the American designer's search for a satisfactory idiom in which to express himself. Architecture of the forties demonstrates the vitality of the unabashedly provincial Greek Revival vernacular. The accumulation in the 1850's of architectural forms which have a vigorous but sometimes bungling Renaissance character betrays a growing artistic awareness of the world beyond New England shores. It marks the beginning of the architect's struggle for archaeological literacy, his valiant though sometimes naïve attempt to master the sophisticated but foreign idioms of the Continent. For more than a decade our Boston architect applies himself to Academic exercises until he has demonstrated to his own satisfaction and that of his clients that he is master of the urbane style of the Second Empire. Then, impatient of Academic restrictions and abounding in self-confidence, he sets forth to create a new architectural style. But soon, astonished at his own intrepidity or perhaps dismayed by the vulgar exhibitionism of some of his products, he returns to the safer ground of the Authentic Revivals; unmitigated self-confidence yields to disciplined erudition. In particular, at the century's end, there develops among Boston architects and their patrons, now thoroughly conversant with the architectural traditions of western Europe, the reassuring realization that despite history's rich artistic treasures, one of the choicest flowers of all had bloomed at home, on Beacon Hill, that the chaste Federal mansions that Bulfinch and his contemporaries had built in the early years of the nineteenth century offered the best models for the modern Boston architect.

The point of view has shifted rapidly: first simple but charming provincialism, then anxious, self-conscious essays at urbanity, next a mood of aggressive, confident self-assertion followed by a quieter mood of erudite eclecticism, and finally a return to a complacent but no longer innocent provincialism.

If the historian found it difficult to categorize in exact historical terms the naïve architectural concoctions of the Back Bay's early decades, by the 1890's he is so burdened with archaeological distinctions that a discussion of them becomes unwieldy. To mention only the main groups, he will identify designs of Italian Renaissance, Plateresque, Chateauesque, Tudor, Jacobean, High Georgian, Adam, Federal, and Louis Quinze derivation. Compared to the individualistic experimentation of the seventies and eighties, it is significant that after 1895 only one large Back Bay house, 395 Commonwealth Avenue, was built in a nonhistoric style—and that was designed by a New Yorker.

Perhaps the most important thing to notice about the new movement is that an ever increasing proportion of the Authentic Revivals is Classical in style or some Renaissance derivation of the Classical. The increasing popularity of this fashion is indicated by the fact that while styles closely related to the Classical accounted for 26 percent of the area's new building between 1885 and 1900, the percentage rises to 91 between 1900 and 1917. Since the speculative builder always follows stylistic innovation at a safe distance, the appearance in 1892 of long rows of quasi-Classical houses and the complete disappearance in new building of picturesque brownstone designs, indicate the decisiveness of the change.[1]

The triumph of the Classical over the individualistic manners of the earlier decades is, of course, not confined to the Back Bay. Symbolized by the Columbian Exposition in Chicago, one observes all over the nation how glaring, white masses of new Classical Revival buildings replace the somber, brownstone forms of the Richardson Romanesque. Significant to our study is the early date at which this new tendency appears in the Back Bay district. Here light-colored stone structures utilizing Classical forms appear at least seven years before the Chicago Exposition of 1893 and some fifteen months before McKim, Mead, and White began the plans for their famed Boston Public Library.[2] Although that New York firm is popularly identified with the Classical Revival in America, their first work in this vein was done for Boston clients. Equally significant is the fact that the Classical innovations by McKim's firm were paralleled chronologically by comparable work from several Boston offices.

We have a photographic record of some 435 residences built or drastically remodeled in the Back Bay between 1885 and 1917. By enumerating the percent of total building that would be classified under each style one can obtain an idea of the relative importance of the various styles in these decades and how their popularity varied.

	1885–1900	1900–1917
Queen Anne (all varieties)	42.6	—
Richardson Romanesque	26.3	—
McKim Classical	15.1	25.5
Federal (American Adam)	6.7	37.6
Italian Renaissance	3.9	1.0
Medieval (nonarchaeological)	2.9	—
Medieval (archaeological)	1.0	3.0
Late Georgian (Adam)	1.0	10.5
High Georgian	0.5	12.4
Louis XV	—	5.0
Other	1.0	5.0

One will see that in making this inventory rather fine stylistic distinctions have been drawn between some of the revivals. This is particularly so in the case of the Federal, Adam, and High Georgian movements—all of which derive from British building of the later eighteenth century. Equally precise archaeological differences could have been made also for the Medieval work represented in the Back Bay, but as that group is so small numerically, no attempt was made to enumerate its various subdivisions. Not every house in the district, of course, fits with equal ease into a precise archaeological category, a fact that is especially true of what we shall term the McKim Classical group. Nevertheless a vast proportion of the designs which date after 1890 invite such distinctions.

ITALIAN RENAISSANCE

Chronologically the first among the late nineteenth century Authentic Revivals in the Back Bay though numerically less important than either the American Federal or the English High Georgian is the Italian Renaissance style. As with the Federal Revival, the earliest hints of this manner in the region are to be found in the work of McKim, Mead, and White. The most orthodox work in this vein, however, was done by Boston firms.

In 1884 the Back Bay's first glimpse of the Italian Renaissance style was provided by the John Andrew house, a handsome four-story, buff brick mansion at 32 Hereford Street, on the corner of Commonwealth Avenue (figs. 189, 190). If not pure Renaissance design from a strict archaeological point of view, there can be no doubt that this style was the architect's principal source of inspiration. Here the New York designers used a number of unmistakably Renaissance features: a heavy Florentine cornice rather than a full Classical entablature; crisply detailed, light-colored stone window frames; continuous string courses at window sill levels; handsome wrought-iron balconies with supporting consoles for the windows of the *piano nobile*. Also Renaissance in derivation, though less imitative in detail, are the heavy iron grilles which protect the basement windows and the somewhat awkward Palladian window above the main entrance. Although the silhouette is contained by the usual heavy horizontal cornice and balustraded parapet, the massing of the facade is not entirely Classical. Such nonsymmetrical forms as the swell-front bay to the left of the axial entrance refer back to Boston's old Greek Revival vernacular, and both the ingenious elliptical corner tower and the clustered chimneys projecting from the hip roof of the building derive from Queen Anne practices.

The importance of this house lies not in the degree of its allegiance to a particular historical style but rather to its historical position as the first indication of the new archaeological interest in Boston. Although the biographer of Charles McKim gives the date of the Andrew house as 1888,[3] the building permit for the structure was issued on July 24, 1884, and city records mention both the installation of a hydraulic elevator in January 1885, and placement of an exterior balcony—presumably the cast-iron grille which came from

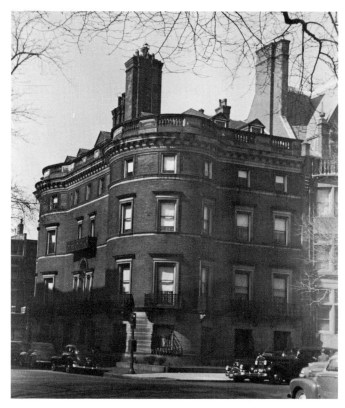

189 Facade of 32 Hereford Street, 1884, by McKim, Mead and White. Although it contains such Queen Anne features as the clustered chimney and corner tower, this design is one of the first indications in America of the approaching revival of the Renaissance style.

the destroyed Tuileries Palace—on the Hereford Street facade in February of the same year (fig. 190). This Back Bay house, therefore, precedes by one year the famous Villard mansions on Madison Avenue and it antedates by three years the celebrated Boston Public Library, a building which is usually considered the spearhead of Classical Reaction in late nineteenth century America.

The Andrew house also established a facade type that the McKim office would often follow thereafter. Entrance is gained through a street-level first floor which contains only minor rooms and which is subordinated to the *piano nobile*. On the facade, windows of the principal story are greatly elongated, but the windows diminish in width

190 Entrance of 32 Hereford Street. This house contained the first grade-level entrance in the Back Bay; the iron balcony on the third floor was salvaged from the Tuileries palace burned in the Paris uprising of 1874.

as well as height on the upper levels and terminate in the attic with stumpy, square openings; the stone cornice provides a strong horizontal note and a balustrade masks the hip roof. Architectural ornamentation is confined to the main cornice, string courses at the level of window sills, and the beautifully detailed window frames. This house is not an example of the usual basement entrance which appears in the Back Bay in 1893 because one ascends (three steps) rather than descends to the entrance hall. As the result of the low elevation of this entry and the fact that the Back Bay basement cannot be placed lower than Grade 12, the basement under the entrance hall is reduced to an almost unusable space with a ceiling height of scarcely six feet.

The general scheme of the Andrew facade was repeated on a larger scale by Stanford White in 1887 for the Algonquin Club.[4] This building, carried up five floors, is framed by octagonal bays at each extremity of the facade, and the central axis is enlivened by superimposed porches and a projecting entrance vestibule (fig. 191). The two upper levels of the facade are treated as a kind of gigantic entablature with a two-layer frieze. The small top-story windows resemble metopes of one frieze which is placed above a second frieze that is filled with sculpture in very high relief. Originally the entire ground story, heavily rusticated as today, projected out to the line of vestibule and bays, thus forming a continuous basement across the whole facade. Under such an arrangement, the three large, floor-length middle windows of the second floor opened onto a terrace which somewhat masked their ungainly proportions; this is still the case of the entrance vestibule and the window above it. Similarly the projecting terrace minimized the unpleasant contrast in scale of these windows and other elements of fenestration. The original basement, projecting beyond the building line for the full eighty-nine-foot width of the facade, was in direct violation of property restrictions, and, as we have seen, the club was ordered by the Commonwealth in 1889 to revise the facade, lawfully restricting each section of projecting bay to the maximum allowed length of eighteen feet. The Palladian windows in the club and the Andrew house are similar in design, both having an awkward quality which results from the difficulty in adjusting the Palladian shape to the mechanical requirements of a double hung window.

Following the Andrew house by two years, the Boston firm of Shaw and Hunnewell did two houses which are notable for their early and accurate use of Renaissance detail. The residence for Elizabeth Skinner at 266 Beacon Street was begun on January 1, 1886, and the Charles Head residence, at 412 Beacon Street, a year later. The white limestone surfaces and the restrained yet accurate detail of these designs appear so advanced that one might assume that they date from the twentieth century. But information given on the building permits corresponds with the present houses, and in 1948 Mr. G. Mott Shaw identified both houses as the work of his father's firm.

The Skinner house, occupying a forty-foot frontage, achieves an impressive monumentality by the sober use of a colossal order run

191   Algonquin Club, 219 Commonwealth Avenue, 1887, by McKim, Mead and White. The first story, which originally projected as far forward as the entrance bay and extended the entire length of the building, was revised in 1889 to conform to the setback regulations established by the Commonwealth.

192   Facade of 266 Beacon Street, 1886, by Shaw and Hunnewell. Executed in white limestone, this is a remarkably restrained design for
the eighties.

through the two upper stories (fig. 192). A balustrade supporting urns masks the attic roof, and the basement story is differentiated from the upper floors by its vermiculated surfaces. Although containing some carved stone ornamentation, the architectural composition of this facade is achieved with relatively few elements, and it is a far better integrated design than either the Andrew house or the Algonquin Club.

Apart from the fourth and fifth stories and the basement entrance, which were added in 1927 when this structure was converted into doctors' offices, the facade of the Charles Head house even more than the Skinner residence resembles work done in the 1920's (fig. 193). Except for the swags and lions heads in the main frieze (the same details appear on the Skinner house), the ornamentation here is restricted to a few architectonic forms. The relief and moldings are delicate and they cast sharp shadows on the light-colored stone. In addition to crisp architrave moldings, window openings are set off from the wall by thin panels which break forward from the wall surface. The tops of these panels are capped by light cornices. Window frames of the first floor are elaborated by consoles which support the separate cornices, by the addition of a banded garland relief on the lintel, and by an egg and dart design on the architraves. The main cornice is supported by modillions as well as a dentil course. The restraint of this design is extraordinary for 1887.

Shaw and Hunnewell were commissioned to design other structures in the Back Bay but they did not again employ the Italian Renaissance style. It is regrettable that, having pioneered so successfully in this idiom, they did not continue to popularize it. Instead it was left to the firm of Peabody and Stearns to exploit the style. Their first attempt in 1892 at 420 Beacon Street was a house for Emily Sears. Enlivened with richly carved areas of Quattrocento ornament about the entrance and in the pediments of the first-story windows, the facade lacks the restraint that distinguishes the work of Shaw and Hunnewell (fig. 194). Here, as in their later houses of Italianate design, Peabody and Stearns fail to rise above a pastiche of richly detailed but often unrelated ornament. One is aware of the indecisiveness of this work when he compares it with the work that the same firm was doing five or six years earlier, houses such as 183 or 251 Marlborough Street, where the designers had used materials with great skill. The district's last Italianate house, 310 Beacon Street, was erected in 1903.

193   Facade of 412 Beacon Street, 1887, by Shaw and Hunnewell. Like the house in fig. 192, this Italian Renaissance design could easily be mistaken for a work of the 1920's. The top two stories and basement entrance were added in 1927.

194   Facade of 420 Beacon Street, 1892, by Peabody and Stearns. A more
      elaborate but less discriminating use of Italian Renaissance details
      than the two houses by Shaw and Hunnewell.

OTHER RENAISSANCE REVIVALS

Following this successful adaptation of the Italian Renaissance, a series
of minor revivals of other Renaissance-derived styles took place in the
Back Bay. At least four of these can be mentioned: Chateauesque,

Plateresque, Tudor, and Louis Quinze. Often these groups number only one or two houses, but they are important to our present study because they illustrate how the architect in the last part of the century sought self-expression through an erudite resuscitation of a historic style, not by creating a new personal manner nor by straining the bonds of old styles.

Deriving inspiration from the sixteenth century chateaux of the Loire Valley are several Back Bay houses that can be labeled Chateauesque.[5] Artistically as well as historically, these examples are less important than Hunt's famous W. K. Vanderbilt mansion on Fifth Avenue or his fabled "Biltmore House" in North Carolina.

The first of the Boston "chateaux" was Carl Fehmer's 1882 residence for Oliver Ames at the corner of Commonwealth and Massachusetts avenues (figs. 195, 196). Perhaps this style was chosen by millionaires because its hybrid character permitted the picturesque massing of the Middle Ages as well as the lavish sculptural decoration of the Renaissance. In the case of the Ames house, the most interesting feature of the exterior is the wealth of exquisitely carved brownstone relief. The delicate pilaster arabesques and friezes filled with floral forms contrast with crisp rectangular architectural forms. One notes especially the panels of relief above the first story windows. Here *putti* intertwine with plant forms and engage in various homey activities relating to the use of the corresponding room inside: eating, playing musical instruments, conversing, and so forth. This as well as several other features of the house had been used somewhat earlier by R. M. Hunt in the Vanderbilt mansion of 1879.[6] The stone carving for the Ames house was done in the Boston yards of the Charles River Stone Company, a subsidiary of Norcross Brothers who operated this plant in addition to their general contracting business. Equally fine stone carving was executed for the Thayer mansion, 239 Commonwealth Avenue, by W. D. Connery and Company in the same year.

In 1889 Andrews and Jacques designed a modified chateau at the corner of Beacon and Hereford streets (448 Beacon). Although they utilized the famous shell cornice of Chambord, the dormer windows seem meager and unstructural since the fronts do not relate to the flanks. More interesting is the quality of the carving which has a flat, lacelike scale that is almost reminiscent of Louis Sullivan's decoration. The designers' choice of tan brick and red sandstone creates so strong a contrast and is so different from the usual color scheme of the

195   Facade of 355 Commonwealth Avenue, 1882, by Carl Fehmer. Inspired by sixteenth century chateaux and constructed for Oliver Ames, this dwelling is one of the most lavish in Boston. Its details illustrate the trend toward archaeological accuracy which became prominent in the late eighties.

Back Bay that it isolates the building. Infinitely more successful in general design, in its use of the corner tower, and in the carved ornamentation surrounding the main entrance is Peabody and Stearns' house of 1886 for Charles Francis Adams at 20 Gloucester Street (fig. 197).

The Burrage mansion at 314 Commonwealth Avenue is the only

Back Bay structure comparable to the Vanderbilt mansion in degree of elaboration (figs. 198, 199). Its massing of picturesque gables and towers and its surcharge of crisp, deeply undercut, stone ornamentation makes this edifice one of the most conspicuous along the avenue. Quite literal in his transcriptions from Chenonceaux, the architect, Charles Brigham, did not achieve anything in this design that Richard Morris Hunt had not accomplished twenty years earlier. Built as late as 1899, the Burrage house serves principally to illustrate how slowly the New York idea of magnificence penetrated Boston. Following its belated flowering in the Burrage mansion, the Chateauesque style left but one more descendant, the remodeled facade of about 1905 at 327 Commonwealth Avenue.

196   Detail of fig. 195. Panels of delicately carved stone relief contain *rinceaux* as well as *putti* engaged in homey activities appropriate to the particular room within. The figure on the left holds a book, those to the right are greeting each other.

197   Facade of 20 Gloucester Street, 1886, by Peabody and Stearns.
        Inspired also by Medieval forms, this dwelling, built for Charles
        Francis Adams, is less concerned with a display of archaeological
        details than the Ames or Burrage mansions.

Julius H. Schweinfurth reverted to sixteenth century Spanish forms
when he designed 304 Commonwealth Avenue in 1895 (fig. 200). The
candelabrum motif, which is worked in bas-relief over the third-story
windows and around the entrance arch suggests specific Plateresque
sources, but the deeply undercut leaf patterns in the archivolts of the
window frames indicate that the designer also admired sixteenth century building of the Loire Valley. If one is curious about the designer's
source of inspiration, he has only to look at Plate XIII of Schwein-

furth's own *Sketches Abroad* to find the designer's field of interest if not his actual model.[7]

Chapman and Frazer were the Back Bay's leading advocates of the late Medieval and early Renaissance styles of England. Number 240 Commonwealth Avenue is a Jacobean pile with a handsome entrance ornamented with pilasters and strapwork (fig. 201). The window treatment in the second story of the bay is an ingenious affair

198   Facade of 314 Commonwealth Avenue, 1899, by Charles Brigham. The Albert Burrage house is one of the few Back Bay houses that aspires to Fifth Avenue magnificence, and it did not set a precedent in Boston.

199   Detail of fig. 198. The architect reproduces details from chateaux of the Loire Valley much as R. M. Hunt had done twenty years earlier in the W. K. Vanderbilt house in New York.

which combines a maximum amount of glass area with a certain archaeological plausibility. The same firm in 1905 designed a large stone Tudor house for William Lindsay at 225 Bay State Road (fig. 202). Provided with an unusually wide lot (seventy-six feet), the architects were able to give this edifice the informal mass of a country dwelling; the main body of the structure is pushed to the rear of the lot overlooking the river, thereby leaving enough space for a projecting ell and a walled garden adjacent to the street in front.

201   Entrance of 240 Commonwealth Avenue, 1903, by
Chapman and Frazer. The
Jacobean entrance for this
house is further evidence
of the variety of archaeological styles found in Boston after 1885.

200   Entrance of 304 Commonwealth Avenue, 1895, by
Julius Schweinfurth. Plateresque Spain inspired portions of the beautiful ornamentation for this house.

202   Facade of 225 Bay State Road, 1905, by Chapman and Frazer. As
        an unusually large lot permitted a freer and more informal massing,
        this Tudor mansion creates the most convincing Medieval effect in
        the whole area.

Although the composition of the Bay State Road house is crowded
with so many features that they compete with one another (at least
the pointed, traceried windows of the first floor bay and two sets of
dormer windows by the main chimney should have been eliminated),
there is a plausibility about this building. Built solidly of stone and
organized as a convincing three-dimensional mass, one is reminded
of a sixteenth century manor house. Clearly the architect knew English architecture first hand, and one could probably find actual prototypes for most of the features included in the design.

Such a composition makes a telling comparison with earlier phases
of Gothic Revival in the Back Bay. The Gothic content of 165 Beacon
Street, built less than forty years earlier (1869), consisted of little more
than pointed arches and tracery that might have been cut out with
a cookie cutter (fig. 110). A somewhat later version of Gothic Revival,
121 Commonwealth Avenue, 1872 (fig. 115)—more Ruskin than Medi-

eval—gains external color and asserts the importance of good crafts-manship by the use of colored tile insets. Both buildings are standard row houses with nothing more to relate them to the Middle Ages than the decoration applied to their front walls, and neither designer singles out a particular moment of the Middle Ages to emulate. In contrast, the 1905 version is more convincing in its massing and use of mate-rials, and its style and details are readily identified as Late Tudor. Although this archaeological accuracy is not necessarily an indication of progress, it does illustrate the change that takes place in American architectural practice during the late nineteenth century.

Finally, in this enumeration of Authentic Revivals, mention must be made of the area's four French houses. In 1904 J. H. Schweinfurth designed twin houses at 426 and 428 Beacon Street (fig. 203). Despite differences in frontage, these houses are skillfully fused into a unified composition. Number 426, twenty-nine feet wide, is arranged with three windows across the front while its neighbor with but twenty-two feet of frontage is given only two. The closer fenestration of the first facade necessitated smaller window heads while the wider win-dow spacing of the second permitted heavy circular pediments filled with sculptural decoration. The variation in window spacing and de-gree of elaboration is carried into the third floor and dormers. Com-mon to both facades are the entrance design, the sturdy stone consoles that support the continuous wrought-iron balcony of the *piano nobile,* the highly ornate entablature and parapet, and the particularly hand-some mansard roof. This design is unmistakably French; one feels it in the complicated stereometry of the ground-floor windows and in the surcharge of cut stone ornament which animates the entablature and the window enframements.

It is instructive to compare this 1904 version of a French building with one erected in the Back Bay forty years earlier (fig. 40). Both designs announce their French allegiance with mansard roofs and stone facades. The earlier brownstone design, though it employs certain theoretically correct profiles and proportions, is rigid and self-conscious; it is drawn according to rule rather than from an easy familiarity with French building. Also there is a thin and timid quality about the stone ornamentation which appears to be skin-deep; the main cornice is wood painted to resemble brownstone. Starting with a for-eign architectural grammar which he had memorized but in which he still felt somewhat alien, the earlier Boston designer instinctively

203   Facade of 426–428 Beacon Street, 1904, by Julius Schweinfurth. The degree to which the feeling of a French building is captured in this design can be understood by comparing it with one built forty years earlier (fig. 40).

fused it with a good deal of his native architectural expression. The result, as we have already seen, is not without merit, but it could never be confused with a building in France.

The architect of the 1904 house had traveled extensively in France as recipient of the Rotch Traveling Fellowship and had sketched and admired the monuments of Paris until he understood their idiom as well as their grammar. In designing 426 and 428 Beacon Street, he infused the facade with a verve lacking in the stiff, academic design of the Civil War building. If the earlier structure had the look of paper architecture with the French Academic ornamentation confined to an eight-inch veneer of brownstone, the later one has a convincing three-dimensional quality. Its robust ornamentation has the feeling of being carved out of the same material as the structural fabric of the building. The elliptical recesses in which are placed the windows and doors of the ground story suggest that the front wall is solidly built of stone; the stone balcony, the heavy window pediments, the strong cornice--all project freely from the facade as though no longer fearful of losing their balance and toppling forward.

Two other French facade houses are located at 128 and 130 Commonwealth Avenue. Built in 1882, these adjacent structures were remodeled about 1905 in the Baroque fashion that had been popularized by the Ecole des Beaux Arts (fig. 204). The files of the city Building Department, usually so complete, fail to mention these alterations. The facades were evidently entirely rebuilt and some new interior paneling and mantels added; the floor system and partitions of the old structures, particularly on the upper levels, were retained, however. Although these designs resemble the Beacon Street houses just discussed in many respects, they recall Paris not so much as they do sections of New York which were fashionable between 1900 and the First World War. These two houses seem rather out of place on Commonwealth Avenue, and, as in the case of the chateauesque Burrage house, their presence serves to remind us of Boston's resistance to Knickerbocker fashions and of her overwhelming allegiance to her native traditions.

THE McKIM CLASSICAL

A rather numerous class of houses must be recognized which do not fall within any precise archaeological category but which are clearly members of the Classical family. Extremely popular in the 1890's, designs of this nature may be grouped under the name of McKim Classical. The term denotes no historic variation of Classical arch-

204   Facade of 128–130 Commonwealth Avenue. Constructed in 1882, the
        facades of these two dwellings were rebuilt about 1905 in the cur-
        rently fashionable Beaux Arts Baroque manner.

itecture but a manner of adapting Classical ornamentation to the requirements of modern building. In structures of this group one finds
an accurate reproduction of Classical detail, but it is used in accord
with the needs of the multiwindowed, many-storied city edifice. Traditional Classical horizontality is recalled by subdividing the facade,
which in cities is almost always vertical, into a number of horizontal

zones in which each zone is a somewhat complete unit of design in itself. Because porticos or even pilasters interfere with a system of fenestration that provides maximum interior lighting, these features are usually eliminated. Such Classical detail as is used is employed chiefly to frame openings and to provide horizontal accents between floors and at the cornice. Otherwise, wall surfaces are usually left plain. Displaying a marked preference for white limestone, poised, symmetrical, and dignified, facades of this class seek monumentality rather than display or liveliness.

A splendid example of this austere Classical manner is the old Nickerson mansion, slightly remodeled but for many years beautifully maintained by the Dudley Pickmans, at 303 Commonwealth Avenue (fig. 205). This house, the last and also the finest residence by McKim, Mead, and White in the Back Bay, was built in 1895. All decorative trivia have been eliminated from its facade. The light-colored granite out of which the edifice is built is appropriate for the reserved, solemn quality of the design. Here the few, large, symmetrically placed windows do not compete with the geometry of the elliptical facade nor with the few areas of decoration around the entrance and along the cornice. Although only thirty-three feet wide—not an unusual size for later mansions along Commonwealth Avenue—the house gives the impression of being larger and more imposing than its neighbors. Indeed, this house is probably the most striking instance in the Back Bay of the individual house attaining an impressive, self-sufficient, yet restrained monumentality.

The interior of the Pickman house attains the same largeness of scale that characterizes the exterior. Axial planning is carefully developed on the first two floors and the use of pilasters and columns in the entrance hall emphasizes this symmetry and imparts a sense of order and spaciousness to what might otherwise have been an insignificant hall area. The principal stair with its handsome bronze railing extends only to the third floor, but a service stair and elevator, each enclosed in a well on the other side of the main hall, communicate with all floors (figs. 206, 207). The dining room on the first floor and both rooms—library and drawing room—on the second, each extending the full width of the house, are spacious areas. In the dining room the richly carved mantelpiece, isolated against a plain panel of Siena marble, imparts a sense of ornamental dignity without descending to active competition with other decorative elements in the room (fig. 208).

205   Facade of 303 Commonwealth Avenue, 1895, by McKim, Mead and
White. The most striking instance in the Back Bay of an individual
house attaining an impressive monumentality.

Peabody and Stearns chose the McKim Classical in 1892 for the
Herbert Sears house at 297 Commonwealth Avenue. Though not abjuring ornamentation to the same extent as its neighbor at 303, this
house attains considerable distinction by reason of the exquisite low
relief decoration around the window and door frames. Seen in the
full force of direct sunlight, this delicate bas-relief "bleaches out,"

but observed in the raking light of early morning or late afternoon it stands out effectively against the plain surfaces of the facade. Also successful is the contrast of heavy patterns of cast iron balconies against the white stone. This facade appears to have directly influenced two smaller houses in the district: 77 Bay State Road (1900) and 285 Commonwealth Avenue (1905).

That a pleasant variation of the McKim Classical can be created even when the style is greatly simplified is demonstrated by 479 Commonwealth Avenue, 1895, and 246 Beacon Street, 1886 (figs. 209, 210).[8] Here only entrance, window trim, cornice, and basement are of stone, the remainder of the facade being carried up in buff or red brick. Intricate relief decoration is all but eliminated and the stone moldings depend for their effect on their proportions and the contrast of materials.

206

Main stair at the first floor, 303 Commonwealth Avenue. The grand stair was retained primarily as a symbol since most of the vertical traffic was carried by an elevator.

207   Main stair at the *piano nobile,* 303 Commonwealth Avenue. The splendid bronze balustrade and the screen of columns add dignity to the
interior.

208   Dining room at 303 Commonwealth Avenue. Running the full 33-foot
width of the house, the spacious dining room is dominated by a
splendid mantel of Siena marble.

209   Facade of 479 Commonwealth Avenue, 1895, by Winslow and Wetherell. A competent example of the McKim Classical, a classification which is not so much a precise archaeological variation of Classical architecture as a manner of adapting Classical ornament to the requirements of a modern, vertically organized, multiwindowed structure.

210   Facade of 246 Beacon Street, 1886, by Peabody and Stearns. This is
       the first example of the popular McKim Classical to appear in the
       Back Bay.

This style unfortunately was often bungled by mediocre designers
and it soon fell into discredit. Typical of such pedestrian work is the
row at 482–490 Beacon Street, an uninteresting creation of light-
colored brick, and the old Minot house at 409 Commonwealth Avenue,
a meretricious edifice without scale and hardly worthy of Peabody

and Stearns. Speculative builders also did their part to run the style into the ground. As early as 1894, a group of three McKim Classical houses were built of ugly yellow brick by a speculator at 349–353 Commonwealth Avenue, and in the late nineties long blocks of undistinguished houses were run up on Bay State Road in the same style. Commercial adaptations of the McKim Classical sometimes have a routine competence, exemplified by the former hotels Lafayette and Tuileries (the latter now a college dormitory, the former a religious hostel) which were built from the same basic *parti* in 1895 and 1896 by McKay and Dunham, architects and contractors (fig. 211).

Along with the Italian Renaissance style to which it is in some respects similar, the McKim Classical makes its debut in 1886. Number 246 Beacon Street (fig. 210), designed by Peabody and Stearns, is

211   Hotel Tuileries, 270 Commonwealth Avenue, 1896, by McKay and Dunham. Built as an apartment hotel, this structure illustrates a routine handling of McKim Classical forms.

both the earliest and one of the most pleasing examples of this manner. The McKim Classical appears for the last time in 1903 at 285 Commonwealth Avenue.

An attempt to establish a terminal date for this style may be arbitrary. After 1900 so few residences were built in the Back Bay—in all, less than a hundred dwellings over a period of fourteen years—that this restricted activity may not offer a completely accurate record of contemporary architectural tastes. In attempting to trace the currents of taste during these late years, we find ourselves on the same uncertain grounds as, in Chapter Four, when we investigated the origins of the French Academic style in the late fifties. Had greater numbers of Back Bay houses been built in the present century, one would probably have discovered slightly different terminal dates for some of the movements treated in this chapter.

THE GEORGIAN REVIVALS

Two general observations should be made regarding the last family of styles which we shall discuss and which we group together as the Georgian Revivals. The three main subdivisions of this movement— High Georgian, Late Georgian or Adam, and Federal—account for over half of the residences (60.5 percent) built in the Back Bay after 1900. One should also remember that Georgian forms were latent in Back Bay architecture long before these three styles appear as relatively pure revivals in the 1890's. Indeed, the critic may question whether it is a Georgian revival or survival. A good case could be made to the effect that Georgian forms had never completely disappeared from the Boston scene.

From our study of Back Bay houses thus far one thing should be clear: that basically the plan and scale of the Back Bay house never varies too greatly from its Beacon Hill ancestor. The style of architecture and the general appearance may change, but the types and numbers of rooms remain substantially the same. One might even argue that the relative sobriety and restraint of Back Bay architecture in the post–Civil War era, characteristics which certainly will impress anyone who compares this district with residential construction elsewhere in America at that time, is due in part to the quiet, restraining influence which Beacon Hill exerted on her younger counterpart down the hill.

Particular attention should be called to the work of Snell and Gregerson who in the sixties and seventies kept alive a good deal of the Beacon Hill spirit in their work. Especially important are the two houses at 58-60 Commonwealth Avenue.[9] The facades of these dwellings, designed as early as 1866 by Snell and Gregerson, employ the old swell front so popular in the 1830's and 1840's (fig. 212). In keeping

212   Facade of 58–60 Commonwealth Avenue, 1866, by Snell and Gregerson. Originally a row of four houses, they illustrate the tenacity of the Georgian tradition in Boston and the fact that it did not die out during the height of Victorian taste.

with Late Georgian practice, pilasters of colossal order were retained as supports for the main cornice and balustrade, the only time this feature was used for a Back Bay house in the sixties. Conspicuous by its absence for the decade in which the houses were built is the mansard roof. Even the entrance porch with its blocky rustication is reminiscent of Georgian—if not Beacon Hill—prototypes.[10] In the case of number 60, where later changes have replaced the original plate glass windows by an eighteen light, double hung sash, the general effect of the exterior is strikingly akin to Beacon Hill.

Although of mixed stylistic antecedents, the Cochrane house at 257 Commonwealth Avenue has Georgian characteristics (fig. 213). Built in 1886, the third of the McKim office's Back Bay commissions, this house reminds us that its designers had already made a sympathetic study of eighteenth century American architecture. But despite the obvious Georgian qualities of his facade the designer was reluctant to give up the Renaissance style entirely, and the design stands midway between the firm's Renaissance Andrew residence of 1884 and its first fully developed Georgian houses of 1890. Characteristically Federal are the graduated story heights and the garlanded window heads capped by cornices on the first floor, the elliptical bay window, and the main cornice topped with a balustrade. In the design of the front entrance, however, the architects avoid Yankee prototypes when they employ a circular pediment of Renaissance design punctuated with a marble oculus and supported with modillions and light pilasters, and they fill the glass panel of the door with a grille of wrought iron. The system of diminishing the widths of upper windows along with their heights is awkward.

Inside the designers made liberal use of eighteenth century details although the general feeling is most un-Georgian. This is especially true of the great, two-story reception hall where the elliptical second-story lantern and skylight, the rectangular shapes of the first- and second-story halls, and the three-story stair cage fuse into a very complex spatial organization (figs. 214, 215). This space with its monumental stairway has a calculated and dramatic quality about it that is closer to Queen Anne living halls than to the matter-of-fact center hall of the eighteenth century mansion with its straight flights of steps. For such details as spiraling newel posts (fig. 216), turned balusters, or the delicately carved trim of the lantern, however, the designer may well have had recourse to the sketch books made nine years before

213   Facade of 257 Commonwealth Avenue, 1886, by McKim, Mead and
      White. Except for the entrance and rather awkward plate glass
      windows, this design recalls Federal architectural forms.

when the associates made their "celebrated sketching trip to the
North Shore." The mantel in the reception room also recalls Adamesque wood carvers at their best (fig. 217), but the hall fireplace with
its yellow marble facing and especially the dining room with its relief
of rinceaux delicately cut in satiny mahogany owe more to Renaissance or even antique precedent than to the eighteenth century.

Keeping in mind these indications of a continuing interest in

214   Stairway at 257 Commonwealth Avenue. Although the space composition of the large central hall conforms to Queen Anne concepts, the detailing of the woodwork is close to Georgian models.

215   Central hall, second floor, at 257 Commonwealth Avenue. The two levels of the hall are connected by a large elliptical well and the area is lighted by a skylight of similar shape.

216   Detail of fig. 214. The balusters and newel post are similar to examples found in New England mansions dating from the third quarter of the eighteenth century.

217   Wooden mantel in the reception room at 257 Commonwealth Avenue is pure Adamesque design.

Colonial architecture, we can proceed to look at three distinct revivals of the 1890's which make scrupulous distinctions between the different phases of eighteenth century work.

THE FEDERAL STYLE

If not chronologically the first, certainly the most important of the late nineteenth century architectural revivals in Boston was the Federal. Making its appearance in 1890, this style leaped into immediate prominence, and by 1917 it had been used for forty-nine houses. Aesthetically, as well as numerically, this group is outstanding, and several of the structures built here on the filled land of the Back Bay region are the artistic peers of the chaste edifices erected eighty years earlier on the slopes of Beacon Hill.

Credit for the movement cannot be ascribed to any one individual as two different architectural firms first produced good Federal houses in the same year. One must admit, however, that a prominent role in this revival was played by McKim, Mead, and White, who used the idiom for three residences built as early as 1890. They also were active in popularizing the movement throughout America.

The year 1890 saw the firm produce three unusually handsome Federal Revival designs in the Back Bay. The largest of these, 199 Commonwealth Avenue, designed for J. A. Beebe, has a striking similarity to the ample, four-square mansions built by early nineteenth century merchants (fig. 218). There is unquestionably a Republican air about this wide, three-storied facade with its balanced swell-front bays, granite basement, simple cornice and balustrade, and handsome portico with recessed fan-lighted entrance. The entrance of this house is not unlike the design of Bulfinch's two splendid houses at 39 and 40 Beacon Street. Indeed, transported to Beacon Hill, this house would elicit the admiration which today it is arbitrarily denied because of its associations with the "Brown Decades." The principal difference between a Bulfinch front and this composition by McKim is the latter's lack of scale caused only by the absence of muntin subdivisions in the large plate glass windows.

The interior of the Beebe mansion also has an early nineteenth century dignity but its plan is handled with more freedom. Instead

218   Facade of 199 Commonwealth Avenue, 1890, by McKim, Mead and
White. Except for the plate glass windows which destroy the scale,
this house would be completely at home on Beacon Hill. The entrance
resembles those at 39–40 Beacon Street designed by Bulfinch.

of the traditional stair placement in the center hall in line with the
front entrance, we find the main stairway in the right rear corner of
the house, displacing the fourth room from its customary place in the
symmetrical eighteenth century plan. In contrast to a Georgian stair
with a straight flight of steps to the second floor, this composition
shows the typical dramatic organization of the late nineteenth century (fig. 219). Recessed behind a screen of Ionic columns and changing
direction three times, it ascends to the upper floor in four easy stages.
Here, as in the Proctor house, the intricately turned newel and balus-

219   Stair hall at 199 Commonwealth Avenue. Although the main stair has a dramatic composition admired by late nineteenth century designers, the detailing derives from eighteenth century models.

ters invite direct comparisons with eighteenth century examples, and the same is true of other details of the hall woodwork.

The second McKim, Mead, and White project of 1890 was a double house at 413–415 Commonwealth Avenue (fig. 220). The spirit of these facades is that of Beacon Hill, though nothing exactly like the rounded, white stone lunettes above the second-story windows can be found there. Especially interesting is the reappearance after an absence of more than two generations of the muntin divisions in the windows and outside shutters.

Several Boston firms did equally important pioneer work in this idiom. Most noteworthy is the work of Little and Browne. In 1890 Arthur Little, who twelve years earlier as an architectural student had been one of the first to raise his drawing pen in praise of old Colonial work, built for himself one of the most charming residences in the Back Bay (fig. 221). The arrangement of the house at 57 Bay State Road with its two-story ballroom is unusual, although it will be remembered that Jonathan Mason's mansion on Mount Vernon Street

220   Facade of 413–415 Commonwealth Avenue, 1890, by McKim, Mead and White. This design is one of the first in the Back Bay to revive the use of muntin divisions in windows in an attempt to emulate Federal precedents.

221   Facade of 57 Bay State Road, 1890, by Arthur Little. Designed by
the architect for himself, this is one of four houses erected in 1890
which uses the Federal style with fidelity.

(destroyed in 1836) had a two-story, ground-floor ballroom lighted by
a great Palladian window. As the Mason house had been designed by
Bulfinch, Mr. Little had good authority for the unusual feature of
his house. Woodwork details, cornices, and the like also demonstrate
familiarity with Federal precedent. Very unlike eighteenth century
American practice, however, is the great freedom shown in the organization of the interior space. No two rooms on any of the first three
floors occur at quite the same level, and the ceiling height of each
room is determined by its functional needs. Although a little tight
in scale because of the restricted size of the Back Bay lot, the flow
of space from the central stair hall to the various rooms opening off
it and the interrelation of the ballroom with a landing of the stair
which also serves as a musicians' gallery is of great architectural interest. The spatial movement of this house is more vertical than the
quieter, horizontal flow found in living halls of Queen Anne country

houses in America. Rather this manipulation of space relates to the mature work of Norman Shaw in various London town houses.

Several other residences in the Federal style were built between 1893 and 1907 by Little and Browne. The large dwelling at 49 Bay State Road (1893) employs a number of familiar Beacon Hill motifs with success: the slightly recessed elliptical arcade of the ground story, the attenuated pilaster strips which run through two stories, and the somewhat ungrammatical manner in which the third-story windows interrupt the architrave of the major entablature (fig. 222). Also Fed-

222   Facade of 49 Bay State Road, 1893, by Little and Browne. This design combines correct Federal detail with an ingenious street-level entrance at the front of the elliptical bay.

eral is the big elliptical bay projecting on the axis of the main facade. For related designs at 117 Bay State Road (1899), 393 Commonwealth Avenue (1899), and 407 Commonwealth Avenue (1901), Arthur Little also returned to the early nineteenth century, though here he moves closer to the Adam tradition with the stone panels filled with swags in bas-relief. Although the disparity in window proportions of these houses reminds us of Queen Anne license, the triple windows do have precedence in small houses built on Beacon Hill in the 1820's.[11]

Another noteworthy specimen of the Federal Revival is the residence at 2 Gloucester Street built in 1893 for W. C. Loring by W. Y. Peters (fig. 223). The exterior of this structure so closely approximates an early nineteenth century appearance that one is rather shocked to discover that the neatly detailed entablature with its delicate pattern of triglyphs and elliptical rosettes is made of stamped metal.

223   Facade of 2 Gloucester Street, 1893, by W. Y. Peters. The exterior detailing of this house has the delicacy of Bulfinch work, yet the main cornice is executed in pressed iron.

224 Doorway in stair hall, main floor, at 2 Gloucester Street. Executed in London Putty, the ornamentation of this door frame outdoes in elaborateness the Federal models it emulates.

The interior of this house, calamitously changed when the structure was converted into apartments, once revealed a profusion of wood trim so skillfully detailed that the only clue to its later date was too great ornateness. The delicate moldings and reliefs were made of an inexpensive mastic known as London Putty which could be cast in intricate designs and glued to the flat wood surface. When covered with several coats of paint, this molded decoration could scarcely be differentiated from more expensive hand-carved trim which had also been painted. Faced with such facility for ornamentation, the designer could not restrain himself. The hall door (fig. 224) has three elements (pilasters, an extremely rich architrave, and an elaborate entablature cap) which crowd each other and compete for attention. Any one of these features would probably have sufficed for a Federal carver. It almost appears as if the latter-day designer was impelled to outdo the models he copied. According to the Loring family, the overmantel in the reception room contains one eighteenth century hand-carved panel (the lower) and one modern replica in mastic (fig. 225). The stair hall, as in the Proctor house by McKim, Mead, and White, follows Georgian models with scrupulous accuracy of detail, but its complicated system of landings and changes in direction and the placement of its Palladian window reveal the aspirations of a generation accustomed to picturesque Queen Anne compositions (figs. 226, 227).

225

Mantel of reception room at 2 Gloucester Street. The economy of molded putty decoration permitted the architect so much freedom to elaborate his design that he often overdid it.

226

Main stair at 2 Gloucester Street. A splendid example of late nineteenth century taste which combines a dramatic stair composition with archaeologically correct details.

227

Main Stair at 2 Gloucester Street, second floor. This fine stair and Palladian window were removed in 1963 when the house was converted into apartments.

Another excellent design by Peters, built in 1899 at 155 Bay State Road, almost achieves the dignity of a house on upper Beacon Street (fig. 228). But the entrance again illustrates the penchant of the revivalist to compound details, each correct in itself but composed in a way that is not characteristic of the period being copied. Here the carved consoles that support the lintel compete with the capitals of the unpleasantly diminutive pilasters that overlay the door jamb. Although the fenestration is excellent, the fan light above the entrance loses its scale in intricacies of design. Another departure from strict Federal usage is the mansard roof. Although the Federal period knew no such feature as the mansard, the client and designer were apparently unwilling to forego the greater attic head room it provided.

Thus it is that the revivalist of the late nineties almost never managed to duplicate exactly the earlier models he admired. Though he had steadfast intentions of adhering to a historic style, he was inevitably affected by intervening architectural forms and current building practices. He could not disregard certain practical features of later movements like the mansard roof; he could rarely resist the temptation to proliferate ornamentation that was so inexpensive to produce by such means as London Putty; and he inevitably infused something of his own dramatic vigor into his compositions.

Between 1890 and 1897, eight different Boston architectural firms produced designs of excellent Federal character in the Back Bay. Unnecessary to discuss all of this work or even to note examples of each office, it is only important to reiterate here the general excellence of these compositions and their mastery of the historical idiom. Archaeological competence was not confined to one office and no single individual can be credited with the revival of the Federal style. As mentioned, the first examples of the style appear in 1890, though there were strong hints of the approaching revival as early as 1868. In 1899 the first group of speculator-built houses was designed in this style, and eventually a number of notable remodeling jobs were also done in the Federal vein. The last Back Bay dwelling to be constructed before the Second World War was designed in a modified version of this style in 1939.[12]

Architecturally speaking, the nineteenth century had been ushered in with the construction of Federal houses on Beacon Hill, and it was now brought to a close by a fresh wave of Federal building in the Back Bay. It seems particularly fitting that Boston's century of great-

228   Facade of 155 Bay State Road, 1899, by W. Y. Peters. Although most details are scrupulously accurate, the designer outdoes Federal precedent in the ornateness of the door frame and fanlight.

ness should end on the same note with which it began, and it is also appropriate that the death knell of the large town house, that symbol of a bygone age, should sound on so conservative and mellow a note as the Federal Revival.

The Adam Style

In addition to the Federal, another phase of late Georgian architecture was revived in the Back Bay. A reasonably accurate reflection of Robert Adam's manner, this style was so much used among American architects of the early twentieth century that one may be rather surprised to find it making its debut in the Back Bay before 1900 under the tutelage of Arthur Little. So precocious, indeed, is the finest specimen of this group, 422 Beacon Street, that one could easily mistake it for a design of the 1920's (fig. 229). Nevertheless the house in its present form agrees with the building permit issued by the city on June 15, 1899, and the street-level entrance and certain decorative motifs on the facade correspond to elements found in other houses designed by Little and Browne about the same time. (There are similar grade entrances at 411 Commonwealth Avenue and 49 Bay State Road, 1893 and 1899; comparable stone reliefs of graceful Adamesque medallions and swags are found at 393 and 401 Commonwealth Avenue, 1899 and 1901.)

Accepting 422 Beacon Street as the product of the late nineteenth century, it is one of the few Back Bay residences whose design seems to have been visibly influenced by the elevator. The entrance is slightly below ground level while the formal living area, as one sees by the greatly elongated front windows, has been raised to the third story. An inspection of the house reveals that from the entrance vestibule one descends a few steps to the customary level of the basement where the cloakrooms and kitchen are located; two large reception rooms and a rear dining room are accommodated on the second story (in actual height above the street this would correspond to the first floor of an older Back Bay house); and a drawing room and library are placed on the third level. Bedrooms and servants' quarters are situated on the upper three floors. In the middle of the house an elevator and service stair communicate through all six levels although the formal stair, preserved primarily as a decorative feature, runs between the first and third levels.

229　Facade of 422 Beacon Street, 1899, by Little and Browne, more reminiscent of Robert Adam in Britain than of Federal work in New England. This design evidences the presence of an elevator because the *piano nobile* is situated two floors above the entrance.

230   Facade of 411 Commonwealth Avenue, 1899, by Little and Browne.
One of the first fireproof residences in the Back Bay of which we have
record. The house follows the organization of floor levels characteristic of Little and Browne.

The same style and general disposition of rooms on the first three
floors was used again by Arthur Little in the Robert Bradley mansion
at 411 Commonwealth Avenue (fig. 230). Built in 1899 also, this house
is interesting to our present study not only because of its advanced
plan and its early fireproof construction but because it preserves two

rooms with their original furniture designed by the architect. The splendid mahogany-paneled dining room is High Georgian and the ballroom a combination of Louis Seize and Adam (figs. 231, 232). The ostentatious ballroom is not entirely successful because the architect, in the process of concocting a decorative scheme from motifs appropriated from the past, rather lost his sense of scale. If the room gives a first impression of being enormous in size, one is abruptly reminded of its actual size by the chairs and benches against the walls or the regulation height bannister placed in the mezzanine windows.

These interiors make interesting comparisons with those of the Mason house of 1883 which also were filled with architect-designed furniture. Although comparably lavish, the Bradley rooms have a much larger scale; ceilings are higher and the sequence of related interior spaces is contrived to produce a formal grandeur. In the earlier Mason house each room is thought of as a separate unit: one in heavy, dark

231   The ballroom at 411 Commonwealth Avenue combines Adam and Louis Seize details. The scale of the room is deceptive as a glance at the railing height of the balcony windows will reveal.

232　　Dining room at 411 Commonwealth Avenue. Arthur Little designed the furniture for this and several other rooms in the house, and it was constructed in Cambridge.

mahogany; the next painted white and quite delicate in feeling; still another cozy and informal, paneled in quartered oak (figs. 173-179). Although these Mason rooms are connected by wide openings and sometimes arranged axially so that a visitor sees two rooms in a glance, they do not seek the earnest formality of the Bradley house. Instead of overwhelming perspectives, each room is a self-contained unit, endowed with a sense of self-conscious inventiveness, even of lighthearted surprise. Whereas the Bradley interiors are constrained by historical precedent, each room of the older Mason house distills its distinct harmony out of highly original decorative forms. It is interesting to note that the special wood paneling and much of the furniture for both sets of interiors were executed by the Boston firm of Davenport and Company.[13]

About this time a splendid music room was added to the Mason house at 211 Commonwealth Avenue.[14] Designed by Arthur Rotch, who was also responsible for the earlier residence, this room is specifically Quattrocento in inspiration, and it has a formal grandeur equal to the Bradley interiors or those of any other residence in Boston (figs. 233–234). The walls of the 30-by-45-foot room are articulated by a series of arches which is carried by light columns and pilasters of plaster painted to resemble marble. These supports rise from a base which is as high as a chair rail. At one end of the room is a sanctuarylike recess that contained a version of a Murillo "Immaculada" which a seafaring ancestor of the family had brought back to New England from Cadiz. Separated further from the room by a railing,

233   Music room at 211 Commonwealth Avenue, about 1897, by Arthur Rotch. The room was added about fifteen years after the house was finished and illustrates the growing magnificence of Boston houses at the century's end. Much of the antique furniture was purchased in Europe for the room.

the recess looks like an altar and therefore belies the festive character of the room. To either side are dead spaces to which no ready access was provided although storage space for chairs is always needed in a room of this sort. The opposite end of the room has a lower, exedra-like bay covered with a coffered ceiling (fig. 234). Opening off the exedra to one side of the entry is a deep alcove with a fireplace which provided a more intimate conversation area. Such eighteenth-century

234   Music room at 211 Commonwealth Avenue. A screen of columns separates the high-ceilinged room from the more intimate conversation alcove with a fireplace.

235 Detail of fig. 233. The low plaster dome is probably the first architectural feature designed specifically for the electric light in the Back Bay.

furniture as was not already in the family was bought for the room in Venice by Miss Mason who was traveling abroad with her friend Mrs. Jack Gardner when the room was being built.

The deep-coffered plaster ceiling of the main room contains at its center a shallow saucer dome designed to provide the major source of illumination for the room (fig. 235). A ring of electric light bulbs set around the base of the dome is shielded from view by the series of free-standing plaster palmettes. The light, which is reflected from the smooth surfaces of the dome, brings into relief the eight *putti* heads worked in stucco. This use of indirect light and the way the light was used to model the architectural features constitute the first design in the Back Bay specifically adapted to the electric light.

HIGH GEORGIAN

Yet another stylistic family among these late nineteenth century revivals refers to British work of the eighteenth century. Houses of this group for the most part are large. It would seem that owners desiring more lavish ornamentation than could be obtained within the chaste Federal idiom chose the heavily laden High Georgian manner. The popularity of this style can also be explained as the influence of the English architect Norman Shaw, who, as we have seen, progressed from the Free Classic to a more formal Georgian manner in his later work.

William Y. Peters produced two of the finest of these designs in 1900 on Bay State Road: number 97 and a block of three dwellings

236   Facade of 145–149 Bay State Road, 1900, by W. Y. Peters. An
almost palatial scale is obtained by combining three residences in a
single design. The facades of the smaller houses at the right are
carried up an extra half story in order to maintain the cornice height
of the corner dwelling.

at 145, 147, and 149. The corner house of the block, the old Weld
mansion at number 149, is almost palatial in scale (figs. 236, 237).
Amplitude is achieved by its lofty exterior proportions and by the
skillful manner in which the house is integrated with adjacent houses
at 145–147. In the interest of unity, a single cornice height has been
retained throughout the group although to do this the entablature of
the smaller dwellings, one unit of which was the home of the designer,
was arbitrarily raised an extra half story. A feeling of considerable
monumentality is attained by means of the robust quoins, alternately
large and small; the use of banded rustication for the ground-level
entrance; the treatment of second-story windows with heavy, sculptural
enframements interrupted by voussoirs of the flat arches; robust stone
balconies; and the strongly accented center axis with free-standing
porch, pedimented window, and a heavily wrought cartouche of the
third story.

Equally elaborate in its interior fittings, this residence is approached from street level through a marble foyer graced with a fountain and a fine divided stairway. On the *piano nobile* the white and gold drawing room with heavy molded ceiling and veined marble mantelpiece connects with the dining room, paneled and carved in the manner of Grinling Gibbons, through a large stair hall (fig. 238). This hall is interrupted in the center by a bronze balustrade which surrounds an

237   Facade of 149 Bay State Road. Ornamented with robust stone architraves and panels of heavy relief, this design illustrates the ponderous High Georgian manner chosen for several of the Back Bay's more elaborate dwellings.

238   Stair hall, second floor, at 149 Bay State Road. Connecting the dining and drawing rooms on the *piano nobile,* this splendid oak-paneled hall contains a bronze balustrade about a well that opens to the entrance hall below.

elliptical opening into the entrance foyer below. Abjuring premolded glued ornamentation, the paneling of both hall and dining room are splendid. The hall is quartered oak, the dining room mahogany. Even the gilt bronze box locks are of exquisite design and workmanship.

The other Peters house, 97 Bay State Road, makes an interesting comparison with its neighbor to the west at number 99 (fig. 239). Of substantially the same size and disposition, these two edifices well illustrate the stylistic differences between the florid High Georgian and simpler Federal manners. The pretentious English Georgian idiom permits the designer to use quantities of heavy stone carving: window enframements, some with pedimental sculpture and volutes, others with projecting keystones; swags within the main entablature; paneled balustrade and urns in the attic. The Federal style house in contrast has a calm, self-effacing mood. Actually somewhat larger than its neighbor, it makes no claim on the attention of the passerby except for the propriety of its proportions, its unusual height, the orthodoxy of its detailing, and the directness of its ancestry to Beacon Hill. There are only seven lavish High Georgian houses in all the Back

239   Facade of 97 (right) and 99 Bay State Road. Both designed in 1900, the first by Rice and Peters and the second by Shepley, Rutan, and Coolidge. These adjacent designs illustrate the more ornate High Georgian and the simpler Federal manners.

240   Facade of 485–487 Commonwealth Avenue, 1897, by R. C. Sturgis.
       A refined design that quotes faithfully from the work of Norman
       Shaw in England.

Bay as opposed to ninety-four Federal designs: Boston householders
once again indicated their preference for a quieter architectural
manner.

In connection with Shaw's influence in Boston, mention should be
made of two medium-sized but very handsome houses designed by R.
Clipston Sturgis in 1897 at 485–487 Commonwealth Avenue (fig. 240).
These fine facades make specific reference to Shaw's work of the eighties
in the segmental window heads crowned with a single brick drip molding, and the design and attenuated proportions of the second-story
windows. Specifically the two oriel windows at 485 and the entrance
at 487 refer to well-known buldings by Shaw in London.[15] Within,

the mingling of Medieval and Renaissance details also recalls Shaw precedent. While on the subject of Shaw's following in Boston, mention might be made that W. Y. Peter's 1900 design for 149 Bay State Road reveals the English designer's latter-day fondness for blocky rustication and heavy broken pediments, such as those he used at "Bryanston" or in his designs for the Regent Street Crescent.

ARCHITECTURAL EDUCATION IN BOSTON

It is not difficult to find reasons for the impressive display of architectural erudition observed toward the century's close in the Back Bay. Ready explanations are found in the increasing availability of such reference material as architectural books and periodicals, the development of inexpensive methods of reproducing architectural illustrations, the higher educational level of the profession in Boston, and the increasing frequency of European travel.

In the 1870's and 1880's the increase in the numbers of architectural books available to the American architect was great. Henry-Russell Hitchcock makes an interesting analysis of Richardson's architectural library, and he notes the increasingly archaeological (if aesthetically less successful) production of the Richardson office as new books on the Romanesque style were added to its library.[16] The growing numbers of these reference books can be gauged by a glance at Boston's several architectural libraries. The Department of Architecture at Massachusetts Institute of Technology, opened in 1868, by 1875 could boast a library of four hundred books. In 1894 the Boston Public Library issued a 150-page catalog of books and magazines on architecture and closely allied subjects in its possession. The avidity with which local reference shelves were stocked is also suggested by the activity of the Boston Society of Architects which, in 1869, voted to allocate between two and three hundred dollars annually for the purchase of foreign architectural publications. In 1885 the society appropriated five hundred dollars to catalog the architectural books in the Public Library.[17]

Periodicals came to play an increasingly important role in the dissemination of architectural knowledge. In 1894 the Public Library listed eighty-three different magazines in the fields of architecture, art, archaeology, antiquarianism, or engineering emanating from nine different countries. Among these were complete sets of three principal British architectural periodicals, one French publication, and ten American magazines.[18]

The Boston Athenaeum also had a good architectural reference library. Although today it catalogs most of the titles just mentioned in the Public Library, it seems unlikely that the various series were acquired as they were published. More probably the back issues were purchased to fill out the series after regular subscriptions had begun.[19] Architectural firms or individuals must also have subscribed to these magazines, but the growth of private libraries is difficult to trace. Hitchcock thinks that Richardson subscribed to *Croquis d'Architecture* and the *Architectural Association Sketch Book,* and he suggests that Richardson must at least have studied the plates in *The Builder* from the 1860's (the last two both British).[20] It is important to remember that all of these magazines placed great emphasis upon architectural history. Every effort was made by publishers to produce illustrations of historical buildings that were accurate enough to be used by the practicing architect in detailing his own designs. Likewise America's first architectural periodical, *American Architect and Building News* (1876), treated its readers to pictures of famous buildings whenever they were available, though far the greater part of the illustrations were of current work. As the magazine was published by the Boston firm of F. R. Osgood Company, many of the projects it carried were by Boston architects.

Photographs also, becoming ever clearer and more commonplace, assisted the architect in his quest for knowledge of historic styles. Various photoengraving processes were developed in the early seventies and it soon became possible to print photography cheaply. In architectural magazines the new Heliotype print began to replace lithographs and woodcuts. The first volume of *American Architect and Building News,* in 1876, carried only one Heliotype illustration, but in succeeding years these prints appeared with ever greater frequency. By 1889 the *Brochure Series* featured each month a folio of Heliotype plates which illustrated some architectural element such as fireplace designs or a collection of Renaissance capitals which could be filed for reference by the architect. In 1894 the Heliotype Printing Company of Boston issued a collection of architectural illustrations, most of which dealt with historical material, under the title *Architectural Odds and Ends,* edited by William Rotch Ware.[21] As the home of scholarly architectural interests, the seat of the country's first important architectural publication as well as its first school of architecture, and the center from which the new Heliotype architectural illustrations were distributed throughout the country, Boston occupied a dominant position on the American architectural scene—a fact which gives added historic importance to the buildings produced at this time in the Back Bay area.

Travel was another factor contributing to an understanding of the historic styles of architecture. An architectural field trip in Europe, not uncommon in the sixties, had by the eighties become the common experience of almost every successful Boston architect. Those who had not been able to make this pilgrimage as students looked forward to the day when they might embark on that coveted journey. Thus we see Stanford White departing for Europe in 1878 as soon as he had accumulated sufficient savings, or Henry Van Brunt, in 1886, making the trip after years of anticipation. Talented students of architecture were materially assisted toward this goal by the establishment in 1883 of the Rotch Traveling Fellowship, a yearly award to a Massachusetts Institute of Technology graduate and the first of its kind in the country.[22] The results of foreign study and diligent travel observations by one young Bostonian is contained in the 1869 sketch book of Robert Peabody published in 1873. He continued to indulge this enthusiasm throughout his life, and in 1912, at the age of 67, he published a second volume, *An American Architect's Sketch Book*. Still other evidences of architectural notes by student-travelers are contained in Julius Schweinfurth's *Sketches Abroad* (1888) or the 1883 and 1890 issues of the *Sketch Book of the Architectural Association of Boston*.[23]

The architectural erudition of the eighties probably resulted also from the higher educational level of practicing architects. In this area the profession had gone a long way since the Boston Society of Architects was founded in 1867. Then, according to the chronicler of the society, "only a handful of architects had a college education," but in 1886 the society was able to establish educational requirements for admission to membership—a college degree or a grade of at least 65 on the Rotch Traveling Fellowship examination.[24] During this same period the curriculum of Massachusetts Institute of Technology's new Department of Architecture was changed to place more emphasis on architectural history. At first the architectural curriculum had consisted largely of engineering subjects with a single course in history reserved for the student's last year, but this situation was soon rectified.[25] In 1874 the revised course of study introduced architectural history in the second year and assigned upper classmen the problem of measuring and drawing selected historical monuments in Boston.

Yet another indication of the relative importance placed upon architectural history at this time can be gathered from the fact that the competitive examination which determined the award of the Rotch Traveling Fellowship, founded in 1883, counted history as one fifth of the total score.[26] It should be remembered that the recipient was chosen not by the schoolmen of Massachusetts Institute of Technology, but by the rank and file of the profession as represented by the Boston Society of Architects.

Two of the above-mentioned measured drawings were reproduced in the January 1875 issue of the *Architectural Sketch Book*. In the same spirit in which this assignment was made, the Boston Society of Architecture next offered cash prizes for the best measured drawings of Colonial work made during the summer vacation in 1878. In 1886 the society voted to direct the Rotch Fellow to spend a portion of his time measuring and drawing a specific unpublished monument which the committee should select.[27] The purpose of this directive was to augment systematically the profession's knowledge of architectural history as well as to give the student a firsthand acquaintance with an important building of the past. The importance of such educational experiences had long been recognized in France and England, and the measured drawings made by young architects there had done much to expand the body of knowledge concerning architectural history which was accumulated at this time.[28] Basically this experience was to the good and its values should not be lost sight of because some students saw only surface details and stylistic clichés. The scrupulous examination of a building which was required to make a measured drawing sharpened the student's eye for scale, his feeling for texture, and his understanding of the sequence of spaces. In giving him experience in distinguishing between two-dimensional drawings and three-dimensional buildings, it helped him to avoid the paper architecture of earlier decades. Only when it offered the student an opportunity to sense the continuity of history did American architectural education reach a mature level. As for its immediate influence, this study of historic examples served to quicken the American student's interest in the traditional architecture of his own country and to hasten the triumph of the Federal Revival.

To return to the subject of the educational level of the profession itself, one is impressed with the literary activities of several local architects as well as the intellectual interests of the Boston Society of Architects. In 1895 two Boston architects were engaged in writing about architectural history. Between that date and 1903 W. P. P. Longfellow and C. A. Cummings brought out their three-volume *Cyclopedia of Works of Architecture in Italy, Greece and the Levant.* Longfellow supplemented this monumental work with *The Column and the Arch* in 1899, and *Applied Perspective* in 1901. In the same year Cummings produced his two-volume *History of Architecture in Italy from the Time of Constantine to the Dawn of the Renaissance,* and immediately thereafter he went to work with Russell Sturgis on the *Dictionary of Architecture and Building.* In 1881 Cummings wrote his invaluable chapter on the architectural development of Boston for the monumental *Memorial History of Boston,* edited by Justin Winsor.

During the last quarter of the century a large number of meetings of the Boston Society of Architects were devoted to historical papers and discussions. The 1876 season was given over to a series of lectures on Renaissance architecture, two lectures each being devoted to the architecture of England, France, and Italy. In February of 1890 Mr. Moore talked on the origins of Gothic architecture. In 1893 Ralph Adams Cram discoursed on the question of style in ecclesiastical architecture; later that year Mr. Longfellow discussed Bramante. In 1897 Langford Warren lectured on the influence of Syrian architecture on that of southern France. And in 1898 Professor Goodyear analyzed the eccentricities in plan of Medieval churches in France.[29] In a more practical way the society assisted historical research by an appropriation in 1878 of three hundred dollars toward the expenses of two young Bostonians, J. T. Clarke and Frank Bacon, to enable them to study the origins of Doric architecture. That was followed, in 1881, by a generous grant of two thousand dollars to an expedition planning to excavate at Assos in Greece. In March of 1890, after the society had heard a report by Mr. Norton and Dr. Tarbell on the projected excavations at Delphi, the society voted a subscription of five hundred dollars and appointed a special committee to solicit individual contributions from Boston architects. Finally, in 1898, another appropriation of five hundred dollars was authorized toward the publication of Sylvester Baxter's pioneer study on *Mexican Renaissance Architecture.*[30]

This record indicates an unusual range of interests on the part of these practicing architects and it again demonstrates the importance which they attached to a sound historical knowledge. It is also interesting to note in passing the concrete concern which these Boston men evinced for classical archaeology more than fifteen years before Charles McKim and his New York friends launched, in 1895, the American School of Architecture in Rome, later to be consolidated in the American Academy.

Once the architectural profession discovered the value of a systematic study of architectural history, it was only a short time before it began to realize that all architectural history had not been made in Europe, that an important chapter had been written in the American colonies prior to and just after the Revolution. By the late 1880's several Boston designers were aware that this particular movement had a special importance for them.

It would appear that Boston had begun to manifest some interest in late Colonial architecture several years before buildings designed in that manner actually appeared along the streets of the Back Bay. As early as 1869 the Boston Society of Architects devoted a program to Charles Bulfinch when the Reverend S. G. Bulfinch addressed the society on Bulfinch's architectural activity and illustrated the talk with his grandfather's original drawings. At the February meeting of the same year, the society's secretary tells us, the values inherent in Colonial architecture were discussed, and in May Mr. Emerson gave a "sermon on his text, the destruction of old New England houses, which he pronounced the only true American architecture which has yet existed." During the 1878 season Mr. Stephenson read a paper on Colonial architecture as illustrated by old houses in Jamaica Plain; Mr. Cabot discussed old houses in North Carolina; Robert Peabody spoke on the pre-Revolution brick architecture of Philadelphia; and an exhibition of Bulfinch drawings was organized.[31]

In 1874 Professor Ware's advanced students at Massachusetts Institute of Technology were for the first time assigned field trips to measure and draw the towers of late Georgian churches in Boston. Two of these projects were published in the 1875 *Architectural Sketch Book*. In May of 1878 the Boston Society of Architects announced a summer contest with cash prizes for measured drawings of early buildings.[32]

Although in the forefront, it must be pointed out that Boston architects were not alone in the rediscovery of Colonial architecture. In

December 1874 *New York Sketch Book* expressed the awakening appreciation for early American architecture in an editorial which accompanied the photograph of a seventeenth century Rhode Island house:

> We offer at this time one of a number of old Newport houses recently photographed by private subscription. The picturesque surroundings and architectural merit of many of these buildings are not to be disputed, nor are they the less deserving of recognition because some people call them "ugly" . . . They are always reasonably simple in outline, frequently show great beauty of detail. Hitherto they have been brought before the public as haunted houses, or as the scene of some story or other, maintained as shadows and admired for their ivy. Now let somebody write about them as architecture.[33]

As early as 1877 the New York architects McKim, Mead, and White and their former partner Bigelow made their "celebrated sketching tour to the North Shore" to study Colonial architecture. This was indeed an influential vacation for, in the estimation of Mr. Mead, "the leaning of the office towards the Classical dates from this trip."[34]

In the same year that the McKim party made its pleasant tour of Marblehead, Salem, Newburyport, and Portsmouth, a young and as yet unknown Boston student named Arthur Little made a similar pilgrimage to study Colonial remains, the fruits of which he published in 1878 under the title *Early New England Interiors*. The pen sketches show the artist to be as yet an unskilled draftsman, hampered by faulty perspective and possessed of a hard and very mechanical technique. If the sketches themselves are of little value, the preface to the volume is an interesting illustration of the awakening interest in Colonial art: "These sketches are the result of a summer's work, undertaken for my own pleasure and instruction, and also with the desire to preserve the relics of a style fast disappearing . . . It is thought by many that with the revival of the so-called Classical style in England, such as the 'Queen Anne' or 'Free Classic,' we on our side of the water should revive our Colonial style . . . With this idea in view, it seemed that some sketches of this work might prove interesting and perhaps useful."[35]

The first work published in Boston in connection with the Georgian Revival, Little's book soon was followed by a flood of architectural publications dealing with the American Georgian and illustrated with a profusion of detailed photographs or measured drawings.[36] These illustrations were designed primarily as references for the practicing architect, an idea which is clearly set forth in the 1891 preface of *Examples of Domestic Architecture in New England:* "The primary object in compiling this work was not to accumulate historical data but rather to present in a form convenient for use and reference by architects . . . some typical examples of the better class of domestic edifices which were erected during the latter half of the eighteenth century . . . The growing appreciation of the aesthetic principles employed in the erecting of these buildings leads us to hope that the publication of these plates may be the means of stimulating closer study in their adaptation to modern domestic work."[37] Between 1876 and 1894, no less than eleven well-illustrated books on American Colonial architecture were published in Boston alone. Between 1896 and 1902 Boston's architectural magazine, *The American Architect and Building News,* issued a supplement entitled *The Georgian Period, Being Measured Drawings of Colonial Work,* an opus whose twelve parts each contained some fifty-six plates of measured drawings or clear Heliotype illustrations but no text.[38]

The growing appreciation for late Georgian architecture is also illustrated by the relative degree of intensity of an early as compared to a later campaign waged to preserve two famous buildings in Boston. In 1865 the city proposed to demolish the Hancock Mansion on Beacon Street and sell the land to satisfy unpaid taxes. Halfhearted and unsuccessful opposition to this action was voiced, the defense of the splendid old mansion being based entirely on grounds of economy or its connection with historic personages.[39] Not one word was uttered about the architectural merits of this building although later critics were to speak of it as the finest house of the early eighteenth century built in New England. In 1895 the Massachusetts legislature, needing larger quarters, proposed that the Bulfinch State House be replaced by a new and more commodious building. This time, however, a veritable wall of protest preserved the old structure. The protest included two communications from the Boston Society of Architects which defended the building on its architectural merits.[40]

The history of the State House traces a full cycle of architectural taste in Boston. The century between its construction in 1793 and its preservation from the indifferent hand of "progress" in 1895 encompasses a complete revolution in architectural fashion. The events which chart this cycle are quite clear. In 1793, when Bulfinch erected his lofty dome, it was the very symbol of modernity and cosmopolitan taste. By 1844 it approached its artistic nadir, and a foremost Boston architect—no other than Arthur Gilman who was to plan the Back Bay area—regarded the structure, now fifty years old, as "flaunting and meretricious."[41] In 1895, four generations after its construction, the edifice again came into its own and was applauded—even by architects. Once again Boston eyes found pleasure in the State House dome and were as gladdened by its gilded surface as on that day it received its first covering of gold leaf. Obviously it was not the dome that had changed—only Boston eyes.

History, at least recent history, seems to have foreordained this destructive pattern, this blind cycle of fashion. It would seem to be a spiritual necessity for a man to deny and destroy what his father and grandfather had achieved in order to affirm himself. For the last two hundred years at least, perhaps since the Renaissance, this has been the pattern of creative self-assertion—with even the process of ultimate rediscovery fortifying the egotism of the fourth-generation which recognizes and corrects the prejudiced and shortsighted judgments of its immediate progenitors.

Before quitting this subject of revived interest in Colonial architecture, one should recall that it was paralleled by a similar feeling for the pictures and furniture of the period. Was it not Oliver Wendell Holmes who, defining a "Bostonian," recollected family portraits by Copley and Blackburn which lined the walls of his hall? W. H. Downes, in his article on "Painting in Boston" for the 1888 *Atlantic Monthly,* noted that three quarters of the private collections in the city contained the work of American painters, mostly portraits. And Robert S. Peabody, in an article in the *American Architect* in 1877, argued for a return to Colonial architectural models because it created a more congruous background for one's heirlooms. "Put our old heirlooms into a Gothic room and they are out of keeping . . . Our heirlooms are tall clocks, Copley or Stuart portraits, Paul Revere tankards, convex mirrors."[42]

Indeed, this return by later nineteenth century Bostonians to Georgian and Early Republican forms is not confined to architecture and the arts. On all sides one is aware of a rediscovery of the merits of eighteenth century life and ways. Several other aspects of this reversion to old values have already been suggested. Boston business chose to content itself with commerce on a familiar and regional scale comparable to what it had known in the earlier nineteenth century; Boston intellectuals basked in the accomplishments of their authors of earlier generations; Boston society preferred to conserve an Early Republican simplicity in its mode of living; Boston First Families consolidated a caste system that is almost unique in America. And now Boston architects reverted to the Federal style of architecture associated with old values that were so much prized. In visual form the Federal style symbolized the privileged position, the bonds of family, and the financial solvency which leading Bostonians had long enjoyed. Boston's way of life having thus remained in so many ways as it was a century earlier, it was appropriate—even desirable—that the old form of architecture should be used to build new homes. The hub of the universe only rotated.

THE BACK BAY AREA
AS AN EXAMPLE
OF CITY PLANNING   8

The Back Bay development began in 1814 when the Massachusetts legislature chartered the Boston and Roxbury Mill Corporation and approved the construction of a long mill dam in the estuary of the Charles River, a dam which would cut off some 430 acres of tidal flats from the channel of the river. The main dam, which exists today beneath the surface of Beacon Street, was a forty-foot earthen dyke faced on the river side by a stone seawall. It stretched from the corner of Charles and Beacon streets in Boston to Gravelly Point in Brookline, a distance of almost a mile and a half. The area thus walled off from the river was subdivided by the Cross Dam into two parts: the Upper or Full Basin and the Lower or Receiving Basin.[1] The Mill Corporation was allowed by its charter to let water into the Full Basin at high tide and to drain the Receiving Basin at low tide into the river, thereby maintaining a difference in water levels of about nine feet. This differential could be utilized to power water mills. The tidal mill was not new in Boston as similar mills had operated in the North Cove in the seventeenth century. The corporation was also licensed to construct a road to Watertown and to operate it in conjunction with the dam as a toll road. Toll was collected on the Mill Dam until December 1865.

The power project, completed in 1821, was no financial success, thanks largely to competition from the more practical steam engine and to the fact that the efficiency of the water-driven mills was soon reduced when the Commonwealth permitted the construction in 1834 of two railroad causeways, which impeded the flow of water in the

Lower Basin. By mid-century the project was manifestly a failure, and there was agitation on all sides to abandon milling operations and to fill the basins.

One strong argument for filling was the fact that the polluted bay constituted a real health menace. From early times Boston had followed the practice of draining her sewage into the harbor; sewers were constructed to the water's edge and the scouring action of the ebbing tide was counted on to sweep the discharge out to sea. As long as the population was small and the tidal flow unimpeded, this primitive arrangement worked well enough. When, however, the Back Bay was cut off from the cleansing flow of the tide while Boston sewers continued to drain into that area, the shallow bay soon became clogged with filth, producing noxious odors.[2] By 1849 the Health Department demanded the fill of the area in the interests of public health.

Meanwhile, the pressure of population within the restricted peninsula of Boston was constantly increasing. With the building of the Louisburg Square section in the 1840's, the last desirable residential area was occupied. Yet the city was growing at a tremendous rate. Between 1840 and 1850 the population jumped an astonishing 47 percent—from 93,000 to 137,000. Within the old area it was necessary not only to provide living quarters for more people, but also to accommodate the growing commercial interests. In the early fifties commerce was forcing householders out of the older residential sections of the city by means of increased land values.[3] Yet because of slow transportation, it was not yet practical for the population to spread to the suburbs. By horsecar, which was not introduced until 1853, it took twenty-five minutes to reach Harvard Square and almost that long to get to Roxbury. South Boston had been laid out in 1804 with high hopes on the part of its promoters that it would attract the city's well-to-do residents. But this section was no more accessible because the bridge to South Boston had been placed disadvantageously: one had to go west along the Neck halfway to Roxbury before turning to cross the South Bay to the new area.[4] East Cambridge had very roundabout horsecar connections with Boston until the 1870's and Charlestown was a long way from the central business districts. In short, there was no place as close to the center of Boston as the Back Bay to look for new home sites.

In addition to these practical considerations, profit was a great incentive for the Back Bay development, since it was to the interests of

all parties that the bay be filled. The Mill Corporation hoped to realize more from the sale of the land than it had from operating the
mill;[5] adjacent property owners viewed the proposed fill as an opportunity for the profitable sale of their holdings; real estate agents
and builders eagerly contemplated the construction of a new section;
the City of Boston saw a chance to lay claim to more free land; and
the Commonwealth of Massachusetts regarded it an an opportunity
to develop its property which was lying idle at the bottom of the
Back Bay. Numerous similar though smaller operations in Boston had
previously proved the economic soundness of filling; and, at the very
time that these discussions were under way, the city was reaping handsome financial benefits from the sale of land in the South End—land
to which it held undisputed title and which it had filled and subdivided in 1850.

All were agreed that the Back Bay must be filled; the only thing
that blocked immediate realization of the scheme was an acrimonious
dispute over the extent of the holdings of the various parties. In 1841
the United States Harbor Commission established a line beyond which
a fill might not encroach upon the harbor. In 1850 Massachusetts
appointed a special commission to investigate her interests in the Back
Bay and to recommend how best these holdings might be developed.
Eighteen months later this first temporary commission reported to
the legislature that the Commonwealth's claim to more than a hundred
acres in the bay could be substantiated, and they recommended the
appointment of a permanent commission empowered to negotiate a
property settlement among the various claimants. They also suggested
that the commission be instructed to contract for the fill of the area,
to lay out its systems of streets, and to sell the Commonwealth's land.

Acting on this recommendation, the legislature, in July 1852, appointed the permanent Commission on Boston Harbor and Back Bay
Lands. The name of this body changed in 1855 to the Commissioners
on Public Lands, and in 1879 to the Harbor and Land Commission.
Beginning in 1853 the progress of the groups concerned with the Back
Bay area is described in annual reports. Among these, the reports of
1854, 1879, and 1886 contain good summaries of various phases of
the commission's activities.[6]

Though briefly noted here, the problem of determining ownership
of the area was a tremendous task, and one which commissioners tried
to solve by means of friendly negotiation rather than by legal con-

test. Basically the problem was decided by riparian ownership (private ownership of coastal property extends as far as low tide; below that title is retained by the state).[7] This simple definition of rights, how-ever, was modified by a mass of grants, privileges, and waivers—often conflicting—such as the rights of property owners to the perpetual benefits of tidal flow, the rights of property owners to dig mud on their tidal flats, rights granted Boston to empty sewers into the bay, or rights granted the Boston and Roxbury Mill Corporation to con-trol forever the tidal flow in the area. This controversy was further complicated by the fact that the area comprising the Back Bay lay within three municipalities: Boston, Roxbury, and Brookline.

After three years of negotiations and despite the shortsighted, un-cooperative attitude of Boston, the tangle of claims and counterclaims was resolved in the main by the Tripartite Agreement of 1856 be-tween the Commonwealth of Massachusetts, the City of Boston, and the Boston and Roxbury Mill Corporation. In this agreement the Mill Corporation was awarded a strip two-hundred feet wide lying parallel to and north of the Mill Dam, the present water side of Beacon Street; the Commonwealth was assured a rectangular plot of one hundred and eight acres in the Lower Basin, bounded (to use present-day landmarks) by the alley between Boylston and St. James streets, a line drawn across the Public Garden at its mid-point, the center of Beacon Street, and a line from Beacon south to the alley behind Boylston—the last line situated about halfway between Exeter and Fairfield streets; the Mill Corporation through its subsidiary, the Boston Water Power Company, was granted the remainder of the two basins which lay below the line of riparian ownership (above that line owner-ship was fairly clear); the City of Boston was awarded some two and three-quarters acres for an addition to the Public Garden, this grant being deducted from the above-described holdings of the Common-wealth. A further agreement was reached for the building of sewers and the maintenance of streets, the entire area having been placed within the territorial limits of Boston.

The grant of land to the city helped to determine that the Public Garden—now one of the finest public parks in America and certainly a splendid ornament to Boston—would indeed be established. We can hardly visualize the city without the Public Garden or imagine that a little over a century ago its very existence was hotly debated. In 1784 the then idle salt marshes west of the Common were given by the town of Boston to a group of rope makers whose yards had just burned. In 1824 the area was bought back by the city with the intention of creating a public garden, an intention which still persisted in 1827, when the city exacted an agreement from the Mill Corporation not to build on the tidal flats in front of the garden. But soon after the attitude of the city fathers toward the project began to vacillate. Their proposal to divide the tract into salable lots was defeated in a municipal election in 1824; in 1839 permission was granted a group of local flower fanciers to build a greenhouse there; in 1850 there was again talk of selling the land; in 1856, after accepting the Commonwealth's two-acre gift for the purpose of enlarging the garden, the city once again threatened to subdivide the new acquisition. Then in 1859, in a special election, the people of Boston agreed to accept the Commonwealth's gift of the area and reserve it in perpetuity as a public garden, but this was not done until the Commonwealth had agreed to indemnify the city by an additional grant of Back Bay land.[8] Finally, in 1859, the matter at long last settled, the city commissioned a local architect, George F. Meacham, to draw up the plans for landscaping the enlarged garden, and that pleasant area that we know today as the Public Garden was created in 1860.

The obstacles of ownership having at last been overcome, the Commissioners on Public Lands next turned to the actual filling of the flats and to laying out a system of streets. The final plan was settled on in 1856, after the commission had persuaded the legislature in 1854 to extend its authority to the line of extreme high tide (rather than mean high tide) so that the entire area, including Gravelly Point, could be planned as a unit.[9] Arrangements were also made for the construction of temporary wooden sewers which would serve until the freshly filled land had settled. In 1856 permission was granted to begin the fill, and in September 1857 filling operations actually got under way.

For this purpose, a special railroad line was built leading to the area to be improved, and by way of tracts belonging to the short Charles River Railroad, this rail line was connected with gravel pits in Needham, some nine miles distance from the fill.[10] Special steam shovels mounted on flat cars were contrived for the excavations and the filling operations soon were under way on a twenty-four-hour schedule (fig. 241).

The Back Bay fill was a tremendous undertaking, the average depth

241   Steam shovel loading gravel cars for the Back Bay fill. The gravel was hauled nine miles from the Needham pits at the rate of some 3500 carloads per day.

of the fill being over twenty feet and the area to be filled more than 450 acres in extent.[11] The filling of the new area contrasts decidedly with previous fills in Boston. Heretofore, most of the earth for fills in Boston had come from the city's own hill tops, dug out by pick and shovel and hauled down to the fills in ox carts. Now, however, these hills were covered with houses, and earth for the fill had to be brought from more distant points. In modern times dredging within the harbor has provided necessary material for fills; but in those days land filled with harbor mud was thought to be unhealthful, and the promoters also lacked the heavy pumps which now make dredging expeditious and relatively cheap. In 1857, therefore, the earth was brought all the way from Needham, a gargantuan task which before the advent of the steam shovel and railroad would have been quite impossible.

Begun at the east end of the bay in the autumn of 1857, the fill had reached Clarendon Street by 1860; it had gone beyond Exeter Street in 1870; by 1876 all of the Commonwealth land had been filled. In 1880 the entire northern part of the Lower Basin was solid ground;

in 1890 filling had gone well beyond Gravelly Point (Kenmore Square) and was continuing west along Bay State Road; before 1900 the last few acres of the Fens, adjacent to Stony Creek and Muddy River, had been covered.[12]

In the new area the streets were filled to the level of the Mill Dam, which was seventeen feet above mean low tide (Grade 17, as it was designated). But because the basements of the houses would be lower than street level, the lots were only filled to Grade 12 (figs. 7, 183). A sanitary sewer system was constructed: branch lines laid in the alleys converged on main sewers situated in alternate streets beginning with Berkeley; these sewers in turn drained directly into the Charles River. The streets of the district were constructed by the Commonwealth but once finished they were maintained by the city. As these first streets were gravel surfaced, the commission report of 1859 found it necessary to defend the dusty condition of the area as at least less unpleasant than the smells which had formerly come from the fetid mud flats.

The financing of this enormous fill was another difficult problem confronting the commission, the more so as the Commonwealth was unwilling to advance any working capital for the project. The commissioners had been empowered to find means of financing the project, but they had only unimproved land with which to bargain, land whose actual value had not yet been established by sales. In 1856 this group negotiated a contract with the firm of Goss and Munson for the fill. The contractors would provide gravel at the rate of forty cents a cubic yard plus forty-one cents per square foot for the area graded; the Commonwealth would reimburse the contractors in filled land at the rate of $1.17 per square foot, titles to parcels of land being exchanged as specific areas of fill were completed. The commissioners also arranged several large sales to individuals, the first of these being the south side of Beacon between Arlington and Berkeley streets which they sold to Goddard and Lawrence in September 1857 for $70,000.[13] Once the land was filled, however, and the public had demonstrated its faith in the new district by actual purchases, the Commonwealth changed its methods of finance; public auctions were substituted for the private sales and the contractors were paid in cash for their work. The auctions were held at such intervals as the commissioners deemed advisable, the first in October 1860, the last in 1879. At these sales the purchaser was required to pay at least 25 percent down and the balance when he took the title. The last piece of Commonwealth property was disposed of in 1886.

The actual financial return to the Commonwealth from the fill was great—a net profit of $3,442,205. Additional grants of almost nine acres had been made to various public institutions which would have yielded another $832,000 if disposed of at the average sale price. The Commonwealth turned one half of its profit into an educational fund which was dispensed to various state schools and colleges as it was collected; the rest reverted to general state funds.[14]

It is interesting to note variations in land values within different sections of the district and also the steady and rapid increase in the average price of Back Bay land. With the inauguration of the first land auction in 1860, the commission established certain minimum prices: $1.375 per square foot for property fronting Marlborough and Newbury streets, $1.62 for corner lots on the same streets; $2.25 for regular lots and $2.75 for corner lots on Commonwealth Avenue. Except for the first auction, prices bid did not exceed these minimums before 1865; in 1868 the schedule of minimum prices was raised almost 10 percent. The 1879 report indicates the rising value of Back Bay property by listing the average yearly prices: $1.05 per square foot in 1857; $1.70 in 1860; $2.39 in 1865; $2.80 in 1870; $3.14 in 1879. In 1886 the Commonwealth disposed of the last of its Back Bay property for $4.35 per square foot, over four times the price it had received for land thirty years earlier. With such consistent and substantial increases in land values (to say nothing of increments in building costs), an investor was fairly certain of always being able to get back his money and therefore did not hesitate to put large sums into his dwelling. The following tabulation gives a rough idea of rising values over a forty-year period. These figures are for new, four-story houses on a twenty-six-foot lot and situated in comparably good locations; they include land costs. The figures are derived from the estimated cost of the house given on the building permit or, for the earlier houses, from the tax record.

Year	Approximate cost of house	Location
1861	$26,000	7 Commonwealth Avenue
1868	45,000	23 Commonwealth Avenue
1877	25,000	63 Commonwealth Avenue
1881	30,000	175 Commonwealth Avenue

Year	Approximate cost of house	Location
1884	$40,000	229 Commonwealth Avenue
1890	35,000	415 Commonwealth Avenue
1900	45,000	77 Bay State Road
1903	60,000	310 Beacon Street

Land values increased more sharply than building costs. The history of two parcels of Back Bay property demonstrate the phenomenal increase in Back Bay land values. John L. Gardner bought a two-hundred-foot plot fronting Marlborough Street (numbers 70 to 87) in October of 1862 for $30,800. The price paid was $1.375 per square foot, the minimum established by the Commission on Back Bay Lands. By 1865 this land was taxed at $50,000, but as the assessed value seems to have been between 85 and 90 percent of actual market value, one may suppose the real value of the property to have been at least $56,200.[15] Within three years Mr. Gardner thus had a paper profit of at least $26,000 on his $30,000 investment, a modest increment of 87 percent. He did not, however, sell the land at that time but built seven residences in 1864 which remained in the Gardner estate as rental property until after his death in 1879.

Another case in point concerns the property at the corner of Commonwealth Avenue and Arlington Street. In December of 1858 this land was acquired at one of the early private sales held by the Commonwealth's land commissioners.[16] Originally the property consisted of two parts, the corner plot sold to John Bates for $13,695 and the adjacent piece to Sam Ward for $10,426. Together, these two parcels brought the Commonwealth $24,121. When the corner house at 12 Arlington Street was finished in 1861, the property was assessed at $56,000 ($19,000, land; $37,000, house); in 1862 its neighbor at 1 Commonwealth Avenue was assessed at $42,500 ($12,500, land; $30,000 house). In 1893 the two residences were thrown together to form one dwelling by Montgomery Sears and have since remained one property. The following tax assessor's values for these houses and land parcels give an idea of the increment in Back Bay values and also the periods in which that increase was most rapid. The unusually large increase in assessed value from 1864 to 1868—more than 50 percent—was not paralleled by significant improvements in the property; it merely reflects the rise in real estate values.

Year	12 Arlington Street	1 Commonwealth Avenue	Combined Property
1861	$ 56,000	$42,200	$ 98,200
1862	56,000		
1863	58,000		
1864	60,000		
1865	66,000		
1866	83,000		
1868	95,000		
1880	100,000		
1881	112,000		
1883	115,000		
1888	125,000		
1893	125,000	80,000	205,000
1894			205,000
1900			220,000
1905			235,000
1910			250,000
1929			250,000

In 1910 the value of this land alone was appraised at $160,200 and the building at $89,800. Thus the land had increased 665 percent in fifty-two years; the building, 243 percent. Is there any wonder that so many conservative Yankees deemed it prudent to reside in Boston's finest residential district?

We have already seen that three sections of land fill had been begun on the fringes of the Back Bay between 1844 and 1857 when the Boylston Street, the Charles Street, and the Beacon Street areas pushed out onto the adjacent mud flats. Each neighborhood was developed independently and its layout was controlled by the streets on the adjacent mainland. These areas were little more than extensions of mainland neighborhoods onto the newly filled land of the bay.

Not until 1853, when the Commonwealth determined to develop its holdings in the Back Bay, was thought given to a plan for the whole area. The system of streets we know today was not arrived at immediately, and it is interesting to trace the slow, painful, and

sometimes fortuitous development of the final layout. This evolution
we can trace in a series of maps dating between 1853 and 1870.

The first hint of a street system for the as yet unfilled area is contained in two maps.[17] One accompanied the *First Annual Report of the
Commissioners on Boston Harbor and Back Bay Lands* in 1854; the other
was prepared for the Boston Water Power Company two years later
(fig. 242). In both maps the whole region is treated as one large, uniform area; streets are laid out on a rigidly rectangular scheme, and
no allowance is made for the interruption of the vast gridiron by
creeks or the two railroads which traverse this area. The district has
no center of interest and no dominant axis.

Gradually, however, this initial concept was modified for various
practical reasons and the vast 450-acre fill was broken down into four
or five sections that were fairly independent of each other. The first
steps in articulating the large tract into separate neighborhoods are
shown by maps of 1860, 1861, and 1863 (figs. 244, 245, 246).[18] In the
former, Columbus Avenue is laid out south of and parallel to the
tracks of the Boston and Providence Railroad; in the latter, Huntington Avenue first appears north of the tracks. Thus, the big filled
area is divided into two sections each with its own axis: the north-
ernmost part (to be called the Back Bay) running parallel to the river
with Commonwealth Avenue as its main axis, and the southernmost
section (which merged with the South End) aligned with the Boston
and Providence tracks and with Columbus and Huntington avenues
as twin centers of interest.

In the light of the subsequent development of the Back Bay as a
high-grade residential district, this articulation of the filled area was
a most fortunate thing. From the reports of the early commissioners,
however, one gathers that it was done reluctantly and out of sheer
necessity since they had envisioned the whole filled region as a homogeneous development. Between 1854 and 1856 the Boston officials,
who had from the first adopted a rather antagonistic attitude toward
the Commonwealth's activities in the Back Bay, blocked the commissioners' plans to connect the streets projected for the Back Bay
with those of the South End.[19] Rather than allow the gridiron system
proposed by the commissioners to intersect Tremont Street, the city
stubbornly prolonged its old pattern of cross streets onto the new land
north of Tremont. As the old system lay at an angle with the new
grid and had a very different scale, it imposed a barrier between the

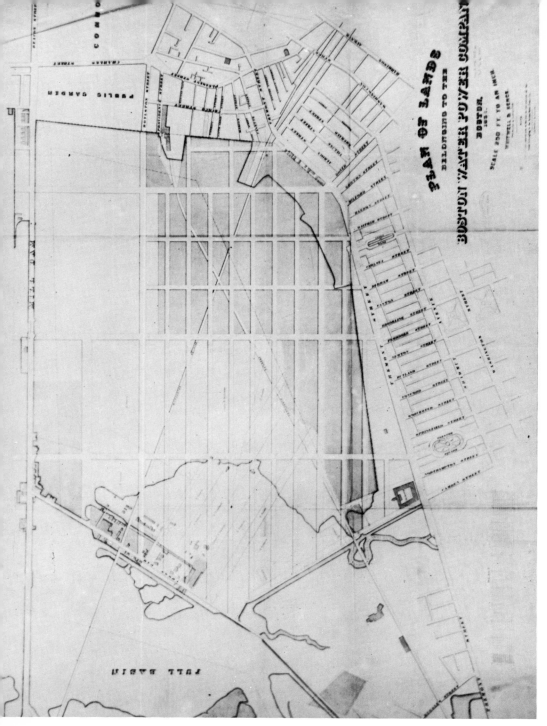

242   Plan projected for the Back Bay area in 1855, prepared by Whitwell and Henck for the Boston Water Power Company.

two systems. As a result, the plan of 1861 treats the Commonwealth's area as a virtual island with only a few of its thoroughfares related to those of adjacent territory.

The insular quality of the Back Bay district in the 1861 plan is least prevalent at the eastern end of the district where both Beacon and Boylston streets continue established thoroughfares into the city, but even here three streets—Newbury, Marlborough, and Commonwealth—are terminated by the Public Garden. On the south, toward the South End, only one Back Bay street, West Chester Park—now Massachusetts Avenue—attempts to make a logical connection with a principal South End street, and only two others bridge the railroad tracks to form roundabout junctions with the South End's pattern of streets.[20] At the district's western end, its streets meet those of Brookline with a singularly arbitrary and inflexible quality. Marlborough, Commonwealth, Newbury, and Boylston bump into Brookline Avenue at an awkward, sharp angle and stop; others merely stop short in the middle of Stony Brook; only Beacon Street continues its westward course (fig. 245). To the north, of course, all Back Bay streets stop at the river bank and no future bridge sites are indicated.

If this 1861 plan is insular in concept, it is also careless or uncertain as to how some details of the plan would be worked out. It would seem that the planner is only explicit about details of the area which are immediately to be built and that he is vague about or indifferent to problems in outlying sections of the district which would not be developed for many years to come. For example, the east-west axis of Commonwealth Avenue, two hundred and forty feet wide, is established with pomp and decision at the edge of the Public Garden but at the district's western end this axis is interrupted by an unmanageable block-long diagonal intersection with railway tracks. Beyond the tracks the axis reasserts itself for a short extension of one and a half blocks only to be choked off by Brookline Avenue. Similarly, the grid plan stops arbitrarily when it reaches the marsh at the juncture of Stony Brook and Muddy River and no egress is provided for the waters of these two streams into the Charles River. On the whole, one sees that the designer's intention is to sketch in the broad outlines of the district and to provide explicit working instructions for the immediate fill, but to leave specific problems concerning more distant areas for future planners to solve once the great fill had progressed that far. At the same time, it is clear that although the 1861 scheme is sometimes sketchy, it makes a deliberate effort to plan the entire northern part of the bay area as a unit. This was possible because the commission in 1854 had secured authority to control the street system of Gravelly Point, an area which lay above average high tide and which was therefore omitted from the 1853–1855 plans for the district.

Having been cut into northern and southern halves in 1861, the great 450-acre fill is subdivided still further in 1881 with the creation of Fenway Park. This action divides the northern half of the new area into eastern and western sections, and it comes about, as we shall see directly, in an effort to provide an outlet for Muddy River into the Charles. The final step in this process of segmentation is reached in 1884, when the Boston and Albany Railroad purchases for use as rail yards the triangular plot bounded by the tracks, Exeter Street, and Boylston Street. This purchase, together with the railroad's right of way, severs the area north of Boylston Street from that lying southwest of the tracks adjacent to Huntington Avenue.

Thus within the bounds of the original bay, four districts are created (fig. 243). Area I, bounded by the Public Garden, the river, Fenway Park, and Boylston Street, is an area that is exclusively residential in character. Area II is bounded by the river, Fenway Park, and the Brookline shore; this area may be subdivided again by the Boston and Albany tracks into a northern part, IIA, whose occupancy is similar to Area I, and a southern part, IIB, which remains undeveloped until the twentieth century. Area III, bounded by Fenway Park, the Boston and Albany tracks, and the Boston and Providence Railroad (now the New York, New Haven, and Hartford line), is mixed residential and commercial. Area IV, south of the latter railroad and bounded by the original shoreline, is really part of the South End neighborhood.

Let us now look more closely at Area I, the section referred to in Chapter One as the "sociological Back Bay." In this area we can also trace an evolution of the street system and of several public parks by means of maps. From the first it was clear that the main roadways would run east-west, and Commonwealth Avenue was planned as a dominant axis as early as 1853. In December of 1856 a system of alleyways was incorporated into the plan, Commonwealth Avenue was increased to its present width of two hundred feet, and setback lines of twenty or twenty-two feet were imposed on all property facing a

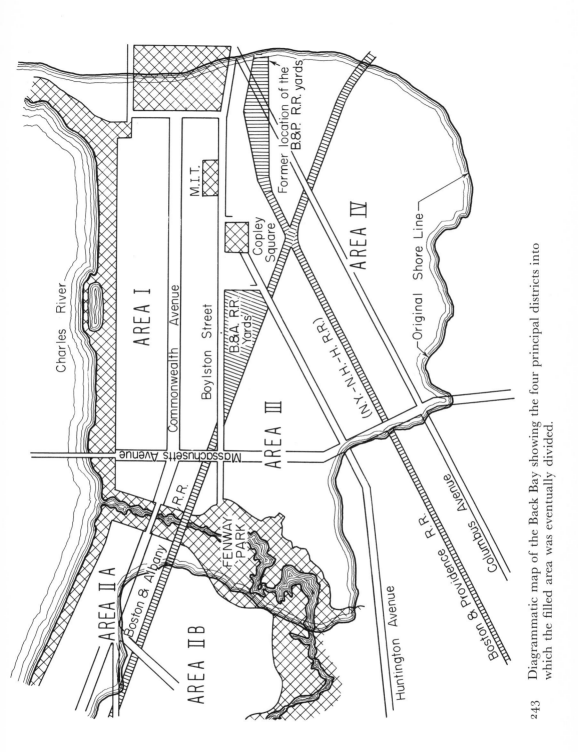

243   Diagrammatic map of the Back Bay showing the four principal districts into which the filled area was eventually divided.

Charles River

AREA I

AREA II A

AREA II B

AREA II

AREA IV

Commonwealth Avenue

Boylston Street

Massachusetts Avenue

M.I.T.

Copley Square

B.&A. RR Yards

(N.Y.-N.-H.-H. R.R.)

Former location of the B.&P. R.R. yards

Original Shore Line

Boston & Albany R.R.

FENWAY PARK

Huntington Avenue

Columbus Avenue

Boston & Providence R.R.

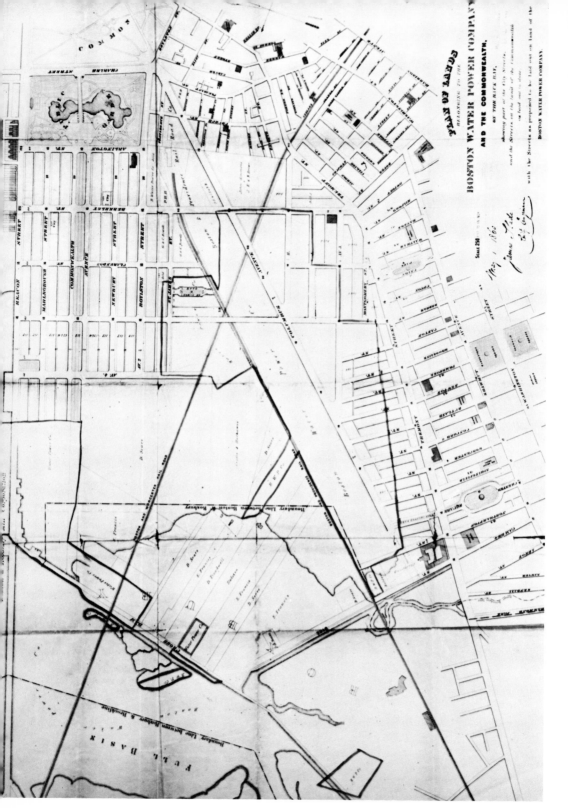

244   Plan for the Back Bay area in 1860, prepared by James Slade, city engineer.

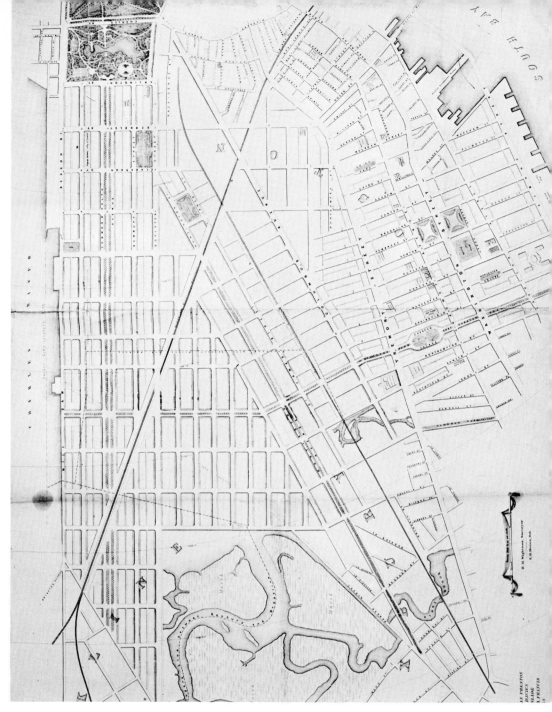

245   Plan for the Back Bay area in 1861, prepared by H. M. Wightman,
       surveyor, and James Slade, city engineer.

main street.[21] In 1861 two additional wide streets besides Commonwealth Avenue appear; one is Huntington Avenue, the other West Chester Park (later Massachusetts Avenue). And at this time West Chester Park is linked to the street system of the South End. Other than West Chester Park, however, the widths of the other transverse streets in Area I seem to have been arrived at without much concern, and no consistent interval was ever established for the blocks that lie between them.

In addition to this strong east-west axial layout it was also determined from the first to enhance the district with several green parks, but the placing and orientation of these areas was a matter of considerable indecision. The most vexing question concerned the location of Copley Square. Although some kind of open and planted area was envisioned in that neighborhood as early as 1860, its shape, location, and name were changed several times. The plan of 1860 shows a narrow residential green similar to Union Park in the South End lying between St. James Street and the Boston and Providence tracks. Named St. James Park, it was small, isolated, and unrelated to the Back Bay street system (fig. 244). One year later two public areas, each a block square, are indicated in the vicinity (fig. 245). Still called St. James Park but considerably larger than its predecessor, one plot faces Huntington Avenue and therefore lies at an angle with the gridiron pattern of Back Bay streets. The second location set aside for public institutions and extending between Berkeley and Clarendon streets, is eventually occupied by the Museum of Natural History and the first M.I.T. building. In this 1861 scheme Dartmouth Street does not carry through to the South End as had been planned a year earlier, thereby restricting direct communication between the two neighborhoods to Berkeley Street and West Chester Park. A third plan, dated February 20, 1863, and issued under the authority of the Back Bay Commissioners, shows Dartmouth Street continuing through to the South End while St. James Park is reoriented toward Boylston Street (fig. 246).

Still a fourth plan of 1870 follows the disposition of streets and squares of the 1863 map, but indicates that the open park has now been allocated to the Fine Arts Museum.[22] With the conversion of St. James Park into a museum site the idea of a green area in the immediate neighborhood seems temporarily to have been eliminated. In 1872 the Commonwealth deeded Massachusetts Institute of Tech-

246   Detail of a plan for the Back Bay area in 1863, prepared by H. M.
        Wightman, surveyor.

nology the triangular plot at the intersection of Huntington Avenue, Dartmouth Street, and Boylston Street (the present Copley Square), and an old building permit exists in the file of the Boston Building Department for an institutional structure on this site. (No other mention is made of the building, whether it was constructed or demolished.) Only in 1883, after the Commonwealth had donated the site (in 1880) of the present Public Library, did the city purchase the triangular plot and call it Copley Square.[23] In 1885 the small triangle in front of Trinity Church was also organized as a park. Eventually with the completion of the New Old South Church and Second Church in 1874, Chauncey Hall School in 1875, the Museum of Fine Arts in 1876, Trinity Church in 1877, and the Public Library in 1891—all facing Copley Square—the area emerged as one of the finest public squares in America. But this final form was arrived at in a most haphazard manner (fig. 247).

A second square was planned initially on Exeter Street between Marlborough and Beacon streets (figs. 244-246). The wall of houses on the north side of Beacon Street was to have been interrupted by an area of water, thus permitting the square direct access to the Charles River. Exeter Street, terminating at its north end at the water, was indicated in early plans of 1860, 1861, and 1863 as considerably wider than Dartmouth Street, but on the 1870 plan Dartmouth was finally established as the principal link with the South End. To accommodate the intersectional traffic, Dartmouth Street was given its present double width (equal to that of West Chester Park or Huntington Avenue) while Exeter Street was demoted to the usual sixty-foot width of a cross street. Although the commissioners' reports are silent on the matter, it is probable that the Exeter Street Square was eliminated in 1870 at the same time that Dartmouth Street was widened in order to compensate the Commonwealth for the loss of salable land. Presumably at the same time or soon after the Mill Corporation was released from its obligations to keep the park frontage open to the river.

In contrast to the halting evolutions of Copley or Exeter squares, the block bounded by Berkeley, Clarendon, Boylston, and Newbury streets was early set aside for public institutions. In 1862 work was commenced on the museum for the Boston Society of Natural History and the following year work began on the first building for the Massachusetts Institute of Technology.

247   A view of Copley Square in 1889 shows Trinity Church without its
later narthex and the original buildings on the north side of Copley
Square. In the foreground are the foundations of the Boston Public
Library.

In these three squares one sees a remnant of the old-fashioned
English system of residential greens scattered through the otherwise
French plan of the Back Bay area. Of these squares, one was entirely
eliminated; Copley Square was pushed out into the intersection of
Huntington Avenue and Boylston Street so that it entirely lost its
feeling of a secluded residential park; and the third was filled with a
museum and school. In the end, therefore, the French extensionist

plan—that of the street-corridor rather than the cell-like residential square—prevailed in the Back Bay even more strongly than Arthur Gilman had originally intended.

In 1881 an important topographical change began to take place in the Back Bay Fens. The creation of Fenway Park commenced with a consideration of the important and difficult problem of Stony Brook and Muddy River flood waters which the early planners had simply ignored. In the late seventies the Boston Park Commission, a body created in 1874, asked several landscape architects for schemes for conducting the waters of these two streams to the Charles River. When in 1879 Frederick Law Olmsted was asked to review these competition designs, he realized that some of the competitors had failed to take into account the flooding of the two streams while others, thinking exclusively of that factor, sought to treat the area as a kind of dry reservoir bounded by stone embankments. Combining aspects of both solutions, Olmsted proposed the present scheme, a parked section in the low-lying areas with roadways built up to form flood dykes along the park's periphery.

Thus a spacious park was created and a permanent open area was established as a western termination for the district—a condition which had always existed in effect because of the large expanses of tidal flats which still remained to be developed. If Fenway Park had not been created, however, the Back Bay residential district would have lacked a clear-cut stopping point, and eventually it would have had to merge with less aristocratic neighborhoods to the west and south.

Fortunately for its homogeneous character and its future stability, the Back Bay was provided with definite boundaries on all four sides: on the north and east sides, the Charles River and the Public Garden; on the west, the open, unimproved tidal flats until these were developed into Fenway Park; on the south, the Boston and Albany Railway yards. Although the west and south boundaries had not been a part of the original concept of the district and did not come into being until 1881 and 1884, they were essential to the later integrity of the district (fig. 243). Functioning as barriers to isolate the Back Bay from the chaos and confusion of the other sections of the city, they enabled the Commonwealth to create a uniformly desirable residential area and to regulate it with strict building restrictions. Even more, these barriers protected the Back Bay for many decades from the creeping blight of contagion from nearby slum or commercial neighborhoods similar to that which has spoiled so many other fine nineteenth century residential districts in America.

The development of Fenway Park brings us to the point where Back Bay problems can no longer be considered in a purely local sense. From this point on plans for the Back Bay must be thought of in terms of their relation to the larger metropolitan area. The solution of the Stony Brook flooding problem had wide repercussions. Within five years of the beginning of the Fenway project, Olmsted had extended the park to a chain of six public parks that stretched from Charlesbank to Jamaica Pond and the Arnold Arboretum. By 1898 this chain had been increased to nineteen green parks which girdled the city.[24] In 1893 the Metropolitan Park Commission replaced the Boston Park Commission, which had been constituted in 1874. Representing thirty-five neighboring towns as well as Boston, the new commission was the first board for regional planning in America. It is interesting, thus, to be able to trace the roots of this historic group to early attempts to solve a local drainage problem in the Back Bay area.

In the same way, the Charles River Basin project began as a local matter and gradually expanded until it became a vital link in the recreation and transportation facilities of Greater Boston. The idea of a basin protected from the fluctuations of the tide by a tidal dam had been under discussion since 1859. Originally, however, the idea was discarded for fear that an obstruction of the natural flow of the tide might cause the main harbor to silt in. Again, in 1876, the Boston Park Commission agitated for such a tidal dam in connection with a sizable fill along the Boston shore of the Charles. As a part of the river improvement they proposed to create a broad parkway and to build a new row of houses fronting park and river. Such effective opposition to the proposal was raised by the householders on the water side of Beacon Street that the entire project was tabled. In 1893 the Commonwealth was persuaded to authorize the construction of a one-hundred-foot-wide concrete promenade beyond the old sea wall and ten years later it approved the construction of the Charles River Dam.[25] Completed in 1910, this dam stabilized the water level of the basin at eight feet above mean low tide, some eighteen inches below mean high tide and seven feet below the mark of very high tides. A further encroachment on the water area of the Back Bay came in 1929-1931 when the Storrow Embankment was constructed to provide a large park immediately north of the promenade. This improvement was conceived as a recreational area for all of Boston but it particularly benefited residents of the adjacent Back Bay. The construction of the Storrow Memorial Drive in 1951, cutting between the residential streets and the river, isolated the Back Bay from the recreational area which for twenty years had contributed so much to the district.

We come, then, to the last stage of the evolution of the Back Bay plan with a discussion of the part that the district plays in the system of traffic ways of modern Boston. It will be recalled that to some extent the area had long served as a link between Boston and the mainland to the west since the Mill Dam, after its completion in 1821, served also as a toll road. During the forty years in which the great fill was being made, the only function of Back Bay streets (except Beacon Street) was to accommodate local traffic; but when the fill reached the far side of the bay, a certain amount of through traffic had to be cared for. The matter came to a head in 1881 when a scheme was needed for continuing Commonwealth Avenue to the Brookline shore. For this vexing problem Olmsted produced his brilliant design which resolved the earlier conflict between the gridiron system of streets and the diagonal pattern of intersecting railroad tracks by bending the axis of Commonwealth Avenue just west of Massachusetts Avenue (fig. 248). By thus averting a clash between the two incompatible systems which seemed to threaten the integrity of the great boulevard, the designer was able to continue the dominant axis of the avenue on the Brookline shore. Almost as important, he furnished Commonwealth Avenue with a visual western limit. For as one looks along the avenue to the west from Gloucester or Hereford street, the buildings along its southern side form a plane that stops one's view and, although foreshortened, this reinforces visually the impression that the district has limits and is a natural unit. Without such a break, Commonwealth Avenue could dissipate its monumentality in endless, tiresome vistas as does that section of the thoroughfare beyond Kenmore Square.

Even before the connection with the western shore had been effected, a vital north-south artery was created out of Massachusetts Avenue. In 1889 that roadway was continued to the Cambridge shore by means of Harvard Bridge. To the south the avenue bridges the railroad tracks

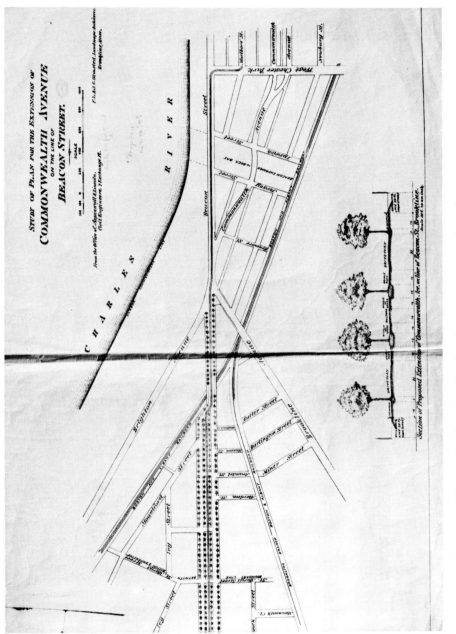

248 Frederick Law Olmsted's plan of 1881 for the western extension of Commonwealth Avenue.

and continues through the South End by means of West Chester Park (now also called Massachusetts Avenue). Thus two arteries, one east-west and the other north-south, were created which were sufficient to carry the relatively light horse and motor traffic of the early 1900's.

In recent times even bigger and more prominent channels of communication have been required. When the construction in 1937 of an underpass on Commonwealth Avenue and the rerouting of traffic along one-way streets in the Back Bay failed to solve the problem created by the motor car, the solution was the construction of Storrow Memorial Drive along the Boston bank of the Charles River. The disadvantages of this addition are that it encroaches still more on the water area of the basin and seriously restricts access from the Back Bay to the embankment recreational areas; indeed it accentuates the insularity of the district. In the same way, the construction of the expressway through the end of Fenway Park nearest the river in 1965 has not impaired the integrity of the Back Bay, though it has desecrated one of the loveliest city parks in America. Instead of a quiet river bank and an inviting park, the north and west boundaries of the district have now stiffened into hostile traffic ways.

In reviewing the topographical development of the area, one realizes that the concept of the Back Bay has always been an enlarging one. Although this process has been gradual, the historian can distinguish four distinct stages in the development of the district. In the 1840's the Back Bay was merely an extension of the mainland onto the newly filled land. Between 1856 and 1880 the district became a kind of island adjacent to the city, an ornamental area of fine homes and handsome public buildings, of prosperous and pleasant prospects that were mercifully isolated from the surrounding chaos of commercial and tenement districts. The third phase commenced in 1881 when the advancing fill reached the Brookline shore and the district began to extend itself onto the mainland, out Bay State Road and along the banks of the Fens. At that point the Back Bay began to lose its insular quality and to function as a link between Boston and the western suburbs. Some of its streets changed from quiet ways carrying only local traffic to through streets charged with traffic for the suburbs. The passage of through traffic, however, was soon choked off by the upsurge of local traffic and parked cars after World War II. By the early 1950's the fourth and present phase of development had begun with the building of Storrow and Embankment drives, and it continued with the extension into the heart of the city of the Massachusetts Turnpike in 1964. Constructed along the already established boundaries of the district, these throughways leave the area more of an island than ever before.

Despite this changing role of the Back Bay within Greater Boston, the district retains certain of its former qualities. Although the streets are now stifled with parked cars and local traffic and despite the heightening silhouette of modern apartment buildings on the area's periphery, the region still is pervaded by sunshine and trees. Even though the open country has receded far beyond the Full Basin or the Brookline shore, the pedestrian within the Back Bay still is aware of open space and greenery that bounds his district on all sides. He retains the impression that open country is not beyond reach. If seventy-five years ago Commonwealth Avenue served as a corridor of space that connected the open expanses of the Public Garden and the Full Basin, it functions today as a spacious, vital link in the chain of green parks that leads from the Public Garden to the Fens, to the Arnold Arboretum, and to the country beyond.

Before leaving the Back Bay plan, brief mention should be made of several unrealized schemes for the development of the area, schemes which were advanced in their day with considerable vigor and with various degrees of practical or artistic justification. One of these was David Sears's plan for Silver Lake which he submitted to the Commonwealth in December 1850. Sears, a capitalist who had bought up great areas of undeveloped tidal flats on the southern shores of the Back Bay, had good reason to see the filling operations speeded.[26] Laboring under the misapprehension that the Commonwealth itself would not claim title to any of the land below the riparian line, Sears offered to deed the Commonwealth thirty-seven and one-half acres of his land provided the legislature would set aside an equal area for a lake as specified on the map which he submitted (fig. 249). Other than the lake, the plan has little to recommend it since it failed as completely as the first commission's schemes of 1853 and 1855 to consider the two railroad tracks which slash through the district in a great X. The four residential squares that he proposed were reminiscent of English developments; but placed on main thoroughfares or cut by a railroad, they could never have provided the genteel seclusion of a successful English residential park. Historically the plan has

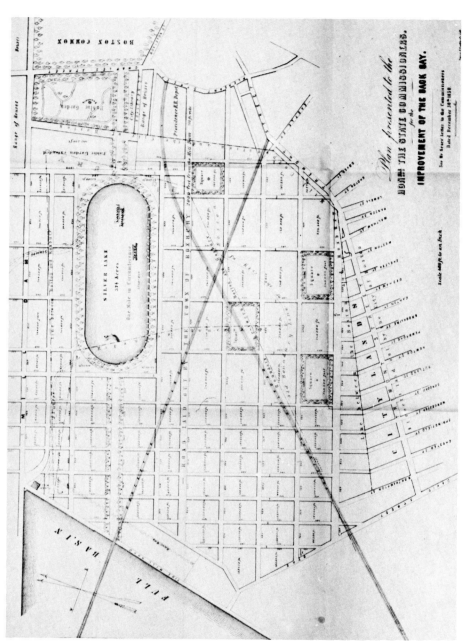

249   David Sears's proposed lake, 1850.

some interest, as the axis projecting through Silver Lake is the first hint of what will become Commonwealth Avenue. The idea of filling the lake by means of sluiceways from the Full Basin presupposed, of course, that that body would remain open water. This well typifies the Boston outlook at mid-century which could not envision that there would ever be a demand for the land occupied by the Full Basin, that is, the area lying west of Hereford Street.

An even more ambitious scheme for preserving an expanse of water in the heart of the district was advocated by George Snelling in 1859. His suggestion was to reserve as open water an area of the Receiving Basin between the present Marlborough and Newbury streets and extending from the present Arlington Street as far west as the Cross Dam.[27] Snelling brought his proposal to the attention of his contemporaries in a thirty-page open letter to the legislature, but his scheme was not given serious attention as the filling of Back Bay lands had been underway for two years and some lots were already sold. Such a generous allotment of space for a lake would have eliminated the Commonwealth's financial profit from the development of the area and it would undoubtedly have been an irresistible target for modern traffic engineers.

Elaborate schemes were envisioned in 1844 and 1856 by Robert Gourlay and by Charles Davenport for the future development of the Charles River Basin. The Gourlay plan is so visionary that it has little to do with the actual problems confronting the builders of the Back Bay.[28] Davenport had a lithographed plan and view prepared which pictured both banks of the Charles River with broad concourses and blocks filled with mansions and churches of the sort that came eventually to occupy the Back Bay (fig. 250). As three-quarters owner of the Cambridge flats, he was somewhat biased in his presentation, but in light of recent developments along the Cambridge embankment, the Davenport concept does not appear so impractical after all.

Despite the disappointment caused by the city's unwillingness to cooperate in developing the entire filled area as a monumental unit, the Commissioners on Public Lands were still determined to lay out the land held by the Commonwealth with all possible dignity and impressiveness. Although the group never recorded their objectives in so many words, it seems clear to the present-day critic that the sponsors had three goals in mind. They wanted the new quarter to be spacious,

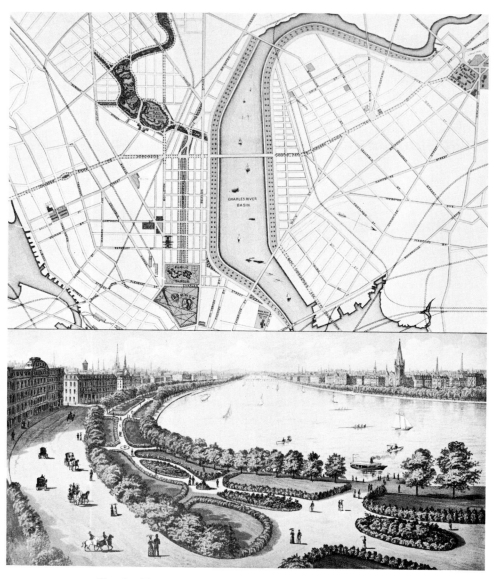

250   Charles Davenport's vision of the Charles River Embankment, 1874.

homogeneous, ornamental. And, of course, it had to be economically profitable.

To secure spaciousness, the planners provided five broad avenues which traversed the area. Varying in width from ninety to two hundred feet, these roadways were amplified by setbacks on abutting property which, in effect, created spatial corridors 112 to 240 feet wide. These wide streets were not created by a mere stroke of the pen; they were attained at considerable sacrifice on the part of the Commonwealth. For example, the planners in 1856 decided to enhance the spacious character of the district by widening Commonwealth Avenue from one hundred and twenty feet to its present two-hundred-foot width. To secure the adherence of the Boston Water Power Company to this revised plan in its section of the fill, Massachusetts had to compensate the company for the loss of salable land by ceding to it twelve acres of state-owned property in the Full Basin. Indeed, of the entire state holdings in the Back Bay, 43 percent of the area was devoted to streets and parks compared to 49 percent to salable building lots.[29] These facts illustrate the practical limits to which the Commonwealth and the commissioners were prepared to go in order to secure an ample residential quarter.

To insure homogeneity, the Back Bay commissioners laid down specific property restrictions and incorporated these into the deeds. Use of property was to be limited; in no part of the district was manufacturing permitted, and along Commonwealth Avenue and parts of Boylston Street commercial uses were proscribed.[30] As a general policy, the planners also discouraged stables in the residential sections. Although the catalogues which advertised the early sales of Back Bay land specifically stated that private stables would not be allowed, no such provision was actually incorporated into the deeds. There seems to have been a kind of gentleman's understanding that a private stable would not be erected if an abutting property owner objected. A number of houses on the water side of Beacon Street had stables that opened upon the alley next to the river, but since lots in this position had been owned originally by the Boston and Roxbury Mill Corporation, they were not subject to all the restrictions imposed on Commonwealth land.

The exterior appearance of buildings was also subject to control to the extent that the edifice had to be at least three stories high, constructed of masonry, and, except for minor appendages, its facade could not project beyond a uniform building line which was established for the entire street. Even after it had disposed of its holdings in the Back Bay, the Commonwealth continued to enforce these property restrictions.

Private enterprise followed the lead of the state in the matter of property restrictions. The Boston Water Power Company and the Boston and Roxbury Mill Corporation, which owned the land west of the Commonwealth's holdings and north of Beacon Street, included restrictions in their title deeds similar to those used by Massachusetts. As late as 1900 the Bay State Road Improvement Society, a group of property owners, voluntarily agreed to a fifty-year prohibition of commercial or industrial uses of property on that street.[31] When this restriction terminated on January 1, 1950, it was not renewed.

A uniformly dignified appearance of the district was also enhanced by the provision of sixteen-foot alleyways which contained necessary service facilities for the houses. In contrast to New York, Boston had frequently employed this practical device in the past. Appearing first in Louisburg Square (1826), it had been uniformly used in the 1850's when the new South End section was laid out. The obvious advantage of the alley is that it leaves the front of the house completely free of kitchen entrance and service areas. In New York, where there are no alleys, the necessary service elements could never be entirely hidden under the high stoop, and in the Back Bay, where there was no long flight of steps leading to the front entrance, the designer would have had even more serious trouble disguising service facilities at the front of the house. The presence of a service alley in the Back Bay, therefore, was a desirable feature, and it kept delivery wagons off the main streets.

In addition to spaciousness and homogeneity, the Back Bay district was "ornamental" as well. In order to create a quarter that was a fitting ornament for Boston, now swollen in population, prosperity, and self-esteem, the Back Bay not only was occupied with the town's newest and finest mansions, it was filled with public buildings and churches and developed as the city's principal cultural area. Within thirty years of the beginning of the fill, the new area was occupied by the Public Library, two colleges, two museums, several clubs and service institutions, five schools, and no less than twelve churches.[32]

This enthusiastic church building in the Back Bay invites particular comment because it was not warranted by the population of the immediate district. Within the area there were about eighteen hundred houses and its population could not significantly have exceeded ten thousand persons (allowing four adults per dwelling and another three thousand inhabitants for the district's thirty-nine hotels and apartment houses). Assuming that half of these people were churchgoers or members of the sects which had churches in the district (there was no Catholic church, for example), this would mean a ratio of a little more than four hundred persons for each church. It is also interesting to note that five of the twelve foundations were Congregational, three Unitarian, three Episcopal.

Several circumstances encouraged the location of congregations in the Back Bay region. There was, of course, the desirability of having one's church within walking distance of home. Churchgoing was a family affair and it fitted both the economical and traditional Sabbath habits of Bostonians to walk to church rather than to ride in carriages. A more practical factor was the high value of real estate in the older sections of the city, especially in the Old South End. This economic pressure encouraged churches along with their parishoners to move to less commercialized sections, and the substantial figure received from the sale of the old church property went a long way toward defraying the expenses of the new site and edifice.[33] The great fire of 1872 burned other congregations out of their old buildings and, faced with rebuilding, they found it expedient to move to a less commercialized locality. Except for the suburbs, which were already supplied with churches, there was no other free area in Boston in which to build. These practical motivations, however, must have been strongly implemented by a desire on the part of the various congregations to ornament the Back Bay—and to be a part of Boston's brightest, newest ornament—a suspicion that may be confirmed by the fact that two congregations moved to the Back Bay in the eighties from the New South End.

Similarly, public buildings were multiplied in the new section. Here again, as in the case of the churches, practical factors encouraged the location of these institutions in the region. As we have seen, this was a period of enormous expansion and development for Boston, a period which saw many new and necessary institutions come into existence. These new organizations, such as the natural history and art museums or Massachusetts Institute of Technology, would surely have found it difficult to secure suitable accommodations in the already congested older sections of the city. In the Back Bay, however, land was available in large parcels, and in many cases it could be obtained without a cash outlay since almost any institution that performed a public service could secure a grant of land from the Commonwealth. In all, Massachusetts donated almost nine acres of Back Bay land, 8 percent of its entire holdings, for public buildings.[34]

Along with the Commonwealth's bounteous gifts of land to various civic institutions there must also have gone the idea that the presence of public buildings was desirable, that they added prestige and distinction to the district in which they were placed. This attitude can be seen in the municipal vote of 1859 to restrict all buildings forever from the Public Garden excepting a city hall. It can be seen also in the endeavors of private citizens to entice various public institutions into a neighborhood with offers of money or free land.[35] It appears that the commissioners for the Commonwealth were aware of the economic advantages of attracting institutions to the Back Bay. Their report of 1863 boasts that the appraised value of property on Newbury Street opposite Massachusetts Institute of Technology and the Natural History Museum had already doubled. Private enterprise was so impressed with the monetary return of such a policy that the Boston Water Power Company donated the site for the old Museum of Fine Arts on Copley Square (the present site of the Copley Plaza Hotel).

It is also clear that these new institutions in the Back Bay filled a cultural need in Boston and that they served the public well. To mention only the activities of the earliest of these, Huntington Hall in the first Massachusetts Institute of Technology building was for many years the scene of the Lowell Lecture series, and it was used for the Handel and Haydn Society concerts.[36] Despite its location on the third story of the old Rogers building, some seventy steps above the street, the hall also served Trinity congregation as a meeting place while the new church edifice was under construction.

Indeed, the cultural center which developed in the Back Bay was probably the result of three factors: the commissioners' deliberate policy of encouragement, the availability of land for building, and the presence in the Back Bay of the city's leading families.[37]

At the very time that the Back Bay was achieving its spacious, its homogeneous, and its ornamental qualities, however, it was failing to develop certain practical facilities which are ordinarily regarded as an essential part of a well-planned community. In the course of time these facilities were added but often in a haphazard fashion. Originally there was, for example, no shopping center in the district. This shortcoming can be explained by the fact that the main retail center of Boston was within easy walking distance. As far as household provisions were concerned, the well-to-do housekeeper in the Back Bay did not go to the tradesman's shop but rather had him bring his ware to the house. The alleyways were busy places of a morning with a long procession of butchers', grocers', and bakers' wagons stopping at the kitchen entrances. The two nearest public markets were on Washington Street, at least a mile beyond the confines of the Back Bay; and S. S. Pierce, that Boston institution, did not build its Dartmouth Street store (now lamentably destroyed) until 1887. The present-day commercial aspect of Copley Square did not emerge until the twentieth century. Originally the square was surrounded by religious edifices, public institutions, and living quarters (fig. 247). In addition to a church, a school, and two apartment hotels, the north side of the square was occupied by eight single-family houses.[38]

Another institution conspicuous in its absence for the first twenty years of the Back Bay's existence was a public school. This situation can only be explained by the fact that the children of most Back Bay families went to private schools. In *Persons and Places* George Santayana retraces in his memory the long walks from his mother's house at 302 Beacon Street to the various public schools he attended in the South End, and he recalls how few neighbor boys accompanied him on this long trek.[39] Not until 1876 was the Prince Public School built at the corner of Exeter and Newbury streets.

For public transportation the Back Bay was somewhat better provided. Although a Massachusetts statute forbade the horsecar to operate on Commonwealth Avenue, a line wended its way through the district via Boylston Street, Arlington, Newbury, Dartmouth, Marlborough, Massachusetts Avenue, and Beacon until it eventually reached Kenmore Square. The main horsecar lines from Boston to Brookline or Roxbury, however, were still carried on Washington, Shawmut, and Tremont streets, routes that had been established in the 1850's when the Back Bay was still open water.

Those Back Bay residents who kept a private carriage but did not have their own stable could keep their horses in two localities. Although up-graded considerably by the addition of the Brimmer Street neighborhood, the area between Charles Street and the river, originally the service area for Beacon Hill, was still occupied by a number of public stables.[40] This section also provided the desired private stables for the Back Bay during the first two decades or so of its growth. After 1875 additional stables were built in the extreme southwest corner of the district on Newbury Street west of Hereford Street, and along West Chester Park south of Commonwealth Avenue.

While admiring the harmonious aspects of the whole Back Bay quarter, it is well to remember that it was by no means the first section in Boston in which an effort had been made to relate a group of buildings to their environment. Numbers of residential squares had been laid out in the English manner (though sometimes, following good English usage, these "squares" were square in name only): Tontine Crescent, built in 1792; Louisburg Square, 1826; Pemberton Square, 1835; Franklin and Blackstone squares, 1849; Chester Square, 1850; Union and Worcester squares, 1851—to name only the most important examples. Before Arthur Gilman laid out Commonwealth Avenue in 1856, Boston had also seen an important example of axial planning in Alexander Parris' Quincy Market group of 1824. Here the center axis was established by the porticoed granite market hall and by the older brick Faneuil Hall of Bulfinch; two minor parallel axes were formed by blocks of four-story granite stores which faced the main market structure. Although the streets on either side of the principal market were not of equal width, one being sixty-five feet wide and the other one hundred and two feet, the individual buildings that were built had, by purchase agreement, to conform to the design which Parris had prepared. The noble and uniform effect of this group of structures may well have encouraged Gilman and the early commissioners to strive for equal congruity in the Back Bay.[41]

Nor were the Back Bay commissioners the first Bostonians to realize the advantages of evoking legal property restrictions. When a group of owners of tidal flats along Albany Street banded together in 1804 to fill their property, they signed an agreement to set all buildings ten feet back from the street. Similarly, in the same year Jonathan Mason and several abutting property owners on Mount Vernon Street decided to accept the facade of Mason's mansion as a building line; in 1821 a legal indenture supplemented this informal agreement.[42]

And mention has just been made of the building requirements in the Quincy Market district.

Any attempt to evaluate the Back Bay plan obliges the critic to consider the district on two levels. He must think of it first as a nineteenth century residential area, and next as an area related to metropolitan Boston of the present day. Briefly summarized, the achievements of the Back Bay plan from the first point of view are these. Arthur Gilman and the three commissioners created a monumental plan for the Back Bay district. The great scheme of axial extension makes a sharp break from the English cell-like, additive scheme of private residential squares which had previously guided Boston's building. Commonwealth Avenue is probably the handsomest boulevard created in nineteenth century United States. Secondly, the early plan was both orderly and flexible. The streets are regular without being monotonous. With one portion fairly well built up before the next was begun, the district possessed an impressive unity at each stage of its development, yet it was flexible enough to grow with Boston for more than half a century. Third, the generous allotment of land for streets and parks was probably unique in mid-century urban planning in America. The sense of spaciousness which permeates the district was further enhanced by the large open areas that existed on all sides. Fourth, provided with definite limits which isolated the Back Bay from other parts of the city, the district was able to develop and later to preserve a distinct and impressive character of its own. Fifth, although possessing a sense of entity and separation, the Back Bay had as many points of contact with adjacent areas as traffic and communication needs required. The most successful of these was Olmsted's brilliant plan for the western end of Commonwealth Avenue which provided a transition from the Back Bay to the heterogeneous areas beyond Kenmore Square and which solved the potential conflict between the gridiron system of streets and the diagonal railway tracks. This excellent solution, as well as the creation of the freight yards along Boylston Street which so effectively separated the district from the nondescript area along Huntington Avenue, were not, be it admitted, a part of the original plan. Sixth, the property restrictions imposed on the Back Bay property were farsighted and they did much to endow the district with a congruous and imposing quality. Seventh, the cluster of educational and religious institutions in the neighborhood of Copley Square created a splendid cultural focus for Boston. This was, in all probability, one of the first civic centers created in a large city in this country.

On the negative side of the ledger there is the failure of the early planners to make the most of the Charles River. The projected Exeter Park with its sliplike approach to the river would not have provided the district with adequate access to the water. In part this defect can be explained by the division in ownership—the water side of Beacon Street was owned by the Boston and Roxbury Mill Corporation whose lands were not controlled by the commission and could not, therefore, be parceled out for civic betterment. More than that, the Charles River in those days was not always beautiful and fragrant. Despite the prestige of the water side of Beacon Street, householders and architects resolutely turned their backs on the water and built their stables there; not until the completion of the Charles Dam in 1910 did the river become a really desirable area. A second failure was the lack of distinction between single-family homes and apartments, as both were classed as residential edifices and allowed in the same area. If such a differentiation had been made and the apartments relegated to a specific section on the periphery of the district, say Boylston and Newbury streets from Dartmouth Street to the Fens, another line of defense could have been added against the infringement of commercial interests and even greater visual unity could have been attained within the district itself. In defense of the early planners, it must be admitted that the apartment was still novel in America and its advantages and disadvantages were not as completely understood as they are today. Third, no shopping center was provided for the district, though in light of the buying habits of Back Bay households in the nineteenth century, this was not a serious drawback. Fourth, judged in terms of the monumental, French, axial plan, the Back Bay scheme lacked focal points at the eastern and western limits of the district. It is true that the open spaces of the Full Basin and then the open Brookline shore formed a kind of objective toward which the eye was drawn and which was balanced on the eastern limit by the similarly open Public Garden, but under the formal Baroque scheme which Gilman had chosen, foci at both ends of Commonwealth Avenue should have been provided. On the other hand, this extensionist attitude, this unwillingness to limit the district, was the

Back Bay's chief asset in terms of future Boston planning.

From the point of view of the modern city planner, the only criticism that can be leveled against the nineteenth century designer is that he could not foresee the staggering requirements of present-day traffic. If he could have done so, he would certainly have laid out a much wider north-south artery (Massachusetts Avenue) to provide for crosstown traffic. Nothing he might have done in terms of broader east-west streets (similar to Commonwealth Avenue) would have solved the present problem of traffic pouring into Boston from Brookline and the suburbs; indeed, to have funneled such quantities of traffic through the Back Bay would have destroyed it as a residential area long ago.

All in all the present century should be enormously grateful for the Back Bay and its authors. The nineteenth century planners preserved the Charles River despite repeated attempts to engulf it in short-sighted real estate profiteering. Moreover, they not only created an orderly district but protected it with clearly defined borders from the creeping contagion of adjacent blighted areas. This enabled the district to retain for a long time its character as a high-grade residential quarter and finally to make an orderly transition to an area of offices and apartments. As a result, the Back Bay has not suffered the drastic changes in value and shifts in population that have overtaken the South End and so many other once-fashionable districts in nineteenth century America. Further, the Back Bay plan preserved essential approaches to the open country. By reason of the district's extensionist plan and because of the spacious proportions of its streets, the door was left open to future growth and development. And finally, in its initial plan and subsequent development the Back Bay retained broad channels of trees and grass and open water that penetrate to the very center of modern Boston. Because of Arthur Gilman's Commonwealth Avenue, because of Frederick Law Olmsted's park system, and because of the open stretches of the Charles River, the twentieth century inhabitant, standing in the heart of the city and looking out onto sprawling modern Boston, can enjoy the restorative qualities of space and greenery so rare in other urban centers. Despite the grime and congestion of a huge metropolis, one senses that he still has a lifeline to the open country even though the country has receded far beyond the visible horizon.

APPENDIX A

BUILDINGS CONSTRUCTED IN THE BACK BAY

Information is given regarding ownership of property when it is known. The number in parentheses following the name of the first owner indicates that the house was still in possession of the original family at the time of the insurance atlases of: (1) 1884, (2) 1889, (3) 1898, (4) 1902, (5) 1908, (6) 1912, (7) 1922, (8) 1928, or (9) when the district was first inspected by the author in 1940.

In a few cases a second name is placed in parentheses below the name of the house builder. This is the first long-term owner of the house. No attempt is made to indicate subsequent ownership no matter for how long a period one family held the property.

As property of women and minors was often held in the name of a trustee, long-term ownership of certain family residences is not indicated on this list. Similarly, a family home inherited by a married daughter is not here recorded.

No study of ownership was made in areas converted to commercial uses (Boylston and Newbury streets), in areas that were constructed late (Bay State Road, for example), or on streets where the house numbers were changed (Charles Street).

Number	Date	Owner	Architect

BEACON STREET, CHARLES STREET TO EMBANKMENT ROAD

CHARLES TO RIVER STREETS, NORTH SIDE

Number	Date	Owner	Architect
67	1845	G. M. Dexter	G. M. Dexter
68	1845	G. M. Dexter	G. M. Dexter
69	1845	G. M. Dexter	G. M. Dexter

RIVER TO BRIMMER STREETS, NORTH SIDE

Number	Date	Owner	Architect
70	1828	H. G. Otis	
71	1828	H. G. Otis	
72	1828	Benjamin Joy	
73	1828	William Sullivan	
74	1828	Jonathan Mason	
75	1828	Jonathan Mason	
76	1847	John Warren	
	1906	Mrs. O. Iasigi	A. W. Longfellow
77	1855	H. Sigourney	
78	1848	Crowninshield	
79	1848	Sam Whitwell	
80	1848	Mifflin	
81	1849	William Appleton	
82	1855	Tisdale Drake	
	1925	10-unit apartment	J. D. Leland
83	1850	Edward Codman	
84	1844	H. G. Otis	
	1911	Bayard Thayer	Ogden Codman

BRIMMER TO BEAVER STREETS, NORTH SIDE

Number	Date	Owner	Architect
85	1844	David Sears (Sidney Morse)	
86	1856	David Sears (Hannah Joy)	
87	1910	H. F. Sears	Wheelwright, Haven
88	1846	Andrew Hall	
	1852	Fox, Standish (S. Payson) (3)	
89	1852	Fox, Standish (E. Parker)	
90	1852	Fox, Turner (James Reed) (3)	
91	1852	Fox, Turner (Richard Parke)	

BEAVER STREET TO EMBANKMENT ROAD, NORTH SIDE

Number	Date	Owner	Architect
92	1849	William Ropes	George M. Dexter
93	1849	Benjamin Curtis	George M. Dexter
94	1849	Arthur Payson	George M. Dexter
95	1849	Sidney Bartlett	George M. Dexter
96	1849	G. M. Dexter	George M. Dexter
97	1849	George Curtis	George M. Dexter
98	1850	William Lawrence	George M. Dexter
99	1852	William Goddard	George M. Dexter

BEACON STREET, EMBANKMENT ROAD TO BERKELEY STREET

NORTH SIDE

100	1856	George Hovey (3)	
	1924	40-unit apartment	
102	1856	Charles Fessenden	C. Allbright
	1938	8-unit apartment	
104	1856	James Beal (8)	
106	1856	John Barnard (2)	
108	1856	J. T. Coolidge (2)	
110	1856	Joseph Coolidge	
112	1856	Nathan Hooper	
114	1856	Robert Hooper	
116	1856	Tom Perkins	
118	1856	R. S. Fay	
	1907	H. P. King	Little, Browne
120	1857	Benjamin Boardman (1)	
	1937	8-unit apartment	Saul Moffie
122	1857	George Upham	
124	1860	Charles Stoddard (2)	
126	1860	John Jeffries (3)	George Snell
128	1860	Francis Manning	George Snell
130	1861	Hollis Hunnewell (4)	George Snell

BEACON STREET, ARLINGTON TO BERKELEY STREETS

SOUTH SIDE

101	1862	Arthur Devins	
103	1862	Sam Tilton (6)	
105	1862	Louisa Adams	
107	1862	Fred Bradlee (8)	
109	1862	George Upham	
111	1863	Eben Dale	
113	1863	John Bradlee (7)	N. J. Bradlee
115	1863	John Bradlee	N. J. Bradlee
117	1864	C. W. Freeland (2)	
119	1865	Charles Blake (1)	
121	1865	Andrew McKinney	
125	1866	Albert Kelsey	
	1937	Apartment	
127	1862	W. C. Wharton (6)	
129	1862	John Dunbar	
131	1861	S. Perkins	
		(Christopher Thayer) (3)	
133	1861	S. Perkins	
		(John Sturgis)	
135	1860	S. H. Russell (4)	
137	1860	Catherine Gibson (9)	
139	1860	George Upham	
141	1860	E. & M. Hooper	
143	1861	J. L. Gardner	Edward Cabot
145	1861	J. L. Gardner	Edward Cabot
147	1861	J. L. Gardner	
		(Randolph Coolidge) (7)	

BEACON STREET, BERKELEY TO CLARENDON STREETS

NORTH SIDE

Number	Date	Owner	Architect
132	1861	David Sears (8)	
134	1860	William Bramhall	
136	1860	Charles Kirby	Charles Kirby
138	1860	Charles Kirby	Charles Kirby
140	1860	Gardner Brewer	
142	1860	George Wales (4)	
	1936	Apartment	
144	1860	John Blanchard	
146	1863	Susan Wells	
148	1860	T. J. Coolidge (6)	
150	1913	George Warren	Parker, Thomas, Rice
	1860	B. T. Loring	
152	1860	David Stewart	
		(Isabella Gardner) (3)	
	1904	E. S. Draper	A. W. Longfellow
154	1861	Peleg Chandler (2)	
156	1861	Charles Kirby	Charles Kirby
158	1861	J. L. Gardner	Charles Kirby
164	1917	Grant Walker	
166	1889	John Homans (6)	
168	1882	George Shattuck	Cabot, Chandler
170	1861	J. L. Gardner	
		(Robt. Cushing) (5)	
	1861	J. L. Gardner	
		(John Cushing) (2)	
172	1900	E. H. Gay	Ogden Codman
174	1861	R. C. Mackay	
	1861	R. C. Mackay	
176	1927	10-unit apartment	Bigelow, Wadsworth
	1863	R. C. Mackay	
178	1862	B. T. Reed (4)	
180	1862	B. T. Reed	

SOUTH SIDE

Number	Date	Owner	Architect
149	1861	Bourne & Leavitt	
151	1861	Bourne & Leavitt	
		(George Lowell) (6)	
153	1861	Bourne & Leavitt	
		(John Morse) (4)	
155	1861	Bourne & Leavitt	
157	1861	Bourne & Leavitt	
		(Thomas Goddard) (2)	
159	1861	Bourne & Leavitt	
161	1863	J. H. Rand	
163	1871	H. Whitwell	
165	1869	Annie Flager	
167	1871	H. Whitwell	
169	1866	Paul Wallis	
171	1866	Paul Wallis	
		(J. B. Moors) (3)	
173	1866	Paul Wallis	
175	1866	Andrew Mudge	
177	1871	Henry Weston (6)	Snell, Gregerson
179	1867	Alfred Hall (6)	Snell, Gregerson
181	1863	H. Whitwell	
183	1863	Nathan Silsbee	
185	1872	John Anderson (2)	
187	1866	James Tobey	
189	1866	John Farrington	
191	1872	James Blake	
		(Frank Thayer) (2)	
193	1872	N. Curtis (2)	
195	1872	James Blake (2)	
197	1867	James Tobey	
199	1867	John Farrington	

BEACON STREET, CLARENDON TO DARTMOUTH STREETS

NORTH SIDE

No.	Date	Owner	Architect
182	1866	J. L. Gardner	
184	1866	J. L. Gardner	
		(T. J. Coolidge) (4)	
186	1869	William Appleton	
188	1864	Fred deHautville	
190	1864	Thomas Cushing	
192	1862	Charles Storrow (4)	
194	1862	George Meyer (5)	
196	1863	George Upton	
	1936	6-unit apartment	
198	1862	John Rollins	
200	1862	John Rollins	
202	1862	John Rollins	
204	1862	John Rollins	
206	1862	John Rollins	
208	1862	John Rollins	
210	1863	Nathan Hubbard (8)	
212	1863	John Sturgis	
214	1863	John Barstow	
216	1863	William Dehon (4)	
218	1863	Alson Tucker (2)	
220	1863	William Tucker	
222	1865	Charles Kirby	Charles Kirby
224	1865	Charles Kirby	Charles Kirby
226	1864	George Upham	
		(Adaline Haskell) (8)	
228	1864	George Upham	
230	1863	William Tucker	
232	1863	Alfred Reed	
234	1863	George Chase	

SOUTH SIDE

No.	Date	Owner	Architect
205	1874	C. W. Freeland	Peabody, Stearns
209	1874	C. W. Freeland	Peabody, Stearns
211	1866	Charles Freeland	
213	1866	Charles Freeland	
215	1866	Charles Freeland	
217	1866	Charles Freeland	
219	1866	Charles Freeland	
		(Mary Mixter) (4)	
221	1870	G. Wheatland	
223	1869	G. Wheatland	
		(J. R. Blake) (2)	
225	1869	G. Wheatland	
227	1869	G. Wheatland	
229	1869	G. Wheatland	
231	1869	William Morland	
233	1869	William Morland	
235	1870	Nathan Silsbee	
237	1870	Nathan Silsbee	
239	1869	Fred Whitwell	
241	1868	H. Whitwell	
		(Julia Ward Howe) (3)	
243	1868	H. Whitwell	
		(Ada Whitney) (3)	
245	1868	H. Whitwell	
247	1868	H. Whitwell	
		(Hannah Bancroft) (8)	
249	1869	H. Whitwell	
		(H. W. Pickering) (4)	
251	1869	H. Whitwell	
253	1869	Charles Goodrich	
255	1872	Charles Galloupe	
	1939	23-unit apartment	Saul Moffie

APPENDIX A BUILDINGS CONSTRUCTED IN THE BACK BAY

BEACON STREET, DARTMOUTH TO EXETER STREETS

NORTH SIDE

Number	Date	Owner	Architect
236	1869	John Slater (Francis Bartlett) (6)	
238	1869	Huntington Wolcott (3)	
240	1871	Edward Bangs (4)	Peabody, Stearns
242	1880	T. D. Boardman	Sturgis, Brigham
244	1882	T. D. Boardman (5)	Sturgis, Brigham
246	1887	Mary West (3)	Peabody, Stearns
250	1887	C. B. Parsons	Peabody, Stearns
252	1871	H. B. Williams	
	1925	19-unit apartment	G. N. Jacobs
254	1871	H. B. Williams	
256	1871	H. B. Williams	
258	1871	H. B. Williams	
260	1871	H. B. Williams	
262	1872	Robert Hooper	
	1938	Apartments	Homer Keissling
264	1872	Robert Hooper	
	1927	Apartments	Bigelow, Wadsworth
266	1886	Elizabeth Skinner (4)	Shaw, Hunnewell
270	1881	C. A. Whittier	McKim, Mead, White
	1956	11-unit apartment	Rich, Tucker
274	1881	H. L. Higginson (3)	H. H. Richardson
	1929	16-unit apartment	G. C. Whiting
276	1874	Francis Bacon	Fred Pope
278	1890	C. W. Amory	
	1938	48-unit apartment	H. L. Feer
280	1877	John Shepard	
	1946	33-unit apartment	H. L. Feer

SOUTH SIDE

Number	Date	Owner	Architect
259	1888	6-unit apartment	Blaikie, Blaikie
261	1888	12-unit apartment	Blaikie, Blaikie
263	1871	G. Wheatland	
265	1871	G. Wheatland	
267	1871	G. Wheatland	
269	1871	G. Wheatland	
271	1876	G. W. Freeland	Peabody, Stearns
273	1876	G. W. Freeland	Peabody, Stearns
275	1876	G. W. Freeland	Peabody, Stearns
277	1876	G. W. Freeland	Peabody, Stearns
279	1881	G. W. Freeland	Peabody, Stearns
281	1881	G. W. Freeland	Peabody, Stearns
283	1885	S. D. Bush (8)	Cabot, Chandler
285	1885	Benjamin Cox (4)	Cabot, Chandler
287	1881	Vinal, Dodge	George A. Avery
289	1881	Vinal, Dodge	George A. Avery
291	1881	Daniel Lane (7)	S. J. F. Thayer
293	1884	Ed Gray	E. Curtis
295	1885	Hotel Royal	S. D. Kelley

NORTH SIDE

No.	Date	Owner	Architect/Builder
282	1872	Caleb Curtis	Theo. P. Briggs
284	1870	W. F. Matchett (3)	
	1927	10-unit apartment	Blackall, Elwell
286	1869	George Barnard (2)	
288	1869	Anne Snelling	
	1945	12-unit apartment	Meyer Louis
290	1869	Anne Snelling	
292	1870	J. L. Stackpole (8)	
294	1870	Stephen Weld	
296	1870	O. W. Holmes (9)	
	1951	7-unit apartment	H. L. Feer
298	1871	Brown, Leavitt	
		(Louis Dabney) (8)	
300	1869	H. Whitwell	
302	1869	H. Whitwell	
		(William D. Howells)	
	1933	5-unit apartment	J. B. Brown
304	1871	Carol Twombly	Charles Kirby
306	1871	Charles Kirby	Charles Kirby
308	1871	Dan Davis	Charles Kirby
310	1871	Dan Davis	Peabody, Stearns
312	1903	J. B. Richmond (8)	
314	1871	Dan Davis	
		(B. G. Boardman) (8)	
316	1885	E. R. Tyler	Cummings, Sears
318	1881	George M. Dana (3)	Allen, Kenway
320	1878	R. M. Staigg	
322	1877	Charles Whitmore (4)	Snell, Gregerson
324	1882	R. D. Evans (2)	Allen, Kenway
326	1890	S. Ballantyne	H. M. Stephenson
328	1885	Otto Dresel	Rotch, Tilden
	1935	9-unit apartment	R. G. Stebbins
330	1871	James Eaton	
332	1871	James Eaton	
	1959	21-unit apartment	Hugh Stubbins

SOUTH SIDE

No.	Date	Owner	Architect/Builder
299	1870	G. Wheatland	Sturgis, Brigham
301	1883	G. E. Niles (3)	Fred Pope
303	1871	Fred Pope	Fred Pope
305	1871	Fred Pope	Fred Pope
307	1871	Fred Pope	Fred Pope
309	1871	Fred Pope	Fred Pope
		(R. M. Rogers) (9)	
311	1871	Fred Pope	Fred Pope
		(Helen Prince) (3)	
313	1871	Fred Pope	Fred Pope
315	1871	Fred Pope	Fred Pope
317	1871	Fred Pope	Fred Pope
319	1871	Fred Pope	Fred Pope
321	1872	Fred Pope	Fred Pope
323	1872	Fred Pope	Fred Pope
325	1872	Fred Pope	Fred Pope
327	1872	Fred Pope	Fred Pope
		(Thomas Proctor) (2)	
329	1874	Fred Pope	Fred Pope
331	1880	Roxana Dabney (7)	Davis & Son
333	1881	S. T. Ames	S. D. Kelley
335	1881	S. T. Ames	S. D. Kelley
337	1881	S. T. Ames	S. D. Kelley
339	1881	S. T. Ames	S. D. Kelley
341	1881	S. T. Ames	S. D. Kelley
343	1873	Fred Pope	Fred Pope
345	1873	Fred Pope	Fred Pope
347	1884	James Converse (2)	J. H. Besarick

BEACON STREET, FAIRFIELD TO GLOUCESTER STREETS

NORTH SIDE

Number	Date	Owner	Architect
334	1871	Fred Pope	
	1907	Remodelled	Cram, Goodhue
336	1876	F. W. Smith (2)	
338	1877	Edwin Morey (5)	B. F. Meacham
340	1880	H. Stackpole (5)	Snell, Gregerson
342	1880	M. Washburn (5)	Allen, Kenway
344	1880	D. C. Knowlton (4)	Allen, Kenway
346	1882	Lucien Carr	Allen, Kenway
348	1886	C. C. Converse (8)	Allen, Kenway
350	1893(?)	Wallace Pierce	
352	1885	Hasket Derby (5)	W. R. Emerson
354	1886(?)	William Vaughan (9)	
	1937	10-unit apartment	H. L. Feer
356	1883	S. T. Ames	
386	1883	S. T. Ames	
388	1872	Brown, Leavitt	
390	1872	Brown, Leavitt	
392	1872	Brown, Leavitt	
394	1872	Brown, Leavitt	
	1926	12-unit apartment	R. H. Doane
396	1872	Brown, Leavitt	
	1953	5-unit apartment	L. L. Furr
398	1872	Brown, Leavitt	
	1964	5-unit apartment	G. Garfinkle
400	1872	Brown, Leavitt	

SOUTH SIDE

Number	Date	Owner	Architect
351	1870	Fred Pope	Fred Pope
353	1870	Fred Pope	Fred Pope
355	1870	Fred Pope	Fred Pope
357	1885	(Sarah Bancroft) (5) H. R. Dalton	Carl Fehmer
359	1886	Albert Stone (8)	Carl Fehmer
361	1872	H. C. Wainwright	F. H. Jackson
363	1872	H. C. Wainwright	F. H. Jackson
365	1872	H. C. Wainwright	F. H. Jackson
367	1886	A. L. Devens	Rotch, Tilden
369	1886	Alden Avery	George Avery
371	1886	Andrew Briggs (5)	Cummings, Sears
375	1886	C. B. Wells (4)	Carl Fehmer
377	1869	Gibson & Pope	Fred Pope
379	1869	Gibson & Pope	Fred Pope
381	1869	Jordan, Pope, Bealls, Cotting, et al.	Fred Pope
383	1869	Jordan, Pope, Bealls, Cotting, et al.	Fred Pope
385	1869	Jordan, Pope, Bealls, Cotting, et al.	Fred Pope
387	1869	Jordan, Pope, Bealls, Cotting, et al.	Fred Pope
389	1869	Jordan, Pope, Bealls, Cotting, et al.	Fred Pope
391	1869	Jordan, Pope, Bealls, Cotting, et al.	Fred Pope
393	1869	Jordan, Pope, Bealls, Cotting, et al.	Fred Pope
395	1869	Jordan, Pope, Bealls, Cotting, et al.	Fred Pope

BEACON STREET, GLOUCESTER TO HEREFORD STREETS

NORTH SIDE

No.	Year	Owner	Architect
406	1887	J. Abbott (8)	Snell, Gregerson
408	1886	R. M. Hodges (3)	Allen, Kenway
410	1886	I. T. Burr	Cabot, Chandler
412	1887	Charles Head (6)	Shaw, Hunnewell
414	1887	M. C. Blake (4)	J. H. Sturgis
416	1890	H. H. Fay	J. T. Kelley
418	1897	H. H. Fay	J. T. Kelley
420	1892	Emily Sears (5)	Peabody, Stearns
422	1899	L. Leland (9)	Little, Browne
424	1904	Ralph Williams	J. Schweinfurth
426	1904	Ruth Sears	J. Schweinfurth
428		Vacant lot	

SOUTH SIDE

No.	Year	Owner	Architect
401	1867	R. M. Pratt	Snell, Gregerson
	1921	5-unit apartment	H. L. Feer
403	1867	J. R. Gregerson (3)	Snell, Gregerson
405	1867	R. M. Pratt	Snell, Gregerson
		(W. M. Hunt)	
407	1867	Anne Fiske	Snell, Gregerson
409	1867	R. M. Pratt	Snell, Gregerson
411	1867	Walter Dabney (6)	
413	1867	Henry Wainwright (5)	
415	1867	Henry Wainwright	
417	1867	Henry Wainwright	
419	1869	Beal, Lilley, et al.	
421	1869	Beal, Lilley, et al.	
		(C. Lilley) (4)	
423	1869	Beal, Lilley, et al.	
		(Helen Child) (4)	
425	1869	Beal, Lilley, et al.	
427	1869	Beal, Lilley, et al.	
429	1869	Beal, Lilley, et al.	
431	1869	Beal, Lilley, et al.	

BEACON STREET, HEREFORD STREET TO MASSACHUSETTS AVENUE

NORTH SIDE

Number	Date	Owner	Architect
448	1889	R. C. Hooper	Andrews, Jacques
450	1895	E. H. Fenno (8)	Shaw, Hunnewell
452	1887	H. P. Quincy	John Sturgis
454	1890	F. B. Rice	Fehmer, Page
456	1886	N. Mathews (8)	Rotch, Tilden
458	1890	T. R. White	Rotch, Tilden
460	1891	G. Davenport (8)	Francis R. Allen
462	1891	W. S. Appleton	Brigham, Spofford
464	1891	Louis Curtis (8)	Rotch, Tilden
468	1891	J. Case (7)	Fehmer, Page
470	1891	J. Case	Fehmer, Page
472	1892	T. A. Hall (8)	W. W. Lewis
474	1891	Nat. W. Pierce	Carl Fehmer
476	1891	E. Frothingham (8)	Fehmer, Page
478	1892	P. V. R. Ely	W. Y. Peters
480	1892	Lucy Ellis (3)	Cabot, Everett, Mead
482	1892	E. H. Fay	E. N. Boyden
484	1892	E. H. Fay	E. N. Boyden
486	1892	E. H. Fay	E. N. Boyden
488	1892	E. H. Fay	E. N. Boyden
490	1892	E. H. Fay	E. N. Boyden
	1891	Mt. Vernon Church	Walker, Kimball

SOUTH SIDE

Number	Date	Owner	Architect
435	1879	H. S. Whitwell	R. S. Bither
441	1887	Alden Avery	George Avery
443	1872	Daniel Davis	Charles Davis
445	1872	Daniel Davis	Charles Davis
447	1872	Daniel Davis	Charles Davis
449	1876	Daniel Davis	Charles Davis
		(Oliver Briggs) (8)	
451	1882	C. A. Dow (5)	Sturgis, Brigham
453	1885	S. T. Ames	S. D. Kelley
455	1886	Asa Caton	J. H. Besarick
457	1886	Asa Caton	J. H. Besarick
459	1887	Asa Caton	J. H. Besarick
461	1887	Asa Caton	J. H. Besarick
463	1887	F. G. Macomber (8)	E. A. P. Newcomb
465	1887	A. G. Weeks	E. A. P. Newcomb
467	1888	Asa Caton	J. H. Besarick
469	1888	Asa Caton	J. H. Besarick
471	1889	J. Shapleigh	J. H. Besarick
473	1889	J. Shapleigh	J. H. Besarick
475	1889	H. M. Caflin	O. F. Smith
477	1889	J. F. Page	Wm. W. Lewis
479	1891	Seth Baker	E. N. Boyden
481	1891	Seth Baker	E. N. Boyden
483	1898	Hotel Cambridge	W. T. Sears

BEACON STREET, MASSACHUSETTS AVENUE TO CHARLESGATE EAST

NORTH SIDE

504	1894	G. Bradford	O. F. Smith
506	1893	V. Y. Bowditch (8)	Shaw, Hunnewell
508	1890	Thomas Nelson	
510		Vacant lot	
512	1890	G. S. Silsbee	Rotch, Tilden
514		Vacant lot	
516		Vacant lot	
	1925	30-unit apartment	Charles Greco
518	1893	Mary Ayer (8)	Rotch, Tilden
520		Vacant lot	
522		Vacant lot	
524		Vacant lot	
	1912	29-unit apartment	F. A. Norcross
526	1894	O. Wadsworth (5)	Walker, Kimball
528	1893	Harold Williams (7)	Rotch, Tilden
530	1908	Charles H. Trazier	George A. Avery
532	1900	Mary Kittridge	Geoffery Hay
534		Vacant lot	
536	1891	W. S. Bryant	W. Y. Peters
	1923	72-unit apartment	E. B. Stratton

SOUTH SIDE

491	1891	Seth Baker	E. N. Boyden
497	1890	4-unit apartment	E. N. Boyden
499	1888	4-unit apartment	S. D. Kelley
501	1888	F. V. Parker	Snell, Gregerson
503	1888	Ed. Burgess	H. W. Stevenson
505	1888	D. Lewis	C. Fehmer
507	1887	H. R. Dalton	C. Fehmer
509	1887	S. S. Allen	C. Fehmer
511	1887	Chadwick, Stillings	S. D. Kelley
513	1887	Chadwick, Stillings (Charles Sherburne) (6)	S. D. Kelley
515	1887	Chadwick, Stillings	S. D. Kelley
517	1887	Chadwick, Stillings	S. D. Kelley
519	1887	Chadwick, Stillings	S. D. Kelley
521	1887	Chadwick, Stillings (Catherine Savage) (7)	S. D. Kelley
523	1887	Chadwick, Stillings	S. D. Kelley
525	1887	Chadwick, Stillings	S. D. Kelley
527	1887	Chadwick, Stillings	S. D. Kelley
529	1887	Chadwick, Stillings	S. D. Kelley
531	1888	Chadwick, Stillings	S. D. Kelley
535	1891	Hotel Charlesgate	J. P. Putnam

BEACON STREET, CHARLESGATE WEST TO RALEIGH STREET

SOUTH SIDE

583	1889	S. R. Baker	E. N. Boyden
585	1889	S. R. Baker	E. N. Boyden
587	1889	S. R. Baker	E. N. Boyden
589	1889	S. R. Baker	E. N. Boyden
591	1889	S. R. Baker	E. N. Boyden

APPENDIX A BUILDINGS CONSTRUCTED IN THE BACK BAY

MARLBOROUGH STREET, ARLINGTON TO BERKELEY STREETS

NORTH SIDE

Number	Date	Owner	Architect
1	1863	William Glidden (2)	
3	1863	George Shattuck	
5	1863	Henry Sargent (6)	
7	1863	J. C. Hooper (6)	
9	1863	Charles Lombard	Charles Kirby
11	1863	George Warren	Charles Kirby
13	1864	E. D. Brigham	Charles Kirby
15	1864	Charles Kirby	Charles Kirby
17	1865	George Howe	
19	1872	George Upton	A. C. Martin
21	1866	Charles Freeland	
23	1866	Charles Freeland	
25	1866	Charles Freeland	
27	1866	Charles Freeland (Mary Richardson) (7)	
29	1870	Samuel Johnson	
31	1870	James Freeland	
33	1870	Stetson Estate (4)	
35	1869	Dodge, Freeland	
37	1869	Dodge, Freeland	
39	1869	Dodge, Freeland (Helen Dodge) (8)	
41	1865	Charles Minot	Snell, Gregerson
43	1865	Charles Minot	Snell, Gregerson
	1923	7-unit apartment	Parker, Thomas, Rice

SOUTH SIDE

Number	Date	Owner	Architect
2	1871	William Richards (6)	
4	1864	William Sheafe	N. J. Bradlee
6	1864	Frank Andrews	G. N. Jacobs
	1924	21-unit apartment	N. J. Bradlee
8	1864	Frank Andrews	
10	1864	William Thomas	
	1905	Arthur Perry	Little, Browne
12	1863	S. T. Morse (8)	
14	1863	James Jackson	
16	1864	John Mixter	
18	1865	John Revere (Anna Torrey) (3)	
20	1865	John Revere (Sarah Linzee) (3)	
22	1863	Thorndike Estate	
24	1863	Thorndike Estate	
26	1863	Thorndike Estate	
28	1863	Thorndike Estate	
30	1863	Thorndike Estate	
32	1864	Benjamin Cheney (8)	

MARLBOROUGH STREET, BERKELEY TO CLARENDON STREETS

NORTH SIDE

53	1867	Edward Codman (4)	
57	1867	Charles Codman (6)	
59	1873	J. M. Crafts (6)	
61	1873	J. M. Standish	
63	1875	C. P. Putnam (6)	J. P. Putnam
65	1876	Francis Minot (4)	
67	1878	R. M. Hodges	Peabody, Stearns
71	1864	J. L. Gardner estate (4)	
73	1864	J. L. Gardner estate (4)	
75	1864	J. L. Gardner estate (4)	
77	1864	J. L. Gardner estate (4)	
79	1864	J. L. Gardner estate (4)	
81	1864	J. L. Gardner estate (4)	
83	1864	J. L. Gardner estate (4)	
85	1864	J. L. Gardner estate (4)	
87	1864	J. L. Gardner estate (4)	
89	1867	J. C. Rogers	

SOUTH SIDE

	1867	First Church, Unitarian	Ware, Van Brunt
66	1870	Charles Kirby (Gridley J. F. Bryant)	Charles Kirby
68	1870	Charles Kirby	Charles Kirby
70	1868	Charles Kirby	Charles Kirby
72	1866	Charles Kirby	Charles Kirby
74	1866	Charles Kirby	Charles Kirby
		(J. C. Philips) (3)	
76	1866	Charles Kirby	Charles Kirby
78	1866	Charles Kirby	Charles Kirby
80	1866	Charles Kirby	Charles Kirby
		(Anna Richards) (3)	
82	1876	James Lawrence	Sturgis, Brigham
86	1872	Charles Joy (8)	Sturgis, Brigham
88	1872	Susan Jackson (6)	
90	1872	Cornelia Winthrop	
92	1870	George Wheatland	

APPENDIX A   BUILDINGS CONSTRUCTED IN THE BACK BAY

MARLBOROUGH STREET, CLARENDON TO DARTMOUTH STREETS

NORTH SIDE

Number	Date	Owner	Architect
101	1872	Augustus Flagg (4)	
103	1866	Catherine Hill (3)	
105	1871	Charles Kirby	Charles Kirby
107	1871	Charles Kirby	Charles Kirby
	1916	Brooks School	J. T. Lee
109	1871	J. Standish	Charles Kirby
111	1872	J. Standish (Clara Barnes) (8)	Charles Kirby
113	1872	Charles Kirby	Charles Kirby
115	1872	Charles Kirby	Charles Kirby
117	1873	J. Standish	
119	1873	James Tobey	George Meacham
121	1877	Charles Freeland	Peabody, Stearns
123	1877	Charles Freeland	Peabody, Stearns
125	1877	Charles Freeland	Peabody, Stearns
127	1877	Charles Freeland	Peabody, Stearns
	1937	10-unit apartment	H. Feer
129	1879	Charles Freeland	Peabody, Stearns
131	1880	Charles Freeland	Peabody, Stearns
133	1880	Charles Freeland	Peabody, Stearns
135	1880	Henry Lee	Cabot, Chandler

SOUTH SIDE

Number	Date	Owner	Architect
104	1866	Albert Sise	
106	1868	Rufus Ellis	
108	1870	William Thomas	
110	1868	Charles Freeland	
112	1868	Charles Freeland	
114	1868	Charles Freeland	
116	1868	Charles Freeland	
118	1868	Charles Freeland	
120	1868	Charles Freeland (A. E. Griswold) (4)	
122	1868	Charles Freeland	
124	1868	Charles Freeland	
126	1868	Charles Freeland	
128	1868	Charles Freeland (Susan Page) (9)	
130	1868	Charles Freeland	
132	1871	John Farrington	
134	1872	John Farrington (Nancy Kimball) (4)	
136	1872	John Farrington	
138	1872	John Farrington	
	1891	G. W. Nason	A. K. Drisko
140	1872	John Farrington	
142	1872	John Farrington	
144	1872	John Farrington	
146	1872	John Farrington (Mary Guild) (3)	
		John Farrington	

MARLBOROUGH STREET, DARTMOUTH TO EXETER STREETS

NORTH SIDE

No.	Year	Owner	Architect
165	1871	T. F. Cushing (2)	Snell, Gregerson
167	1878	Charles Gordon (6)	J. P. Putnam
169	1878	Parkman Shaw (3)	Shaw, Shaw
171	1881	G. B. Upton	C. Fehmer
173	1881	G. B. Upton	C. Fehmer
175	1871	Silas Merrill	
177	1871	Silas Merrill (William Gaston) (7)	Clark, Curtis
179	1881	H. G. Curtis (8)	Clark, Curtis
181	1881	J. S. Thorndike (8)	Shaw, Shaw
183	1882	J. E. Peabody (3)	Peabody, Stearns
185	1884	Edward Grew (8)	Peabody, Stearns
189	1906	Henry Porter (8)	Winslow, Bigelow
191	1881	Edward Dwight (3)	C. Fehmer
193	1882	S. T. Ames	S. D. Kelley
195	1883	F. W. Chandler (8)	Cabot, Chandler
197	1891	R. S. Bradley	J. L. Faxon
199	1890	7-unit apartment	E. N. Boyden

SOUTH SIDE

No.	Year	Owner	Architect
164	1870	Benjamin Crowninshield (8)	H. H. Richardson
166	1874	Eben Jordan	
168	1874	Eben Jordan	
170	1874	Eben Jordan	
172	1874	Eben Jordan	
174	1876	Eben Jordan	
176	1876	Eben Jordan (Effie Ellis) (7)	
178	1879	R. Sullivan	Cabot, Chandler
180	1880	Chadwick, Stillings	S. D. Kelley
182	1925	5-unit apartment	
182	1880	Chadwick, Stillings	S. D. Kelley
184	1881	T. B. Curtis	Clark, Curtis
186	1886	J. W. Shapleigh	
188	1884	James Minot	
190	1881	Russell Sturgis	Sturgis, Brigham
192	1881	Samuel Stillings	
194	1881	Samuel Stillings	Sturgis, Brigham

APPENDIX A BUILDINGS CONSTRUCTED IN THE BACK BAY

MARLBOROUGH STREET, EXETER TO FAIRFIELD STREETS

NORTH SIDE

Number	Date	Owner	Architect
225	1873	George Wheatland	L. Weissbein
227	1873	George Wheatland	L. Weissbein
229	1873	George Wheatland	L. Weissbein
231	1873	George Wheatland	L. Weissbein
233	1874	George Wheatland	
235	1874	George Wheatland	
237	1874	George Wheatland	
239	1874	George Wheatland	
241	1884	S. T. Ames	S. D. Kelley
245	1883	G. R. Minot (4)	Cabot, Chandler
247	1881	J. Bradlee (3)	T. M. Clark
249	1880	O. Norcross (7)	Bradlee, Winslow
251	1886	F. H. Appleton (8)	Peabody, Stearns
253	1883	J. F. Curtis (7)	Carl Fehmer
255	1883	Robert Bradley	
257	1883	William Simes	Cabot, Chandler
259	1884	J. C. White (8)	Peabody, Stearns
261	1887	H. A. Whitney	Charles Brigham
275	1886	G. H. Binney (2)	Carl Fehmer
277	1873	Fred Pope	Fred Pope
279	1873	Fred Pope	Fred Pope

SOUTH SIDE

Number	Date	Owner	Architect
220	1892	6-unit apartment	Fred Pope
224	1892	12-unit apartment	Fred Pope
226	1881	C. J. Blake (6)	W. W. Lewis
228	1879	W. F. Whitney (8)	W. W. Lewis
230	1880	S. T. Ames	S. D. Kelley
232	1880	S. T. Ames	S. D. Kelley
234	1880	S. T. Ames	S. D. Kelley
236	1881	S. T. Ames	S. D. Kelley
		(Emily Osborn) (3)	
238	1881	S. T. Ames	S. D. Kelley
240	1881	S. T. Ames	S. D. Kelley
242	1881	S. T. Ames	S. D. Kelley
244	1882	S. T. Ames	S. D. Kelley
246	1883	S. T. Ames	S. D. Kelley
248	1885	Wilbur Parker (6)	Hartwell, Richardson
252	1885	S. T. Ames	S. D. Kelley
254	1887	S. W. Merrill	
256	1887	S. W. Merrill	
258	1887	S. W. Merrill	
272	1883	W. S. Bartlett (6)	W. W. Lewis
274	1879	Charles Wood	F. R. Allen
276	1884	J. T. Morse, Jr.	Cabot, Chandler
	1930	8-unit apartment	Bigelow, Wadsworth

MARLBOROUGH STREET, FAIRFIELD TO GLOUCESTER STREETS

NORTH SIDE

No.	Year		
285	1871	Fred Pope	
		(H. M. Reed) (6)	
287	1871	Fred Pope	
289	1871	Fred Pope	
291	1872	Fred Pope	
		(H. Goddard) (5)	
293	1872	Fred Pope	
295	1872	Fred Pope	
		(M. Sleeper) (5)	
297	1872	Fred Pope	
299	1872	Fred Pope	
301	1877	J. B. Ames	E. A. P. Newcomb
303	1877	J. B. Ames	E. A. P. Newcomb
309	1877	D. W. Beckler	
311	1877	D. W. Beckler	
313	1877	D. W. Beckler	
315	1877	D. W. Beckler	
317	1874	D. W. Beckler	
319	1874	D. W. Beckler	
321	1873	Herbert Barney	F. H. Moore
323	1873	Herbert Barney	F. H. Moore

SOUTH SIDE

No.	Year		
282	1872	G. M. Gibson	Ware, Van Brunt
284	1872	G. M. Gibson	Ware, Van Brunt
286	1872	G. M. Gibson	Ware, Van Brunt
288	1872	G. M. Gibson	Ware, Van Brunt
290	1872	G. M. Gibson	Ware, Van Brunt
292	1872	G. M. Gibson	Ware, Van Brunt
		(Henry Van Brunt) (1)	
294	1877	J. B. Ames	E. A. P. Newcomb
296	1877	J. B. Ames	E. A. P. Newcomb
298	1878	S. T. Ames	
300	1878	S. T. Ames	
302	1878	D. W. Beckler	F. H. Moore
304	1878	D. W. Beckler	F. H. Moore
306	1878	D. W. Beckler	F. H. Moore
308	1878	D. W. Beckler	F. H. Moore
310	1878	D. W. Beckler	F. H. Moore
		(F. Skinner) (3)	
312	1879	T. S. Perry (8)	Cabot, Chandler
314	1879	S. T. Ames	S. D. Kelley
320	1879	S. T. Ames	S. D. Kelley
322	1872	W. T. Sears (3)	Cummings, Sears

Number	Date	Owner	Architect	Number	Date	Owner	Architect

MARLBOROUGH STREET, GLOUCESTER TO HEREFORD STREETS

NORTH SIDE

Number	Date	Owner
337	1872	Hiram Gerrish
		(J. McIntire) (5)
339	1872	Hiram Gerrish
341	1872	Hiram Gerrish
		(Susan Wales) (7)
343	1872	Hiram Gerrish
345	1872	Hiram Gerrish
347	1872	Hiram Gerrish
349	1872	Hiram Gerrish
351	1872	Hiram Gerrish
353	1872	Hiram Gerrish
		(W. L. Daggett) (5)
	1959	2-unit house
355	1872	Hiram Gerrish
357	1872	Hiram Gerrish

Architect for unnumbered 1959 entry: Krokyn, Krokyn

SOUTH SIDE

Number	Date	Owner	Architect
334	1872	Hiram Gerrish	J. H. Besarick
336	1882	S. T. Ames	
338	1876	H. S. Whitwell	
340	1876	H. S. Whitwell	
342	1876	H. S. Whitwell	
344	1877	H. S. Whitwell	
346	1877	H. S. Whitwell	
348	1878	George Wheatland	
350	1878	George Wheatland	
352	1878	George Wheatland	
354	1879	George Wheatland	
356	1879	George Wheatland	
358	1879	George Wheatland	
360	1879	George Wheatland	
362	1879	George Wheatland	

MARLBOROUGH STREET, HEREFORD STREET TO MASSACHUSETTS AVENUE

NORTH SIDE

363	1872	J. F. Richardson	
365	1887	S. Richardson (4)	
369	1879	George Wheatland	Fred Pope
371	1879	George Wheatland (E. Russell) (7)	
373	1879	George Wheatland	
375	1880	George Wheatland (Annie Odin) (6)	
377	1880	George Wheatland (Hannah Osgood) (7)	
379	1880	George Wheatland	
381	1880	George Wheatland (A. Calef) (7)	O. F. Smith
383	1880	George Wheatland	O. F. Smith
385	1880	George Wheatland	O. F. Smith
387	1880	George Wheatland (H. M. Dexter) (8)	O. F. Smith
389	1880	George Wheatland	O. F. Smith
391	1880	George Wheatland	O. F. Smith
393	1883	John Shapleigh	
395	1883	John Shapleigh	
397	1883	John Shapleigh	
399	1884	W. H. Rollins (8)	J. P. Putnam
401	1885	William Simes	Cabot, Chandler
403	1886	Charles Tilton (4)	John Fox
405	1889	6-unit apartment	S. D. Kelley
407	1889	6-unit apartment	S. D. Kelley
409	1890	12-unit apartment	S. D. Kelley
411	1890	6-unit apartment	S. D. Kelley

SOUTH SIDE

364	1879	S. T. Ames	R. S. Bither
370	1880	W. Williamson (8)	Cabot, Chandler
372	1880	F. H. Skinner	Kirby, Lewis
374	1880	A. E. Harding	Kirby, Lewis
376	1880	E. & A. Sever (7)	Carl Fehmer
378	1880	Frank Jones	
380	1881	Charles Sprague	Cummings, Sears
382	1881	J. M. Hubbard (5)	Peabody, Stearns
384	1881	Mary Boardman	Shaw, Shaw
386	1882	C. E. Hubbard	Allen, Kenway
388	1885	A. P. Sears	Cummings, Sears
390	1885	J. Shapleigh	S. D. Kelley
392	1885	J. Shapleigh	S. D. Kelley
394	1886	J. Shapleigh	S. D. Kelley
396	1887	Sarah Davis (5)	Cummings, Sears
398	1887	Crowninshield, Cabot	Peabody, Stearns
400	1887	Crowninshield, Cabot	Peabody, Stearns
402	1887	Crowninshield, Cabot	Peabody, Stearns
404	1888	Charles Cotting (7)	Snell, Gregerson
406	1888	Fred Dexter (4)	Shaw, Hunnewell
416	1895	32-unit apartment	W. T. Sears

APPENDIX A BUILDINGS CONSTRUCTED IN THE BACK BAY

MARLBOROUGH STREET, MASSACHUSETTS AVENUE TO CHARLESGATE EAST

NORTH SIDE

Number	Date	Owner	Architect
421	1889	6-unit apartment	S. D. Kelley
423	1889	4-unit apartment	S. D. Kelley
425	1886	George Wheatland	O. F. Smith
427	1886	George Wheatland	O. F. Smith
429	1886	George Wheatland	O. F. Smith
431	1885	Chadwick, Stillings	
433	1885	Chadwick, Stillings	
435	1885	Chadwick, Stillings	
437	1885	Chadwick, Stillings	
439	1885	Chadwick, Stillings	
441	1885	Chadwick, Stillings	
443	1885	Chadwick, Stillings	
445	1885	Chadwick, Stillings	
447	1886	F. J. Parker	W. P. Wentworth
449	1887	George Wheatland	O. F. Smith
451	1887	George Wheatland	O. F. Smith
453	1887	George Wheatland	O. F. Smith
455	1887	George Wheatland	O. F. Smith
457	1887	George Wheatland	O. F. Smith
459	1889	G. M. Barnes	Rotch, Tilden
463	1889	G. M. Barnes	Rotch, Tilden
		(Incorporated in Hotel Charlesgate)	

SOUTH SIDE

Number	Date	Owner	Architect
424	1889	W. D. Vinal	S. D. Kelley
426	1887	George Wheatland	O. F. Smith
428	1886	A. H. Morse	Cummings, Sears
430	1885	George Wheatland	O. F. Smith
432	1885	George Wheatland	O. F. Smith
434	1885	George Wheatland	O. F. Smith
436	1885	George Wheatland	O. F. Smith
438	1885	George Wheatland	O. F. Smith
440	1885	George Wheatland	O. F. Smith

COMMONWEALTH AVENUE, ARLINGTON TO BERKELEY STREETS

NORTH SIDE

No.	Year	Name	Architect
1	1861	Samuel Ward	
3	1861	B. S. Rotch (2)	
5	1861	Abbott Lawrence (4)	
7	1912	Walter Baylies	Parker, Thomas, Rice
	1861	Samuel Johnson (6)	
9	1861	R. Greenleaf	
		(O. Norcross) (8)	
	1937	14-unit apartment	
11	1868	F. Bradlee	N. J. Bradlee
		(E. Abbott) (4)	
13	1868	F. Bradlee (2)	N. J. Bradlee
	1907	Anna Nowell	Parker, Thomas, Rice
15	1867	William Pickman (2)	Snell, Gregerson
17	1866	William Gardiner (1)	
19	1867	T. C. Amory (2)	
21	1868	J. A. Burnham (5)	
23	1868	Daniel Spooner (1)	
25	1861	Samuel Hooper (1)	
27	1861	Samuel Hooper	
		(Thornton Lothrop) (9)	

SOUTH SIDE

No.	Year	Name	Architect
2	1864	James Little (2)	
4	1864	William Brown (2)	
6	1864	A. Abbe	
		(William Weld) (6)	
8	1864	Erastus Bigelow (1)	
10	1864	Thomas Appleton (1)	
12	1870	Samuel Gookin	
14	1871	Charles Kirby	Charles Kirby
	1927	40-unit apartment	
16	1864	Charles Woodbury (2)	G. N. Jacobs
18	1864	Samuel Ward	
		(C. Dorr) (6)	
20	1861	Samuel Ward	Bryant, Gilman
22	1861	Edward Motley (9)	Bryant, Gilman
24	1861	E. E. Snelling (2)	Bryant, Gilman
26	1861	H. Saltonstahl (3)	Bryant, Gilman
28	1861	G. T. Bigelow (1)	Bryant, Gilman
30	1861	Jonas Fitch (2)	Bryant, Gilman
32	1861	Miles Standish (3)	Bryant, Gilman
34	1861	M. A. Edwards (2)	Bryant, Gilman
36	1861	Ezra Lincoln (1)	Bryant, Gilman
38	1862	Nathan Gibbs (1)	
40	1862	John Sharp (1)	
42	1864	F. W. Sayles (1)	
44	1864	R. E. Robbins (7)	
46	1864	Samuel Gookin	
48	1864	William Chadbourne	

APPENDIX A BUILDINGS CONSTRUCTED IN THE BACK BAY

COMMONWEALTH AVENUE, BERKELEY TO CLARENDON STREETS

NORTH SIDE

Number	Date	Owner	Architect
29	1864	J. Stetson	
	1894	10-unit apartment	J. P. Putnam
31	1864	J. Sawyer (2)	
33	1864	C. H. Dalton (6)	
35	1873	Elisha Atkins	N. J. Bradlee
37	1872	Elisha Atkins (3)	N. J. Bradlee
39	1872	I. Farnsworth (2)	N. J. Bradlee
41	1869	Elizabeth Drew	
43	1869	Elizabeth Drew	
	1902	A. R. Williams	J. A. Schweinfurth
45	1869	Elizabeth Drew	
47	1869	Elizabeth Drew	
49	1877	Charles Torrey (4)	Cummings, Sears
51	1876	G. A. Gardner (8)	Cummings, Sears
55	1875	J. T. Bailey (2)	Cummings, Sears
57	1874	J. A. Burnham (8)	Carl Fehmer
59	1874	A. A. Lawrence (9)	Carl Fehmer
61	1879	S. E. Lawrence (2)	Carl Fehmer
63	1877	Annie Warren (4)	Snell, Gregerson
65	1877	Charles Rollins	Snell, Gregerson
	1925	14-unit apartment	McLaughlin, Burr

SOUTH SIDE

Number	Date	Owner	Architect
50	1868	John Hogg (2)	
	1925	40-unit apartment	G. N. Jacobs
52	1872	Edward Browne (3)	
54	1866	John Sharp (7)	Snell, Gregerson
56	1866	Willard Sayles (8)	Snell, Gregerson
	1930	22-unit apartment	G. N. Jacobs
58	1866	Henry Sayles	Snell, Gregerson
60	1866	J. P. Putnam (1)	Snell, Gregerson
62	1872	Henry Williams	
64	1872	Henry Williams	
66	1872	Henry Williams	
		(J. W. Clark) (6)	
68	1869	David Whitney (6)	Snell, Gregerson
70	1869	Catherine Brewer (2)	N. J. Bradlee
72	1869	J. R. Brewer (5)	N. J. Bradlee
74	1870	Laura Sayles	
76	1872	Charles Fox	
78	1872	Charles Fox	
	1922	7-unit apartment	John Craig
80	1872	Charles Fox	
82	1872	Edward Page (2)	T. P. Briggs
84	1872	Sarah Burnham (7)	Emerson, Fehmer
86	1874	Cornelia Thomas	T. P. Briggs
88	1881	Henry Keyes (7)	
90	1879	Nathaniel Walker (4)	
	1925	24-unit apartment	G. N. Jacobs

COMMONWEALTH AVENUE, CLARENDON TO DARTMOUTH STREETS

NORTH SIDE

No.	Date	Owner	Architect
107	1869	Hotel Hamilton	Ware, Van Brunt
109	1879	J. M Forbes (9)	
111	1872	H. Whitwell	
113	1872	H. Whitwell (3)	
115	1876	Walter Hastings	Cummings, Sears
	1937	7-unit apartment	
117	1876	Walter Hastings	Cummings, Sears
119	1876	Walter Hastings	Cummings, Sears
121	1879	R. C. Brown (5)	Bradlee, Winslow
123	1872	Charles Wood	Cummings, Sears
125	1872	Elizabeth Kendall	W. G. Preston
127	1872	George Tuxbury	W. G. Preston
	1871	William Weld	
		(S. M. Pratt) (3)	
129	1871	Charles Ellis	
131	1880	Gideon Scull (7)	Carl Fehmer
133	1879	William Wharton (3)	Snell, Gregerson
135	1878	Francis Jacques	Snell, Gregerson
151	1876	Robert G. Shaw (6)	Shaw, Shaw

SOUTH SIDE

No.	Date	Owner	Architect
114	1871	First Baptist Church	H. H. Richardson
116	1874(?)	H. Daggett	
118	1872	James Case	Emerson, Fehmer
120	1873	Laura Case	Emerson, Fehmer
122	1871	Laura Case	Emerson, Fehmer
		(William Lawrence) (8)	
124	1871	Martha Cowing (1)	Emerson, Fehmer
126	1871	Elias Merwin (1)	Emerson, Fehmer
128	1882	William Shapleigh	S. D. Kelley
	1905?	Remodeled	
130	1882	William Rand	S. D. Kelley
	1905?	Remodeled	
132	1885	J. B. Glover (4)	Cummings, Sears
144	1880	William Atherton (7)	G. W. Pope
146	1876	S. E. Westcott (2)	G. W. Pope
148	1876	F. L. Fay (5)	G. W. Pope
150	1879	R. Baker (6)	Peabody, Stearns
152	1870	Jarvis Williams	

APPENDIX A   BUILDINGS CONSTRUCTED IN THE BACK BAY

COMMONWEALTH AVENUE, DARTMOUTH TO EXETER STREETS

NORTH SIDE

Number	Date	Owner	Architect
161	1873	J. D. Bates (4)	C. R. Kirby
163	1874	J. D. Bates	C. R. Kirby
165	1879	John Erskine	Cummings, Sears
167	1880	E. R. Morse (2)	Sturgis, Brigham
169	1879	J. S. Fay (7)	Peabody, Stearns
	1928	I. T. Burr	Parker, Thomas, Rice
171	1879	A. Lowell (3)	Snell, Gregerson
173	1879	Roger Walcott (7)	Peabody, Stearns
	1917	Harleston Parker	Parker, Thomas, Rice
175	1881	Charles Merriman (4)	Peabody, Stearns
177	1882	J. Q. Adams (9)	Snell, Gregerson
179	1879	William Bradley (4)	Carl Fehmer
181	1878	Charles Whitney	C. E. Luce
183	1878	Frank Merriman (8)	Snell, Gregerson
185	1883	William Bradley (incorporated into Hotel Agassiz)	James Smith
191	1872	Hotel Agassiz	Weston, Rand

SOUTH SIDE

Number	Date	Owner	Architect
	1871	Hotel Vendome	W. G. Preston
	1881	Hotel Vendome (addition)	J. F. Ober
172	1885	C. S. Bartlett (4)	J. H. Besarick
174	1893	L. M. Merrill	Lewis, Paine
176	1883	W. F. Wesselhoeft (5)	Charles Atwood
178	1883	J. B. Bell (7)	Charles Atwood
180	1883	W. S. Rand	S. D. Kelley
182	1879	O. M. Wentworth (7)	W. F. Wentworth
	1925	32-unit apartment	G. N. Jacobs
184	1889	6-unit apartment	McKay, Smith
186	1890	18-unit apartment	McKay, Smith
188	1890	18-unit apartment	McKay, Smith
190	1881	H. S. Whitwell	
192	1872	Louise Hubbell	Emerson, Fehmer
	1926	8-unit apartment	Bigelow, Wadsworth

COMMONWEALTH AVENUE, EXETER TO FAIRFIELD STREETS

NORTH SIDE

No.	Year	Owner	Architect
195	1881	F. C. Haven (1)	J. P. Putnam
197	1881	T. M. Rotch (9)	Rotch, Tilden
199	1890	J. A. Beebe (6)	McKim, Mead, White
203	1883	Leopold Morse (7)	L. Weissbein
	1929	Facade	W. M. Cox
205	1882	Endicott Peabody (2)	Peabody, Stearns
207	1883	Winthrop Sargent	Rotch, Tilden
211	1883	W. P. Mason (9)	Rotch, Tilden
213	1881	C. T. White (8)	Peabody, Stearns
215	1883	J. Lawrence (1)	Rotch, Tilden
219	1887	Algonquin Club	McKim, Mead, White
223	1883	G. Higginson	Cabot, Chandler
225	1884	W. L. Richardson (3)	Peabody, Stearns
227	1884	N. S. Bartlett (8)	Peabody, Stearns
229	1882	F. R. Sprague (4)	Peabody, Stearns
231	1885	J. C. Rogers (6)	Rotch, Tilden
233	1886	W. C. Rogers (4)	Rotch, Tilden
235	1882	G. Wheatland	O. F. Smith
239	1882	Nath. Thayer (8)	Sturgis, Brigham
	1937	21-unit apartment	H. Feer

SOUTH SIDE

No.	Year	Owner	Architect
196	1881	D. N. Spooner (2)	Peabody, Stearns
198	1880	Annie Mathews (8)	Allen, Kenway
200	1882	J. A. French	Allen, Kenway
202	1882	Sara Stratton (3)	Allen, Kenway
204	1888	W. S. Rand	S. D. Kelley
206	1885	D. Flagg (3)	Allen, Kenway
208	1885	H. C. Jackson (7)	Allen, Kenway
212	1879	B. W. Munroe (3)	Peabody, Stearns
214	1879	S. T. Ames	Peabody, Stearns
		(G. H. Quincy) (3)	
216	1879	George McKay	R. S. Bither
218	1879	George McKay (4)	R. S. Bither
220	1879	Robert McKay (2)	
222	1879	B. F. Guild (8)	W. Whitney Lewis
224	1879	F. J. Doe (4)	W. Whitney Lewis
226	1881	Asa Caton	
228	1881	C. W. Parker (6)	G. A. Avery
230	1881	C. W. Parker	G. A. Avery
232	1880	A. A. Wheelock	G. A. Avery
234	1889	H. W. Wadleigh	W. Whitney Lewis
236	1879	H. W. Wadleigh (2)	W. Whitney Lewis
238	1879	C. B. Wilson (2)	G. A. Avery
240	1879	William Baker	G. A. Avery
	1903	Rollin Allen	Chapman, Frazer

COMMONWEALTH AVENUE, FAIRFIELD TO GLOUCESTER STREETS

NORTH SIDE

Number	Date	Owner	Architect
245	1877	Elenor Emmons (7)	W. Whitney Lewis
247	1878	Uriel Crocker (4)	Bradlee, Winslow
	1905	Emily Mandell	William Rantoul
249	1878	W. S. Rand	S. D. Kelley
251	1880	J. S. Bigelow (8)	Shaw, Shaw
253	1880	N. B. Mansfield (3)	W. Whitney Lewis
255	1880	H. O. Roberts	W. Whitney Lewis
257	1886	A. Cochrane (9)	McKim, Mead, White
261	1880	A. Hunnewell (8)	Shaw, Shaw
263	1880	Charles Lovering	Snell, Gregerson
265	1880	F. H. Appleton (3)	Peabody, Stearns
267	1880	Charles Boyden (4)	Snell, Gregerson
269	1881	C. A. Kidder (2)	Allen, Kenway
273	1891	T. E. Proctor (8)	Hartwell, Richardson

SOUTH SIDE

Number	Date	Owner	Architect
246	1880	G. A. Avery	G. A. Avery
248	1878	J. W. Shapleigh	S. D. Kelley
250	1878	J. W. Shapleigh	S. D. Kelley
	1925	25-unit apartment	G. N. Jacobs
252	1879	S. Shapleigh	S. D. Kelley
254	1879	G. A. Avery	G. A. Avery
256	1879	Uriah Coffin	
258	1879	J. Shapleigh	S. D. Kelley
260	1879	J. Shapleigh	S. D. Kelley
262	1880	J. Shapleigh	S. D. Kelley
264	1882	J. Shapleigh	S. D. Kelley
266	1883	J. Shapleigh	S. D. Kelley
270	1896	Hotel Tuileries	McKay, Dunham
274	1885	H. M. White	S. D. Kelley
276	1885	W. Sherburne	S. D. Kelley
278	1883	Asa Caton	J. H. Besarick
280	1894	John Hogg	Walker, Kimball
282	1884	Alex. Moseley (3)	Allen, Kenway

COMMONWEALTH AVENUE, GLOUCESTER TO HEREFORD STREETS

NORTH SIDE

No.	Date	Owner	Architect
283	1879	H. S. Whitwell	
285	1881	H. S. Whitwell	
	1903	H. J. Bradbury	Winslow, Bigelow
287	1892	H. M. Sears (8)	Rotch, Tilden
291	1884	W. H. Allen (9)	Allen, Kenway
293	1890	E. B. Horn	S. D. Kelley
297	1899	James Draper (7)	Peabody, Stearns
303	1895	G. A. Nickerson (3)	McKim, Mead, White
305	1884	Mrs. N. Thayer	Peabody, Stearns

SOUTH SIDE

No.	Date	Owner	Architect
284	1880	Sumner Mead	Kirby, Lewis
286	1880	W. S. Rand	S. D. Kelley
288	1880	W. S. Rand	S. D. Kelley
290	1890	Fred Pope	Fred Pope
294	1880	J. Shapleigh	S. D. Kelley
296	1880	J. Shapleigh	S. D. Kelley
298	1880	J. Shapleigh	S. D. Kelley
300	1880	Uriah Coffin	O. F. Smith
302	1881	Uriah Coffin	O. F. Smith
304	1895	Clark, Weld	J. H. Schweinfurth
306	1896	J. G. Webster	Dwight, Chandler
308	1889	12-unit apartment	S. D. Kelley

APPENDIX A BUILDINGS CONSTRUCTED IN THE BACK BAY

COMMONWEALTH AVENUE, HEREFORD STREET TO MASSACHUSETTS AVENUE

NORTH SIDE

Number	Date	Owner	Architect
311	1877	Thomas Dana	W. Whitney Lewis
	1924	14-unit apartment	Funk, Wilcox
313	1877	Warren Hobbs (7)	Whitney Lewis
315	1878	D. Chamberlain	G. F. Meacham
317	1878	J. G. Abbott	O. F. Smith
319	1878	Asa Caton	
321	1879	Asa Caton	
323	1879	Asa Caton	
325	1879	Frank Thayer	G. F. Meacham
	1900(?)	Facade	W. G. Preston
327	1880	James Tobey	Kirby, Lewis
329	1895	George Wheatland	O. F. Smith
333	1895	Hotel Lafayette	McKay, Dunham
337	1880	Asa Caton	Kirby, Lewis
339	1880	Asa Caton	Kirby, Lewis
341	1880	Asa Caton	Kirby, Lewis
		(N. W. Rice) (8)	
343	1882	G. G. Crocker (8)	Bradlee, Winslow
345	1925	10-unit apartment	F. A. Norcross
347	1888	M. B. Mason (5)	Allen, Kenway
349	1894	L. M. Merrill	G. W. Lewis
351	1894	L. M. Merrill	G. W. Lewis
353	1894	L. M. Merrill	G. W. Lewis
355	1882	Oliver Ames (7)	Carl Fehmer

SOUTH SIDE

Number	Date	Owner	Architect
314		Vacant lot	
316	1881	Frank Thayer	O. F. Smith
314	1899	Albert Burrage	Charles Brigham
318	1881	J. Shapleigh	S. D. Kelley
320	1881	J. Shapleigh	S. D. Kelley
322	1882	George Wheatland	Bradlee, Winslow
324	1882	George Wheatland	Bradlee, Winslow
326	1882	George Wheatland	Bradlee, Winslow
328	1888	R. S. Gill	A. H. Drisko
330	1889	I. J. T. Edmunds	Winslow, Wetherill
332	1878	Benjamin Fitch (4)	
334	1879	William Noble	G. A. Avery
336	1881	Vinal, Dodge	G. A. Avery
338	1882	George Wheatland	Bradlee, Winslow
340	1882	George Wheatland	Bradlee, Winslow
342	1883	George Wheatland	O. F. Smith
344	1883	George Wheatland	O. F. Smith
346	1883	George Wheatland	O. F. Smith
348	1883	George Wheatland	O. F. Smith
350	1883	George Wheatland	O. F. Smith
352	1883	George Wheatland	O. F. Smith
354	1883	George Wheatland	O. F. Smith
356	1883	George Wheatland	O. F. Smith
358	1883	George Wheatland	O. F. Smith
360	1883	George Wheatland	O. F. Smith
362	1889	10-unit apartment	Richards, Richards
366	1889	6-unit apartment	Richards, Richards

COMMONWEALTH AVENUE, MASSACHUSETTS AVENUE TO CHARLESGATE EAST

NORTH SIDE

371	1892	10-unit apartment	McKay, Dunham
373	1892	21-unit apartment	McKay, Dunham
375	1892	H. M. Jernegan	G. A. Avery
377	1889	A. Knowlton	A. H. Drisko
379	1889	A. Knowlton	A. H. Drisko
381	1885	George Wheatland	O. F. Smith
383	1885	George Wheatland	O. F. Smith
385	1885	George Wheatland	O. F. Smith
387	1885	George Wheatland	O. F. Smith
389	1885	George Wheatland	O. F. Smith
391	1885	George Wheatland	O. F. Smith
393	1899	Wirt Dexter (8)	Little, Browne
395	1899	Fred Ayer (7)	A. J. Manning
399	1924	Moorland Apartments	H. B. Andrews
401	1901	A. T. Brown (4)	Peabody, Stearns
403	1901	Samuel Carr (8)	Shepley, Rutan, Coolidge
405	1900	Loren duBois (8)	S. D. Kelley
407	1901	William Amory (7)	Little, Browne
409	1898	W. Minot (4)	Peabody, Stearns
411	1899	R. S. Bradley (8)	Little, Browne
413	1890	F. D. Amory (8)	McKim, Mead, White
415	1890	Richard Olney (5)	McKim, Mead, White

24 Charlesgate East
| 1891 | W. Minot, Jr. | Peabody, Stearns, |

SOUTH SIDE

374	1912	Harvard Club	Parker, Thomas, Rice
378	1883	Park Entrance Land Co.	Peabody, Stearns
380	1883	Park Entrance Land Co.	Peabody, Stearns
382	1895	The Colonial	A. H. Vinal
384	1896	6-unit apartment	A. H. Vinal
386	1899	6-unit apartment	A. H. Vinal
388	1899	6-unit apartment	A. H. Vinal
390	1908	The Puritan	E. B. Stratton
400	1897	Hotel Somerset	A. Bowditch

APPENDIX A   BUILDINGS CONSTRUCTED IN THE BACK BAY

Number	Date	Owner	Architect

COMMONWEALTH AVENUE, CHARLESGATE WEST TO BEACON STREET

NORTH SIDE

Number	Date	Owner	Architect
461	1891	J. H. Thompson	S. D. Kelley
463	1891	J. H. Thompson	S. D. Kelley
465	1891	J. H. Thompson	S. D. Kelley
467	1891	J. H. Thompson	S. D. Kelley
469	1891	J. H. Thompson	S. D. Kelley
471	1891	J. H. Thompson	S. D. Kelley
475	1923	Offices	F. A. Norcross
477	1892	W. B. Allen (7)	Stephenson, Ballantine
479	1895	George Willcomb (6)	Winslow, Wetherell
481	1897	Charles Thorndike (8)	W. Y. Peters
483	1897	Charles Throndike	W. Y. Peters
485	1897	George Harvey (4)	R. C. Sturgis
487	1897	A. Coolidge (7)	R. C. Sturgis
491	1898	T. J. Coolidge	Shaw, Hunnewell
493	1895	T. Frothingham (7)	A. H. Vinal
495	1895	Alice Carpenter (7)	Walker, Kimball
497	1895	Charles Rollins (7)	Walker, Kimball

SOUTH SIDE

Number	Date	Owner	Architect
464	1916	46-unit apartment	Blackall, Clapp, Whittemore
468	1892	J. Bennett (5)	J. F. Ober
470	1897	Horace Packard (8)	Winslow, Wetherell
472	1900	S. Shapleigh	S. D. Kelley
474	1900	S. Shapleigh	S. D. Kelley
476	1900	S. C. King	W. Whitney, Lewis
478	1903	E. S. Wallace	Kilham, Hopkins
480	1901	E. C. Stanwood (6)	Chapman, Frazer
482	1898	L. A. Wright (6)	Dwight, Chandler
484	1895	L. D. Merrill	G. Wilton Lewis
486	1895	L. D. Merrill	G. Wilton Lewis
488	1895	L. D. Merrill	G. Wilton Lewis
490	1914	Chester Bliss	A. W. Longfellow
	1915	Kenmore Hotel	Blackall, Clapp, Whittemore

COMMONWEALTH AVENUE WEST OF KENMORE STREET

SOUTH SIDE

504	1897	S. Vorenberg	J. S. Kelley
506	1898	C. E. Jenkins	Peters, Rice
508	1897	A. Boothby	C. W. Kingsbury
510	1892	E. H. Fay	S. D. Kelley
512	1892	E. H. Fay	S. D. Kelley
514	1892	E. H. Fay	S. D. Kelley
516	1892	E. H. Fay	S. D. Kelley
518	1892	E. H. Fay	S. D. Kelley
520	1892	E. H. Fay	S. D. Kelley
522	1892	E. H. Fay	S. D. Kelley
524	1892	E. H. Fay	S. D. Kelley

NEWBURY STREET, ARLINGTON TO BERKELEY STREETS

SOUTH SIDE

4	1870	Henry Kidder	N. J. Bradlee
6	1866	John Webster	
8	1866	David Webster	Strickland, Blodget
	1928	Store, offices	
10	1865	James Standish	Blackall, Elwell
		(Benj. French) (3)	

NORTH SIDE

3	1864	Fox, Studley
5	1864	Fox, Studley
	1931	Ritz Hotel
7	1864	Fox, Studley
9	1863	Francis Vose
	1924	Store, offices

APPENDIX A BUILDINGS CONSTRUCTED IN THE BACK BAY

Number	Date	Owner	Architect	Number	Date	Owner	Architect
11	1863	Clarisa Kittredge (2)		12	1865	James Standish (J. A. Dodd) (2)	
	1926	Store front			1926	Store front	
13	1864	Samuel Hinckley		14	1864	Andrew Weeks (2)	
	1937	Sunday School, Emanuel Church		16	1864	Eliz. Kendall	Little, Russell
	1862	Emanuel Church	A. R. Estey		1928	Store, offices	
27	1875	Fox, Studley		18	1873	Miles Washburn	Peabody, Stearns
	1920	Chapel, Emanuel Church	Allen, Cullen		1927	Store, offices	F. A. Norcross
29	1874	J. Erskine	Fred Pope	20	1867	Hiram Bean	
31	1872	Lucy Crehore		22	1867	Hiram Bean	
	1926	Store front	J. F. Cullen	24	1867	Hiram Bean	
33	1881	Alden Avery	George Avery		1925	Store front	Strickland, Blodget
	1922	Store front		26	1872	J. D. Ball	
35	1870	A. D. Sinclair		28	1870	R. C. Greenleaf	
	1929	Store, offices			1911	National Academy Arts and Sciences	Page, Frothingham
37	1872	William Sheaf	J. R. Hall	30	1870	R. C. Greenleaf	
	1922	Store front		32	1871	Ann Badger	
39	1889	4-unit apartment	C. R. Beal		1922	Store front	
	1924	Store front		34	1871	E. A. Studley	
					1922	Store front	
				36	1869	James Standish	
				38	1869	James Standish	
				40	1869	James Standish	
				42	1868	James Standish	
					1928	Store, offices	H. B. Allen
				44	1868	James Standish	
				46	1868	James Standish	
				48	1869	Hotel Kempton	
					1927	Store, offices	H. B. Allen

NEWBURY STREET, BERKELEY TO CLARENDON STREETS

SOUTH SIDE

1862	Museum of Natural History	W. G. Preston
1864	First building, Massachusetts Institute of Technology	W. G. Preston
1883	Second building, Massachusetts Institute of Technology	
1939	New England Mutual Insurance Building	Carl Fehmer Cram, Ferguson

NORTH SIDE

	1866	Central Congregational Church	
69	1869	Charles Freeland	R. M. Upjohn
	1919	Store front	
71	1869	Charles Freeland	
	1927	Store front	
73	1869	Charles Freeland	
	1905	Store front	
75	1874	Charles Freeland	Peabody, Stearns
	1921	Store front	
77	1874	Charles Freeland	Peabody, Stearns
	1928	Store front	Wetherell, Ross
79	1876	Charles Freeland	Peabody, Stearns
81	1876	Charles Freeland	Peabody, Stearns
	1939	Store front	
83	1876	Charles Freeland	Peabody, Stearns
	1925	Store front	
85	1876	C. P. Wilson	Charles Kirby
	1926	Store front	
91	1872	Eben Jordan	Fred Pope
	1925	Store front	J. R. Ward
93	1872	Eben Jordan	Fred Pope
95	1872	Eben Jordan	Fred Pope
	1925	Store front	
97	1872	Eben Jordan	Fred Pope
	1921	Store front	H. B. Allen
99	1882	Charles Lauriat	
101	1882	Charles Lauriat	
	1928	Bank	Henry, Richmond
103	1881	J. Avery Richards	Louis Weissbein
	1939	Store front	

APPENDIX A BUILDINGS CONSTRUCTED IN THE BACK BAY

NEWBURY STREET, CLARENDON TO DARTMOUTH STREETS

NORTH SIDE

Number	Date	Owner	Architect
109	1871	C. A. Cummings	Cummings, Sears
	1923	Store windows	
113	1883	G. R. Shaw	George R. Shaw
115	1887	W. S. Rand	S. D. Kelley
	1932	Store front	J. E. Bennett
117	1887	W. S. Rand	S. D. Kelley
119	1873	Charles Underwood	F. H. Moore
121	1873	S. G. Palmer	F. H. Moore
123	1873	N. Morse	F. H. Moore
	1927	Store front	
125	1873	F. H. Moore	F. H. Moore
127	1873	F. H. Moore	F. H. Moore
129	1877	J. W. Tobey	
	1927	Store front	
131	1877	J. W. Tobey	
	1927	Store front	
133	1877	J. W. Tobey	
	1924	Store front	
135	1877	William S. Rand	
137	1877	William S. Rand	
139	1877	John Shapleigh	
141	1876	Asa Caton	
	1929	Store, offices	
143	1876	Asa Caton	H. B. Allen
	1927	Store, offices	H. B. Allen

SOUTH SIDE

Number	Date	Owner	Architect
110	1877	James Standish	
112	1876	James Standish	
114	1876	J. Farrington	
116	1876	J. W. Tobey	Funk, Wilcox
	1928	Store, offices	
118	1876	J. W. Tobey	
120	1886	William S. Rand	W. S. Rand
122	1886	William S. Rand	W. S. Rand
124	1886	William S. Rand	W. S. Rand
126	1886	William S. Rand	W. S. Rand
128	1927	Store, offices	Shepard, Stearns
	1877	Charles Freeland	Peabody, Stearns
130	1877	Charles Freeland	Peabody, Stearns
	1927	Store front	E. B. Stratton
132	1877	Charles Freeland	Peabody, Stearns
	1927	Store offices	H. B. Allen
134	1877	Charles Freeland	Peabody, Stearns
136	1877	Charles Freeland	Peabody, Stearns
	1927	Store front	H. B. Allen
138	1883	Alden Avery	Avery, Page
	1927	Store front	W. T. Aldrich
140	1883	Alden Avery	Avery, Page
	1929	Store front	
	1886	Victoria Hotel	J. L. Faxon

NEWBURY STREET, DARTMOUTH TO EXETER STREETS

NORTH SIDE

149	1883	5-unit apartment	W. G. Preston
153	1876	H. S. Whitwell	
155	1876	H. S. Whitwell	
157	1888	4-unit apartment	
159	1888	4-unit apartment	
161	1888	4-unit apartment	
163	1886	A. A. Pope	G. W. Clarke
165	1885	S. G. Hayward	G. W. Clarke
	1927	Store front	
167	1881	Silas Merrill	
169	1881	Silas Merrill	
171	1881	Silas Merrill	
	1928	Store front	
173	1881	Silas Merrill	
175	1886	Silas Merrill	
177	1886	Silas Merrill	
179	1885	R. H. Allen	S. D. Kelley
	1884	Spiritualist Church	Hartwell, Richardson

SOUTH SIDE

152	1884	Boston Bicycle Club	G. F. Meacham
154	1889	4-unit apartment	A. H. Drisko
156	1889	4-unit apartment	A. H. Drisko
158	1889	4-unit apartment	A. H. Drisko
160	1888	5-unit apartment	S. D. Kelley
162	1884	Silas Merrill	
	1925	Store front	
164	1884	Silas Merrill	
166	1884	Silas Merrill	
168	1880	Ernest Cushing	George Avery
170	1881	Henry Cushing	George Avery
172	1885	Silas Merrill	G. Wilton Lewis
174	1885	Silas Merrill	G. Wilton Lewis
	1936	Store front	
176	1890	C. P. Searle	G. F. Magnitzky
	1888	Horace Mann School	A. H. Vinal
	1883	Hollis Street Church	G. F. Meacham

APPENDIX A   BUILDINGS CONSTRUCTED IN THE BACK BAY

NEWBURY STREET, EXETER TO FAIRFIELD STREETS

NORTH SIDE

Number	Date	Owner	Architect
	1876	Exeter Schoolhouse	G. A. Clough
205	1881	Silas Merrill	
207	1881	Silas Merrill	
209	1881	Silas Merrill	
211	1880	Silas Merrill	
213	1880	Silas Merrill	
215	1880	Silas Merrill	
217	1880	Silas Merrill	
219	1880	Silas Merrill	
221	1880	Silas Merrill	
223	1880	Silas Merrill	
225	1880	Silas Merrill	
	1916	Basement store	
227	1879	Silas Merrill	Rubin Rand
229	1879	Silas Merrill	Rubin Rand
231	1879	Silas Merrill	Rubin Rand

SOUTH SIDE

Number	Date	Owner	Architect
	1883	Normal Art School	Hartwell, Richardson
206	1886	Silas Merrill	
208	1886	Silas Merrill	
210	1885	W. S. Rand	S. D. Kelley
212	1885	W. S. Rand	S. D. Kelley
	1936	New facade	
214	1885	W. S. Rand	S. D. Kelley
216	1884	W. S. Rand	S. D. Kelley
218	1884	W. S. Rand	S. D. Kelley
220	1884	J. Shapleigh	S. D. Kelley
222	1884	J. Shapleigh	S. D. Kelley
224	1884	W. S. Rand	S. D. Kelley
226	1884	W. S. Rand	S. D. Kelley
228	1882	Chadwick, Stillings	S. D. Kelley
230	1882	Chadwick, Stillings	S. D. Kelley
232	1882	Chadwick, Stillings	S. D. Kelley
234	1882	Chadwick, Stillings	S. D. Kelley
236	1886	S. W. Merrill	
238	1886	S. W. Merrill	
240	1886	S. W. Merrill	
	1928	Office building	J. H. Ritchie

NEWBURY STREET, FAIRFIELD TO GLOUCESTER STREETS

NORTH SIDE

No.	Date		
245	1884	W. C. Nash	
247	1884	A. J. Webster	Cabot, Chandler
249	1881	John Briggs	John Briggs
251	1881	John Briggs	John Briggs
253	1882	Prescott Hall	G. Wilton Lewis
255	1882	Herbert Nash	G. Wilton Lewis
257	1882	Herbert Nash	G. Wilton Lewis
259	1882	Silas Merrill	G. Wilton Lewis
261	1881	Alden Avery	George Avery
263	1881	Alden Avery	George Avery
	1927	Basement store	
265	1884	J. Shapleigh	S. D. Kelley
267	1881	A. T. Lowe	W. Whitney Lewis
269	1881	William Lewis	W. Whitney Lewis
271	1884	S. T. Ames	S. D. Kelley
273	1884	S. T. Ames	S. D. Kelley
275	1884	S. T. Ames	S. D. Kelley
	1922	New facade	
279	1882	C. A. Morse	S. D. Kelley

SOUTH SIDE

No.	Date		
242	1880	Alden Avery	George Avery
244	1880	Alden Avery	George Avery
246	1884	Alden Avery	George Avery
248	1884	Alden Avery	George Avery
250	1884	Alden Avery	George Avery
252	1884	Alden Avery	George Avery
254	1882	Silas Merrill	G. Wilton Lewis
256	1882	Silas Merrill	G. Wilton Lewis
258	1882	Silas Merrill	G. Wilton Lewis
260	1882	Silas Merrill	G. Wilton Lewis
262	1882	Silas Merrill	G. Wilton Lewis
264	1882	Silas Merrill	G. Wilton Lewis
266	1882	Silas Merrill	G. Wilton Lewis
268	1882	Silas Merrill	G. Wilton Lewis
270	1882	Silas Merrill	G. Wilton Lewis
272	1882	Silas Merrill	G. Wilton Lewis
274	1882	Silas Merrill	G. Wilton Lewis
276	1882	Silas Merrill	G. Wilton Lewis
278	1882	Silas Merrill	G. Wilton Lewis
280	1882	Silas Merrill	G. Wilton Lewis
282	1880	Alvah Burrage	W. Whitney Lewis
284	1920	Office building	A. D. Boyle

APPENDIX A   BUILDINGS CONSTRUCTED IN THE BACK BAY

NEWBURY STREET, GLOUCESTER TO HEREFORD STREETS

NORTH SIDE

Number	Date	Owner	Architect
281	1886	U. F. Coffin	O. F. Smith
283	1886	U. F. Coffin	O. F. Smith
285	1884	U. F. Coffin	O. F. Smith
287	1884	U. F. Coffin	O. F. Smith
289	1886	U. F. Coffin	S. D. Kelley
291	1886	U. F. Coffin	S. D. Kelley
293	1885	Elizabeth Post	William Dabney
295	1885	George Edwards	William Dabney
297	1889	Alden Avery	George W. Avery
299	1887	Alden Avery	George W. Avery
301	1887	Alden Avery	George W. Avery

SOUTH SIDE

Number	Date	Owner	Architect
284	1884	Silas Merrill	G. Wilton Lewis
286	1885	Silas Merrill	G. Wilton Lewis
288	1885	Silas Merrill	G. Wilton Lewis
290	1885	Silas Merrill	G. Wilton Lewis
292	1885	Silas Merrill	G. Wilton Lewis
294	1885	Silas Merrill	G. Wilton Lewis
296	1885	Silas Merrill	G. Wilton Lewis
298	1886	Silas Merrill	G. Wilton Lewis
300	1886	Silas Merrill	G. Wilton Lewis
302	1886	Silas Merrill	G. Wilton Lewis
304	1888	Chadwick, Stillings	S. D. Kelley
306	1888	Chadwick, Stillings	S. D. Kelley
308	1888	Chadwick, Stillings	S. D. Kelley
	1926	Store in basement	
314	1885	Ed. B. Horn	S. D. Kelley
316	1885	Store, 4-unit apartment	S. D. Kelley

NEWBURY STREET, HEREFORD STREET TO MASSACHUSETTS AVENUE

Street built up with stables. Record omitted.

BOYLSTON STREET, PARK SQUARE TO CHURCH STREET

New	Old*		
182	76	1850	Jonathan Preston
184	77	1850	Jonathan Preston
188	78	1850	Jonathan Preston
192	79	1850	Jonathan Preston
	80	1848	Carr, Emerson
194		1885	White Building
200	81	1848	N. A. Thompson
	82	1848	N. A. Thompson
	83	1850	N. Sturtevant
202		1885	Potter Building	S. J. F. Thayer
	84	1850	N. Sturtevant
212		1890	Store building	Winslow, Wetherell
	85	1848	T. B. Wales
214		1891	Store building	S. D. Kelley
	86	1848	Alex Twombly
220		1890	Store front
222	87	1845	I. A. Carey
	88	1848	Lincoln, et al.
	89	1848	Lincoln, et al.
228		1921	Bradbury Building	Blackall, Clapp
	90	1848	Lincoln, et al.
	91	1848	Lincoln, et al.
	92	1848	Lincoln, et al.
240		1885	Thorndike Hotel	S. J. F. Thayer

*New street numbers for buildings on Boylston Street were assigned in 1890–91.

BOYLSTON STREET, CHURCH STREET TO ARLINGTON STREET

New	Old		
	93	1849	Peter Goodman
	94	1849	J. Foster

APPENDIX A BUILDINGS CONSTRUCTED IN THE BACK BAY

Number	Date	Owner	Architect
248	1888	Store, offices	S. J. F. Thayer
95	1911	Store, offices	J. A. Schweinfurth
	1849	R. Appleton	
252	1890	Store front	
96	1845	T. J. Lodbel	
	1899	Store front	Irving, Casson
254	1921	Store front	
97	1845	T. J. Lodbel	
98	1845	Samuel Guild	
260	1888	Store front (Women's Educational and Industrial Union)	
99	1849	Samuel Guild	
268	1925	Store front	
100	1849	Samuel Guild	
272	1922	Store front	
101	1849	Eben Sears	
276	1922	Store front	
102	1849	A. Wentworth	
103	1849	Eben Sears	
	1884	Store front	
280	1928	Store front	
288	1846	Luther Drew	
104	1846	Luther Drew	
292	1863	Davenport	
105	1863	Davenport	
296	1858	L. Burnham	
106			
300			
107			
108			
306	1929	Store, offices	I. Richmond
109	1858	Mary Parkman	
310	1912	Store, offices	Peabody, Stearns
110	1858	Elizabeth Guild	Demolished 1902 to cut Arlington Street
111	1861	George Peters	Demolished 1902 to cut Arlington Street
112	1861	A. Cheney	Demolished 1902 to cut Arlington Street

BOYLSTON STREET, ARLINGTON TO BERKELEY STREETS

NORTH SIDE

New	Old	1860		
357	121	1860	Arlington St. Church	Arthur Gilman
361		1872	Dr. George Lyman	
	123	1863	Charles Sheafe	Peabody, Stearns
	125	1864	George Morey	
363		1909	Office building	Arthur Gray
	127	1864	George Morey	
	129	1864	George Morey	
	131	1864	George Morey	
367		1902	Standish Building	Winslow, Bigelow
	133	1864	George Morey	
379		1902	Store front	
	135	1864	George Morey	
383		1899	Store front	
	137	1866	Elizabeth Blise	
	139	1866	Elizabeth Blise	
	141	1867	Fox, Studley	
393		1903	Store, offices	W. G. Rantoul
	143	1867	Fox, Studley	
	145	1867	Fox, Studley	
	147	1867	Fox, Studley	
399		1924	Store front	
	149	1867	Fox, Studley	
	151	1867	Fox, Studley	
	153	1868	Fox, Studley	

BOYLSTON STREET, ARLINGTON TO BERKELEY STREETS

Arlington Street not cut through until 1902

SOUTH SIDE

New	Old	1860		
	113	1860	A. Bowditch	
	114	1861	C. Ellis	
	115	1863	Thomas Cushing	
334		1904	Store building	W. G. Rantoul
	116	1863	J. Preston	W. G. Preston
	117	1863	E. Manton	W. G. Preston
336			Store front	
	118	1863	F. Cushing	
	119	1864	R. Huntington	
334		1890	Store front	
	120	1864	J. Farrington	W. G. Preston
	122	1865	J. Preston	W. G. Preston
	124	1865	J. Preston	Parker, Thomas, Rice
360		1906	Mayflower Bldg.	
	126	1867	J. Preston	W. G. Preston
	128	1867	James Paul	W. G. Preston
368		1926	Store, offices	H. B. Allen
	130	1868	Henry Holt	
	132	1868	Henry Holt	
	134	1868	Henry Holt	
376		1894	Eldridge Building	W. T. Sears
	136	1868	Henry Holt	
380		1927	Store, offices	
384	138	1866	Henry Holt	
	140	1861	Fox, Studley	Little, Russell

APPENDIX A   BUILDINGS CONSTRUCTED IN THE BACK BAY

Number	Date	Owner	Architect	Number	Date	Owner	Architect
419	1896	Warren Chambers	Ball, Dabney	390	1896	Store front	George Abbot
155	1868	Fox, Studley		142	1861	Fox, Studley	
423	1919	Store front		392	1921	Store front	
157	1868	Fox, Studley		144	1861	Fox, Studley	
429	1917	Store front		396	1911	Store front	
159	1868	Fox, Studley		146	1861	Fox, Studley	
431	1918	Store front	L. Greenleafe	402	1908	Store, offices	A. H. Bowditch
161	1869	Fox, Studley		148	1861	Fox, Studley	
439	1910	Store, offices	A. H. Bowditch	150	1861	Fox, Studley	
163	1869	Fox, Studley		152	1861	Fox, Studley	
165	1869	Fox, Studley		154	1871	Hotel Berkeley	
449	1918	Stores, offices		420	1905	Office building	Codman, Despradelle

BOYLSTON STREET, BERKELEY TO CLARENDON STREETS

NORTH SIDE

Date	Owner	Architect
1862	Museum of Natural History	W. G. Preston
1864	First building Massachusetts Institute of Technology	W. G. Preston
1883	Second building Massachusetts Institute of Technology	Carl Fehmer
1939–42	New England Mutual Life Insurance Building	Cram and Ferguson

SOUTH SIDE

Old	New	Date	Owner	Architect
462	170	1882	Y.M.C.A.	Sturgis, Brigham
470	178	1875	I. S. Craft	
472	180	1875	I. S. Craft	
476	182	1869	Robert Stover	
		19—	Office building	
480	184	1869	Ralph White	
484	186	1871	L. A. Wright	
486	188	1871	Francis Brooks	
490	190	1870	Fanny Mackay	
492	192	1870	Fanny Mackay	
498	194	1874	James Tobey	
504	196	1875	George Moffatt	W. Whitney Lewis
		1877	Brunswick Hotel annex	Peabody, Stearns
		1873	Brunswick Hotel	Peabody, Stearns

BOYLSTON STREET, CLARENDON TO DARTMOUTH STREETS

NORTH SIDE

541	225	Hotel Bristol	1879	L. Newcomb
543	233	Hotel Cluny	1876	J. P. Putnam
	235	Charles Freeland	1877	
551		Store front	1924	
553	237	Charles Freeland	1877	
559	239	D. W. Cheever	1878	
561	241	J. Farrington	1877	
565	243	J. Farrington	1877	
		Second Church Society	1873	N. J. Bradlee
		Unitarian		
569		Office building	1915(?)	
585		Chauncy Hall School	1873	A. C. Martin
		Office building	1915(?)	
601	261	T. A. Taylor	1877	
603	263	Sam Carlton	1879	
607	265	Sam Carlton	1879	

APPENDIX A   BUILDINGS CONSTRUCTED IN THE BACK BAY

BOYLSTON STREET, DARTMOUTH TO EXETER STREETS

NORTH SIDE

New	Old	Date	Owner	Architect
		1874	New Old South Church	
		1872	New Old South Church Parsonage	
647	285	1886	Silas Merrill	
651	287	1886	Silas Merrill	
657	289	1886	Silas Merrill	
661	291	1888	Silas Merrill	
665	293	1888	Silas Merrill	
669	295	1888	Silas Merrill	
673	297	1888	Silas Merrill	
675	299	1888	Silas Merrill	
687	307	1884	Hotel Kensington	

SOUTH SIDE

Number	Date	Owner	Architect
	1887	Boston Public Library	McKim, Mead, White Ware, Van Brunt
	1881	Harvard Medical School	Cummings, Sears
	1890	Harvard Medical School addition	Cummings, Sears

BOYLSTON STREET, EXETER TO FAIRFIELD STREETS

NORTH SIDE

Number	Date	Owner	Architect
705	1892	Stone Building	G. W. Pope
715	1890	Silas Merrill	
719	1890	Silas Merrill	
723	1890	Silas Merrill	
727	1890	Silas Merrill	
731	1895	Hayes Building	G. W. Pope
735	1897	G. F. Fabyan	

Buildings beyond Fairfield Street are not listed; all are commerical or apartment buildings.

ARLINGTON STREET

No.	Year	Building / Owner	Architect
1	1861	J. L. Simmons	probably G. F. J. Bryant
		(Wm. Weld)	
2	1861	J. L. Simmons	probably G. F. J. Bryant
		(John Faulkner) (2)	
3	1861	J. L. Simmons	probably G. F. J. Bryant
		(S. T. Dana)	
4	1861	Henry Atkins (5)	
5	1861	Seth Simmons	
6	1861	Josiah Abbott	
7	1861	William Lawrence	
	1929	Junior League Club	Strickland, Blodget
8	1870	Barney Corey	
9	1861	Oliver Brewster	
10	1861	Sarah Cazenove	
11	1861	John Homans	
12	1860	John Bates	
13	1860	William Moreland	R. M. Hunt
14	1860	H. H. Williams	R. M. Hunt
15	1860	H. H. Williams	R. M. Hunt
	1931	Ritz Carlton Hotel	Strickland, Blodget
16	1869	W. G. Preston	W. G. Preston
17	1864	A. F. Conant (6)	W. G. Preston
18	1861	E. H. Clark	
19	1864	Benjamin Bates (5)	
	1860	Arlington Street Church	Arthur Gilman

BERKELEY STREET

No.	Year	Building / Owner	Architect
	1862	Museum of Natural History	W. G. Preston
243	1869	Hotel Kempton	H. B. Allen
	1927	Store, offices	
247	1869	C. A. Wood (F. H. Peabody) (6)	
249	1869	C. A. Wood	
	1924	Store front	
	1866	Central Congregational Church	R. M. Upjohn
255	1864	William Chadbourne	
299	1877	J. C. Philips	Peabody, Stearns
	1959	Lutheran Church	Pietro Belluschi
	1867	First Church, Congregational	Ware, Van Brunt
300	1867	George Wheatland (C. S. Dana) (7)	
301	1865	Charles Minot (4)	Snell, Gregerson
	1923	7-unit apartment	
302	1867	George Wheatland (Sarah Jackson) (5)	Parker, Thomas, Rice
304	1869	Mariana Crafts	

APPENDIX A BUILDINGS CONSTRUCTED IN THE BACK BAY

CLARENDON STREET

Number	Date	Owner	Architect
	1883	M.I.T., Second building	Carl Fehmer
220	1883	12-unit apartment	M. W. Brown
232	1872	Uriah Coffin	
233	1879	Trinity Church Rectory	H. H. Richardson
234	1871	Newton Talbot	
236	1871	Newton Talbot	
	1929	Store front	
260	1871	Brattle Square Church	H. H. Richardson
261	1869	Hotel Hamilton	Ware, Van Brunt
	1876	F. L. Fiske (7)	Cummings, Sears
263	1925	14-unit apartment	McLaughlin, Burr
	1870	George Wheatland	
265	1870	George Wheatland (A. L. Mason) (3)	
267	1870	George Wheatland (Annie Parker) (2)	
270	1873	James Chadwick (4)	Weston, Rand
271	1869	George Wheatland	
273	1869	George Wheatland	
275	1869	George Wheatland	
277	1869	George Wheatland	
279	1869	George Wheatland	
278	1870	F. W. Hunnewell (6)	
285	1864	Mrs. Thomas Perkins (2)	

DARTMOUTH STREET

Number	Date	Owner	Architect
	1874	Old South Church	Cummings, Sears
270	1881	Boston Art Club	W. R. Emerson
275	1886	Hotel Victoria	J. L. Faxon
280	1871	Stephan Stoddard	
282	1871	Stephan Stoddard	
284	1871	Stephan Stoddard	
277	1878	J. P. Putnam (5)	J. P. Putnam
279	1871	James Standish	
281	1871	James Standish	
283	1871	James Standish	
	1871	Hotel Vendome	W. G. Preston
	1881	Hotel Vendome enlargement	J. F. Ober
303	1876	Arthur Hunnewell (8)	Shaw, Shaw
306	1872	S. V. R. Thayer	John Sturgis
	1882	Oakes Ames	
312	1871	George Wheatland	
314	1871	George Wheatland	
315	1870	Hollis Hunnewell	
317	1870	George Wheatland	
	1925	7-unit apartment	
319	1869	George Wheatland	
321	1869	George Wheatland	
326	1872	George Wheatland	Snell, Gregerson
328	1872	George Wheatland	Snell, Gregerson
330	1889	8-unit apartment	Blaikie, Blaikie

EXETER STREET

No.	Year	Owner / Building	Architect
1	1870	George Wheatland	
3	1870	George Wheatland	
5	1870	George Wheatland	
7	1872	George Wheatland	Peabody, Stearns
9	1872	George Wheatland	Peabody, Stearns
11	1872	George Wheatland	Peabody, Stearns
16	1886	E. P. Bradbury (3)	W. Whitney Lewis
17	1881	H. C. Haven (stable)	
	1915	Residence	
18	1885	W. S. Dexter (4)	Snell, Gregerson
25	1882	Nathan Mathews	Peabody, Stearns
	1884	Spiritualist Temple (Exeter Theatre)	Hartwell, Richardson
	1876	Exeter Schoolhouse	G. A. Clough
	1883	Normal Art School	Hartwell, Richardson
	1887	Boston Athletic Assn.	John Sturgis
	1889	Copley Hotel annex	T. M. Clark
	1890	Copley Hotel	Fred Pope

FAIRFIELD STREET

No.	Year	Owner	Architect
1	1871	H. C. Wainwright	
		(A. Hinckley) (2)	
3	1871	H. C. Wainwright	Ware, Van Brunt
5	1871	H. C. Wainwright	Ware, Van Brunt
7	1872	G. M. Gibson	
9	1872	G. M. Gibson	
		(E. H. Morse) (8)	
8	1879	H. L. Higginson	Sturgis, Brigham
10	1879	H. L. Higginson	Sturgis, Brigham
		(C. G. White) (5)	
12	1879	Georgiana Lowell (7)	Cabot, Chandler
18	1878	Elizabeth Grinnell (6)	Peabody, Stearns
20	1875	Elizabeth Allen (7)	W. Whitney Lewis
21	1880	G. P. King	W. Whitney Lewis
29	1876	Asa Potter	W. Whitney Lewis
30	1883	W. G. Saltonstahl (5)	Peabody, Stearns
31	1877	Asa Potter	Ober, Rand
33	1877	Asa Potter	Ober, Rand
35	1878	Asa Potter	Ober, Rand
37	1878	Asa Potter	Ober, Rand
32	1878	Asa Potter	Ober, Rand
34	1878	Asa Potter	Ober, Rand
36	1879	Asa Potter	Ober, Rand
38	1879	Asa Potter	Ober, Rand
39	1880	Alden Avery	George Avery
41	1880	Alden Avery	George Avery
40	1886	Silas Merrill	
42	1886	Silas Merrill	
44	1886	Silas Merrill	

APPENDIX A BUILDINGS CONSTRUCTED IN THE BACK BAY

GLOUCESTER STREET

Number	Date	Owner	Architect	Number	Date	Owner	Architect
1	1870	C. E. Cook	W. G. Preston	48	1882	George Wheatland	Bradlee, Winslow
2	1893	W. C. Loring (9)	W. Y. Peters	50	1882	George Wheatland	Bradlee, Winslow
3	1872	F. H. Moore	F. H. Moore	52	1882	George Wheatland	Bradlee, Winslow
5	1872	F. H. Moore	F. H. Moore	54	1882	George Wheatland	Bradlee, Winslow
7	1872	F. H. Moore	F. H. Moore	56	1882	George Wheatland	Bradlee, Winslow
4	1871	H. C. Wainwright		49	1883	George Wheatland	O. F. Smith
6	1871	H. C. Wainwright		51	1883	George Wheatland	O. F. Smith
8	1871	H. C. Wainwright		53	1883	George Wheatland	O. F. Smith
	1912	7-unit apartment	Parker, Thomas, Rice	55	1883	George Wheatland	O. F. Smith
9	1872	W. T. Sears	Cummings, Sears				
11	1872	W. T. Sears	Cummings, Sears				
13	1872	W. T. Sears	Cummings, Sears				
15	1872	W. T. Sears	Cummings, Sears				
10	1872	Hiram Gerrish	J. H. Besarick				
12	1872	Hiram Gerrish	J. H. Besarick				
14	1872	Hiram Gerrish	J. H. Besarick				
17	1886	E. V. R. Thayer	Sturgis, Brigham				
20	1886	C. F. Adams (2)	Peabody, Stearns				
29	1882	C. A. Morse	S. D. Kelley				
31	1882	C. A. Morse	S. D. Kelley				
33	1882	C. A. Morse	S. D. Kelley				
35	1882	C. A. Morse	S. D. Kelley				
30	1880	W. S. Rand					
32	1880	W. S. Rand					
34	1880	W. S. Rand					
36	1880	W. S. Rand					
42	1884	Silas Merrill	G. Wilton Lewis				
44	1884	Silas Merrill	G. Wilton Lewis				
46	1884	Silas Merrill	G. Wilton Lewis				

HEREFORD STREET

7	1879	E. E. Chapin	R. S. Bither
9	1879	E. E. Chapin	R. S. Bither
11	1879	E. E. Chapin	R. S. Bither
12	1869	Caroline Sawyer	
13	1872	J. F. Richardson	
15	1872	J. F. Richardson	
17	1872	J. F. Richardson	
14	1871	G. Gibson	
16	1871	G. Gibson	
18	1871	G. Gibson	
20	1871	G. Gibson	
27	1879	S. T. Ames	R. S. Bither
29	1879	S. T. Ames	R. S. Bither
31	1879	S. T. Ames	R. S. Bither
32	1884	John Andrew (9)	McKim, Mead, White
40	1886	F. S. Sargent (8)	Shaw, Hunnewell
45	1882	George Wheatland	Bradlee, Winslow
47	1882	George Wheatland	Bradlee, Winslow
49	1882	George Wheatland	Bradlee, Winslow
51	1882	George Wheatland	Bradlee, Winslow
53	1882	George Wheatland	Bradlee, Winslow
46	1885	E. B. Horn	E. N. Boyden
48	1885	E. B. Horn	E. N. Boyden
50	1885	E. B. Horn	E. N. Boyden
52	1885	E. B. Horn	E. N. Boyden

MASSACHUSETTS AVENUE

| 7 | 1888 | 13-unit apartment | O. F. Smith |
| 29 | 1889 | Brooks Adams | |

APPENDIX A BUILDINGS CONSTRUCTED IN THE BACK BAY

Number	Date	Owner	Architect	Number	Date	Owner	Architect

BAY STATE ROAD, CHARLESGATE WEST TO RALEIGH STREET

Number	Date	Owner	Architect
7	1895	Chadwick, Stillings	S. D. Kelley
9	1895	Chadwick, Stillings	S. D. Kelley
11	1895	G. F. D. Paine	F. R. Allen
13	1889	Chadwick, Stillings	S. D. Kelley
15	1889	Chadwick, Stillings	S. D. Kelley
17	1889	Chadwick, Stillings	S. D. Kelley
19	1889	Chadwick, Stillings	S. D. Kelley
21	1889	Chadwick, Stillings	S. D. Kelley
23	1889	Chadwick, Stillings	S. D. Kelley
25	1889	Chadwick, Stillings	S. D. Kelley
27	1889	Chadwick, Stillings	S. D. Kelley
29	1889	Chadwick, Stillings	S. D. Kelley
31	1891	Chadwick, Stillings	S. D. Kelley
33	1891	Chadwick, Stillings	S. D. Kelley
35	1891	Chadwick, Stillings	S. D. Kelley
37	1891	Chadwick, Stillings	S. D. Kelley
39	1892	Chadwick, Stillings	S. D. Kelley
41	1892	Chadwick, Stillings	S. D. Kelley
43	1892	Chadwick, Stillings	S. D. Kelley
45	1892	Chadwick, Stillings	S. D. Kelley
47	1893	Chadwick, Stillings	S. D. Kelley
49	1893	Lester Leland	Little, Browne

BAY STATE ROAD, RALEIGH TO DEERFIELD STREETS

NORTH SIDE

No.	Year	Owner	Architect
57	1890	Arthur Little	Arthur Little
59	1893	Edmund Wheelwright	Wheelwright, Haven
61	1893	John E. Devlin	Wheelwright, Haven
63	1894	Fred H. Curtiss	F. M. Makefield
65	1895	J. W. Wheelwright	J. W. Wheelwright
67	1897	Mrs. E. B. Osgood	Fehmer, Page
69	1897	Andrew Weeks	Chapman, Frazer
71	1899	Charles F. Lyman	Chapman, Frazer
73	?	Thorndike	
75	1901	Alfred Bowditch	Peters, Rice
77	1900	Ezra Thayer	Peters, Rice
79	1902	Charles Hubbard	
81	?	Joslin	
83	1900	C. H. Tyler	Fox and Company
87	1923	Sheraton Hotel	Strickland, Blodget, Lane
97	1900	William Gaston	Peters, Rice
99	1900	R. Saltonstahl	Shepley, Rutan, Coolidge
2 Deerfield	1900	P. C. Brooks	Shepley, Rutan, Coolidge

SOUTH SIDE

No.	Year	Owner	Architect
52	1913	Fred Johnson	Murdock Boyle
56	1900	Lorin Deland	Andrews, Jacques, Rantoul
58	1895	Wheatland, Vinal	Arthur H. Vinal
60	1895	Wheatland, Vinal	Arthur H. Vinal
62	1895	Wheatland, Vinal	Arthur H. Vinal
64	1895	Wheatland, Vinal	Arthur H. Vinal
66	1895	Wheatland, Vinal	Arthur H. Vinal
68	1895	Wheatland, Vinal	Arthur H. Vinal
70	1896	Wheatland, Vinal	S. D. Kelley
72	1896	Wheatland, Vinal	S. D. Kelley
74	1896	Wheatland, Vinal	S. D. Kelley
76	1896	Wheatland, Vinal	S. D. Kelley
78	1896	Wheatland, Vinal	S. D. Kelley
80	1896	Wheatland, Vinal	S. D. Kelley
82	1899	George Wheatland	S. D. Kelley
84	1899	George Wheatland	S. D. Kelley
86	1899	George Wheatland	S. D. Kelley
88	1899	George Wheatland	S. D. Kelley
90	1899	George Wheatland	S. D. Kelley
92	1899	George Wheatland	S. D. Kelley
94	1899	George Wheatland	S. D. Kelley
96	1905	10-unit apartment	A. H. Vinal

APPENDIX A   BUILDINGS CONSTRUCTED IN THE BACK BAY

Number	Date	Owner	Architect

BAY STATE ROAD, DEERFIELD TO SHERBORN STREETS

NORTH SIDE

Number	Date	Owner	Architect
105	1893	F. C. Welch	Ball, Dabney
109	1900	Thom Lockwood	Winslow, Wetherell
111	1933	Dr. Wolfsen	Arthur Rosenstein
113	1897	Louise Winslow	Winslow, Wetherell
117	1899	Frank Snow	Little, Browne
119	1899	E. W. Burdett	Winslow, Wetherell
121	1899	Mrs. Alice Childs	Winslow, Wetherell
125	1899	Miss Sophie Moen	Winslow, Wetherell
127	1905	John Farlow	James Kelley
129	1936	R. Dresser	William Galvin
131	1900	Edwin Curtis	Stickney, Austin
133	1900	Ellen Sturgis	John Lavalle
135	1902	James Pendergast	James Mulcahy
137	1895	E. W. Harding	W. Whitney Lewis
139	1895	William A. Hayes	Longfellow, Alden
141	1900	Charles Dwight	Fehmer, Page
143	1900	William Y. Peters	Peters, Rice
145	1900	Gorham Peters	Peters, Rice
149	1900	Charles G. Weld	Peters, Rice

SOUTH SIDE

Number	Date	Owner	Architect
108	1939	William Beetham	Oliver Barker
110	1910	Lillian Nutting	E. B. Stratton
112	1910	Lillian Nutting	E. B. Stratton
114	1910	Lillian Nutting	E. B. Stratton
116	1910	Lillian Nutting	E. B. Stratton
118	1910	Lillian Nutting	E. B. Stratton
120	1913	Mark Lewis	Hurd, Gore
122	1913	Mark Lewis	Hurd, Gore
124	1913	Mark Lewis	Hurd, Gore
126	1913	Mark Lewis	Hurd, Gore
128	1913	Mark Lewis	Hurd, Gore

BAY STATE ROAD, SHERBORN TO GRANBY STREETS

NORTH SIDE

No.	Year		
153	1893	Charles Pitman	Wheelwright, Haven
155	1899	Elinor Harding	Peters, Rice
157	1903	William E. Rotch	Putnam, Cox
159	1902	George Wheatland	S. D. Kelley
161	1902	George Wheatland	S. D. Kelley
163	1902	George Wheatland	S. D. Kelley
165	1902	George Wheatland	S. D. Kelley
167	1902	George Wheatland	S. D. Kelley
169	1902	George Wheatland	S. D. Kelley
171	1900	George Wheatland	E. M. A. Machado
173	1900	George Wheatland	E. M. A. Machado
175	1900	George Wheatland	E. M. A. Machado
177	1900	George Wheatland	E. M. A. Machado
179	1900	George Wheatland	E. M. A. Machado
181	1900	George Wheatland	E. M. A. Machado
183	1899	George Wheatland	E. M. A. Machado
185	1899	George Wheatland	E. M. A. Machado
187	1899	George Wheatland	E. M. A. Machado
189	1899	George Wheatland	E. M. A. Machado
191	1897	James Means	Little, Browne
193	1899	George Wheatland	E. M. A. Machado
195	1899	George Wheatland	E. M. A. Machado
197	1899	George Wheatland	E. M. A. Machado
199	1899	George Wheatland	E. M. A. Machado
201	1899	W. D. Vinal	A. H. Vinal
203	1899	W. D. Vinal	A. H. Vinal
205	1899	W. D. Vinal	A. H. Vinal

SOUTH SIDE

No.	Year		
152	1902	Albert Storey	Fehmer, Page
154	1896	Ed. D. Peters	William Y. Peters
156	1899	George Bosworth	George Bosworth
158	1900	Ada Vinal	Arthur Vinal
160	1900	Ada Vinal	Arthur Vinal
162	1900	Ada Vinal	Arthur Vinal
164	1900	Ada Vinal	Arthur Vinal
166	1900	Cecil Caverly	Arthur Vinal
168	1900	Ada Vinal	Arthur Vinal
170	1901	Vacant lot	
172	1902	George Wheatland	S. D. Kelley
174	1902	George Wheatland	S. D. Kelley
176	1902	George Wheatland	S. D. Kelley
178	1902	George Wheatland	S. D. Kelley
180	1902	George Wheatland	S. D. Kelley
182	1904	George Wheatland	S. D. Kelley
184	1906	George Wheatland	S. D. Kelley
186	1906	George Wheatland	S. D. Kelley
188	1906	George Wheatland	S. D. Kelley
190	1906	George Wheatland	S. D. Kelley
192	1907	George Wheatland	S. D. Kelley
194	1907	George Wheatland	S. D. Kelley
196	1900	W. D. Vinal	Arthur H. Vinal
198	1900	W. D. Vinal	Arthur H. Vinal
200	1900	W. D. Vinal	Arthur H. Vinal
202	1900	W. D. Vinal	Arthur H. Vinal
204	1899	W. D. Vinal	Arthur H. Vinal

APPENDIX A BUILDINGS CONSTRUCTED IN THE BACK BAY

Number	Date	Owner	Architect		Number	Date	Owner	Architect
207	1899	W. D. Vinal	A. H. Vinal		206	1899	W. D. Vinal	Arthur H. Vinal
209	1899	W. D. Vinal	A. H. Vinal		208	1899	W. D. Vinal	Arthur H. Vinal
211	1899	W. D. Vinal	A. H. Vinal		210	1899	W. D. Vinal	Arthur H. Vinal
213	1899	W. D. Vinal	A. H. Vinal		212		Vacant lot	
215		Vacant lot			214		Vacant lot	
217	?	Bemis						
25 Granby								
	1895	W. P. Wilson	J. P. Rinn					

BAY STATE ROAD, GRANBY TO ASHBY STREETS

NORTH SIDE

Number	Date	Owner	Architect
225	1905	William Lindsay	Chapman, Frazer
231	1904	Lorin Deland	Andrews, Jacques, Rantoul
233	1902	Cornelia Upham	Warren, Smith, Briscoe

SOUTH SIDE

Number	Date	Owner	Architect
232	1913	?	Nathan Douglas
236	1913	A. L. Rudnick	F. A. Norcross
		Vacant lots	
264	1913	Davis, Sherman	Frank, Wilcox
270	1913	Davis, Sherman	Frank, Wilcox
280	1913	Davis, Sherman	Frank, Wilcox
		Vacant lots	
304	1901	George Mackey	G. Wilton Lewis
306	1901	Luther Merrill	G. Wilton Lewis
308	1901	Luther Merrill	G. Wilton Lewis
310	1901	Luther Merrill	G. Wilton Lewis

BRIMMER STREET

WEST SIDE

No.	Year	Owner	
1	1870	Hasket Derby	
3	1869	E. J. Hale	John Bemis
	1897	21-unit apartment	Henry Savage
5	1888	Seth Baker	
9	1867	F. Wainwright	
11	1867	G. W. Braman	
15	1884	E. L. Clark	S. E. Tobey
17	1882	Robert Codman	Sturgis, Brigham
19	1869	Mary Wales	Snell, Gregerson
21	1869	Mary Wales	Snell, Gregerson
23	1870	?	
25	1870	Henry Foote	
27	1870	Susan Oliver	
29	1881	C. Faulkner	Bradlee, Winslow
31	1869	S. W. Swett	Snell, Gregerson
33	1869	Fred D. Allen	Snell, Gregerson
35	1869	A. H. Hardy	Snell, Gregerson
37	1869	E. A. Strong	Snell, Gregerson
39	1869	George Higginson	Snell, Gregerson
41	1869	Charles E. Ware	Ware, Van Brunt

EAST SIDE

No.	Year	Owner	
2	1868	Silas Merrill	
4	1868	Silas Merrill	
6	1868	Silas Merrill	
8	1868	Silas Merrill	
10	1868	Silas Merrill	
12	1868	Silas Merrill	
14	1868	Silas Merrill	
16	1868	Silas Merrill	
18	1868	Silas Merrill	
20	1868	Daniel Davis	
22	1868	Daniel Davis	
24	1868	Daniel Davis	
26	1868	Daniel Davis	
28	1868	Daniel Davis	
	1879	Church of the Advent	Sturgis, Brigham
50	1912	Brimmer Street Trust	R. A. Fisher
52	1912	Brimmer Street Trust	R. A. Fisher
54	1912	Brimmer Street Trust	R. A. Fisher
56	1912	Brimmer Street Trust	R. A. Fisher
58	1912	Brimmer Street Trust	R. A. Fisher

CHESTNUT STREET

No.	Year	Owner
94	1845	William Sullivan
96	1839	A. S. Johnson
98	1839	A. S. Johnson
100	1839	A. S. Johnson
102	1856	David Sears
104	1856	David Sears
106	1856	J. P. Warren

OTIS PLACE

No.	Year	Owner	
1	1870	Mary Pickering	
2	1870	R. E. Althorp	
3	1872	A. C. Martin	A. C. Martin
4	1872	A. C. Martin	A. C. Martin
5	1872	School for Mrs. Martin	A. C. Martin
6	1872	Otis Estate	A. C. Martin
7	1872	Otis Estate	A. C. Martin
8	1872	Otis Estate	A. C. Martin

APPENDIX A BUILDINGS CONSTRUCTED IN THE BACK BAY

Number	Date	Owner	Architect

MOUNT VERNON STREET

Number	Date	Owner	Architect
156	1871	Otis Estate	
158	1871	Otis Estate	
160	1871	Otis Estate	
162	1871	Otis Estate	
129	1870		
131	1870		
133	1870		
135	1870		

PINKNEY STREET

Number	Date	Owner	Architect
94	1867	Daniel Davis	
96	1867	Daniel Davis	
98	1867	Daniel Davis	
100	1867	Daniel Davis	
127	1843	P. G. Rounds	
129	1871	C. W. Parker	

RIVER PLACE

Number	Date	Owner	Architect
1	1869	Braman, Davis	
2	1869	Braman, Davis	
3	1869	Braman, Davis	
4	1869	Braman, Davis	

RIVER STREET

Number	Date	Owner	Architect
2	1845	D. Rubbles	
3	1846	D. Rubbles	
4	1846	D. Rubbles	
5	1846	A. Mayhew, rooming house	
7	1858	Samuel Neal	
8	1858	Samuel Neal	
9	1858	Samuel Neal	
10	1858	Samuel Neal	

CHARLES RIVER SQUARE

	1910	Frank R. Bourne	

WEST HILL PLACE

	1916	Coolidge, Carlson	

CHARLES STREET, MOUNT VERNON TO PINKNEY STREETS

WEST SIDE

New	Old*		
101	76	1856	
99	78	1856	
97	80	before 1839	
95	82	1866	Silas Merrill
93	84	1866	Silas Merrill
91	86	1866	Silas Merrill
89	88	1866	Silas Merrill
87	90	1866	Silas Merrill
85	92	1866	Silas Merrill
83	94	1866	Silas Merrill
81	96	1866	Silas Merrill
79	98	1866	Silas Merrill
77	100	1866	Silas Merrill
75	102	1866	George Derby

CHARLES STREET, PINKNEY TO REVERE STREETS

73	108	1845	Stable, changed to shop in 1855
71	110	1855	Governor Andrew
69	112	1855	Governor Andrew
67	114	1857	Remodeled as residence, Moses Grant
65	116	1857	Remodeled as residence, Moses Grant
63	118	1857	Moses Grant
61	120	1857	Moses Grant
59	122	1864	Trustees of Assn. Relief Aged Females
57	124	1864	Trustees of Assn. Relief Aged Females
55	126	1864	Trustees of Assn. Relief Aged Females

*The numbering on Charles Street was changed in 1866.

APPENDIX A   BUILDINGS CONSTRUCTED IN THE BACK BAY

CHARLES STREET, REVERE TO CAMBRIDGE STREETS

Number		Date	Owner	Architect
53	122	1841		
51	130	1843		
49	132			
47	134			
45	136			
43	138			
41	146	1855	John Hoppin	
39	148	1855	John Hoppin (James Field residence)	
37	150	1855	John Hoppin	
35	152	1855	John Hoppin	
33	154	1855	John Hoppin	
31	156	1855	John Hoppin	
29	158	1840	Tenements	
27	160	1840	Tenements	
25	162	1840	Tenements	
23	164	1840	Tenements	
21	166	1858	O. W. Holmes	
19	168	1858	Hasket Derby	

APPENDIX B

CHURCHES IN THE BACK BAY

Date	Church	Architect
1860	Arlington Street Church (Congregational)	Arthur Gilman
1862	Emanuel Church (Episcopal)	A. R. Estey
1866	Central Church (Congregational)	R. M. Upjohn
1867	First Church (Unitarian)	Ware, Van Brunt
1871	Brattle Square Church (Unitarian; taken over by Baptists, 1881)	H. H. Richardson
1873	Second Church (Unitarian; demolished about 1915)	N. J. Bradlee
1874	New Old South Church (Congregational)	Cummings, Sears
1875	Trinity Church (Episcopal)	H. H. Richardson
1879	Church of the Advent (Episcopal)	Sturgis, Brigham
1883	Hollis Street Church (Congregational; now Copley Methodist Episcopal Church)	G. T. Meacham
1884	Spiritualist Temple (now Exeter Street Theatre)	Hartwell, Richardson
1891	Mount Vernon Church (Congregational)	Walker, Kimball
1959	Lutheran Church	Pietro Belluschi

APPENDIX C

SCHOOLS, PUBLIC BUILDINGS, AND CLUBS IN THE BACK BAY

Date	Building	Architect
1862	Museum of Natural History	W. G. Preston
1864	Massachusetts Institute of Technology	W. G. Preston
c. 1870	Convent and School, Sisters of Notre Dame (by 1873 atlas)	
1873	Chauncey Hall School (private)	A. C. Martin
1874	Museum of Fine Arts	Sturgis, Brigham
1875	Prince School (public)	G. A. Clough
1879	Massachusetts Charitable Mechanics Association Hall	W. G. Preston
1881	Boston Art Club	W. R. Emerson
1882	Young Men's Christian Association (now converted into offices, southwest corner of Boylston and Berkeley)	Sturgis, Brigham
1882	Harvard Medical School (now Boston University)	Ware, Van Brunt
1883	Normal Art School	Hartwell, Richardson
1883	Second M.I.T. building on Boylston Street	Carl Fehmer
1884	Bicycle Club (building incorporated into Boston Art Club, 1889)	G. T. Meacham
1885	Fire Station	
1886	Police Station	
1887	Boston Public Library	McKim, Mead, White
1887	Algonquin Club	McKim, Mead, White
1887	Boston Athletic Club	John Sturgis
1888	Horace Mann School for Deaf (now Boston University School of Music)	A. H. Vinal

NOTES

CHAPTER I   INTRODUCTION

1. This comment does not apply to the handsome branch office of the Shawmut National Bank, completed in 1964.

2. Clarence D. Long, Jr., *Building Cycles and the Theory of Investment* (Princeton, 1940), p. 152. Long traces four major building cycles in the United States on a national scale. These correspond fairly closely to the waves of building activity in the Back Bay. He indicates a low point in the middle nineties with recovery beginning in 1901 and nearing a high between 1905 and 1916. This recovery is indicated in the Back Bay somewhat earlier, 1899, but the continued prosperity after 1900 is not reflected in the Back Bay because house building in the area was dying out.

3. This figure concerns only new private houses; it does not include apartments or structures built as offices, nor does it include remodeled houses.

CHAPTER 2   THE CULTURAL BACKGROUND OF THE BACK BAY DEVELOPMENT

1. Population of the area which is now within the limits of Boston Proper, United States census figures:

1800	24,937	1860	177,840	1900	560,892
1825	58,277	1870	250,526	1930	781,118
1840	93,383	1880	362,839	1950	790,863
1850	136,881	1890	448,477	1960	697,197

2. An excellent summary of Boston maritime development is contained in Hamilton Hill, "Trade, Commerce and Navigation of Boston," *A Memorial History of Boston*, ed. Justin Winsor (Boston, 1881), IV, 222.

3. For a discussion of Boston railroad building and financing, see Charles Francis Adams, Jr., "Canal and Railroad Enterprise in Boston," *A Memorial History of Boston*, ed. Justin Winsor (Boston, 1881), IV, 111–150.

4. Carroll D. Wright, "Industries in the Last One Hundred Years," *A Memorial History of Boston*, ed. Justin Winsor (Boston, 1881), IV, 95. The figures are for goods manufactured in Suffolk County.

5. John T. Morse, Jr., *Oliver Wendell Holmes, His Life and Letters* (Boston, 1896), pp. 83 and 149.

6. Information about the Lawrence Collection in Mabel M. Swan, *The Athenaeum Gallery, 1827–73*, Boston Athenaeum (Boston, 1940), p. 173. For a catalogue of the Appleton engravings, *The Tosti Engravings*, Boston Public Library (Boston, 1871), p. 24.

7. For a comprehensive discussion of painting and picture collecting in Boston just after the Civil War, see William Howe Downs, "Painting in Boston," a series of six articles in the *Atlantic Monthly*, July to December 1888. Reference to the Appleton picture collection, 62:778 (December 1888).

8. See John S. Dwight, "Music in Boston," *A Memorial History of Boston*, ed. Justin Winsor (Boston, 1881), IV, 414–464.

9. *The Builder*, 7:207 and 8:290. They are practically the only notices of American buildings to appear in the British periodical during these years.

10. For a description of horsecar lines see Richard Herndon, *Boston of Today* (Boston, 1892), p. 24. For the advent of gas lighting see John Koren, *Boston, 1822–1922*, City of Boston Printing Department (Boston, 1922), p. 155. For the development of the city's water supply see Eugene C. Hultman, "History of Boston's Water Supply," *Proceedings of the Bostonian Society* (1948), p. 48. On penny postage see Courtney Guild, "Men and Market," *Proceedings of the Bostonian Society* (1927), p. 30. For a description of bridge building and early filling operations see Edward Stanwood. "Topography and Landmarks in the Last One Hundred Years," *A Memorial History of Boston*, ed. Justin Winsor (Boston, 1881), IV, 31–35.

11. For a comparison of bank clearings see *Annual Report of the Comptroller of the Currency to the Forty-Eighth Congress*, Government Printing Office (Washington, D.C., Dec. 3, 1883), p. 53. The yearly totals of bank clearing houses in Boston and New York:

	Boston	New York
1857	$1,000,000	$ 8,333,226
1880	3,300,000	37,128,126
1883	3,540,980	40,293,165

For a thorough description of Boston financial interests see Henry P. Kidder and Francis Peabody, "Finance in Boston," *A Memorial History of Boston*, ed. Justin Winsor (Boston, 1881), IV, 151–178.

12. A contemporary warning of Boston's faltering economic pace was expressed by Otis Clapp, *A Letter to Abbot Lawrence and Robert Gould Shaw on the Present Condition and Future Growth of Boston* (Boston, 1853), p. 4. The incident concerning the proposed rail merger related by Frederic J. Stimson, *My United States* (New York, 1931), p. 84.

13. Stimson, *My United States*, pp. 76–77.

14. For account of failure to purchase the controlling interest in the New York Central line see Adams in Winsor, *Memorial History*, IV, 143.

15. This is a synthesis of his text. H. G. Wells, *The Future of America* (New York, 1906), pp. 224, 227–228, and 230. Here Wells uses Boston only as the personification of this particular intellectual attitude which he sometimes encountered in America, but he also intended his strictures to apply specifically to Boston.

16. Howells quoted by Van Wyck Brooks, Introduction to *A Hazard of New Fortunes* (New York, 1960), p. v.

17. Cleveland Amory, *The Proper Bostonians* (New York, 1947); the curfew date, p. 53; the ancestral requirements, pp. 43 and 54. For a description of a late nineteenth century sewing circle see Clara K. Rogers, *Memories of a Musical Career* (Boston, 1932), pp. 418–419.

18. Regarding the number of banks in 1880, see William Leahy, *Fifty Years of Boston, A Memorial Volume*, Boston Tercentenary Committee (Boston, 1932), p. 245. In 1898 the first of the large Boston bank mergers took place; nine banks consolidated to form the Shawmut National Bank with total deposits of $20,000,000.

19. Boston's architectural tastes were as impeccable as her literary preferences. As William Dean Howells observed, she "would rather perish by fire and sword than be suspected of vulgarity; a critical, fastidious Boston, dissatisfied with the rest of the hemisphere." Howells in *A Chance Acquaintance,* quoted in *Fifty Years of Boston,* p. 303.

20. Henry James, *The American Scene* (New York, 1907), p. 237.

CHAPTER 3   TOPOGRAPHICAL DEVELOPMENT OF BOSTON

1. A delightfully written and complete account of the changing topography of the city is given in Walter Muir Whitehill, *Boston, A Topographical History* (Cambridge, Mass., 1963).

2. The standard reference on topographical development of Beacon Hill is Allen Chamberlain's *Beacon Hill, Its Ancient Pastures and Early Mansions* (Boston, 1925). It is the source of most of the information presented here on cutting down the summits of Tremont, the laying out of streets and squares, and the building of houses. The height of the hill was 153.7 feet above city base; of the Bulfinch column, 157 feet (pp. 33 and 30).

3. For characteristic columnar monuments of the 1790's see Allais, et al., *Projects d'architecture qui ont merités les grands prix* (Paris, 1806).

4. Population figures for surrounding towns from *Heads of Families, First Census of the United States, 1790* (Washington D.C., 1908), p. 10. Information on Cambridge in Wendell Garrett, "The Topographical Development of Cambridge, 1793–1896," *Proceedings, Cambridge Historical Society* (1961–63), 39:108–125.

5. For descriptions of the town and Long Wharf, see Thomas Pemberton, "Topographical and Historical Description of Boston in 1794," *Collection of the Massachusetts Historical Society for 1794,* (Boston, 1810), III, 248–250, and Gilbert R. Payson, "Long Wharf and the Old Water Front," *Proceedings of the Bostonian Society (1926),* p. 23.

6. For a description of the early condition of Boston Neck, see Nathaniel B. Shurtleff, *A Topographical and Historical Description of Boston,* printed at the request of the City Council (Boston, 1871), pp. 138–140.

7. Chamberlain, *Beacon Hill,* pp. 213–235.

8. Francis Cabot Lowell, "History of the Gardiner Greene Estate," *Proceedings of the Bostonian Society,* series 1, vol. XII, p. 51. The Greene house was built in 1758. For detailed account of the changes on Cotton Hill, see Chamberlain, *Beacon Hill,* p. 156.

9. The Mount Vernon Proprietors were Harrison Gray Otis, Jonathan Mason, Benjamin Joy, and Mrs. Swan. Charles Bulfinch, originally a partner, had to withdraw because of financial difficulties resulting from his disastrous Tontine Crescent venture.

10. Concerning the incline "railroad," Chamberlain, *Beacon Hill,* p. 80, quotes N. I. Bowditch, "Cleaver Articles," *Boston Evening Transcript,* 1855. Shurtleff, *Topographical Description,* p. 121, describes the Charles Street activity. Of the two freestanding mansions on Beacon Hill only the (second) Harrison Gray Otis house stands today; the Jonathan Mason house was demolished in 1836 to provide space for numbers 59–67 Mount Vernon Street. By verbal agreement the property owners on the north side of the street bound themselves to a thirty-foot set back from the

street. This agreement was confirmed by a legal action in 1820. Chamberlain, *Beacon Hill*, p. 89.

11. Chamberlain, *Beacon Hill*, p. 27, summarizes the confusing evidence regarding the original height of Beacon Hill.

12. Chamberlain, *Beacon Hill*, pp. 32–33.

13. For descriptions of early nineteenth century changes in Boston's market area, see Shurtleff, *Topographical Description*, p. 120, and Payson in *Proceedings of the Bostonian Society* (1928), pp. 33–36. For a description of the Tremont House, see William H. Eliot, *A Description of Tremont House* (Boston, 1830), p. 31.

14. For the railway construction, see Adams, "Canal and Railroad Enterprise in Boston," *A Memorial History of Boston*, ed. Justin Winsor (Boston, 1881), IV, 123–126. Charles S. Damrell, *A Half Century of Boston's Building* (Boston, 1895), pp. 50–52, describes the stations, designates the architects, and includes pictures of most of the stations.

15. Edward Stanwood, "Topography and Landmarks in the Last One Hundred Years," *The Memorial History of Boston*, ed. Justin Winsor (Boston, 1881), IV, 28–33.

16. Stanwood in Winsor, *Memorial History*, describes these fills in detail. The story is retold in a clear and delightful fashion by Whitehill, *Topographical History*, chaps. iv and v.

17. Payson in *Proceedings of the Bostonian Society*, pp. 23–40. Atlantic Avenue follows for a way the approximate line of the old Barricade, the seventeenth century harbor fortification.

18. James R. Bruce, "Filling of the Back Bay," *Proceedings of the Bostonian Society* (1940). His map facing page 24 best summarizes in a visual manner the various fills of Boston Harbor. Whitehill, *Topographical History*, chap. vii.

19. That is, 1000 feet at low tide; at extreme high tide the Neck was almost inundated. In 1785 a company was licensed to build a stone causeway along the Neck to make travel easier during periods of extreme high tide (Shurtleff, *Topographical Description*, p. 141).

20. Albert Mathews, article in *Boston Transcript*, June 22, 1935.

21. Shurtleff, *Topographical Description*, pp. 385–387, and Whitehill, *Topographical History*, chap. v. Whitehill questions the status of the South End as a fashionable district and observes that few Boston leaders ever lived there.

22. The progress of the Back Bay fill at ten-year intervals is shown in a set of blue prints prepared in 1881 by Fuller and Whitney, Back Bay engineers, and preserved in the Boston Public Library.

23. Bruce, *Proceedings of the Bostonian Society*, map, p. 24, and Stanwood in Winsor, *Memorial History*, IV, 39–48.

24. William Leahy, *Fifty Years of Boston, A Memorial Volume*, Boston Tercentenary Committee (Boston, 1932), p. 43. By 1912 Boston reached the limits of her geographical extension. Further expansion by land was blocked by adjoining cities like Brookline and Cambridge which did not choose to incorporate with the city, and there remained no more harbor area that could be filled.

25. For the horsecar lines, see Richard Herndon, *Boston of Today* (Boston, 1892), p. 24, and Foster M. Palmer, "Horse Car, Trolley, and Subway," *Proceedings of the Cambridge Historical Society*, 1961–63, 39:78–108. Also Leahy, *Fifty Years of Boston*, p. 270. The first horsecar line was opened in 1853 to Cambridge; in 1857 the seventh and last line was constructed by the Metropolitan Company to Brookline. Scollay Square was the main horsecar center; other terminals were Bowdoin and Haymarket Squares. When the system was consolidated there were totals of 235 miles of track, 1841 cars, and 7728 horses.

26. In 1900 Boston proper contained 560,892 inhabitants; Greater Boston, 1,116,209. In 1950 the city itself contained 790,863; Greater Boston, 2,354,507. *United States Bureau of the Census, Seventeenth Census, 1950*, Government Printing Office (Washington, D.C., 1950), I, 32.

27. Edward Stanwood, *Boston Illustrated*, James R. Osgood (Boston, 1872), pp. 51–52, gives a good description of the business district before the fire. Damrell, *Half Century of Boston's Building*, pp. 46–78, includes notices of the construction of Boston's major buildings between 1880 and 1895. Arranged haphazardly and not indexed, this material seems to be a fairly literal transcription from the building permits of the city's Building Department. The most important house-mover of the period was William Blair who moved the seven-story Hotel Pelham.

28. K. S. Bartlett, "When Boston Had a Station for Each of Its Eight Railroads," Boston Sunday *Globe*, June 13, 1948. The present North Station, built in 1928, was preceded by another union station built on the same site in 1894.

CHAPTER 4   THE TRANSITIONAL PERIOD

1. In 1857 property on Franklin Street sold at $7 to $10 a square foot; in the first auction of Back Bay lands, property sold at $1.37 to $2.25. *Boston Directory*, 1860, p. 159.

2. The history of the negotiations and of the fill is given in Chapter Eight. In a number of instances construction was begun on adjacent private land somewhat earlier than 1859.

3. Information from examination of city tax records.

4. Of considerable interest are passing references to the house that stood at 194 (formerly 80) Boylston Street, and to the life that was lived there, in the memoirs of Alice B. Coolidge, "My Early Reminiscences," 1923, an unpublished manuscript, Boston Athenaeum, pp. 25–30.

5. Russell Sturgis, *Homes in City and Country* (New York, 1893), p. 16.

6. Information from examination of city tax records between 1825 and 1875.

7. City tax records for 1829 indicate that six contiguous houses at the west end of Beacon Street were under construction but not finished. Although street numbers had not yet been assigned, it is clear that they are the present row at 70–75. The first two were owned by Harrison Gray Otis, the next two by Benjamin Joy and William Sullivan respectively, the last two by Jonathan Mason. As the tax records usually lag behind actual improvements, we can safely say that the houses were designed and begun in 1828. As an example of the time lag, the contracts for houses at 92–99 Beacon Street were signed in March, 1848, but the houses first appear on the tax rolls in 1849 as "unfinished."

8. Asher Benjamin, *The Practical House Carpenter* (Boston, 1829), plate 32. On the same page appears the guilloche (really a circular fret) that is very similar if not quite identical to the one in the cornice.

9. The aesthetic superiority of the dark mortar joint is seen by comparing it with modern pointing in which white mortar has been used. White mortar minimizes the warm color of the brick masonry, and the sheer quality of the brick surface is also destroyed.

10. George M. Dexter, *Oeuvre*, vol. X: pages not numbered. In 1967 little remains of this very handsome block. Numbers 98 and 99 were demolished to provide access to Embankment Drive; numbers 94 and 97 were replaced by an apartment

building. Even the two dwellings that remain, 95 and 96, have suffered a good deal of remodeling. Bound with the drawings for the houses is an alternative scheme which utilizes the familiar swell-front facade.

CHAPTER 5   THE PERIOD OF ACADEMIC HEGEMONY

1. Commonwealth of Massachusetts, *Eighth Annual Report of the Harbor and Land Commission for 1886* (Boston, 1887), p. 3.

2. Gridley J. F. Bryant to Jury for Competition for Boston Free Hospital, April 12, 1861, in *Documents of the City of Boston,* document 34, vol. II, p. 31. Emphasis added.

3. John Summerson, *Georgian London* (New York, 1946), pp. 23–26.

4. The schedule of streets for Beacon Hill was laid out by Mather Withington in 1799. Charles Bulfinch also produced a plan providing for a square 190 by 460 feet, but this scheme was not used. (Allen Chamberlain, *Beacon Hill, Its Ancient Pastures and Early Mansions,* Boston, 1925, p. 70.) S. P. Fuller laid out Louisburg Square in April 1826 (*ibid.,* p. 188). The Pemberton Square development was controlled by Patrick Jackson; no other surveyor or planner is mentioned in connection with the square's development (p. 156). The plan for the New South End was drawn by the city engineer, E. S. Chesbrough and William Parrot (see Richard Herndon, *Boston Today,* Boston, 1892, p. 74).

5. The swell front was used for most of the houses constructed in Pemberton Square soon after 1835 and for those on Louisburg Square, which was built up between 1834 and 1844. It was also employed, as we saw in Chapter Four, for houses along Boylston Street constructed in the early fifties.

6. Whitehill, *Topographical History,* figs. 67 and 68, reproduces two row house projects which are typical of the New South End yet they were designed and built, so one of the drawings informs us, in 1857–58 by N. J. Bradlee. Although not a strong artistic personality, Bradlee was one of the founders of the Boston Society of Architects and therefore a "respectable" figure. Interestingly enough when Bradlee designed houses for the Back Bay (for example, two houses for Frank Andrews at 6 and 8 Marlborough Street, 1864), they are in the Academic French manner. Marjorie Drake Ross, *The Book of Boston, The Victorian Period* (New York, 1964), p. 135, illustrates a swell-front house in Chester Square designed in 1858 by Luther Briggs, Jr., another B.S.A. member about whom less is known.

7. For a brief discussion of Haussmann's boulevards, see Sigfried Giedion, *Space, Time and Architecture,* (Cambridge, Mass., 1941), pp. 468–478. For a description of nineteenth century architectural education, see A. J. Bloor, *Architectural and Other Art Societies of Europe,* American Institute of Architects (New York, 1869), p. 100.

8. Henry-Russell Hitchcock, Jr., *The Architecture of H. H. Richardson and His Times* (New York, 1936), pp. 40–43.

9. Thumbnail sketches of the most prominent Boston architects' lives, training, and work are scattered throughout Richard Herndon, *Boston of Today* (Boston, 1892).

10. Preston's work is mentioned in Herndon, *Boston of Today.* However, a far more important picture of his work and of the changing concepts of American architecture in the second half of the nineteenth century is derived from a study of the forty-eight bound volumes of Preston's work preserved in the Boston Public Library. Volume One is devoted to Preston's sketches and drawings for the Massachusetts Institute of Technology building. One watercolor sketch is signed, "W.

G. Preston, architect, Paris, France," another dated "Paris, 1863." The actual working drawings date from 1865. The drawings for the Museum of Natural History, bound in Volume Three, are dated May 31, 1862; plans for the Conant house, in the same volume, are dated December 30, 1863. The pages of these volumes are not numbered and the opus is not indexed.

11. Walter H. Kilham, *Boston after Bulfinch* (Cambridge, Mass., 1946), p. 79. Viollet-le-Duc, *Discourses on Architecture;* translated by and with an introductory essay by Henry Van Brunt (Boston, 1875).

12. For Gilman's design of the Back Bay see *King's Dictionary of Boston* (Cambridge, Mass., 1883), p. 44, and Arthur Gilman, *The Story of Boston* (New York, 1889), p. 454. The architectural relationship between Gilman and Gridley Bryant is not entirely clear. The *Boston Directory* indicates that they shared offices at 4 Court Street, Boston, from 1860 to 1867, but it does not indicate a partnership as existed in several other contemporary Boston offices. In 1868 Bryant formed an actual partnership with L. P. Rogers which is indicated in the *Directory*. It would probably be correct to refer to Bryant and Gilman as associates. For Gilman's earlier architectural criticism, see his article "Architecture in the United States," *North American Review,* 58:436 (April 1844).

13. Quoted in William D. Austin, "History of the Boston Society of Architects" (1942), unpublished manuscript in the Boston Athenaeum, chap. vii, p. 29.

14. Charles A. Cummings, "Architecture in Boston," *A Memorial History of Boston,* ed. Justin Winsor (Boston, 1881), IV, 48. Date of house from inspection of city tax records.

15. Edward Stanwood, *Boston Illustrated* (Boston, 1872), p. 83, and *The Builder,* 11:721–722 (November 26, 1853).

16. The *Boston Directory* shows Edward P. Deacon residing in this house for the first time in 1848.

Mr. David T. Van Zanten has recently called my attention to a water color rendering of the Deacon mansion preserved in the Boston Athenaeum. Dated 23 August 1846, it accompanied the mason's contract for the house, and it was signed by the owner, Mr. E. P. Deacon, and G. J. F. Bryant as architect. This would indicate that M. Lemoulnier, who is traditionally credited with the design, had some kind of professional working agreement with Mr. Bryant.

17. Information about painters, collectors, and dealers contained in W. H. Downes, "Boston Painters and Paintings," *Atlantic Monthly,* 62:779–781 (December 1888).

18. Although Richardson was connected with the design of the hospital (Hitchcock, *H. H. Richardson,* p. 43), he can hardly be identified as the architect of the Back Bay houses as he was still living in Paris at the time of their construction in 1863.

19. Montgomery Schuyler, "A Review of the Works of Richard Morris Hunt," *Architectural Record* 5:97–108 (October 1895). A photograph of the group of houses faces page 103 but the text contains no references to it. City tax records indicate that the buildings were already under construction in 1860.

20. The Deacon mansion, referred to above, had a mansard roof as early as 1848, but it was unique in many ways. A random sample of houses built on Union Park as late as 1854 used traditional ridge roofs. The block of six houses built for Hollis Hunnewell at 1654–1672 Washington Street in 1854 also had ridge roofs; see Robert Rettig, "The Mansion at 1682 Washington Street," an unpublished graduate paper, Department of Fine Arts, Harvard University.

As yet unpublished for the Cambridge Historical Commission research by Mrs. Antoinette Downing and Miss Eleanor Pearson reveals the presence on the Continent well before the Civil War of still another architect from Greater Boston. Henry Greenough, 1807–1883, brother of the more famous Horatio Greenough, lived in Europe on two occasions, 1831–3 and 1845–50, and he is known to have studied in Florence. He designed several mansard roof houses in Cambridge which predate 1857, heretofore thought to be the earliest date, save for the Deacon mansion of 1846–48, for that roof in Boston. As yet incomplete research reveals four mansard roof houses by Greenough: the Louis Agassiz house of 1853 on the site of the present Fogg Museum, the Sabra Parsons house of 1854 at 64 Linnaean Street, his own house of 1855 (destroyed) at 1737 Cambridge Street, and the Edward Loring house of 1856 at 4 Kirkland Place.

21. We have a record of 304 single-family houses still standing or photographed which were built between 1857 and 1869. Fifty-three percent of these (161 dwellings) were four stories to their main cornice (that is, organized on six levels including basement and attic).

22. Cummings in Winsor, ed., *Memorial History*, IV, 482. For an indication of the rise in property values late in the century, see below, page 368.

23. The lot size of the town house, or as the British call it, terrace house, seems to have been standardized very early in its development. When Bloomsbury Square, London, was laid out in 1661 the unit of the subdivision was twenty-four feet. (Summerson, *Georgian London*, p. 24.) There was only one instance of a redivision on Commonwealth Avenue of lots sold at auction by Massachusetts; at 76, 78, 80 Commonwealth Avenue three houses are built on two regular lots. Sometimes, however, by individual negotiation the division line between adjacent lots was shifted so that one lot was wider than standard, the other narrower. Examples of this readjustment are 8–10 and 118–120 Commonwealth Avenue.

Such a division into standard size lots did not, of course, preclude an investor's right to consolidate a large plot of land through the purchase of several consecutive plots sold at auction. After a buyer had bid on one lot at auction he had the privilege of taking as many adjacent lots for the same price as he wished. Thus a few large parcels were acquired, usually for the purpose of erecting a hotel or apartment house, for example, Hotel Vendome, Hotel Agassiz, and the Hotel Hamilton. It should also be understood that land in the western end of the district, owned by the Boston Water Power Company, was not auctioned in plots of equal size. Here, especially along the north side of Commonwealth Avenue, lots were frequently wider than twenty-six feet.

24. It should be recalled also that English architecture provided a precedent for this type of design. Unified blocks of terrace houses had long been popular in Britain, and as early as 1793 Bulfinch had introduced this system to Boston in his famous Tontine Crescent.

25. This figure is for houses built in pairs; it does not concern groups of more than two units.

26. Susan Hale, *T. G. Appleton, Life and Letters* (New York, 1885), p. 319. The author states that Appleton chose a foremost Boston architect to design the house but fails to mention his name.

27. Originally 132 Beacon Street had a similar facade design (see the Boston Athenaeum's Southworth and Hawes Collection of old photographs of Boston). Both of these designs would appear to violate the building restrictions imposed by the Commonwealth.

28. The Union Club did not open its ladies' restaurant until 1898. For the conservative quality of Boston society vis-à-vis that of New York, see Cleveland Amory, *The Proper Bostonians* (New York, 1947), pp. 276–279.

29. On occasion this room was converted into a first-floor study.

30. *The Builder,* September 16, 1865, p. 654.

31. Numbers 1 and 16 Arlington Street illustrate the typical entrance arrangement with the door on the narrow front. Side entrances at 132 and 147 Beacon Street are typical of the many alterations which moved the entrance to the side wall of the basement. The small house at 271 Clarendon Street, 1869, was the first to have its entrance on the long side of the building; the first relatively large houses to place the entrance there are 164 and 165 Marlborough Street, 1870 and 1871 respectively.

32. Examples of houses with a side yard on Beacon Hill are 29A Chestnut Street (1801), 55 Mt. Vernon Street (1804), and a number of small wooden houses on Revere and Myrtle streets. Only two Back Bay houses were free standing: 299 Berkeley Street (1877; demolished in 1939), and 105 Bay State Road (1893).

33. Record high tides of fifteen feet are mentioned by Eugene Hultman, "The Charles River Basin," *Proceedings of the Bostonian Society* (1940), p. 39. The present water level in the Basin has been stabilized at eight feet above low tide (Grade 8).

34. The first-floor kitchens are generally found in houses designed by Snell and Gregerson, for example, 165 Marlborough Street and 177 Commonwealth Avenue; and by Shaw and Shaw, for example, 151 Commonwealth Avenue and 303 Dartmouth Street. With the completion of the better sewer system in 1884 (John Koren, *Boston, 1822–1922,* City of Boston Printing Department, Boston, 1922, p. 254) basement kitchens as well as basement entrances became perfectly practicable.

35. Occasionally one of the main rooms on the second floor would be utilized as a bedroom if the family were large, but no toilet facilities were provided on this level. See George Santayana, *Persons and Places* (New York, 1944), p. 143. The organization of the main stair varied considerably as in a group of eleven similar houses at 110–130 Marlborough, built by Charles Freeland. In some cases the stair stops at the second floor, occasionally it goes to the fourth. The Calvin Page family selected number 128 specifically because of the latter arrangement.

36. Thirty volumes of N. J. Bradlee's works, dating 1853–1881, preserved in the Athenaeum and 48 volumes of Jonathan Preston's work, dating 1863–1886, in the possession of the Boston Public Library. Number 6 Marlborough Street and 4 Newbury Street, both designed by N. J. Bradlee and now destroyed, contained billiard rooms on the third floors.

37. Coolidge, "My Early Reminiscences," pp. 25–30.

38. Carroll D. Wright, "History of Wages and Prices in Massachusetts, 1752–1883," *Massachusetts Bureau of Statistics of Labor,* 16th Annual Report (Boston, 1885), p. 29. When compared to the earnings of shop or factory girls, the housemaids wages plus food and lodging put her in a relatively good position. The average weekly earnings of girls employed in commerce, allowing for layoffs, was $4.91, while the average cost of living for working girls was $5.02 per week in 1883. *Fifty Years of Boston, A Memorial Volume,* Boston Tercentenary Committee (Boston, 1932), pp. 208–210 and 228–231.

39. In 1948 the contract plans and building specifications for this house, the latter of which has since disappeared, were in the possession of Warren Motley, a descendant of the original owner, Edward Motley. The plans were signed by the carpenter and masonry contractor, the architect, and the owner. They bore the

contract date, July 7, 1860, called for the completion of the house by August 1, 1861 (13 months), and specified a contract price of $13,400.

40. An interesting notebook in the possession of the late Dr. Calvin Page records the expenses incurred by his father in fitting out the house at 128 Marlborough Street, immediately after he had purchased it, in 1869. The itemized list is given here in full.

April 9, 1869 house	$27,000.00
Insurance, Mechanics Mutual	54.00
Insurance, Union Mutual	54.00
Stamps on mortgage	17.25
D. Healy, window cleaning	6.00
W. Hewitt, paper hanger	106.30
Bliss & Perkins, gas fixtures	346.76
Sweetser & Abbot, carpets	747.82
J. P. Blumstead, paper hangings	244.77
William McPherson, decorating	192.00
William McPherson, 2 mirrors	69.16
Blue Room, Brussels carpet	115.00
Armstrong, odd jobs	112.00
Armstrong, sinks and screens	121.32
Whitcomb, carpenter work	53.74
Seth Fuller, speaking tube	49.00
Armstrong, odd jobs	43.70
Faucett & Hawks, ventilator repair	9.25
Ironing stove	15.00

41. William P. Blake, *Reports of the United States Commissioner to the Paris Universal Exposition of 1867*, Government Printing Office (Washington, D.C., 1860), p. 58.

42. Lorado Taft, *The History of American Sculpture* (New York, 1903), p. 537. In 1858 the *Boston Directory* listed twenty-five marble workers and four marble dealers. Verbal account of Fabricotti's activities from his great-grandson in Carrara.

43. On cost of fixtures, see above, note 40. Information on chandeliers at the Gibson House Museum from Mr. Charles H. Gibson in 1948.

44. Hitchcock, *H. H. Richardson*, p. 81. Numbers 312–314 were erected by the speculative builder George Wheatland, as were a number of Back Bay houses.

44a. Robert B. Rettig calls my attention to the fact that 130 Beacon Street was designed by George Snell, see Hollis H. Hunnewell, *Life and Letters of Horatio H. Hunnewell* (privately printed, 1906), Vol. I. Numbers 126 and 128, likewise demolished in 1964, were clearly designed by the same architect.

45. For Hotel Hamilton information, see Charles S. Damrell, *A Half Century of Boston's Building* (Boston, 1895), p. 262; Schuyler, "Richard M. Hunt" in *Architectural Record*, 5:103 (October 1895). Other attributions are derived from the often incomplete building permits of Boston for 1872 (before the permits were kept).

46. Cummings in Winsor, *Memorial History*, IV, 482.

47. City of Boston Building Permit no. 1888-339 for 204 Commonwealth Avenue records that S. D. Kelley was architect for the facade of the house only.

48. George Snell is first listed in the *Boston Directory* in 1851; he was joined by James R. Gregerson in 1862; the firm disappears after 1895. Snell's chief commission was the Music Hall of 1852. He was an early occupant of the Studio Building on Tremont Street where William Morris Hunt had his first Boston studio. The firm seems to have specialized in residential work.

49. The designs attributed to Snell and Gregerson are: 179 Beacon Street (1869), 401–409 Beacon Street (1867), 41–43 Marlborough Street (1865; now destroyed), 106 Marlborough Street (1869), 165 Marlborough Street (1871), 236–238 Dartmouth Street (part of the design of 165 Marlborough), 58–60 Commonwealth Avenue (1866), 68 Commonwealth Avenue (1869). Designs of this office which are documented by records of the Building Department are: 322, 340, and 406 Beacon Street; 165 and 404 Marlborough Street; 63, 133, 135, 171, 177, 183, 263, 267 Commonwealth Avenue; 18 Exeter Street.

50. The 1830 figure is from the *Boston Almanac*. In 1857, according to the *Boston Directory*, Boston had 49 architects; in 1869 the number had grown to 72, a ratio of one architect to approximately every 3400 persons.

51. John Ruskin, *The Seven Lamps of Architecture* (London, 1849), pp. 31–37; Edward M. Barry, *Lectures on Architecture* (London, 1881), p. 8.

52. For the Ware and Van Brunt atelier, see Clare T. Evans, "Biography of William Robert Ware," an unpublished manuscript, Avery Library, Columbia University. For the beginning of the Department of Architecture at Massachusetts Institute of Technology, Arthur C. Weatherhead, *The History of Collegiate Education in Architecture in the United States* (New York, 1941), pp. 34–36.

53. For a brief account of the life and work of Gridley Bryant, see H. T. Bailey, "An Architect of the Old School," *New England Magazine*, 25:429 (November 1901). Bryant's as well as Arthur Gilman's office was at 4 Court Street. The *Boston Directory* also lists Luther Briggs at that same address between 1857 and 1861, but gives no indication of a partnership with Bryant. Hammatt Billings is sometimes mentioned as a Bryant associate, but at no time after 1843 (when the *Boston Directory* began publication) did they have offices at the same address.

54. William Austin, "A History of the Boston Society of Architects," an unpublished manuscript in the Boston Athenaeum, 1942, is the source of most of the information on the members, formation, activities, and interests of that association. The objectives of the two groups in founding the organization are discussed in Chapter Two.

55. Austin, "Society of Architects," iii, 19, for a resumé of early programs; xvi, 10, for a discussion of the deliberations on architectural ethics; xii, 3, for the society's assistance to the department of architecture at Massachusetts Institute of Technology.

CHAPTER 6   THE DECADES OF INDIVIDUALISM

1. A simpler classification would group them in four main styles: Academic style (including Brownstone Academic, Academic Brick, Panel Brick); Gothic Revival (including Brownstone Gothic, Ruskin Gothic, Late Gothic); Richardson Romanesque; Queen Anne style (including groups interested in the expressive potential of material and in a purely decorative use of Queen Anne motifs).

2. Although these facades were not built entirely of brick, the impression that they create is one of homogeneity of color and building material. White or grey granite was customarily used for the basement walls and the front steps, but white was not introduced above the level of the first floor. A mellow brownstone that blended nicely with the brick color was used to frame the front door and for window lintels.

3. A better total picture of the entire postwar period would be obtained if one considered the thirty-year period 1869–1900. In this case the distribution of styles would be: Academic styles, 39 percent; Queen Anne styles, 29 percent; Classical and Georgian styles, 13 percent; Romanesque style, 13 percent; Gothic styles, 6 percent.

4. Numbers 49–51 Commonwealth Avenue, erected in 1876 and 1877, are the last houses of handsome Academic design built in brownstone in the Back Bay district. The exception to single designs is 311–319 Beacon, 1871, a group of five Academic houses constructed of brownstone and organized symmetrically about a central projecting pavilion.

5. Numbers 57–59 and 61 Commonwealth Avenue (1874 and 1879) by Carl Fehmer; 63–65 Commonwealth Avenue (1877) by Snell and Gregerson.

6. Other examples are: 4–8 Gloucester Street (1871); 62–66 Commonwealth Avenue (1872); 1–5 Fairfield Street (1871); 361–365 Beacon Street (1872).

7. Other examples of first-floor kitchens are found at 303 Dartmouth Street; 151, 177, and 183 Commonwealth Avenue; and 322 Beacon Street. This, however, is not a complete list of this arrangement.

8. Snell and Gregerson made similar use of columns in the stair halls at 177 and 263 Commonwealth Avenue and at 322 Beacon Street.

9. Information obtained from Mrs. Endicott in 1948.

10. The last example is 18 Exeter Street, 1885, by Snell and Gregerson. Subsequently the firm experimented with materials in a Queen Anne manner.

11. William D. Austin, "History of the Boston Society of Architects," 1942, an unpublished manuscript, Boston Athenaeum, chap. v., p. 10. Carroll D. Wright, *A History of Wages and Prices in Massachusetts, 1752–1883,* Massachusetts Bureau of Statistics and Labor, Sixteenth Annual Report (Boston, 1885), p. 14.

12. Austin, "Society of Architects," chap. viii, p. 15.

13. For a mason's wage in America and England, see Wright, *History Wages and Prices,* pp. 14 and 279. For French wages, see William P. Blake, *Reports of the United States Commissioners to the Paris Universal Exposition of 1867* (Washington, D.C., 1870), p. 36. For Austrian wages, see Robert H. Thurston, *Reports of the Commissioners of the United States to the International Exposition at Vienna* (Washington, D.C., 1876), vol. IV, sec. D, p. 22.

14. The building permit for 165 Commonwealth Avenue is complete in all details except for the name of the architect.

15. Hudson H. Holly, *Modern Dwellings in Town and Country* (New York, 1876), p. 25.

16. The house was illustrated in *American Architect and Building News,* 1:19 (January 15, 1876), and 1:109 (April 1, 1876). According to the first article, the tiles were made in Spain.

17. Henry-Russell Hitchcock, *The Architecture of H. H. Richardson and His Times* (New York, 1936), pp. 21, 252, 283. Hitchcock notes that Richardson made sketches for three unrealized Back Bay structures: a house for Oliver Ames (this house as finally built by Carl Fehmer in 1882 bears no relation to the study by Richardson that Hitchcock reproduces, fig. 81); a house for Mr. Borland; and an apartment building for B. W. Crowninshield which was probably planned for 349–351 Commonwealth Avenue. In March 1882 Richardson was commissioned to do the Ames Building at Kingston and Bedford streets (Hitchcock, pp. 252, 283).

18. Hitchcock, *H. H. Richardson,* p. 251.

19. Illustrated in Hitchcock, *H. H. Richardson,* fig. 121.

20. Charles S. Damrell, *A Half Century of Boston's Building* (Boston, 1895), an advertisement on p. 443. Other prominent Back Bay structures using Sands' bricks were the Boston Art Club and the State Armory on Columbus Avenue.

21. The rectory's recessed entrance was repeated in three other Back Bay houses: 25 Exeter Street (1882), 30 Fairfield Street (1883), and 29 Fairfield Street. Although 29 Fairfield was built in 1876, the recessed entrance on Fairfield Street was not added until 1890 when the house was drastically remodeled and the front door was moved from Commonwealth Avenue to Fairfield Street.

22. Reginald Blomfield, *Richard Norman Shaw* (London, 1940), gives a very clear explanation of the origins of the Queen Anne movement in England and he illustrates the principal works mentioned here.

23. Hitchcock, *H. H. Richardson*, figures 46, 47, and 50. R. Norman Shaw, *Sketches for Cottages and Other Buildings* (London, 1878), 50 plates.

24. There is only one example of half-timber gables in the Back Bay area; here, however, the timberwork is covered, as required by fire laws, with pressed metal. A good example of Tudor Revival is John Russell Pope's "Bonnycrest" of 1914 at Newport, Rhode Island.

25. "Georgian Houses in New England," *American Architect and Building News*, 2:338–339 (October 20, 1877). This article is signed "Georgian"; an accompanying sketch is signed RSP, which undoubtedly refers to Robert S. Peabody, who defended the old manner on more than one occasion. The article argues for a revival of Georgian forms in this way: "Just as the English Queen Anne architects, without thought of purity of style, have not hesitated to borrow from the past, let us in America not hesitate to draw on our Colonial past; let us not merely copy Queen Anne forms, for that would only add another revival to our repertoire; let us seek inspiration in American Georgian architecture and thereby give the style we develop native roots."

26. Austin, "Society of Architects," chap. viii, pp. 19–20, for the debate in the Boston Society of Architects. *American Architect and Building News*, 2:133 and 2:320–322; the first of these articles is a summary of Robert Peabody's talk at the Boston Society of Architects, the second is signed "J.M.B." The first Queen Anne style house was begun in 1878 at 18 Fairfield Street by Peabody and Stearns. The following year fifteen more houses in the same style were built, six of them at 369–79 Marlborough Street, by the speculative builder George Wheatland.

27. Several details which were very popular with American designers between 1875 and 1890 are closely identified with the Queen Anne style. The sunburst or sunflower motif has already been mentioned. Another cliché is the bay window whose area of glass is divided into two sections, the central part of which is a large sheet of plate glass cut to resemble somewhat the shape of a Palladian arch while the upper surrounding areas are divided into numerous small panes by thin wooden muntins (see, for example, the remodeled bay window at 76 Beacon Street, about 1883). Another detail is the stepped or curvilinear gable. Deriving ultimately from Dutch Renaissance work and much used in London during the 1870's, this feature was used for the first time in the Back Bay at 284–292 Marlborough Street in 1872 and most picturesquely at 8–10 Fairfield Street (1879).

28. Other exaggerated examples of this superficial decoration are 245–247 Marlborough Street (1881–83) and 247 Newbury Street (1884).

29. Other examples of this simple but effective use of materials are found at 373, 451, and 503–509 Beacon Street; 190, 252, 259, and 401 Marlborough Street; and 297–301 Newbury Street.

30. Austin, "Society of Architects," chap. v, p. 25.

31. Courtney Guild, "Men and Market," *Proceedings of the Bostonian Society* (*1927*), p. 40. Gilbert Payson, "Long Wharf and the Old Water Front," *Proceedings of the Bostonian Society* (*1928*), p. 35. James L. Bruce, "The Filling in of the Back Bay," *Proceedings of the Bostonian Society* (*1940*), p. 34.

32. Numbers 39–45 Bay State Road, S. D. Kelley, architect.

33. John P. Comer, *New York City Building Control, 1800–1941* (New York, 1942), p. 8.

34. City of Boston, *Digest of the Statutes Relating to the Survey and Inspection of Buildings in Boston* (Boston, 1873), pp. 16–19. "All party walls shall be carried up to a height of not less than two and one-half feet above the roof covering with the full thickness of the party wall, and shall be capped with stone or iron. Where there is a flat, hip, or pitch roof, the party wall shall be carried up to a height not less than two and one-half feet above the roof covering, at every part of said roof . . . Where the roof is a mansard or any style excepting as above specified, unless the same is constructed of fire-proof materials, the party wall shall be carried to a height of not less than two and one-half feet above the flat or upper slope and shall extend through the lower slope at least eighteen inches distant from and parallel with the roof covering . . . [The party wall above the roof level] shall be corbelled at least twelve inches, or to the outer edge of all projections on the front and rear walls of the building . . . If a gutter stone of suitable dimensions and properly balanced shall be inserted, it shall be equivalent to corbelling." (Acts for 1872, chap. 371, sec. 11)

"No mansard shall be constructed more than one story in height nor more than twenty feet from the upper floor of the building unless the mansard is constructed of fireproof material . . . All external parts of the building which are more than forty-five feet above sidewalk level shall be made of or covered with non-combustible materials . . . And all exterior wooden cornices that shall hereafter require to be replaced shall be constructed with some non-combustible material . . . No bay window shall be constructed of wood which shall extend more than three feet above the second story from the street." (Acts for 1872, chap. 371, sec. 19)

"Every building greater than thirty feet wide except public buildings, etc. shall have one or more brick partition walls running from front to rear and carried up to a height not less than the second floor joists . . . these walls so located that the space between any second floor bearing walls shall not be greater than twenty-five feet . . . Iron or wooden girders, supported on iron or wooden columns may be substituted for the bearing walls." (Acts for 1873, chap. 289, sec. 63)

"All main partitions supporting in any manner the floor beams or rafters shall be placed directly over each other." (Acts for 1873, chap. 289, sec. 64)

35. This setback was twenty feet on Commonwealth Avenue and the north side of Beacon Street; it was twenty-five feet on Boylston Street between Berkeley and Clarendon streets; otherwise it was twenty-two feet.

36. The property restrictions inserted in the first deeds read as follows: "This conveyance is made upon the following stipulations and agreement: that any building erected on the premises shall be at least three stories high . . . that the front wall thereof on a main street or avenue shall be set twenty (or twenty-two) feet from said street or avenue provided that steps, windows, porticos, and other projections appurtenant thereto are to be allowed in said reserved space of twenty (or twenty-two) feet."

After January 28, 1863, the following restrictive clause was added to the above provision: "subject to the following limitations, namely: 1. that no projection of any kind other than steps and balustrades connected therewith and also cornices at the roof of the building will be allowed to extend more than five feet from said front wall into said space; 2. that no projection in the nature of a bay window, circular front or octagonal front with a foundation wall sustaining same . . . will be allowed unless any horizontal section of said projection would fall within the external lines of a trapezoid whose base upon the rear line of foresaid space does not exceed seven-tenths of the whole front of the building nor exceed eighteen feet in any case, and whose side lines shall make an angle of forty-five degrees with the base; and each house in a block shall be considered a separate space within the meaning of this limitation." Commonwealth of Massachusetts, *Tenth Annual Report of the Commissioners on The Back Bay*, 1863.

37. The Algonquin Club case is reported in the *Fourteenth Annual Report of the Harbor and Land Commission*, 1892. The Hotel Kensington case is reported in the *Seventh Annual Report*, 1885.

38. *Sixteenth Annual Report*, 1894.

39. The records of the Building Department are silent on this remodeling. The information given here was supplied by Mrs. Edwin Webster, present owner of the house. Benjamin Constant (1845–1902), an Academician, attained considerable fame in the late nineteenth century. Several times a medalist at the Salon, he executed important ceiling decorations for the Hotel de Ville, the new Sorbonne building, and the Opera Comique in Paris. In addition to his decorative work, he was a popular portrait painter. Thieme-Becker, *Allgemeines Lexikon der Bildenden Kunstler* (Leipzig), vol. 7, pp. 323–324.

40. This intermediate wall was mandatory if the span was more than thirty-five feet (Acts for.1873, chap. 289, sec. 64).

41. The larger timbers and spacing were specified in the Dexter plans for 90–99 Beacon Street (1849). Current size requirements, Federal Housing Authority, *Minimum Property Requirements* (October 1964).

42. Another early residence of fireproof construction is 411 Commonwealth Avenue, 1899.

43. *Digest of Statutes Relating to Buildings in Boston*, p. 10.

44. *Ibid.*, p. 12. Comer, *New York City Building Control*, p. 52.

45. Walter Kilham, *Boston after Bulfinch* (Cambridge, Mass., 1946), p. 39. As the pressed brick were somewhat thinner than the common brick, it was very difficult to integrate the courses of the two masonry shells. Metal clamps were avoided possibly because they made it difficult to keep the mortar joints as thin ($\frac{3}{16}$ of an inch) as desirable.

46. Illustrated, *American Architect and Building News*, 1:28 (January 22, 1876).

47. Information on the Medical College furnace from Kilham, *Boston after Bulfinch*, citing the *New England Journal of Medicine and Surgery* for 1816. Information on Mount Vernon Street houses from Allen Chamberlain, *Beacon Hill, Its Ancient Pastures and Early Mansions* (Boston, 1925), p. 208. Information on Back Bay furnaces from city building permits which indicate that many Back Bay houses contained two furnaces. The eleven furnace makers of 1859 contrast with six in 1846. There is a description of the soapstone registers in Alice B. Coolidge, "My Early Reminiscences," unpublished manuscript, Boston Athenaeum, 1923.

48. For advent of gas lighting in Boston see John Koren, *Boston, 1822–1922* (Boston, 1922). Information on cost of private systems and the installation of electric lights in Hotel Vendome from an advertisement in *Kings Dictionary of*

Boston (Cambridge, Mass., 1883). As for early electrical installations in the area, the Building Department reported 106 permits to install electric light systems in all of Boston in 1882, 41 permits in 1883, 69 in 1884, 51 in 1885. City of Boston, *Annual Report of the Inspector of Buildings for 1886* (Boston, 1887), p. 28.

49. The first residential elevator installation of which we have record is at 29 Fairfield Street in 1876. The house was remodeled in 1890 and the original installation modified. A city building permit in 1873 refers to two elevators in the Hotel Agassiz, designed by Weston and Rand. Plans of the Hotel Hamilton of 1869 preserved in the Boston Public Library indicate an elevator there. The second and third elevators in Back Bay residences were installed at 179 Commonwealth Avenue (1879) and 135 Marlborough Street (1880). According to the City of Boston, *Annual Report of the Inspector of Buildings, 1886,* p. 11, there were 140 hydraulic elevators installed in Boston in 1886 alone; building permits exist for only five Back Bay elevators in that year. This latter figure, which comes from remaining Building Department records, does not seem to give a true picture of the total installations for the early years. An instance of one elevator that is not documented is 22 Commonwealth where an old hydraulic elevator, still used in 1948, is neither shown in contract plans for the house nor recorded in alteration permits.

50. In a number of large early houses one section of the attic was reserved for purposes other than servants' bedrooms or service areas. The Bradlee plans for 6 Marlborough Street (1864) and 4 Newbury Street (1870)—both houses destroyed —had billiard rooms on the top floors but no plumbing. Attic billiard rooms are also found at 17 Gloucester Street (1886) and 32 Hereford Street (1884), both houses with elevators.

51. Chamberlain, *Beacon Hill,* p. 208.

52. The value of the land from city tax records for that year.

53. Wright, *History of Wages and Prices,* pp. 278, 279, 73, and 244, and *Construction Costs, 1874–1935,* no editor (New York, 1936), p. 15.

54. Plumbing fixtures on the upper floors of Beacon Hill houses were, of course, a physical impossibility before the construction of the water reservoir atop Beacon Hill in 1848 provided the requisite pressure to force water to such heights.

55. Lewis Mumford, *The Brown Decades* (New York, 1931), p. 266.

CHAPTER 7   THE AUTHENTIC REVIVALS AND TRIUMPH OF THE GEORGIAN STYLE

1. Numbers 482–490 Beacon Street constitute a row of large, nondescript, Classical-style houses, built by E. H. Fay. The last non-Classical houses, both begun in 1892, are 510–524 Commonwealth Avenue, also built by Fay, and 39–45 Bay State Road, built by Chadwick and Stillings.

2. A permit to build the Elizabeth Skinner house at 266 Beacon Street was granted January 1, 1886; the Boston Public Library was commissioned March 30, 1887.

3. Charles Moore, *Life and Times of Charles F. McKim* (Boston, 1929), p. 338.

4. The Algonquin Club was commissioned on February 3, 1887, almost two months before the architectural contract for the Boston Public Library was awarded. Charles C. Baldwin, *Stanford White* (New York, 1931), p. 316.

5. In this connection attention should be called to a group of sixteen different houses built during the 1880's which are greatly influenced by chateau architecture

but are not sufficiently archaeological in their approach to be classified among the Authentic Revivals. Certainly they cannot be grouped with Brownstone Gothic or Ruskin Gothic, considered in Chapter Six, but actually they fall somewhere between those categories and the Authentic Revivals. An example is 497 Commonwealth, 1895.

6. A similar use of exterior carved *putti* above windows was used in the Vanderbilt house. John Van Pelt, *The W. K. Vanderbilt House* (New York, 1925), plates 27–31.

7. Julius H. Schweinfurth, *Sketches Abroad* (Boston, 1888).

8. The entrance of 479 Commonwealth, designed by Winslow and Wetherell in 1895, is copied almost directly from the McKim, Mead, and White apartment on the corner of Beacon and Charles streets, built in 1890.

9. There were originally four houses in this group; numbers 54 and 56 were demolished in 1930.

10. Similar rusticated window frames with exaggerated keystones are found in drawings for the St. Giles and Bloomsbury public baths, London, by Baly and Pownall, *The Builder*, July 23, 1853, p. 473.

11. Carl J. Weinhardt, Jr., "Domestic Architecture of Beacon Hill, 1800–50," *Proceedings of the Bostonian Society*, 1958, p. 24.

12. The speculator-built houses at 82–94 Bay State Road were designed by S. D. Kelley and constructed by George Wheatland. The late example is a combined apartment and doctor's office at 108 Bay State Road.

13. Information obtained in 1948 from Miss Fannie Mason and Mrs. Rouaux, née Bradley.

14. There is no mention of the addition of the music room wing in the building permits of the Building Department, but from insurance atlases we can establish that it was erected between 1888 and 1898. Several friends of the late Miss Mason think that the room was added in the middle nineties. Mr. David McKibbin, Fine Arts Librarian at the Boston Athenaeum, suggests the date of 1897 because of the presence of a set of eighteenth century Venetian chairs in the room. A set of identical chairs in Fenway Court is known to have been bought by Mrs. Gardner in that year; it is probable that Miss Mason acquired her chairs at the same time to furnish the new room.

15. Photographs reproduced in Reginald Blomfield, *R. Norman Shaw* (London, 1940). The door resembles one at 170 Queens Gate (1888), fig. 42; the windows duplicate those at "Swan House" (1876), fig. 49; the rustication recalls "Bryanston" (1890), fig. 22.

16. Henry-Russell Hitchcock, Jr., *H. H. Richardson and His Times* (New York, 1936), pp. 101–102, 182–185.

17. For size of Massachusetts Institute of Technology architectural library, see Arthur C. Weatherhead, *The History of Collegiate Education in Architecture in the United States* (New York, 1941), p. 26. For the Boston Public Library holdings, see *Catalogue of Books Relating to Architecture, Construction, and Decoration in the Public Library of the City of Boston, November 1, 1894* (Boston, 1894). For the book purchases of the Boston Society of Architects, see William Austin, "A History of the Boston Society of Architects," an unpublished manuscript in the Boston Athenaeum, 1942, chap. v, p. 15, and chap. xiii, p. 15.

18. The three British periodicals: *The Architect, The Architectural Association Sketch Book,* and *The Builder;* the French magazine: *Croquis d'Architecture;* the American journals: *American Architect and Building News, American Builder, Architectural Review, Architecture and Building, Brochure Series, Builder and Woodworker, Decorator and Furnisher,*

Inland Architect and News Record, Manufacturer and Builder, Technology Architectural Review.

19. On the flyleaf of volume 1 (1846) of the Athenaeum's *Builder* is the date 1869. In the opinion of Miss Margaret Hackett, the reference librarian, this may well be the date at which the back issues of the periodical were acquired. Other than that, there is no record at the Athenaeum of when the subscription to the magazine began.

20. Hitchcock, *H. H. Richardson,* pp. 91–92 and 98.

21. The term "Heliotype" is apparently a trade name, for a perusal of several late nineteenth century histories of photoengraving did not mention the process. The *Brochure Series* was published in Boston by the Architectural Association from 1889–1892.

22. Austin, "Society of Architects," chap. xii, p. 3, and chap. ix, p. 3.

23. *The Sketch Book of the Architectural Association of Boston,* issued in 1883 and again in 1890 under the editorship of R. D. Andrews is not to be confused with the *Architectural Sketch Book* published by the Portfolio Club of Boston between 1873 and 1876.

24. Austin, "Society of Architects," chap. xiii, p. 11.

25. Weatherhead, *Collegiate Education in Architecture,* p. 25.

26. The examination was proportioned among the following subjects: architectural design, 30 percent; architectural history, freehand drawing, and construction, 20 percent each; French, 10 percent. Austin, "Society of Architects," chap. xii, p. 4.

27. Austin, "Society of Architects," chap. ix, p. 8, and chap. xiii, p. 15.

28. The Prix de Rome was established by the French government in 1720 to give the student an opportunity to study and absorb the lessons of Classical architecture in Rome. In England once the romantic imagination had been awakened to the beauties of the Middle Ages, architectural students commenced an examination of Medieval monuments. The British *Architectural Association Sketch Book,* published first in 1867, was largely dedicated in its early years to the reproduction of measured drawings of British student-travelers.

29. This summarizes chapters 8, 9, 13, and 17 in Austin's account of the Boston Society of Architects' meetings.

30. Austin "Society of Architects," chap. x, pp. 2 and 12; chap. xiv, pp. 10–11; and chap. xvii, p. 28.

31. Austin, "Society of Architects," chap. v, pp. 8–9 and 15; chap. ix, pp. 7 and 8.

32. Austin, "Society of Architects," chap. ix, p. 8.

33. *New York Sketch Book* (Boston, 1874), vol. I, no. 12, pl. 45.

34. Moore, *Charles F. McKim,* p. 41, and Baldwin, *Stanford White,* p. 113.

35. Arthur Little, *Early New England Interiors* (Boston, 1878), pages not numbered.

36. In 1877, one year previous to the appearance of Little's work, a book was published in Philadelphia by T. Westcott entitled *The Historic Mansions of Philadelphia.* This is the earliest publication on American Colonial architecture listed in the 1894 catalogue of the Boston Public Library, and perhaps the earliest volume on that subject to appear.

37. James M. Coner and E. E. Soderholtz, *Examples of Domestic Architecture in New England* (Boston, 1891).

38. *Catalogue of Books Relating to Architecture in the Boston Public Library.* The supplement entitled *The Georgian Period* was clearly designed to meet the requirements of the drafting room. It is interesting to note that some of the drawings reproduced here bear dates as early as 1888.

39. "Report of the Committee on the Preservation of the Hancock House," *City of Boston Document, 1863*, document 56, pp. 1–14.

40. Austin, "Society of Architects," chap. xvi, p. 26.

41. Arthur Gilman, "Architecture in the United States," *North American Review*, 58:436 (April 1844).

42. William H. Downes, "Boston Painters and Paintings," *Atlantic Monthly*, 62:650 (November 1888). Robert S. Peabody, "Georgian Houses in New England," *American Architect and Building News*, 2:338–339 (October 20, 1877).

CHAPTER 8   THE BACK BAY AREA AS AN EXAMPLE OF CITY PLANNING

1. Nathaniel B. Shurtleff, *A Topographical and Historical Description of Boston* (Boston, 1871), p. 432. Edward S. Stanwood, "Topography and Landmarks in the Last One Hundred Years," *The Memorial History of Boston*, ed. by Justin Winsor (Boston, 1881), IV, 35. James Bruce, "Filling in the Back Bay," *Proceedings of the Bostonian Society*, 1940, map facing p. 23. Walter Muir Whitehill, *Boston, A Topographical History* (Cambridge, Mass., 1963), chap. vii. Shurtleff states that some 450 acres of the Back Bay were cut off from the Charles River by the construction of the Mill Dam; Bruce's map gives 570 acres as the total of the Back Bay fill. The latter figure includes areas lying north of Beacon Street, that is, the "water side" of Beacon Street, the Bay State Road section, the Brimmer Street filled area, and the Storrow Embankment.

The Cross Dam was an earthen dyke about 50 feet wide and faced on each side with granite walls, which were supported by a grillage of logs six layers deep and held together by wooden pins. Wilbur Davis, "The History of Boston as Disclosed in Digging of the Commonwealth Avenue Underpass," *Proceedings of the Bostonian Society*, 1938, p. 30.

2. George Santayana, *Persons and Places* (New York, 1944), p. 143. Santayana mentions the unpleasant odors rising from the flats but adds that most Back Bay residents were away in the summer months when the odors were worst. Also William Lawrence, *Memories of a Happy Life* (Boston, 1926), p. 3.

3. *Boston Directory, 1860*, p. 159. An article notices the changes currently taking place in the Tontine Crescent in Franklin Street. This property sold at $7 to $10 per square foot and was then built with six-story, granite stores designed by Gridley Bryant. It is instructive to contrast these prices with the $1.37 to $2.75 minimum prices placed on Back Bay property in the same year.

4. Foster M. Palmer, "Horse Car, Trolley, and Subway," *Proceedings of the Cambridge Historical Society* (1961–63), 39:84. On the bridge to South Boston, Shurtleff, *Topographical Description*, p. 472.

5. *Second Annual Report of the Commissioners on Boston Harbor and Back Bay Lands*, 1854. The commissioners reported that the Boston and Roxbury Mill Corporation had invested over $2,800,000 in the water power and toll road projects and that their return had been less than one-tenth the legal rate.

6. *Second Annual Report of the Commissioners on Boston Harbor and Back Bay Lands*, 1854, contains a summary of the various property claims in the Back Bay and of the commissioners' efforts to settle them. The 1879 report includes a summary of the yearly sales of Back Bay property by the commission. The 1886 report also summarizes land sales as well as grants of land in the area to public institutions. A briefer summary of the negotiations for ownership and the arrangements for

filling the land is given by Stanwood in Winsor, *Memorial History of Boston,* IV, 35.

7. An early Colonial statute gave the Commonwealth ownership of all tidal flats below the line of private right. This private right was low watermark or 100 rods below high watermark, whichever was less. Bruce, *Proceedings of the Bostonian Society,* 1940, p. 26.

8. Christopher Eliot, "The Boston Garden," *Proceedings of the Bostonian Society,* 1939, pp. 27–45. On July 1, 1853, the city of Boston was awarded two tracts of land at Newbury and Berkeley and Marlborough and Berkeley streets in compensation for relinquishing its right to sell the Public Garden. The value of this land was then estimated at $67,000. *Fifth Annual Report of the Commissioners on the Back Bay,* 1857.

9. The commissioners who authorized the generous allotment of land for streets and parks and who supported Arthur Gilman's plan for the district were Stephen Fuller, Thomas B. Hall, and E. C. Purdy.

10. *Fifth Annual Report of the Commissioners on the Back Bay,* 1857.

11. The average fill needed was 20.15 feet, *Fourth Annual Report of the Commissioners on the Back Bay,* 1856.

12. A set of fifteen blueprints preserved in the Boston Public Library (Atlas 21.392, 1881) and prepared by Fuller and Whitney, Back Bay engineers, shows the development of the Back Bay fill at ten-year intervals from 1814 to 1881.

13. In 1857 the commission recommended that the Commonwealth make a $20,000 appropriation to set the filling operations in motion. When this proposal was rejected, the commissioners resorted to the system of reimbursing the filling contractor with improved land. The price paid by Goddard and Lawrence at the private sale of 1857 was approximately $1.05 per square foot.

14. *Eighth Annual Report of the Harbor and Land Commission,* 1886.

15. A record of the sales of the Commissioners on Public Lands is preserved in six bound volumes which were stored in 1942 on the fourth floor of the Registry of Motor Vehicles building on Causeway Street. The sale to Gardner is recorded in volume 1. The Calvin Page house at 128 Marlborough Street was bought for $27,000 in 1869 (above, Chap. V, note 40), but the tax assessment for that year was $24,000, or 89 percent of the value.

16. *Fifth Annual Report of Commissioners on the Back Bay,* 1857.

17. Massachusetts Commission on Boston Harbor and Back Bay, "Plan of the Receiving Basin Showing Certain Avenues and Lines of Releases, prepared from surveys made under the direction of the Commissioners," April 12, 1853, S. P. Fuller. "Plan of Lands Belonging to the Boston Water Power Company," 1855, Whitwell and Henck.

18. "Plan of Lands Belonging to the Boston Water Power Company and the Commonwealth on the Back Bay," May 1, 1860, James Slade, City Engineer. "Plan of Lands in the Back Bay Belonging to the Boston Water Power Company, the Commonwealth and Other Parties, Showing the Streets, Grades and Sewers Laid Out and Recommended by the Back Bay Commissioners," December 31, 1861, H. M. Wightman, Surveyor, and James Slade, City Engineer. "Plan of Back Bay, Streets, Grades, and Sewers as Laid Out and Recommended by the Back Bay Commissioners," February 20, 1863, H. W. Wightman, surveyor.

19. *Second Annual Report of the Commissioners on Boston Harbor and Back Bay Lands,* 1854. The criticism of the Boston City Council is also made by Stanwood, in Winsor, *Memorial History,* IV, 34.

20. Apparently not envisioned in 1860, West Chester Park first appears in the plan of 1861.

21. Plan appended to the first commissioners report of 1853. In this plan the street that eventually becomes Commonwealth Avenue is designated as Avenue V, and it is only slightly wider than the two parallel adjacent streets but no wider than Avenue II (Boylston Street). The 1856 plan is appended to the *Fifth Annual Report of the Commissioners on the Back Bay*, 1857, as Appendix E.

22. "Plan of Boston with Additions and Corrections," 1870, Thomas W. Davis, city surveyor.

23. *Second Annual Report of the Harbor and Land Commission*, 1880.

24. Charles E. Eliot, II, "The Boston Park System," *Fifty Years of Boston, A Memorial History*, Boston Tercentenary Committee (Boston, 1932), pp. 657–671.

25. Eugene Hultman, "The Charles River Basin," *Proceedings of the Bostonian Society*, 1940, pp. 39–48.

26. "Report of the Committee on the Petition of David Sears and Others in Respect to the Drainage of the Back Bay," *City of Boston Document*, 1850, document 14. According to a member of the Sears family, David Sears acquired his holdings from families of Revolutionary War veterans whose services had been recompensed by the Commonwealth with grants of land. Some of this land was subject to tidal flow and was worthless for agricultural purposes. Sears was thus able to buy it for very little.

27. George Snelling, *Proposed Modification of the Plan for the Back Bay Territory* (Boston, 1860), 20 pp.

28. Robert F. Gourlay, *Plans for Enlarging and Improving the City of Boston* (Boston, 1844). The plan is reproduced in Whitehill, *Topographical History*, p. 146.

29. *Third Annual Report of the Commissioners on Boston Harbor and Back Bay Lands*, 1855, Appendix E, explains the arrangement to widen Commonwealth Avenue. Using the average price of $2.19 per square foot for land sold by the Commonwealth between 1857 and 1886 as the basis for evaluation, the property given to the Water Power Company was worth about a million dollars. The percentage of land devoted to public purposes is given in *Eighth Annual Report of the Harbor and Land Commission*, 1886. The remaining 8 percent of the land was donated for schools, museums, and other public institutions.

30. *Fifth Annual Report of the Harbor and Land Commission*, 1883. This report contains a good summary and interpretation of the property restrictions in the light of intervening court rulings. Commercial interests seem to have first invaded the Back Bay about 1890. In 1898 property owners on Boylston Street petitioned for and received releases from the clause which proscribed commercial activities on that street. One can follow the course of commercial building in the district through the building permits which record remodeling or new commercial construction. See above, pp. 432–434, 439–441.

31. See a typical property deed, as for 108 Bay State Road. Suffolk County Registry, 1939, vol. 5823, p. 461.

32. See above, pp. 459, 461, for the complete list.

33. Whitehill, *Boston Topography*, pp. 164–170, traces the whereabouts of many of the churches and organizations before they settled in the Back Bay.

34. *Eighth Annual Report of the Harbor and Land Commission*, 1886. This land would have sold for about $833,500.

35. Shurtleff, *Topographical Description*, p. 466, reports that a Mr. Evans offered a large sum of money to the Free Hospital, provided it would locate in the South End.

36. James L. Bruce, "The Rogers Building and Huntington Hall," *Proceedings of the Bostonian Society*, 1941, p. 149.

37. Whitehill, *Boston Topography*, pp. 135–138, discusses the early ascendency that the Back Bay gained over the New South End. After citing Albert B. Wolfe's account of the marked decline of the South End following the Panic of 1873, he goes on to indicate that few Boston leaders had ever settled in the South End. Whitehill feels that when the old and established families were forced out of their old homes by the encroachments of commerce, they moved to the Back Bay, not the South End.

38. The Hotel Bristol (1879), the Hotel Cluny (1876), the Second Church Society (1873), and Chauncey Hall School (private; 1873). See above page 444.

39. Santayana, *Persons and Places*, p. 149. See also a letter of Albert Mathews to Mrs. J. C. Perkins, Nov. 1, 1932, MSS L 176, Boston Athenaeum, in which Mathews recalls neighborhood friends on Commonwealth Avenue who attended Noble and Greenough School in the 1870's.

40. According to *Sanborn's Insurance Atlas of Boston* for 1868, there were 47 livery stables on Byron, Chestnut, and Lime streets.

41. It is interesting to note that this project was also built on filled land. There is a further similarity: the wide and narrow market streets correspond to the different width of Commonwealth Avenue and adjacent streets.

42. The Albany Street restrictions are reported by Stanwood, in Winsor, *Memorial History*, IV, 31; the Beacon Hill agreement, Allen Chamberlain, *Beacon Hill, Its Ancient Pastures and Early Mansions* (Boston, 1925), p. 145.

INDEX